DEVOTIONS *and* DESIRES

DEVOTIONS *and* DESIRES

Histories of
SEXUALITY *and* RELIGION
in the Twentieth-Century
UNITED STATES

Edited by Gillian Frank,
Bethany Moreton, and
Heather R. White

THE UNIVERSITY OF NORTH CAROLINA PRESS

Chapel Hill

This book was published with the assistance of the
Anniversary Fund of the University of North Carolina Press.

© 2018 The University of North Carolina Press

All rights reserved

Manufactured in the United States of America

The University of North Carolina Press has been a member
of the Green Press Initiative since 2003.

LIBRARY OF CONGRESS CATALOGING-IN-PUBLICATION DATA
Names: Frank, Gillian, editor. | Moreton, Bethany, editor. |
White, Heather Rachelle, 1974– editor.
Title: Devotions and desires : histories of sexuality and religion in the twentieth-century
United States / edited by Gillian Frank, Bethany Moreton, and Heather R. White.
Description: Chapel Hill : The University of North Carolina Press, [2018] |
Includes bibliographical references and index.
Identifiers: LCCN 2017030398 | ISBN 9781469636252 (cloth : alk. paper) |
ISBN 9781469636269 (pbk : alk. paper) | ISBN 9781469636276 (ebook)
Subjects: LCSH: Sex—United States—Religious aspects—History—20th century. |
Sex customs—United States—History—20th century. | Americans—Sexual
behavior—History—20th century. | United States—Religion—History—
20th century. | Religion and politics—United States—History—20th century.
Classification: LCC HQ18.U5 D48 2018 | DDC 306.70973—dc23
LC record available at https://lccn.loc.gov/2017030398

Material in Judith Weisenfeld's chapter, "Real True Buds: Celibacy and Same-
Sex Desire across the Color Line in Father Divine's Peace Mission Movement,"
originally appeared in her book *New World A-Coming: Black Religion and
Racial Identity during the Great Migration* (New York: NYU Press, 2017).

CONTENTS

Acknowledgments ix

Introduction: More than Missionary:
Doing the Histories of Religion and Sexuality Together
Gillian Frank, Bethany Moreton, and Heather R. White
1

Winnifred Wygal's Flock: Same-Sex Desire
and Christian Faith in the 1920s
Kathi Kern
17

Subversive Spiritualities: Yoga's Complex Role in the Narrative
of Sex and Religion in the Twentieth-Century United States
Andrea R. Jain
34

Purity and Population: American Jews, Marriage, and Sexuality
Rebecca L. Davis
54

Sex Is Holy and Mysterious: The Vision of Early
Twentieth-Century Catholic Sex Education Reformers
James P. McCartin
71

Real True Buds: Celibacy and Same-Sex Desire across the
Color Line in Father Divine's Peace Mission Movement
Judith Weisenfeld
90

Sexual Diplomacy: U.S. Catholics' Transnational
Anti–Birth Control Activism in Postwar Japan
Aiko Takeuchi-Demirci
113

Modernizing Decency: Citizens for Decent Literature
and Covert Catholic Activism in Cold War America
Whitney Strub

133

Family Planning Is a Christian Duty: Religion,
Population Control, and the Pill in the 1960s
Samira K. Mehta

152

From Women's Rights to Religious Freedom: The Women's League
for Conservative Judaism and the Politics of Abortion, 1970–1982
Rachel Kranson

170

Fascinating and Happy: Mormon Women, the LDS
Church, and the Politics of Sexual Conservatism
Neil J. Young

193

The Making of Gay and Lesbian Rabbis in
Reconstructionist Judaism, 1979–1992
Rebecca T. Alpert and Jacob J. Staub

214

Founding New Sodom: Radical Gay
Communalist Spirituality, 1973–1976
Daniel Rivers

234

We Who Must Die Demand a Miracle: Christmas 1989 at
the Metropolitan Community Church of San Francisco
Lynne Gerber

253

Afterword
John D'Emilio

277

Recommended Reading 283
Contributors 289
Index 293

ILLUSTRATIONS

Father Divine and the second Mother Divine, late 1940s *92*

A devotional collage made by a follower of Father Divine, n.d. *98*

Dorothy L. Moore in 1946 *103*

Happy S. Love, 1949 *107*

Elizabeth Bolton, a student at Reconstructionist Rabbinical College, 1993 *227*

Kittredge Cherry and Audrey Lockwood at their "holy union" wedding ceremony, 1987 *266*

ACKNOWLEDGMENTS

The editors would very much like to thank the contributors to this volume, all of whom brought their passion and expertise to bear on the questions of religion and sexuality. Some of our authors revised their chapters multiple times in order to integrate reader suggestions and to dialogue with other chapters as they developed. We are grateful for their patience and dedication to this project and for helping us to build a robust conversation about the histories of religion and sexuality.

We also wish to thank the scholars who contributed to this project by offering feedback and conversation, especially the two anonymous readers for the University of North Carolina Press and Wallace Best, Rebecca Davis, John D'Emilio, Ann Gleig, Katie Lofton, Anthony Petro, Tim Retzloff, Stuart Sarbacker, and Stuart Smithers.

Our thanks go out to Gail Patten for her careful editing and administrative support.

We are grateful to Alan Zwickler and the Phil Zwickler Charitable and Memorial Foundation Trust for supporting this project.

The Center for the Study of Religion at Princeton University provided us with an excellent venue for our workshop and editing sessions.

Our sincere appreciation goes to Elaine Maisner, our editor at UNC Press, who cheered enthusiastically for this project at the outset and gave us outstanding support until its completion.

DEVOTIONS *and* DESIRES

INTRODUCTION

More than Missionary: Doing the Histories of Religion and Sexuality Together

GILLIAN FRANK,
BETHANY MORETON,
AND HEATHER R. WHITE

The lines seem so clearly drawn: A white evangelical minister stands in front of his California congregation on a Sunday morning. In one hand he holds a Bible. In the other is the text of the U.S. Supreme Court decision in *Obergefell v. Hodges* extending civil marriage rights to same-sex couples throughout the country. "It's time to choose," he thunders to thousands of believers in the stadium-style worship center. "Will we follow the Word of God or the tyrannical dictates of government?" His declaration "This is who I stand with" is met with applause from the faithful as he dramatically flings the Court's decision to the ground and tramples on it, waving the Bible in his upraised hand.[1]

If ever there were a moment in U.S. history when the categories of "religion" and "sexuality" seemed diametrically opposed, it was the Sabbaths that followed the Court's historic "gay marriage" decisions on a Friday in June 2015. Not an hour after the announcement that same-sex partners must be admitted to civil marriage in all fifty states, the Union of Orthodox Jewish Congregations of America released an official statement to the press. It reiterated "the historical position of the Jewish faith, enunciated unequivocally in our Bible, Talmud and Codes, which forbids homosexual relationships and condemns the institutionalization of such relationships as marriages."[2] At the *National Review*, culture warrior George Wiegel counseled fellow Roman Catholics to interpret their post-*Obergefell* position as analogous to that of their persecuted predecessors in Elizabethan England, holding out as a particularly apt symbol the "gutted, dismembered" body of a sixteenth-century Jesuit martyr.[3] Not to be outdone, evangelicals likewise broadcast their dissent. One hundred evangelical representatives signed an open letter titled "Here We Stand: An Evangelical Declaration on Marriage." The signatories included leaders of the multiethnic Kainos Movement, the Gospel Coalition, and the National Hispanic Christian Leadership Conference alongside representatives of historically white institutions like the Moody Bible Institute and the Southern Baptist Theological Seminary.[4] And the theological responses were not limited to official spokesmen: in the first twenty-four hours after the decision, Google logged an enormous spike in searches for the terms "Sodom," "Leviticus," "End Times," "Abomination," and "Romans 1," the New Testament epistle in which Saint Paul inveighs against "sexual impurity" in highly specific terms.[5]

But below the fold, a more complex story emerged. As fast as the Orthodox could condemn the decision, the Conservative and Reform rabbinical bodies applauded it.[6] The Hindu American Foundation and Muslims for Progressive Values "celebrated" and "rejoiced," respectively.[7] One hundred *other* evangelical leaders—representing churches and organizations like the Gay Christian Network and Patheos Progressive Christian—signed a different letter "in celebration of this major step toward justice and equality" and exhorted fellow believers to address other forms of discrimination against their LGBTQI brothers and sisters.[8] The ten most popular Bible verses retweeted in response to *Obergefell* were almost evenly divided between the supportive, like top-ranked 1 Corinthians 13:13 ("But the greatest of these is love"), and the critical, like Galatians 6:7 ("God cannot be mocked").[9] Religious bodies had filed amicus briefs on both sides of the historic case. Lined up in defense of self-styled "traditional" marriage were the United States Conference of Catholic Bishops, the National Association of Evangelicals, the Southern Baptist Convention, and the Church of Jesus Christ of Latter-day Saints—all familiar voices from forty years of a sex-focused, religious "culture war." The National Coalition of Black Pastors and Religious Leaders explicitly protested the *Obergefell* petitioners' attempt to equate "so-called homosexual marriage" with the moral claims in *Loving v. Virginia*, which struck down state bans on interracial marriage in 1967.[10] But while the official faith-based support for gay marriage was smaller in sheer numbers of members represented, it was impressive in its breadth: the Episcopal bishops' brief in favor of civil recognition for same-sex marriage was signed by the United Church of Christ, the Union of Reform Judaism, Muslims for Progressive Values, and the Unitarian Universalist Association. In all, almost two thousand faith leaders signed onto the argument that "no one 'religious' view" could be allowed to define civil marriage.[11]

This wide-angle attention to religious involvement in the *Obergefell* case spotlights the varied and passionate forms of religious involvement and activism around sexuality. Across the political spectrum, Americans have brought their religious convictions about birth control, abortion, interracial marriage, and queer sex into courtrooms, statehouses, and public demonstrations.[12] These varied political involvements also correspond with even more complex forms of lived religious practice. From dating websites like Christian Mingle to advice books like *Kosher Sex*, even the most conservative and orthodox of American religious groups have innovatively recast seemingly secular sexual ideals and practices into specifically religious projects.[13]

Just as a flashpoint like the *Obergefell* case can alert us to intertwined religious and sexual politics in the present, longer narratives of religion and sexuality can reward thoughtful observers with a far more complex account of the American past. Foundationally, this volume's contributors challenge a narrative that deems religiosity as a conservative and repressive force. They reject the zero-sum account of secular sex locked in a struggle for human liberation from repressive religion as well as its flipside, the jeremiad against corrupting, immoral desire that destroys the freedom to worship and corrupts the soul. Instead, the historians in this volume are among those who have brought nuance and context to the public discussion of American passions, both sexual and religious. Each of these contributors insistently thinks about religion and sexuality *together*, as categories that create and impinge upon each other. Though the authors collected here are not the only scholars to stress this open approach, this volume seeks to break new ground by systematically appraising its consequences for understanding broad changes of America's twentieth century.[14]

In much historical writing, the modern sexual system is understood to be a direct consequence of the putative decline of religion in modern America, or secularization. Whether this thesis is directly stated or tacitly assumed, it informs many historians' understanding of the relationship between the two zones of historical experience. According to the landmark survey of the history of U.S. sexuality *Intimate Matters* by John D'Emilio and Estelle B. Freedman—still the only book of its scope—the modern period is characterized by "a commercialized sexuality," and "sexual relations are expected to provide personal identity and individual happiness, apart from reproduction." In identifying the engines of change, these authors cite "the economy, the family and politics" as helping to drive what they refer to as sexual liberalism: the acceptance of sexual pleasure as key to personal happiness, the separation of sex from procreation, the privileging of heterosexual pleasure within and outside of marriage (so long as the latter is nonprocreative), all the while emphasizing the centrality of marriage itself.[15] In her reflections on the state of the field, Margot Canaday has noted that for LGBT history, "the overriding narrative might have much more to do with the halting and uneven move from acts to identities; [with] the formation of urban subcultures; and finally, with the (related) establishment of a homo/hetero binary."[16] And yet, whether it is the history of sexuality in general or LGBT history in particular, religion, notably, has been left off this list of influential social institutions in making the modern sexual order.

To approach religion as a key analytic term in the recent history of sexuality means rethinking a presumed teleology of recent historical change. Religion, no less than sexuality, has been a site for invention, contestation, and change during the twentieth century. These changes further intersect with a range of processes that have forged twentieth-century culture and politics, especially racialization, state formation, gender construction, and economic organization. Our task in this volume is to show the active role of religious ideas, institutions, and practitioners in shaping received meanings and practices of sexuality.

Such an approach upturns textbook overviews of American religious history and the history of sexuality, both of which tend to undertheorize the other category, resulting in "jack-in-the-box" representations of the other field. Historian Jon Butler's comment about religion could similarly be made about sexuality: each "pops up colorfully on occasion," but "as with a child's jack-in-the-box, the surprise offered by the color or peculiarity of the figure is seldom followed by an extended performance, much less substance."[17] From *Intimate Matters* to numerous groundbreaking edited volumes to primary source teaching collections, religion "pops up" as an oppositional force: a residual but waning source of regulation in the face of progressive change and a forceful auxiliary to conservative sexual politics. Overviews of modern American religion offer symmetrical but reversed coverage of sexuality, focusing on religious conflict and change as a response to the "popping up" of feminist and LGBT social movements. This treatment links sexuality to nonreligious social, technological, and political developments, which religious groups subsequently challenge, adapt, or embrace.[18] These unruly forces emerge from outside the sustained frame of analysis. Consequently, we are left on both sides with a perplexing oil-and-water narrative: religion and sexuality are each present primarily in the other's absence.

This mutual absence in the respective histories of religion and sexuality has come into being even as scholars in each field have traced similar historical developments and engaged in parallel conceptual conversations. Historians working in both fields have identified the twentieth century as a time of transformation that gave rise to ideologies of personal choice and increased visibility for marginalized outsiders—broad trends that scholars of sexuality address in terms of "sexual liberalism" and that religion scholars conceptualize as "religious pluralism."[19]

In conceptualizing this diversity, historians of sexuality and religion have worked carefully to define and historicize their respective categories of inquiry, effectively showing that religion and sexuality are not neutral descriptive labels for unchanging, natural phenomena but terms with classificatory dynamics that reflect political and ideological struggles between insiders and outsiders. These genealogical inquiries challenge the political norms and cultural assumptions that define both categories as private and personal and open up analysis of how a respective history of religion or history of sexuality connects to broad social, demographic, and political developments.

Bringing together the critical work in each field provides an essential foundation for thinking about the histories of religion and sexuality in new ways. An important place to begin a synthetic analysis of religion and sexuality is with some deceptively simple questions about basic categories: What are we talking about when we call something religious? What acts, attitudes, or attributes are we describing as sexual? The commonsense answers to these questions, in many contexts, suggest interior truths: Religion pertains to a person's beliefs about morality and higher beings; sexuality refers to feelings of desire and attraction. Both reflect intensely personal experiences, and both are often invisible to outsiders unless they are outwardly expressed—by the wearing of a recognizably religious symbol like a crucifix or by an expression of affection like kissing. However, expressions that appear sexual or religious demand analysis and contextualization; a kiss is never just a kiss, just as a cross is never just a cross. Because many students approach these categories with an attitude of "I know it when I see it," identifying the history and politics of the assumed definitions of religion and sexuality is crucial.

Religious and sexuality studies scholars argue that the commonplace assumptions about religion and sexuality in the present day are not natural facts. They are ideas with a history. In the late nineteenth century, new modes of thinking about sexuality and religion emerged in Europe and the United States. The new therapeutic sciences of psychology and psychiatry, which circulated novel terms like "sex inversion" and "heterosexuality," shifted how people apprehended sexual identities and desires.[20] An emergent understanding of "sexuality" as a separable, conceptually distinct category was reinforced by the therapeutic sciences, which presented individual personality as the dynamic product of family relationships and biological sex drives. Complementing the rise of sexual sciences was a burgeoning popular culture that provided vernacular terms with which to describe sexual acts, identities, and subcultures.[21] This emergent paradigm framed sexuality as a profoundly interior yet also broadly encompassing human attribute—a constitutive aspect of individual personality and also a determining force on one's subsequent social roles and interpersonal interactions.[22]

Scholars in religious studies have also analyzed a similar kind of innovation in the modern category of religion. Concurrent with the science of sexuality, the new discipline of anthropology imagined "religion" as a universal property of human culture. Against the backdrop of sixteenth-century European colonization, Enlightenment thinkers sought to fit multiple colonized cultures into an intellectual framework based on European historical experience. This framework borrowed its component categories from a Christian paradigm, which was expanded in generic, universalizing terms: all human societies offered some notion of supernatural beings, recounted myths about the origins of the world, and formed ritual practices for marking human life cycle transitions. Just as everyone now had a sexuality, so too did everyone have a religion—and in both cases, some were clearly superior to others. The emergent anthropological understanding of "religion" framed it as a universal category that could be found in parallel forms across all major human societies, arrayed in a hierarchy of congruence with the ideal. Western Christian conceptions of interior "belief" served as a supposedly generic component of religion everywhere. In other words, even as everyone now had a religion, this religion was supposed to be private and separated from politics.[23]

These interconnecting discourses on religion and sexuality were not just descriptive. They were also normative. They shaped a modern terminology and set of evaluations for "true religion" and "good sex" that were freighted with expectations of shoring up much larger domains of healthy society. Conceptions of "true religion" and "good sex" connected to broader preoccupations about the social order: what counted as "true religion"—that is, practices and beliefs perceived to be spiritually authentic and socially beneficial—was that which also supported and encouraged "good sex," or forms of erotic expression and kinship structures that were socially valued. These intertwined dynamics of religion and sexuality were carried onward in both the profoundly personal and the most broadly encompassing politics of the twentieth century. Not only are religion and sexuality not merely personal; they are also co-constructed with race, gender, class, and nation as governing dynamics of modern social and political life.[24]

Historicizing religion and sexuality together—as this volume does—confirms the centrality of religion and sexuality to shaping twentieth-century American culture and politics. The chapters of this collection are presented chronologically as a way to foreground this volume's intervention in broad narratives about widespread sexual and religious transformations. At the same time, the essays might also productively be read under thematic groupings, which cut across the overarching narrative. Our overview aims to introduce broad historiographical interventions while also highlighting alternative schema and distinct subthemes.

When it comes to religion, many historians of sexuality in the twentieth-century United States have not fully shed what Michel Foucault calls the "repressive hypothesis." When historians have paid attention to religious institutions, activists, and faiths, they have too often viewed them as a repressive force characterized by "prohibition, censorship, and denial."[25] The contributors to this volume, conversely, historicize the ways in which religious beliefs and institutions simultaneously regulated, channeled, and incited sexual expression. Put another way, they show how religious actors and institutions helped shape the contours of sexual liberalism. This twentieth-century shift, toward a view of sexuality as good in itself, was a value that many religious groups embraced and rearticulated as a divinely created good. Indeed, even groups that stood firmly on tradition as the guide for rightly ordered sex invested sexual pleasure with spiritual value. Thus, in many cases sexual liberalism fit perfectly with the defense of traditional marriage and family.[26]

Religious groups, our contributors show, were active champions of many modern sexual reforms. Early in the twentieth century, for example, Roman Catholics worked to deliberately synthesize moral teachings with ideals of sexual health. James P. McCartin's chapter, "Sex Is Holy and Mysterious: The Vision of Early Twentieth-Century Catholic Sex Education Reformers," analyzes Catholic sex education efforts from the 1910s through the 1930s. His chapter foregrounds an array of Catholic educators and trained moral theologians who sought to counter the effects of an emergent heterosocial urban leisure culture not with silence or censorship but with forthright sexual instruction for youth. These Catholic educators hoped to reverse adolescents' misconception that "sex is unclean and vulgar" while affirming that "the body is good and sacred in all its parts" and instilling a "simple and truthful narrative of the sacred story of life." Amid a purported upsurge in adolescent promiscuity, the church's official representatives committed themselves to containing secular forces that were disseminating sexual values. While it would be easy to paint such efforts as conservative and reactionary because of clergy's distrust of commercialized sexual cultures, such efforts, McCartin avers, were met with a Catholic sex education effort that was theologically sophisticated and pedagogically up-to-date.

Mainline Protestants proactively advanced ideals of sexual liberalism by coupling marital sexuality with an ethos of pleasure. Samira K. Mehta's chapter, "Family Planning Is a Christian Duty: Religion, Population Control, and the Pill in the 1960s," demonstrates how mainline Protestants at midcentury supported the birth control pill in order to separate sex from reproduction and foster marital sexual intimacy. To justify the need for reproductive control, leading clergy drew from religious tradition and texts, couching support for birth control firmly within existing white middle-class Protestant discourses and creating a new, ecumenical position on fertility control and the Christian family. These Protestants constructed birth control as a moral choice that bespoke Christian responsibility and a social obligation to care for the planet by controlling population growth. Mehta's chapter underscores that support for birth control and moves toward sexual liberalism were not simply effects of secular forces but in fact deeply rooted in Protestant theology.

Contributors to this volume show that conservative religious traditions have not had a simple or oppositional relationship to sexuality. Rather, religious tradition has served as a paradoxical channel for sexual change. Whitney Strub's chapter, "Modernizing Decency: Citizens for Decent Literature and Covert Catholic Activism in Cold War America," demonstrates how Citizens for Decent Literature, an ecumenical antipornography group with Catholic roots, was not simply antisex. CDL worried that pornography undermined moral and social order by perverting viewers and vigorously sought to contain what it defined as obscenity. However, like the mainline Protestant supporters of birth control described in Mehta's chapter and the politicized conservative housewives described in Neil J. Young's chapter, CDL endorsed sexual liberalism by celebrating desire and pleasure when it was contained within heteronormative marital arrangements. CDL's sexual liberalism, Strub argues, was articulated and legitimated through frequent references to a "Judeo-Christian heritage," an ecumenical strategy that joined Catholics, Protestants, and Jews into a shared sexual politics that paved the way for the rise of the New Right. Together these essays give weight to the argument that sexual politics is not simply a Manichaean binary with the forces of secular liberalism lined up on the side of sexual freedom and the forces of religious conservatism lined up on the side of regulation and repression. Instead, they invite us to think further on the complex and contradictory cultural and political positions that different individuals and groups take in relation to both religion and sexuality.

Just as it is necessary to refute frameworks that render religion as an unyielding repressive force, so too is it vital to attend to the plurality of religious traditions and practices that have shaped the history of sexuality. Doing so moves historians away from a dominant cultural bias that conflates religion with Protestantism and sexuality with heterosexuality. In this vein, contributors to our volume emphasize the religious and sexual variance at work during the twentieth century and how a variety of religious actors articulated competing sexual norms, identities, and practices. Rachel Kranson's chapter on the Women's League for Conservative Judaism examines how liberal Jewish women struggled for abortion rights within an emergent conservative order that was being increasingly shaped by evangelicals and traditionalist Catholics. Kranson focuses on the Women's League's engagement with the issue of reproductive rights during the 1970s and early 1980s, as the hardened ideological positions that would later come to characterize the national debates over abortion were only just beginning to form. By tracking how the Women's League modified arguments that it used to justify access to abortion, the chapter deftly spotlights how these rhetorical shifts revealed the crucial impact that the anti-abortion activism of the Christian right had on less conservative, even non-Christian, religious groups.

Likewise, Aiko Takeuchi-Demirci's chapter, "Sexual Diplomacy: U.S. Catholics' Transnational Anti–Birth Control Activism in Postwar Japan," examines how Catholic activism over abortion and contraception was fueled domestically and internationally by competition with mainline Protestant policy makers. Amid Cold War tensions, American Catholics formed a powerful lobby as the occupation government sought to navigate Japanese demands for birth control and abortion access. Even as Takeuchi-Demirci's chapter complicates easy labels like "religious conservative" and "liberal," she foregrounds how sexual values were negotiated between confessional traditions.

Together the abovementioned chapters move us away from the formulation that religion is a repressive and singular entity. The histories they offer instead invite us to ask open-ended questions: How do different religious groups construct sexual values? What are the debates within and between denominations over sexual norms? What are the relationships between religious and sexual identities?

Many of our contributors take up the latter question and analyze the twentieth-century co-construction of religious and heterosexual identities through reforms aimed to promote marriage. In their respective chapters, Rebecca L. Davis and Neil J. Young demonstrate the ways in which marriage and heterosexuality were religious projects undertaken to achieve faith-based cultural and political goals. Davis's "Purity and Population: American Jews, Marriage, and Sexuality" investigates the Jewish investment in marriage, exposing how Jewish Americans promoted cultural and religious continuity through reproduction. Marriage and sexuality, Davis shows, shaped the ways in which Jewish Americans practiced and valued their faith. In turn, the religious investment in marriage, by Jews and other people of faith, contributed to national conversations about the sanctity and value of marital stability and constituted heteronormative sexualities.

Young's chapter, "Fascinating and Happy: Mormon Women, the LDS Church, and the Politics of Sexual Conservatism," investigates how Mormon women's marriage promotion activities shaped the development of Mormonism's conservative sexual and gendered culture. By examining Mormon theology, popular prescriptive literature, and women's political activism, Young maps how LDS women constructed heterosexual family structures and empowered other women to seek happiness through wifely submission and marital sexual pleasure. This religious-sexual project, Young argues, was not confined to Mormon homes but instead turned outward to the nation to counter sexual and religious beliefs that directly opposed their moral vision and ideological worldview. In historicizing sexuality and religion together, Davis and Young actively blur the boundaries between the categories themselves. Together their contributions reveal how sexual norms and religious norms converged to support heterosexual politics, identities, and practices.

Many religious groups, however, did not wed spiritual practice to heteronormativity; rather, they shaped religious institutions and remade definitions of the sacred to embrace countercultural visions of sexuality. Judith Weisenfeld's chapter, "Real True Buds: Celibacy and Same-Sex Desire across the Color Line in Father Divine's Peace Mission Movement," explores how religious spaces engendered cross-racial and same-sex intimacies in the Peace Mission—a gender-segregated, predominantly African American and racially integrated new religious movement that flourished in the 1930s and 1940s. Weisenfeld examines the practices of celibacy among black and white women in Father Divine's movement to show that a practice that we might think of as absent of sexuality in fact has much to illumine. The chapter's close analysis of the correspondence between these "real true buds" makes clear that there is a great deal of queer history to be found in new religious movements. As Weisenfeld deftly shows, this innovative religious community challenged and reconfigured dominant meanings of family, sexuality, and race by fostering same-sex spiritual kinship and interracial camaraderie.

Weisenfeld's chapter joins contributions to the volume by Rebecca T. Alpert and Jacob J. Staub and by Lynne Gerber that demonstrate how twentieth-century sexual minorities reshaped religious institutions and practices. In "The Making of Gay and Lesbian Rabbis in Reconstructionist Judaism, 1979–1992," Alpert and Staub offer a nuanced picture of the process by which lesbian and gay inclusion became a value embraced by the Jewish Reconstructionist tradition. Their chapter focuses on the history of policy debate surrounding the ordination of Jewish rabbis and highlights the ways in which gays and lesbians sought to remake their religious communities and broaden religious traditions.

Likewise, Gerber's "We Who Must Die Demand a Miracle: Christmas 1989 at the Metropolitan Community Church of San Francisco" illustrates the co-constitution of sacred and sexual identities. Gerber focuses on urban gay politics during the AIDS epidemic and on ways in which sexual communities forge religious rituals. Her nuanced investigation of the Metropolitan Community Church of San Francisco—an independent Christian space that affirmed homosexuality and recognized gay relationships—immerses readers in the history of the MCC and its changing theological and sexual politics as well as in the broader institutional and political responses to HIV/AIDS. The chapter offers a rich case study of how one church struggled to maintain a gay- and sex-positive position in the face of AIDS while using AIDS as an opportunity to draw upon the Christian tradition for spiritual sustenance and to challenge its adequacy in the face of the crisis.

Gerber's attention to the urban context of this gay religious community reminds us that religion and sexuality have geographies. Her chapter can be read productively alongside the contributions by Daniel Rivers, Kathi Kern, and Andrea R. Jain, which likewise attend to the dynamics of place in sexual and religious practice. Rivers's contribution, "Founding New Sodom: Radical Gay Communalist Spirituality, 1973–1976," immerses us in the world of gay male communalists across the United States in the mid-1970s and in the ways these sexual communities embraced a cosmology that was rural, sexually vibrant, gay male, New Age, and often pagan. The chapter investigates the rural world of men who fled urban centers and created alternatives to gay bar scenes of the cities. These communalists, Rivers shows, offered a vision of free sexual expression in spiritual terms amid nature, which they saw as the harbinger of revolutionary action, the true successor to early gay liberation. This historical analysis of rural liberationist spirituality expands our understanding of sexual liberation and the construction of gay male identities outside of urban communities and established religious traditions.

Just as some of our contributors invite an exploration of the histories of sexuality and religion outside of urban centers, so too do they encourage an analysis of the ways in which religion and sexuality exceed national borders and complicate our notion of a bounded United States. At the heart of Jain's chapter, "Subversive Spiritualties: Yoga's Complex Role in the Narrative of Sex and Religion in the Twentieth-Century United States," is a story of how yoga arose from an ongoing cultural exchange between India and the United States. Like Takeuchi-Demirci's chapter on transnational Catholic networks, Jain's contribution shows how international networks forged sexual and religious ideas. Immigration, travel, and the sharing of books undergirded a transnational yoga movement. Jain's chapter details how architects of the modern yoga movement, such as the celibate Swami Vivekananda and the free-love advocate Ida Craddock, challenged sexual and religious norms of this period, which emphasized reproductive marriages and women's sexual accessibility within marriage. These yogis, Jain argues, blurred religious and national boundaries and challenged mainstream Christianity.

Kern's chapter, "Winnifred Wygal's Flock: Same-Sex Desire and Christian Faith in the 1920s," likewise focuses on American engagement with Indian culture and the religious and sexual encounters that arose through these cultural exchanges. Kern studies Winnifred Wygal, a leading member of the professional staff of the Young Women's Christian Association who prepared contemporary, nondenominational worship materials for the organization. Kern reveals the hidden history of female sexual networks within the prewar YWCA. In Kern's narrative, Wygal constructed an erotic life in India that challenged both the conventions of heterosexual "companionate marriage" and the concomitant emergence of homosexual "pathology." Intervening in an established body of literature about romantic friendships at the dawn of the medical category "lesbian," Kern shows how religious spaces allowed for sexual variance even as religious language became an expressive vehicle for same-sex desire within the context of religious enterprises overseas.

Our volume ends with an afterword by the eminent U.S. historian John D'Emilio. For close to a decade, D'Emilio has urged the fields he helped establish—LGBT history and the history of sexuality—to devote more attention to religious themes and actors in the modern period especially. Indeed, the chapters in our volume point to complex stories of devotion and desire that counter the thinness of the usual narratives about twentieth-century religion and sexuality. However, the map we offer has many blank spaces that range from well-known and exhaustively studied traditions, like white evangelical Protestantism, to relatively marginalized U.S. religious groups such as Islam, Native American traditions, and African and Asian religions. To complement our chapters, we therefore include a recommended reading list that highlights key research in these areas as well as in the intersecting sexual and religious histories of Asian Americans, Latinx communities, and Americans of Middle Eastern descent, among others. This volume seeks to join this growing body of historical scholarship in demonstrating that the histories of sexuality and religion are not niche concerns. Rather, in their specificity and at their intersections, these are histories that undergird many of our shared, contested, foundational narratives.

For many readers, devotion and desire may seem like strange bedfellows. It is our hope that these chapters reveal that religion and sexuality have been longtime and intimate companions. Understanding these intertwined histories, moreover, reveals that the American past, no less than its present, is both sexually and religiously diverse. This past contains unusual positions, porous boundaries, and dangerous liaisons and—as this volume shows—is so much more than missionary.

NOTES

1. "Conservative Pastors Deliver Sharp Criticism of Same-Sex Marriage," National Public Radio, June 29, 2016, http://www.npr.org/2015/06/29/418641115/conservative-pastors-deliver-sharp-criticism-of-same-sex-marriage.

2. "Orthodox Union Statement on Supreme Court's Ruling in *Obergefell v. Hodges*," Orthodox Union Advocacy Center, June 26, 2015, http://advocacy.ou.org/2015/orthodox-union-statement-supreme-courts-ruling-obergefell-v-hodges/.

3. George Wiegel, "Lessons, after *Obergefell*, from Catholics Who Were Persecuted under Elizabeth I," *National Review*, June 29, 2015, http://www.nationalreview.com/article/420442/after-obergefell-lessons-from-persecuted-catholics.

4. "Here We Stand: An Evangelical Declaration on Marriage," *Christianity Today*, June 26, 2015, http://www.christianitytoday.com/ct/2015/june-web-only/here-we-stand-evangelical-declaration-on-marriage.html.

5. Stephen Smith, "Sodom, Leviticus, and *Obergefell*: The Bible after Friday's Decision," *Christianity Today*, June 29, 2015, http://www.christianitytoday.com/ct/2015/june-web-only/how-internet-responded-to-supreme-court-same-sex-marriage-d.html.

6. The Rabbinical Assembly, "Conservative Rabbis Applaud SCOTUS Same-Sex Marriage Decision," The Rabbinical Assembly, June 26, 2015, http://www.rabbinicalassembly.org/story/conservative-rabbis-applaud-scotus-same-sex-marriage-decision?tp=25; Central Conference of American Rabbis, "Supreme Court Decision One Step Toward Recognizing We Are All Made in God's Image," Central Conference of American Rabbis, June 26, 2015, http://www.ccarnet.org/about-us/news-and-events/

supreme-court-decision-one-step-toward-recognizing-we-are-a/. Conservative Judaism is so named for its original defining commitment to conserving Hebrew-language services and, more generally, halacha, not for allegiance to sociopolitical conservatism.

7. Hindu American Foundation, "HAF Commends Supreme Court Affirmation of National Marriage Equality," Hindu American Foundation, June 26, 2015, http://www.hafsite.org/whats-new/haf-commends-supreme-court-affirmation-national-marriage-equality; Muslims for Progressive Values, "Rejoicing the U.S. Supreme Court's Decision on Marriage Equality," PRLog, June 26, 2015, http://www.prlog.org/12469814-muslims-for-progressive-values-rejoicing-the-us-supreme-courts-decision-on-marriage-equality.html.

8. Brandan Robertson, "Evangelical Leaders Affirm SCOTUS Ruling, Say There Is Still Work to Do," NOMAD: Thoughts on Faith and Culture, June 26, 2015, http://www.patheos.com/blogs/revangelical/2015/06/26/evangelical-leaders-affirm-scotus-ruling-say-there-is-still-work-to-do.html.

9. Smith, "Sodom, Leviticus, and *Obergefell*."

10. *Obergefell v. Hodges*, Amicus Briefs, 14-556, "Brief for the National Coalition of Black Pastors and Christian Leaders," https://www.supremecourt.gov/ObergefellHodges/AmicusBriefs/14–556_National_Coalition_of_Black_Pastors_and_Christian_Leaders_REPRINT.pdf (accessed September 27, 2016). For historical analysis of the relationship between various black Christianities and gay rights movements, see the contributions to Josef Sorett, ed., *The Sexual Politics of Black Churches* (Durham: Duke University Press, forthcoming); Russell K. Robinson, "Marriage Equality and Postracialism," *UCLA Law Review* 61, no. 4 (2014): 1010–81; and Amy L. Stone and Jane Ward, "From 'Black People Are Not a Homosexual Act' to 'Gay Is the New Black': Mapping White Uses of Blackness in Modern Gay Rights Campaigns in the United States," *Social Identities* 17, no. 5 (September 2011): 605–24.

11. *Obergefell v. Hodges*, Amicus Briefs, 14-556, "Brief for Freedom to Marry as Amicus Curiae Supporting Petitioners," https://www.supremecourt.gov/ObergefellHodges/AmicusBriefs/14-556_Freedom_to_Marry.pdf (accessed September 27, 2011).

12. Leslie Woodcock Tentler, *Catholics and Contraception: An American History* (Ithaca: Cornell University Press, 2004); Daniel K. Williams, *Defenders of the Unborn: The Pro-Life Movement before Roe v. Wade* (New York: Oxford University Press, 2016); Fay Botham, *Almighty God Created the Races: Christianity, Interracial Marriage, and American Law* (Chapel Hill: University of North Carolina Press, 2009); Sarah Barringer Gordon, *The Spirit of the Law: Religious Voices and the Constitution in Modern America* (Cambridge, Mass.: Belknap Press of Harvard University Press, 2010).

13. Christian Mingle, https://www.christianmingle.com (accessed September 22, 2016); Shmuel Boteach, *Kosher Sex: A Recipe for Passion and Intimacy* (New York: Doubleday, 1999).

14. For notable scholarship on approaching religion and sexuality as co-constructed categories, see Janet R. Jakobsen and Ann Pellegrini, *Love the Sin: Sexual Regulation and the Limits of Religious Tolerance* (New York: New York University Press, 2003); Linell Elizabeth Cady and Tracy Fessenden, *Religion, the Secular, and the Politics of Sexual Difference* (New York: Columbia University Press, 2013); Marie Griffith, "Sexing Religion," in *The Cambridge Companion to Religious Studies*, ed. Robert A. Orsi

(Cambridge: Cambridge University Press, 2011), 338–59; Megan Goodwin, "Thinking Sex and American Religions," *Religion Compass* 5, no. 12 (2011): 772–87; and Anthony Michael Petro, "Religion, Gender, and Sexuality," in *The Columbia Guide to Religion in American History*, ed. Paul Harvey and Edward Blum (New York: Columbia University Press, 2012), 188–212.

15. John D'Emilio and Estelle B. Freedman, *Intimate Matters: A History of Sexuality in America* (New York: Harper and Row, 1989), 300.

16. Margot Canaday, "LGBT History," *Frontiers* 25, no. 1 (2014): 11.

17. Jon Butler, "Jack-in-the-Box Faith: The Religion Problem in Modern American History," *Journal of American History* 90, no. 4 (March 2004): 1359.

18. Most American religions textbooks address sexuality as an issue within "culture war" politics; see Frank Lambert, *Religion in American Politics: A Short History* (Princeton: Princeton University Press, 2008), 189; and Sydney E. Ahlstrom and David D. Hall, *A Religious History of the American People* (New Haven: Yale University Press, 2004), 1117. More nuanced treatment is found in Edwin S. Gaustad and Leigh Eric Schmidt, *The Religious History of America* (San Francisco: Harper San Francisco, 2007), 382–93.

19. For a historical overview of American religious pluralism, see William R. Hutchinson, *Religious Pluralism in America: The Contentious History of a Founding Ideal* (New Haven: Yale University Press, 2003). For a critical genealogy of the category, see Courtney Bender and Pamela E. Klassen, eds., *After Pluralism: Reimagining Religious Engagement* (New York: Columbia University Press, 2010).

20. George Chauncey, "From Sexual Inversion to Homosexuality: Medicine and the Changing Conceptualization of Female Deviance," *Salmagundi* 58/59 (1982): 114–46; Jonathan Katz, *The Invention of Heterosexuality* (Chicago: University of Chicago Press, 2007); Harry Oosterhuis, *Stepchildren of Nature: Krafft-Ebing, Psychiatry, and the Making of Sexual Identity* (Chicago: University of Chicago Press, 2000); Jennifer Terry, *An American Obsession: Science, Medicine, and Homosexuality in Modern Society* (Chicago: University of Chicago Press, 1999); John D'Emilio, "Capitalism and Gay Identity," in *Families in the US: Kinship and Domestic Politics*, ed. Karen V. Hansen and Antia Ilta Garey (Philadelphia: Temple University Press, 1983), 131–41.

21. Chad Heap, *Slumming: Sexual and Racial Encounters in American Nightlife, 1885–1940* (Chicago: University of Chicago Press, 2008); George Chauncey, "Christian Brotherhood or Sexual Perversion? Homosexual Identities and the Construction of Sexual Boundaries in the World War One Era," *Journal of Social History* 19, no. 2 (1985): 189–211; George Chauncey, *Gay New York: Gender, Urban Culture, and the Making of the Gay Male World, 1890–1940* (New York: Basic Books, 1995); Kathy Peiss, *Cheap Amusements: Working Women and Leisure in Turn-of-the-Century New York* (Philadelphia: Temple University Press, 1986); Judith R. Walkowitz, *City of Dreadful Delight: Narratives of Sexual Danger in Late-Victorian London* (Chicago: University of Chicago Press, 1992).

22. Robert A. Padug, "Sexual Matters: On Conceptualizing Sexuality in History," *Radical History Review* 20 (Spring/Summer 1970): 3–23; Carol Vance, "Social Construction Theory: Problems in the History of Sexuality," in *Homosexuality, Which Homosexuality?*, ed. Dennis Altman, Nierkerk A. van Kooten, and T. Van Der Meer (Amsterdam: An Dekker, 1989), 13–34.

23. Talal Asad, *Genealogies of Religion: Discipline and Reasons of Power in Christianity and Islam* (Baltimore: Johns Hopkins University Press, 1993); Tomoko Masuzawa, *The Invention of World Religions, or, How European Universalism Was Preserved in the Language of Pluralism* (Chicago: University of Chicago Press, 2005); J. Z. Smith, "Religion, Religions, Religious," in *Critical Terms for Religious Studies*, ed. Mark Taylor (Chicago: University of Chicago Press, 1998): 269–84; Tisa Joy Wenger, *We Have a Religion: The 1920s Pueblo Indian Dance Controversy and American Religious Freedom* (Chapel Hill: University of North Carolina Press, 2009).

24. On normative discourses and politics in sexuality, see Lauren Berlant and Michael Warner, "Sex in Public," *Critical Inquiry* 24, no. 2 (Winter 1998): 547–66; Lisa Duggan, "Queering the State," *Social Text* 39 (Summer 1994): 1–14; Roderick Ferguson, *Aberrations in Black: Toward a Queer of Color Critique* (Minneapolis: University of Minnesota Press, 2004); Jasbir Puar, *Terrorist Assemblages: Homonationalism in Queer Times* (Durham: Duke University Press, 2007); and Gayle Rubin, "Thinking Sex," in *Pleasure and Danger: Exploring Female Sexuality*, ed. Carole S. Vance (Boston: Routledge and Kegan Paul, 1984), 267–319. On the "good religion"/"bad religion" problem, see Robert Orsi, *Between Heaven and Earth: The Religious Words People Make and the Scholars Who Study Them* (Princeton: Princeton University Press, 2005), 177–204. On the co-construction of religious and sexual normativities, see Janet R. Jakobsen, "Ethics after Pluralism," in *After Pluralism: Reimagining Religious Engagement*, ed. Courtney Bender and Pamela E. Klassen (New York: Columbia University Press, 2010), 31–57.

25. Michel Foucault, *The History of Sexuality, Volume 1: An Introduction* (New York: Pantheon Books, 1978).

26. D'Emilio and Freedman, *Intimate Matters*, 241, 300.

WINNIFRED WYGAL'S FLOCK

Same-Sex Desire and Christian Faith in the 1920s

KATHI KERN

Frances' letter plunged me into torture. I went away and wept as I have not in a year.... For 24 hours I wallowed in agony but I got hold of myself this morning. I must face facts. Facts in this case are 1. That for 11 years I have [generally] speaking centered my life around Frances Perry and everything at present indicates that that will continue to be as always. Nobody can take or touch her place. All this tho I adore Helen and need her and love so deeply Jane and Ruth F and Leslie—ad infinitum. The second fact is that it is good for FP and good for me to be independent in many ways. That effort is harder on me than on her. I am in love with Frances. She loves me only. I am calmer today. My! My!... I must stand in the presence of God, of the sun, of silence, of people—yet apart.[1]

No one would mistake Winnifred Wygal (1884–1972), a career Young Women's Christian Association worker, for a bohemian sex radical of the 1920s. Yet as the passage above suggests, the author and reformer forged an erotic life that challenged both the conventions of heterosexual "companionate marriage" and the concomitant emergence of homosexual "pathology" that characterized early twentieth-century domestic relations. Her perception of the boundless capacity of God's love emboldened Wygal to engage romantically with a number of different women, including Frances Perry, her companion from 1910 to 1940, as well as multiple other women who became, as she sometimes put it, part of her "fold."[2]

Rather than seeing Christian commitment as constraining of human and sexual connection, Wygal maintained that personal relationships were intimately "related to our sense of God." She adamantly rejected the idea that her nonmonogamous, same-sex sexuality was abnormal and instead longed to find God's love through people and work.[3] Wygal's diary provides a rare window on a Christian's negotiation of her sexuality and underscores a central contribution of this book: religious faith played a shaping role in validating same-sex desire in the first half of the twentieth century.

Writing in the wake of Michel Foucault's *The History of Sexuality*, historians of sexuality initially embraced Foucault's hypothesis that the modern sexual subject was constructed through secular discourses.[4] Mining medical journals and the writings of sexologists, as well as police and court records, for evidence of queer ancestors, scholars searched for same-sex desire where they were persuaded they would find it. Foucault's emphasis on secular discourses shifted scholars' attention from religious contexts. Drawing evidence from a range of temporal and geographical contexts, however, historians of religion and sexuality subsequently challenged this tendency by illuminating the various ways in which religious faith created a venue for same-sex expression.[5] Offering vocabularies of spiritual intimacy, religiously affiliated homosocial spaces, intimate rituals, and powerful theological concepts that transcended stigmas of deviance, religious faith played a pivotal yet still largely unappreciated role in the history of same-sex desire. Wygal's life provides an opportunity to clearly delineate the impact of religion on same-sex desire in each of these ways.

Wygal's diary stretches our historical imagination and challenges our received wisdom in several ways. Within the course of her lifetime, she negotiated a cultural transition that historians have done so much to document: the erosion of social acceptance of romantic friendships between women at the turn of the century and the emergence of new categories of "types" of people who were frequently stigmatized for their same-sex desire.[6] Scholars concede that the remarkable fluidity and relatively "unproblematic status" that characterized nineteenth-century intimate female friendships receded in the face of new psychological classifications of sexuality. Women of the early twentieth century experienced this dislocation in various ways. Some women, protected by class and race privilege, continued to live their lives largely unmolested by the new popular and medical denunciations of same-sex affection, although many adopted a more private stance toward public acknowledgment of their love. Fearing exposure, some public figures, like the prison reformer Miriam Van Waters, made a preemptive strike by burning personal correspondence and "strategically" invoking an earlier discourse on the innocence of female friendship. Still others, whether as a strategic decoy or not, deployed the language of pathology themselves. Jeanette Marks, a teacher of English at Mount Holyoke, despite her fifty-two-year relationship with Mount Holyoke president Mary Woolley, published a book in 1911 warning of the dangers of romantic friendship among women.[7]

Wygal took a different path, grounding her same-sex desire in her practice of mainline Christianity. Wygal's experience demonstrates that the emergence of a scientific paradigm of pathology, as well as popular warnings against "mannish lesbians," did not eliminate religious faith as a space for same-sex desire among women in the 1920s.[8] In fact, not only did Wygal find in her faith the strength to resist popular and medical denunciation, but she also understood her need to love multiple women as an expression of God's boundless love. Wygal's extraordinary diary provides a glimpse into such a residual space and, moreover, illustrates the unexamined capacity of Christian faith as a source of self-affirmation for a woman like Wygal.

This chapter explores the residual spaces opened up by Wygal's evolving theology, particularly how her concept of God positioned her to ground her understanding of both race and sexuality in a Christian context. In a literal sense, new horizons emerged from Wygal's international travel, bringing her a heightened perspective on the United States from afar and an opportunity to apply her social justice theology to the places and people she encountered. Wygal's travels to India, the setting for this chapter, allowed her the "psychological space" to fully appreciate how God's love transcended difference. The distance from home, as well as her reliance on correspondence and journaling, created space and opportunity for Wygal to explore her own identity as a white woman who loved other women.

Wygal's theology, particularly her concept of God's all-encompassing love, was refined by her work in the YWCA and the international travel that affiliation afforded. Wygal's career-long association with the YWCA put her in constant proximity of like-minded women from around the world. Following her graduation from Drury College in 1906, Wygal pursued graduate work at various institutions, including Columbia University, where she earned a master's degree in history and economics in 1912. The renowned Christian theologians Reinhold Niebuhr and Paul Tillich mentored her at Union Theological Seminary.[9] For twenty-five years, from 1919 to 1944, Wygal served as a member of the professional staff of the YWCA, a uniquely significant organization in American history. The YWCA, known today primarily as a fitness facility, began in 1858 as a Christian social service organization that offered a wide array of services to women in a rapidly industrializing world, including employment services, housing for women workers, temporary lodging for women travelers, and health and sex education programs. The YWCA was biracial and international in scope and played a supportive role in social movements of the twentieth century, including women's suffrage and civil rights.[10] Wygal focused her efforts on the student movement within the YWCA, the National Student Council Staff, where she rose through the ranks to become "executive" of the council. Her primary intellectual project centered on preparing contemporary, nondenominational worship materials for religious services for the YWCA.[11]

From her home base in New York City, Wygal traveled extensively on behalf of the international YWCA, an experience that positioned her to reflect from a distance on the race and sex politics of her home country. In the pages of her diary, Wygal interrogated what it meant to be a follower of Jesus Christ in America. Her international travel brought her into contact with varied religious traditions and with international leaders of note, including Mahatma Gandhi and Rabindranath Tagore. Like other religious liberals of the period, she carved out an expansive and cosmopolitan theology, one that embraced progressive social change and valued religious ideas from other traditions.[12] Unlike many Americans of the time who traveled to Asia and became immersed in Hinduism or Buddhism, Wygal always returned to the foundations of her Christian faith, applying what she learned abroad to clarify her commitment as a Christian in the United States.

Wygal regularly reflected on the concept of God's love. She understood God's love as an intimate presence in her life. In fact, there was little that happened on a day-to-day basis that did not require God's intimate involvement. When she experienced flu symptoms in Tokyo, Wygal urged herself "to get hold of God more on this health business."[13] With self-awareness, Wygal chastised herself in the diary for lapsing too easily into "a sort of confidential intimacy" with God. She prodded herself to remember his "absolute overpoweringness."[14]

Wygal's intimate conversations with God and her reliance on his love as an agent in her life reflected a larger trend in American religious life. God and Jesus over the course of the nineteenth century became less formidable and more human in scale, more personal, less angry. Jesus, for many American religious liberals, became an "iconic figure of niceness."[15] For Wygal, however, Jesus was a catalyst for change, an uncompromising advocate for justice, and a tireless presence in the lives of others. Exercising his power from the margins, Jesus understood what it meant to be misunderstood; he grasped, as she put it, what it meant to be "queer."[16]

Those two recurring concepts—an intimate, loving God and an uncompromising, openhearted Messiah—propelled Wygal to carve out a life in opposition to the dominant culture of 1920s America, both racially and sexually. The concept of a boundless Christian love allowed her to challenge white privilege, to contextualize her same-sex desire, and to love multiple women unapologetically. As she wrote in her diary, "Is there anything to hold to but to love people and keep clean and do right as far as I know how? What can we do in such a world? What *is* right?"[17] As a Christian, what was "right" to Wygal was, for instance, to take aim at Jim Crow. Convinced that she should return from her time abroad a "different person," Wygal reaffirmed her commitment to apply her Christian principles to homegrown American injustice.[18]

Wygal's ever-sharpening analysis of the privileges of whiteness was honed by her time abroad. Her trip to India in 1927 was part of a sabbatical world tour on behalf of the YWCA and made in the company of one of her intimate friends, a younger woman named Ruth Fertig. Before the two arrived in India, they had visited Hawaii, Japan, China, and the Philippines. From the vantage point of the 1950s, Wygal continued to endorse ship travel as affording visitors a pace that encouraged both in-depth discovery of new places and "infinite time for reflection."[19] Travel was indispensable to Wygal's evolving views, both on race and sexuality, and she admitted that it was a strategy to "broaden the psychological space around" her. While Wygal recognized that travel might simply "confirm our prejudices," she saw the potential for something deeper: "the most sensitive of our travelers returns home loving his country more, thankful to be an American but fervently wishing that America had the composite virtues he has seen elsewhere and feeling more creatively critical of his land than he has been before."[20]

Wygal's time in India was particularly rich because she managed to "free herself" from European and American friends and was hosted by an Indian colleague whose connections brought her into conversation with Mahatma Gandhi and Rabindranath Tagore.[21] At Gandhi's ashram in Ahmedabad, Wygal's sense of her own "calling" crystallized. As Americans, Wygal and Fertig were greeted at the ashram with a judicious mixture of welcome and suspicion. Their tour in India came just one year after the momentous publication of American Katherine Mayo's *Mother India*.[22] Regarded as the height of imperialist propaganda by Indian readers, Mayo's book sparked both an internal dialogue for Wygal and many conversations with Indians as she toured the country. Wygal, who found the book appalling, quickly ascertained that her credibility among Indians depended on a quick, timely condemnation of Mayo.[23]

Wygal experienced a conversion at Gandhi's ashram, but not to Hinduism. Rather, the time with Gandhi clarified her political commitments as a Christian.[24] As Wygal prayed at Gandhi's ashram, she became convinced that the missionary impulse was misplaced.[25] Christians should not waste their energy trying to win conversions among Hindus. Similarly, Christians should not adopt Hinduism, a detour Wygal described as "the path of least resistance." "Isn't it easier," she asked, to join an ashram than "to stick to the needy west and try to find simplicity and God amid the complexity of the very very needy United States?" Was it possible to do this?, she asked Gandhi. "He was careful to say twice that he did not say that one could not live simply and spiritually in the complexity of modern life, but that he had found he could not.... The seductions of modern society are so subtle and numerous as to make it extremely difficult."[26]

For Winnifred Wygal, a brief exchange with Gandhi would have profound consequences. Wygal left Gandhi, in her words, "more devoted to Jesus Christ than I ever was in my life" but also more convinced that Gandhi's lived religion should inspire Christians to apply their theology to daily life, to remedying the complex social problems that blighted American democracy. Her exposure to diverse groups of people and different ways of living constantly positioned Wygal to question the normativity of American racism, particularly Americans' obsession with miscegenation. She puzzled in her diary about "racial mixtures": "Honolulu and Ceylon as laboratories, much success. Why are Philippine Chinese or Dutch Singalese [sic]—accepted when the Anglo Saxon mixture is still so frowned upon?"[27]

Unlike some Americans who would come to embrace Gandhi as "the Christ of our Age"—the conduit from Jesus to Martin Luther King Jr.—Wygal's position was more nuanced.[28] She allowed in her diary that Gandhi directed so much of his energy to building and sustaining his ashram, whereas Jesus had led with an idea, not an institution. "I think that Jesus was righter than Gandhi because he established an attitude but not a regime.... Jesus' attitudes are thoroughly practical. Nothing more practical than love."[29] On a visit to Rabindranath Tagore's school in Shantiniketan, Wygal recorded a conversation about "the Christian way" with Tagore's secretary, Ariam Williams. He impressed Wygal with the idea that Jesus was "less talk, more action."[30] Jesus's relentless action in the world, an expression of his boundless love, was the overarching paradigm that Wygal sought to realize in all aspects of her life. For Wygal, love was as indispensable to justice as fair housing, privacy, and the right to a living wage. As she spelled out her political commitments decades later, she listed love—"love i.e. the opportunity to love and be loved, for all men need love in order to survive"—alongside these other factors.[31]

Reluctant to leave India, Wygal wrote with a heavy heart of her departure, of her privilege in being able to simply sail away from the burdens of poverty, hunger, and imperial rule. "Are we, Ruth and I, under India's burden? Do I really care? Do I ache with Gandhi, with God or do I slip carelessly freely away after an interesting holiday? Can I ever be the same again?" Leaving behind the beauty, the history, the mountains, but especially the people—"women more fearless than we of the West"—Wygal reaffirmed her commitment: "Our part is to learn of them! To love them; to weep over our failure to understand them; to be brothers to them; above all to go home and get under our own misery, our own cruelty, our own ignorance and there to live."[32] In the context of India, Gandhi, and Hinduism, Wygal's commitment to Christianity deepened. Her sense of herself as a Christian whose purpose was to "get under our own misery" came into sharp focus in her time there. God's love provided the through line, the continuity that allowed her to process all she had witnessed and to forge a plan for the future. On board, she worked and reworked her theology in the pages of her diary: "I believe completely in God, God is the Essence; the Source; the Quality; the Unity; the Self; the All there is. I adore God. I stand with the historical Jesus; him I also adore . . . as the picture of what man has the potentiality to be, a lifting of humanity up to God not a dragging of Jesus down to earth." Affirming the "God in us," Wygal recognized that pain was also a function of God, writing, "Pain is used to redeem, pain is inherent in love."[33]

The redemptive power of pain allowed Wygal to contextualize both the sins of racism and her struggles to find love. For a Christian like Wygal, God's love wielded power. Her understanding of God's capacious love also shaped Wygal's sexuality. As she wrote in her diary, "The real philosophy of Jesus is to find life, not to lose it." And for Wygal, "finding life" was intimately bound up with her love of women.[34]

The danger when one discovers traces of same-sex desire in a historical figure is to impose contemporary categories onto the past, to shape it into something recognizable. As scholars, we need to tread carefully among our sources to preserve the "fundamental otherness" of past sexual practice.[35] Judith Weisenfeld, for example, cautions us in this volume to not simply impose the category "lesbian" on the same-sex desire expressed by women in Father Divine's Peace Mission. The implication of such a label—although rendering the past more legible—would undermine the legitimacy of the women's own religion position. Their commitment to celibacy was honored by triangulating their expressions of love and desire for each other through the "Father in me." Similarly, Winnifred Wygal defies convenient labeling. A map of her complex emotional and erotic universe included her maintenance of both a primary relationship and a cluster of satellite relationships that moved in and out of her orbit. Between 1916 and 1942, Wygal continued a primary relationship with Frances Perry, fostered a budding romance with Helen Price, traveled to Asia and Europe with Ruth Fertig, and cultivated several other intimate relationships through correspondence and occasional visits.

Wygal's entangled emotional commitments overlapped on the pages of her diary, as thoughts of one woman inevitably reminded her of yet another. In a passage written during her visit to Agra, she reflected on the exquisite beauty of the Taj Mahal in the moonlight. Lying on her back, gazing at the moon and stars, she contemplated "beauty" and asked rhetorically, "Am I making it with Ruth? O not in the usual sense. We are very devoted. But what am I doing to her? What is she like? I do not understand her very well. I wish I did, I love her though." In the beauty and tranquility of the night, awash in a feeling of being "at home" in the garden of the Taj Mahal, Wygal conjured her coterie of intimates, focusing alternately on her traveling companion, Ruth; her new love, Helen Price; and her abiding love for Frances Perry: "O if Helen Price could see it [the Taj Mahal]! She would so understand and appreciate. . . . How I love Helen Price these days. She is a comfort. And Frances—my far off beautiful Frances—a Taj Mahal of life to me is Frances—always I adore her, remote Frances, who shows me my place. No wonder Helen has been a new lifegiving experience during 1927. I waited 4 years for Frances and she could not. It must have been my fault. It was all my fault. Frances is very loyal but she gives herself elsewhere."[36]

Was Wygal "making it with Ruth?" she asked rhetorically; "O not in the usual sense." Historians of sexuality have cautioned against the requirement of "genital proofs" of sexual contact among those we study, arguing that it creates an unfair burden imposed primarily on historical figures perceived to be "queer."[37] While the archive does not answer these questions definitively, Wygal did in fact conceptualize the capacity of a spiritual relationship with other women to include physical contact. In a telling passage in her diary, Wygal detailed an experience of taking Communion on a May Sunday morning in 1928. The church service was reportedly "dull," but Wygal achieved a moment of "ecstasy" kneeling at the Communion rail, receiving the "symbols" with the familiar refrain "The body of our Lord Jesus Christ which was given for thee, preserve thy body and soul unto everlasting life.

Take and eat this in remembrance . . . that Christ died for thee . . ." The familiar invocation of Christ's sacrifice, the performance of an intimate, holy ritual, called to mind Wygal's most personal relationships: "I thought about Ruth F and her temperament and needs. About Frances Perry." Of the latter, Wygal considered (her mind clearly straying from the ritual at hand), "I wonder what she would think if I asked her not to kiss me?" Wygal transported herself to a painful memory years earlier, a moment shared with Frances Perry under a tree in Windermere. Perry announced that kissing Wygal elicited no feelings from her and was, in fact, no different than kissing "a block of wood." She meant, Wygal elaborated, that Perry experienced "no passion." Wygal cautioned that she did "not believe 'passion' is necessary or even right. But I do believe that a deep spiritual unity and a rare faith between two women friends will express itself in natural and warm humor and physical contact. Nothing abnormally erotic but natural, spontaneous, tender . . . as the case may be."[38]

Wygal's phrase "nothing abnormally erotic" opens a space to consider Wygal's self-scrutiny of her sexual desire. Erotic physical contact—as long as it was not *abnormally* erotic—was natural between women, "wholesome," as she often described her connections to other women. Does the phrase "abnormally erotic" signal her awareness of an encroaching discourse of pathology? Wygal's diary is riddled with self-interrogation: she contemplates her "sin," her "smallness," her "weakness," her "wickedness," her anti-Semitism, her disappointments as a writer, and, most frequently, her failure to be "god-like."[39] Yet throughout, Wygal resisted a tone of defensiveness about her same-sex love. In fact, her interrogation of her sins often centered on her incapacity to love a woman fully. After seeking sustenance in her devotional reading—a combination of Harry Fosdick and the books of John and Mark—Wygal pronounced herself "depressed with my own sin, my own smallness, my own restlessness. God fill me with the peace of Galilee, of Jesus. Ruth doubts that I love her. It bothers me. O if only I were better! I mean bigger, more poised, more radiant, more serene, more very, very God-like."[40] Her faith in God emboldened her to see these relationships as natural, wholesome, and reflective of the love of God. "I am not guilty of any overt sins," she wrote in her diary in March 1928, yet she was never more convinced of "how good was Jesus and how bad I was."[41]

Free of sin, physical contact should be natural and wholesome between two women who shared "a rare faith." The trouble was, there was something inauthentic about Frances Perry's kisses, and it bothered Wygal. "I have wished for two years that FP wouldn't kiss me until there came a time when she wanted to or couldn't help it. To me it is sacrilegious to use a kiss as a concession to conventionality."[42] A kiss could devolve into a concession to conventionality, or it could signify something more precious: the intersection of divine and human love.[43] For Wygal, the love of God and a spiritual unity between women friends based on that love were mutually constitutive, indistinguishable.

What seems less clear is whether or not Frances Perry (and the other women Wygal loved) shared her commitment to a spiritually inspired, physical intimacy. Frances Perry's kisses lacked passion, but her letters alternately raised Wygal's romantic hopes and dashed them irrevocably. The remote "Taj Mahal of Life" sometimes confused and frightened Wygal: "My letter from FP raises again questions. I cannot quite see why I become confused on the score of Frances and her ideals. I am so afraid of her. . . . Why do I resist being prayed for? O I am so wicked. . . . Frances writes of her belief in celibacy! I cannot believe in it, she means celibacy for some not all. She is a rare person."[44] Wygal's snide aside—"celibacy for some not all"—suggests that Perry may have withheld pleasures that Wygal found to be natural and spontaneous between two women sealed in a common faith.[45] In passage after passage in her diary, Wygal counsels "self control" and bemoans the loss of something crucial between them: "Can I myself be one of the lost? I love Frances Perry. I look at her picture. I wish things had been different between us. She is beautiful but I am not yet straight on it all."[46] In a letter from Perry that Wygal attached to the inside of her diary of 1927, Perry addressed Wygal as "My Other Soul," yet her prescriptions suggest that the two women may have held conflicting perspectives on the carnal nature of spiritual love: "O Winnifred Wygal this friendship of ours is something made beautiful by being in a crucible of fire, of pain, of agony. If we can increasingly strip it of impurities burned away by fire it will be a thing in time of utter loveliness. Do you know what I am saying? Tell me you understand."[47]

Wygal carefully managed the flow of information regarding her various connections, yet all roads led through the troubled waters that were Frances Perry. The source of both pleasure and agony, Perry was Wygal's mainstay, although, as the diary passage that opened this chapter indicates, she adored and needed Helen, Jane, Ruth F., and Leslie—"ad infinitum." Women in the satellite relationships were sometimes relied upon to provide emotional support during times of conflict with Perry. A passage in her diary details a night Wygal spent with another woman on the "ad infinitum" list—Leslie—to whom she confessed (presumably delicately) her simultaneous love of both Frances Perry (FP) and Helen Price (HP):

> It was a relief to *see* her. I love her and trust her. She was frank with me. I stayed overnight with her, we talked to 3am. I told her more about FP than I've ever told anyone. It is hard to admit to L[eslie] that there has been ever a situation re FP but likely she guessed it. She told me that it was evident that FP was bothered re HP. It's a wholesome situation but a hard love. I love them both but oh so differently. FP need not fear, she loses me not yet she has been careless with my affections for five years. . . . I feel sort of at loose ends spiritually.[48]

Wygal at times struggled to manage so many loves, each unique and indispensable, a process enabled by her international travel and the well-oiled machine of the postal system that conveyed the bounty of her love, a wealth of letters gathered and sent as precious cargo at each port of call.[49] Her travel meant that Wygal was not tightly bound to a single place; it also meant that she was not exclusively tied to a single person. What was manageable through correspondence, however, could prove taxing in person. In her diary, Wygal chastised herself for her failure to love with a Christlike abundance and capacity: "I got to thinking of my sins. I wrote a bit to Leslie. I wept. I am so wicked. I am frightened that I get so nervous and cross and I do not want to at all. I love them all, oh so! Jesus! Was he ever cross or nervous[?]"[50]

Wygal struggled to manage her loves in the here and now, but she also tended the flock of past loves when called upon. An aspect of Wygal's "fundamental otherness" was her sense of Christian obligation in maintaining intimate connections with women, long after her erotic interest in them had subsided. In her diary she wrote with exasperation of one such encounter, regretting that she "gave one full week to Louise Huff." Describing the week as essentially wasted when she had important work to do, Wygal did not feel at liberty to "turn down Louise's longings." Citing a covenant she had entered into years before as a junior at Drury College—"Having girls once I must continue to be fair"—Wygal took the ethical high ground. She spent a sleepless week "lolling about" and "squeezing hands," listening to the "pretty and so well-dressed" Louise Huff's late-night testimony on the liberating impact of Harry E. Fosdick's *Modern Use of the Bible*.[51] There was no question that Huff had grown intellectually into "a far more interesting and able person than I ever dreamed or hoped in 1912," but the obligation took its toll on Wygal. She "loved" Huff, would "love her always," but disappointed her classmate by spending only two nights with her. ("One would have been better for me," Wygal sighed.)[52]

Ultimately, Winnifred Wygal's diary—a complex text dense with self-recriminations, theological observations, racial commentary, romantic travel narratives, and expressions of same-sex desire—makes a compelling case for a Christian paradigm for both same-sex love and nonmonogamy. Wygal was unrepentant in her embrace of other women. In fact, she worried over her friends who could not absorb the theological truth that intimate relations were an expression of the divine. Poor Martha Dennison, who "wasn't very attractive" and "does not attract many people and I suppose men never," stayed up late with Winnifred bemoaning her "cut-offness" from God. Women like Martha, Winnifred allowed, saw men and marriage as the only logical outlet: "O we must get above that kind of loneliness. I wish they all cared as little as I for men and marriage. Yet in a way I have wanted and needed it as much as any. I am not abnormal. How can I say it? I *long* for love and life and people and labor that is all a part of God and yet I am so contented with my present state."[53] And in her refusal to see herself as "abnormal," Wygal resisted the emerging popular and medical paradigms of deviance that would offer such explanatory power in the history of the twentieth century. Two points are worth underscoring here. Many of the historical protagonists for whom spirituality provides a lexicon for same-sex desire participated in marginal or alternative religions.[54] But Wygal was squarely, thoroughly mainstream in her Presbyterian upbringing and her liberal Protestant theology. Buoyed by a relentless, socially conscious Jesus and the capaciousness of God's love, Wygal embraced racial justice and her romantic longings for the love of particular women. In fact, both her love of God and her love of other women shared a common emotional texture, her admission of "confidential intimacy."[55]

The second point regards chronology. Most of the scholarship mapping out the intersection of spirituality and same-sex desire contends that by the 1920s, expressions of homoeroticism, however couched in religious metaphor, were viewed with suspicion. George Chauncey has marked the period in which Wygal was writing and building a life as a "veritable 'Heterosexual Counterrevolution.'" He and other scholars have argued that with the waning of a Victorian paradigm of women's sexual passivity, the cultural acceptance of same-sex desire between women actually constricted. Greater sexual liberalization for women was firmly tied to heterosexuality.[56] So Wygal's experience may provide both more evidence of religious faith as an antidote to medical pathology and popular discourses and an example of the persistence of such resistance into a later era.[57] In her diary, Wygal offered sympathy to a woman who "feels the new psychology knocked her." The friend had lost her ability to pray, a powerful tool of resistance for Wygal.[58] Yet even Wygal's religiously inspired resistance to medical pathology may not have lasted much past 1930. As early as 1932, she quarreled with Frances Perry over the latter's insistence that she destroy their letters, the letters of Helen Price, and the multivolume diary on which this chapter is based. Wygal reluctantly complied in part with Perry's demand. Perry's ostensible reason for destroying the correspondence was Wygal's "small closet space," but Perry was apparently also concerned that Wygal could die suddenly, "saddling others with the private and sorry job" of examining the personal letters.[59] Composing her autobiography as a seventy-year-old in the 1950s, Wygal no longer attempted to account for the religious impulse of her same-sex desire. Rather, she deleted the episodes entirely and asserted, "Sex and boys excited and haunted me from the age of eight on until that time thirty-five years later when the pattern fell into place and a sense of peace and destiny ensued." In the context of Cold War homophobia, Wygal explained her unmarried status as an outgrowth of the repressions of an earlier historic moment.[60]

Perhaps the most significant finding is not that Wygal used religion as a protective buffer against the encroachments of medical pathology and popular discourses that stigmatized same-sex desires but rather that she organized an erotic life that lay outside the dominant paradigm of serial monogamy. She did this self-consciously and with Christian conviction. As she reassured Frances Perry of the pivotal place in her constellation, Wygal relied on a biblical parable to seal her point: "You *are* the lamb of my bosom. You have been since 1918 and will be till we die ... but I have other sheep not of this fold and there are times when the precious lamb must wait while one goes among the ninety and nine."[61] This familiar refrain from Luke, the parable of the lost sheep, provided Wygal with a justifiable framework for nonmonogamy, for temporarily abandoning her "precious lamb" in search of a lost sheep in need of her rescue. Bolstered by her religious faith, Wygal crafted a life where the love of women (plural) grew out of her love of God. In the spring of 1928 in the pages of her diary, Wygal offered a prayer: "May I learn to live in the world but differ from it enough to be of value to it."[62] This passage encapsulated Wygal's theological stance. Her Christianity empowered her to achieve an elusive balance, to be of the world but not to conform to it. God's love provided the sustenance to be different, both as social justice advocate and as a lover of women. Difference, in Wygal's prayer, was not something to be simply tolerated; it was a catalyst for transformation, the power by which humanity was lifted up to God.

NOTES

For helpful comments and conversations, I am indebted to Dwight Billings, Kate Black, Bruce Dorsey, Phil Harling, Joanne Pope Melish, Karen Tice, Judith Weisenfeld, and the Works in Progress Series in the University of Kentucky Department of History. Finally, I wish to thank the tireless work of research assistants Nyoka Hawkins, David Lai, and Ashley Sorrell for their excellent efforts on behalf of this project.

1. Winnifred Wygal Diary, August 12, 1928, Winnifred Wygal Collection, Arthur and Elizabeth Schlesinger Library on the History of Women in America, Radcliffe College (hereafter Wygal Diary).

2. Wygal Diary, July 15, 1928; October 3, 1932.

3. Ibid., February 6, 1928. See H. G. Cocks, "Religion and Spirituality," in *The Modern History of Sexuality*, ed. H. G. Cocks and Matt Houlbrook (New York: Palgrave Macmillan, 2006), 169.

4. Michel Foucault, *The History of Sexuality, Volume 1: An Introduction* (repr., New York: Vintage, 1990).

5. See Molly McGarry, *Ghosts of Futures Past: Spiritualism and the Cultural Politics of Nineteenth-Century America* (Berkeley: University of California Press, 2008), 5; Kevin P. Murphy, "Socrates in the Slums: Homoerotics, Gender, and Settlement House Reform," in *A Shared Experience: Men, Women, and the History of Gender*, ed. Laura McCall and Donald Yacavone (New York: New York University Press, 1998), 273–96; Seth Koven, *Slumming: Sexual and Social Politics in Victorian London* (Princeton: Princeton University Press, 2004); Sue Morgan, "'The Word Made Flesh': Women, Religion and Sexual Cultures," in *Women and Religious Cultures in Britain, 1800–1940*, ed. Sue Morgan and Jacqueline deVries (New York: Routledge, 2010), 159–87; and Martha Vicinus, *Intimate Friends: Women Who Loved Women, 1778–1928* (Chicago: University of Chicago Press, 2004).

6. At the same time, in the nineteenth century, same-sex desire was not entirely free of judgment. As Gillian Frank has observed, anxieties about women's desire for one another clearly was not only the preserve of medical experts but also a widespread public concern. For example, see a remarkable two-part series of advice columns by Anne McDowell, which was published in the *Saturday Evening Post* in January and February 1871. The *Saturday Evening Post* was one of the highest circulating and oldest journals in the United States with upward of fifty thousand national subscribers in the 1870s.

7. For an overview, see Leila Rupp, *A Desired Past: A Short History of Same-Sex Love in America* (Chicago: University of Chicago Press, 1999), 76–84; Estelle B. Freedman, "'The Burning of Letters Continues': Elusive Identities and the Historical Construction of Sexuality," *Journal of Women's History* 9, no. 4 (Winter 1998): 181–200; and Linda W. Rosenzweig, *Another Self: Middle-Class American Women and Their Friends in the Twentieth Century* (New York: New York University Press, 1999), 125–35.

8. Morgan, "'Word Made Flesh,'" 178.

9. See Columbia University catalogue, 1911–12, http://www.ebooksread.com/authors-eng/columbia-university/catalogue-volume-19111912-ulo/page-28-catalogue-volume-19111912-ulo.shtml (accessed March 27, 2013).

10. See Nancy Marie Robertson, *Christian Sisterhood, Race Relations, and the YWCA, 1906–46* (Urbana: University of Illinois Press, 2007); and John Donald Gustav-Wrathall, *Take the Young Stranger by the Hand: Same-Sex Relations and the YMCA* (Chicago: University of Chicago Press, 2000).

11. Prior to her death in 1972, Wygal bequeathed to the YWCA her work-related papers as well as an array of her publications, including titles such as *Jesus: A Brief Study*, *We the Peoples of the Ecumenical Church*, and *How to Plan Informal Worship*. The sixteen-volume diary on which this chapter is based escaped a purge of Wygal's personal papers in 1932 and can be found at the Arthur and Elizabeth Schlesinger Library on the History of Women in America housed at Radcliffe College.

12. On the cosmopolitanism of religious liberals, see Leigh E. Schmidt and Sally M. Promey, eds., *American Religious Liberalism* (Bloomington: Indiana University Press, 2012).

13. Wygal Diary, October 24, 1927.

14. Ibid., March 24, 1928.

15. Carrie Tirado Bramen, "The Christology of Niceness: Harriet Beecher Stowe, the Jesus Novel, and Sacred Trivialities," in *American Religious Liberalism*, ed. Leigh E. Schmidt and Sally M. Promey (Bloomington: Indiana University Press, 2012), 39; Stephen Prothero, *American Jesus: How the Son of God Became a National Icon* (New York: Farrar, Straus, and Giroux, 2004), 55.

16. Wygal Diary, February 2, 1928. From the context in which she is railing against racial prejudice toward Chinese on board her ship, it seems that Wygal is using "queer" to mean "different."

17. Ibid., December 27, 1927.

18. Ibid., January 14, 1928.

19. Winnifred Wygal, unpublished autobiography, n.d., chap. 5, p. 1, box 3, folder 11, Winnifred Crane Wygal Papers, Sophia Smith Collection, Smith College.

20. Ibid., p. 12.

21. Wygal befriended a Mr. Vakil who served as the Inspector of Education for the Bombay presidency on the ship between Hong Kong and Colombo. See Winnifred Wygal, February 5, 1928, transcription of a letter recounting a visit to Gandhi's Ashram, box 3, folder 4, Winnifred Crane Wygal Papers, Sophia Smith Collection, Smith College.

22. For more on Katherine Mayo, see Mrinalini Sinha, *Specters of Mother India: The Global Restructuring of an Empire* (Durham: Duke University Press, 2006).

23. Wygal Diary, January 6, 1928.

24. Winnifred Wygal, unpublished autobiography, chap. 7, p. 2.

25. The YWCA had a complicated stance toward missions. On the one hand, YWCA workers qualified for "missionary rates" while traveling and worked within a framework of the Christian-inspired Social Gospel. On the other hand, many active workers within the YWCA saw themselves in a separate endeavor from that of the missionaries, emphasizing the ecumenical nature of their project and their freedom from male authority. Like many feminists of the period who worked for women's rights internationally, Wygal was generally critical of missionaries and wrote extensively of their collective hubris and their

inability to appreciate local culture and conditions. See Nancy Boyd, *Emissaries: The Overseas Work of the American YWCA, 1895–1970* (New York: Woman's Press, 1986), 5.

26. Winnifred Wygal, February 5, 1928, typed transcript of a journal account of Wygal's visit to Gandhi's Ashram, Winnifred Crane Wygal Papers 105, box 3, folder 4, Sophia Smith Collection, Smith College, Northampton, Massachusetts.

27. Wygal Diary, January 4, 1928.

28. John H. Holmes of the War Resisters League dubbed Gandhi the "Christ of Our Age." See Scott Bennett, *Radical Pacifism: The War Resisters League and Gandhian Nonviolence in America, 1915–1963* (Syracuse: Syracuse University Press, 2003), 29.

29. Wygal Diary, February 8, 1928.

30. Ariam Williams, a Ceylonese Christian of Tamil origins, taught at Tagore's school from 1924 to 1943. He served as Tagore's secretary in 1927 and 1930. See Krishna Dutta and Andrew Robinson, eds., *The Selected Letters of Rabindranath Tagore* (Cambridge: Cambridge University Press, 1997), 385n4.

31. Winnifred Wygal, unpublished autobiography, chap. 5, p. 13.

32. Wygal Diary, February 16, 1928.

33. Ibid., May 12, 1928.

34. Ibid. Wygal appeared never to have engaged in a romantic relationship with a man.

35. Cocks, "Religion and Spirituality," 167.

36. Wygal Diary, January 28, 1928.

37. Blanche Wiesen Cook, "The Historical Denial of Lesbianism," *Radical History Review* 20 (1979): 60–65; Leila Rupp, "Imagine My Surprise: Women's Relationships in Historical Perspective," *Frontiers: A Journal of Women Studies* 5, no. 3 (Autumn 1980): 61–70. Cook argues that straight men and women were not held to the same burden of "genital proof" to confirm their heterosexuality. Other scholars have documented religiously inspired sexual contact among women that required management, balance, and atonement. See, for example, Freedman, "'Burning of Letters Continues'"; and Pauline Phipps, "Faith, Desire and Sexual Identity: Constance Maynard's Atonement for Passion," *Journal of the History of Sexuality* 18, no. 2 (May 2009): 265–86.

38. Wygal Diary, May 13, 1928.

39. Laments such as these appear throughout the multiple volumes of the diary. These particular examples are drawn from March 8, 1928.

40. Ibid., March 8, 1928.

41. Ibid.

42. Ibid., May 13, 1928.

43. Sue Morgan has argued that "the familiar, heartfelt language of spiritual love" allowed women to articulate "dissident, same-sex subjectivities." See Morgan, "'Word Made Flesh,'" 175.

44. Wygal Diary, June 15, 1928.

45. This passage read in concert with another one in which Wygal says Perry "gives herself elsewhere" raises the possibility that Perry was romantically involved with someone else and chose celibacy as the basis of her relationship with Wygal.

46. Wygal Diary, June 29, 1928.

47. Frances Perry to Winnifred Wygal, undated letter attached to Wygal Diary, October 1927.

48. Wygal Diary, August 26, 1928.

49. Wygal saw her letter writing as her "vocation" (ibid., March 30, 1928) yet worried that she wrote too extensively to people. Ibid., June 6, 1928.

50. Ibid., March 7, 1928.

51. Harry E. Fosdick, *Modern Use of the Bible* (London: Macmillan, 1925).

52. Wygal Diary, July 15, 1928.

53. Ibid., February 6, 1928. In her diary of 1928, Wygal occasionally expresses frustration over Ruth's interest in men.

54. See, for example, McGarry, *Ghosts of Futures Past*, 159, on the queerness of Spiritualism; Murphy, "Socrates in the Slums," 275; and Cocks, "Religion and Spirituality," 171.

55. Wygal Diary, March 25, 1928.

56. George Chauncey Jr., "From Sexual Inversion to Homosexuality: The Changing Medical Conceptualization of Female 'Deviance,'" in *Passion and Power: Sexuality in History*, ed. Kathy Peiss and Christina Simmons (Philadelphia: Temple University Press, 1989), 107. See also Morgan, "'Word Made Flesh,'" 173. Linda W. Rosenzweig's treatment of the Wygal-Perry relationship focused primarily on the tension, pain, and dissolution of the relationship as well as on Wygal's capitulation to the burning of their letters, an indication of Wygal's growing awareness of the growing social unease about same-sex love. See Rosenzweig, *Another Self*, 138–39.

57. See Koven, *Slumming*, 239, 275. H. G. Cox writes: "Whereas nineteenth-century religion had been allowed to be truly queer, in the sense that its cultural prestige and immense social authority meant that it might cover a variety of polymorphous and unspecific transgressions of gender and sexuality, by the early twentieth century religion had come under suspicion and fallen into decay as one of the principal locations for sexual expression of all kinds." See Cox, "Religion and Spirituality," 175. Also see Rosenzweig, *Another Self*, 147, on the persistence of romantic friendships among women into the mid-twentieth century.

58. Wygal Diary, February 15, 1928.

59. As quoted in Rosenzweig, *Another Self*, 139.

60. Winnifred Wygal, unpublished autobiography, chap. 1, p. 4. On homophobia in the 1950s, see Margot Canaday, *The Straight State: Sexuality and Citizenship in Twentieth-Century America* (Princeton: Princeton University Press, 2009), 168.

61. Wygal Diary, September 13, 1932. For the parable of the lost sheep, see Luke 15:3–7.

62. Wygal Diary, May 22, 1928.

SUBVERSIVE SPIRITUALITIES

Yoga's Complex Role in the Narrative of Sex and Religion in the Twentieth-Century United States

ANDREA R. JAIN

For most of the twentieth century, yoga advocates challenged the dominant U.S. social order when it came to sexual norms and their religious justifications. The twentieth-century United States provided rich soil for the re-creation of "exotic" Indian devotions into idiosyncratic forms of yoga, promoting modes of spirituality through which participants subverted mainstream cultural templates for sexuality. While the Protestant moral establishment sought to channel the new era's innovations in contraception, companionate marriage, and increased public visibility of heterosexuality into the older Christian sanctification of family-centered, reproductive marital sexuality, yoga advocates across the United States offered starkly contrasting sacred sexual values: sexual renunciation on the one hand or sexual liberty on the other.

Multiple diverse representations of yoga emerged in the United States through the efforts of several early twentieth-century subversive spiritual figures and movements. Transcendentalism, Theosophy, New Thought, Christian Science, and the Vedanta Society were among the movements that assimilated and syncretized ideas and practices from Protestant liberalism, modern science, and mind cure, as well as yoga and other South Asian traditions.[1] The architects of this spiritual practice of modern yoga thus blurred religious boundaries and challenged mainstream Christianity as they also subverted sexual norms.[2] However, this decidedly countercultural image shifted markedly by the end of the twentieth century.[3] For this reason, yoga provides a unique exemplar of the intertwined transformations of twentieth-century religion and sexuality. Initially largely perceived as a perverse and heathen challenge to the Protestant moral establishment, yoga by the century's end typified ascendant cultural ideals of bodily and spiritual health.

This chapter contributes to the ongoing effort to situate yoga within the realm of U.S. spirituality in the twentieth century and illuminates yoga's subversive sexual legacies through several case studies of "unchurched" forbears of American yoga.[4] Those responsible for appropriating and re-creating yoga as a mode of subversive spirituality varied as widely as the turn-of-the-century sex reformer Ida C. Craddock (1857–1902), the Hindu-Indian nationalist Vivekananda (1863–1902), the tantric guru Swami Muktananda (1908–82), and the devotional guru Daya Mata (1914–2010). I also explain the routes through which yoga, while remaining within the realm of spirituality, eventually came to play a very different social role, reflecting sexual and gender norms in the popular imagination in the late twentieth century. In the last few decades of the twentieth century, dominant ideas and institutions increasingly influenced some schools of yoga, which resulted in the mirroring of sexual normativity. For most of yoga's story in the twentieth-century United States, however, its advocates were more concerned with God-realization or self-realization through celibacy or, on the flipside, with sexual liberty than with the pursuit of cultural ideals of health, beauty, or sexual prowess. Consequently, the role of yoga and its various sexual cultures have a significant place in the narrative of sex and religion in the twentieth-century United States.

TWO SUBVERSIVE LEGACIES IN THE FIRST HALF OF THE TWENTIETH CENTURY

In 1902, when yoga advocates Swami Vivekananda and Ida C. Craddock died, they left behind two legacies that would shape U.S. visions of yoga and in turn influence twentieth-century sexual attitudes and ideas. Of particular significance to their stories is the Protestant moral establishment, which historian David Sehat argues functioned as the cultural and legal standard in much of the United States at the turn of the century.[5] This period witnessed vigorous attempts to enforce fundamentalist interpretations of what it meant to be a "Christian nation." Postal inspector and founder of the New York Society for the Suppression of Vice Anthony Comstock played a significant role in this movement.[6] Beginning in 1873, Comstock used his position in the postal service to battle ideas and practices he deemed a threat to the Protestant morals he identified as American, including Craddock's subversive teachings on yoga and sex. The normative religious standard upheld by Comstock and the broader movement for the "suppression of vice" denounced the pursuit of sexual pleasure, instead identifying reproduction as the legally protected and religiously sanctioned purpose of sex. For these Protestant reformers, the outrage that Craddock represented primarily hinged on her severance of the connection between marital sex and reproduction.[7]

Born in Philadelphia, Craddock was raised by a mother who had an enthusiasm for evangelical Protestantism and moral reform and sent her daughter to a Quaker school.[8] Despite her mother's rigid conservatism, Craddock repeatedly challenged social and religious norms from a young age and actively pursued spiritual, social, and political interests. She taught typing and stenography classes at the Women's Educational and Industrial Union and joined a Unitarian church. She studied spiritualism, adopting one of the few modes of power available to women: communication with the spirit world. Over time, she built an impressive psychical and spiritualist repertoire, drawing from her experience as a research assistant for the metaphysical magazine *Borderland*, her interest in the Society for Psychical Research, and her studies of Theosophy, Christian Science, New Thought, and additional occult topics. She eventually declared herself a priestess and pastor of the Church of Yoga. As historian Leigh Schmidt argues, "Craddock's abandonment of her Protestant identity was one part of a much larger yogic challenge to evangelical Christianity's power to define the nation's sexual and religious norms."[9]

Craddock opened an office in Chicago where she counseled and taught correspondence courses to married couples, educating them on the sacred nature of sex and natural birth control. In a move that irreversibly stamped her with the legal and medical charge of insanity, the unmarried Craddock maintained that her explicit sexual knowledge came from her nightly psychical experiences with her angel-husband, Soph. She became a public figure in 1893 at the World's Columbian Exposition in Chicago, a massive fair held in honor of the four hundredth anniversary of Europeans' arrival in the Americas and the United States' subsequent "progress" and imperialism.[10] There, Craddock courted controversy by defending the "Danse du Ventre," a belly-dancing performance, against Comstock's onslaughts in the name of decency.

In her writings, Craddock combined the goals of marital union and tantric yoga with a Christian theology that she believed undergirded both, making them mutually desirable and reinforcing spiritual pursuits. She discovered tantra by reading The Esoteric Science and Philosophy of the Tantras, Shiva Sanhita, an English translation of one of the earliest and best-known hatha yoga texts, the fifteenth-century Shiva Samhita. In its pages, she encountered the esoteric, tantric components of hatha yoga. Craddock homed in on the idea that sex could facilitate divine realization through certain tantric techniques, most notably the *vajroli mudra* or "urethral suction." This practice required the male partner in intercourse to control ejaculation and functioned as a hydraulic technique through which male and female sexual fluids were transformed within the male body in order to bring about "an immortal yet concrete *diamond body* that transcends the laws of nature."[11]

Craddock reconstructed those ideas and techniques into a new system, requiring restricted seminal emissions, for enhancing pleasure within heterosexual marital intercourse, reducing the incidence of unwanted pregnancy, and simultaneously advancing the state of the soul in relation to God.[12] In a creative redefinition of tantra's sacralization of sex, Craddock formulated a new vision of marital intercourse that considered God to be a third partner in the union, suggesting, "Only those who have experienced the bliss of taking God into the marital partnership in its most intimate relation can be said either to be truly wedded or to truly realize what it is to love God, and be in return beloved by Him."[13]

In her 1900 book *The Wedding Night*, Craddock explains that yoga is central to her vision of divine sexual union between husband and wife: "To the average uninstructed man or woman, there is no apparent relation between the honeymoon and that philosophy which I prefer to call 'yoga.' And yet, if yoga were properly understood and practiced in the marital embrace by every newly married couple, their sex life would be, from the start, so holy, so healthy, so happy, that they would never care to descend to the methods commonly practiced among married people today."[14] Then-common birth control methods that Craddock implicitly critiqued would have included primarily condoms, douching, and spermicidal preparations, but her emphasis on male continence, or intercourse without ejaculation, had a long American religious history independent of this yogic rebranding. In promoting this form of extreme self-control as a path to spiritual communion through sex, Craddock was drawing on the earlier works of Christian utopians like John Humphrey Noyes, founder of the communalist Oneida Community. Her innovation lay in trying to teach it more broadly and in the context of yoga rather than reserving the discipline of continence for a tiny community of adepts.[15]

Her emerging system of yoga included a set of techniques for simultaneously achieving sexual pleasure, birth control, and closeness to God, goals that were ordinarily considered antithetical. She disseminated her scandalous ideas primarily through pamphlets sent by U.S. mail. This distribution method brought down the wrath of the new postal inspection regime: Comstock brought charges against her for attempting to spread "obscene" literature.[16] In 1899, Craddock faced federal indictment in Chicago for using the post to distribute a tract on appropriate sexual relations between husband

and wife. In 1902, after being convicted, this time in a New York trial on similar charges, Craddock spent three torturous months in prison. Upon her release, an upcoming federal trial for distribution of *The Wedding Night* threatened additional prison time. Craddock responded by taking her own life in order to die a free woman. Her efforts to promote yoga as a sexual and spiritual method, even if prescribed within the boundaries of heterosexual marriage and offered as a more God-centered alternative to barrier methods of birth control, were too radical for her time and place.

Like the path-breaking Craddock, Pierre Bernard (1865–1955) was a social radical and tantric yogi who prescribed yoga as a legitimate and effective sexual-spiritual mode of bodily pleasure.[17] Unlike Craddock, Bernard viewed yoga as a sexual-spiritual practice useful both within and outside of marriage. Bernard succeeded in attracting many disciples who, in some cases, continued his legacy and shaped yoga in the United States. Bernard discovered yoga in his boyhood when he met an Indian yogi by the name of Sylvais Hamati in Lincoln, Nebraska. Hamati became Bernard's guru and taught him hatha yoga techniques. In turn, Bernard became a teacher of sexual yoga who was nicknamed in the press "the Omnipotent Oom" and the "Loving Guru." For years, he and his students were run out of city after city for their heterodox teachings and practices.

By avoiding the prosecution that had ensnarled Craddock and doomed her proselytizing efforts, Bernard managed to draw a substantial following despite a far more radical sexual value system. Though rumors of sexual rituals followed him wherever he and his students settled, he kept the details of his nonmonogamous, nonmarital sexual-spiritual practices secret by not allowing the public to observe them and not explicitly prescribing them in any published records. In the single issue of his journal, *International Journal of the Tantrik Order*, for example, he discussed sex's centrality to religion—he went as far as asserting that humanity's underlying power resides in "the sexual instinct," which "finds its grandest and most exalted expression in religion"— but he did not advocate transgressive sexual practices or provide detailed sexual instructions like those found in Craddock's essays.[18] Since federal obscenity law in the Comstock era was grounded in distribution prohibitions, Bernard and his students were able to successfully resist attempts to halt their face-to-face instruction of students and their scandalous experiments with yoga postures and other rituals. In one notorious episode of 1910, there were accusations that Bernard forced young women to engage in his sexual rituals. The scandal was inflamed by the then-current panic over "white slaving," or the rumored kidnapping of white women for forced prostitution. While awaiting trial for the alleged crimes, Bernard was imprisoned in "the Tombs," a New York prison famous for its horrific living conditions, for more than three months. But since the testimony of two of his former disciples was the only evidence against him—the rituals took place in privacy, and there were no documented records of them—Bernard was released when his followers suddenly dropped all charges and fled the state.[19]

Bernard and his fellow practitioners of tantra established the Tantrik Order in America in 1905. In 1918, they settled in Nyack, New York, and built an esoteric rural retreat, the Clarkstown Country Club, where followers received instruction in hatha yoga and secret tantric initiations. This secrecy left much to the press's imagination, resulting in dramatic and probably largely fictitious accounts of the rituals. The club flourished for thirty years thanks to the abundant financial support of rich and famous individuals and families, most notably the Vanderbilts. It was also famous for scenes of men and women wearing tight-fitting clothing and contorting their bodies into onerous postures on the front lawn, as well as for opulent circuses that were open to the public.

Bernard's club represented a reawakening of the sacralization of the body that pervaded mainstream culture.[20] The YMCA, for example, provided a context in which physical fitness was perceived to enhance an ascetic and Protestant notion of self-control, moral development, and purity. The Clarkstown Country Club differed, however, from the YMCA and other mainstream physical-culture organizations because of its emphasis on the body as the locus of erotico-mystical experience and pleasure. Bernard's novel rendition of yoga combined the physical techniques of modern hatha yoga, the erotico-mysticism of tantra, and a communal ethic based on a nondualist philosophy, or the view that everything in existence is formed from the same underlying, unifying divinity. This vision countered the mainstream twentieth-century American theological template, which reflected the Protestant notion that God is utterly distinct from his creation. Yoga, according to Bernard, was first and foremost about celebrating divinity within oneself by improving health and increasing bodily pleasures.

Much of the criticism leveled against Bernard in the popular media was fueled by widespread stereotypes about tantra and hatha yoga. First, abilities to contort the body into what were considered bizarre postures were also associated with the abilities of Western contortionists.[21] Consequently, commentators reduced the yogic postures, which signified spiritual traditions, to crass entertainment. Second, the supposed *siddhis* or magical powers of some such yogis resulted in the association of hatha yoga with occult magic.[22] Most scandalous of all, tantra became associated with sex magic. Bernard was one of the first yogis to reconstruct tantra as a mode of sexual pleasure and generated a lot of criticism from his contemporaries for doing so.[23] Because they received nearly obsessive attention in the writings of travelers, journalists, and scholars, derogatory visions came to represent hatha yoga to mainstream Americans. Mass-circulation writings on yoga reified colonialist and orientalist conceptions of hatha yoga as particularly mysterious, bizarre, uncivilized, and threatening to modernity and rationality. Mark Singleton describes the situation: "As mass-circulation print media brought images of yogic austerities to a wider audience, the *hatha* yogin's reputation as the eccentric extreme of the Indian religious spectrum was increasingly cemented."[24]

Given this emerging matrix of radical ideas about sexual freedom and expression, Craddock, Bernard, and their fellow travelers were less convenient forebears for American yoga than a celibate Indian guru. The yoga advocate often identified as the "father" of modern yoga was the celibate monk, Hindu reformer, missionary to the United States, and Indian nationalist Swami Vivekananda.[25] Vivekananda prescribed a narrow vision of yoga that he termed *raja yoga* or "royal yoga," which primarily constituted a meditative practice combined with what he called "Practical Vedanta," a democratic form of Hindu spirituality based on an ethical imperative for social service with the personal quest for union between the self and the singular absolute.[26]

Vivekananda was born Narendranath Datta to a prosperous family in Calcutta. As a young adult, he joined the Brahmo Samaj, a Hindu reform movement that promoted monotheism, and later became a disciple of the Hindu mystic Ramakrishna. He took vows of renunciation, traveled throughout India, and built upon his conglomerate of religious, social, and nationalist concerns, seeking Hindu reform and revivalism for India. Upon hearing about the Parliament of the World's Religions to be held in Chicago in 1893, Vivekananda decided it served as an opportunity to garner Westerners' support for his cause of reforming India. Vivekananda arrived in 1893 at the Parliament of the World's Religions and delivered a speech on the universal truth of Hinduism that made him famous.[27] His teachings on modern Vedanta—that there is a singular and unifying divinity that the individual can experience through meditation and chastity alongside other ascetic practices—was unlike Craddock's sacralization of marital sexual intercourse or Bernard's divinization of the human body and the "sexual instinct."

Vivekananda's teachings appealed to a wide range of Americans who rejected mainstream institutional forms of religion for new unchurched forms of spirituality that competed in the religious market, such as Spiritualism,

Theosophy, and mind cure. Attracted to his individualistic, democratic ideas and to his vision of Hinduism as the panacea for the problems of modern materialism, many students of spirituality and the unchurched welcomed Vivekananda as a spiritual master. Like Vivekananda, these U.S. seekers all sought to wed metaphysics to modern ideas and values and shared the aim of "self-realization," imagined by Vivekananda to entail realization of the unity between one's self and divinity. Inspired by an ancient Indian philosophical concept (*atmajnana*), self-realization as a modern spiritual goal developed its own nuances in the twentieth century, characterizing a "therapeutic ethos" that came to dominate the moral climate of consumer culture.[28] With his newly acquired fame among spiritual seekers, Vivekananda quickly transformed his mission from one focused on raising money for Hindu reform and revivalism in India to creating a global movement based on Hinduism's universal truths.

Vivekananda attempted to construct yoga in ways deemed compatible with contemporary moral agendas by eliding certain aspects of yoga and emphasizing others.[29] Because of hatha yoga and tantra's associations with what were considered bizarre yoga postures, extreme asceticism, magic, sexual obscenity, and popular entertainment, Vivekananda censored both, instead emphasizing the ethical, philosophical, or meditational components of what became known as raja yoga.

Vivekananda and his disciples embraced a "yoga from the neck up," largely stopping short of the most controversial of yoga practices, those unsavory bodily postures and the sexual rituals associated with tantra.[30] In part because Vivekananda's "yoga from the neck up" was a meditative and ascetic yoga, stripped of the sexuality of hatha yoga and tantra, he was successful in drawing many Americans as he lectured across the United States, followed by private yoga lessons and the famous two-month meeting with a dozen of his closest disciples at Thousand Island Park in New York, widely cited as the first yoga retreat. His disciples were largely disillusioned with churched religious orthodoxy but were not compelled to flout moral norms. His achievements in popularizing yoga in this form included the 1895 establishment of U.S. centers for what he called the Vedanta Society, an organization for the dissemination of yoga across the United States, and the notable success of his book *Raja Yoga* (1896). In *Raja Yoga*, he equated his yoga system with the yoga of the most widely cited ancient text on classical yoga to this day, Patanjali's Yoga Sutras (circa 350–450 CE). The book sold out in a matter of months.[31] In this way, Vivekananda also mythologized, and in the process validated, raja yoga.[32]

Despite censoring yoga of controversial pretzel-twisting postures and sexual techniques, Vivekananda and the Vedanta Society nevertheless challenged mainstream cultural templates for sexuality by actively recruiting women into a celibate order, therefore challenging normative women's roles within sex- and kinship-based families. Most significant, in the period that historians of sexuality have located the rise of an intensified investment in heterosexual companionate marriage and growing social penalties for those outside of it, the Vedanta Society posed ascetic challenges to marriage, providing an alternative life to the burdens of marriage and reproduction that included celibacy and spiritual advancement.[33] Vivekananda connected women's spiritual capacities with unconventional women's roles. Vedanta convert Christine Greenstidel, known in her Vedantic circle as Sister Christine, credited Vivekananda with initiating women into monasticism, despite knowing the decision would result in his Indian peers' criticism for mixing men and women in a coed monastic order.[34] In terms that resonated with Victorian women's attacks on the sexual double standard, the yogi described chastity as the preeminent virtue, encouraging any man who aspired to live a religious life to look upon all women as his mother.[35] Vivekananda taught yoga as a path toward enhancing life, not through the body's pleasures but through chastity, meditation, and self-realization, equally available to men and women but ideally outside of the patriarchal family.

Many who remained on the side of the Protestant moral establishment, however, still thought such movements were a danger to all they considered decent, pure, and godly.[36] In forthrightly misogynist and xenophobic tones, critics eventually targeted all varieties of yoga for fear that exotic India, in the form of charismatic gurus and sex-crazed appropriators of yoga, was luring women away from the patriarchal family. In 1909, even the spiritually and socially radical Theosophical Society banned all conversation on yoga. Madame Helena Blavatsky and Colonel Henry Steel Olcott had founded the Theosophical Society in 1875 in New York City. It was a spiritualist organization countering religious orthodoxies and seeking religious reform by means of synthesizing Asian and Western metaphysical traditions. By 1901, there were five hundred active chapters in forty-two countries. The Theosophical Society was a "community that had heavily invested in reinscribing the traditional lore of India in the scientific terms of the modern, British-inspired West."[37] It promoted the ethical ideals and meditative practices associated with the Yoga Sutras, conflating its yoga system with raja yoga. This valorization of one strand of yogic practice helped confirm the U.S. association of hatha yoga with moral danger and of raja yoga, in contrast, with the culmination of spiritual progress. Among the Theosophical Society's major contributions to the popularization of a morally elevated, uncarnal version of yoga was its publication of an English translation of the Yoga Sutras in 1907. Another Theosophist, William Judge (1851–96), provided a commentary on the Yoga Sutras in which he warned of the dangers of hatha yoga's physical techniques, which he believed were "not spiritual."[38]

These moves to conflate yogic traditions generally with the specific, respectable form of raja yoga make the Theosophical Society's ultimate reversal even more significant. Annie Besant (1847–1933), president of the American Theosophical Society at the time it banned yoga, described women who practiced it as "animalistic."[39] A 1911 headline in a *Washington Post* Sunday special on controversies surrounding yoga succinctly evidences the general conflation of yoga with the antithesis of social mores: "This Soul Destroying Poison of the East: The Tragic Flood of Broken Homes and Hearts, Disgrace and Suicide That Follows the Broadening Stream of Morbidly Alluring Oriental 'Philosophies' into Our Country."[40] Soon, the federal government began an investigation to reveal just how many people in the United States, especially women, had been seduced and cheated by yoga.[41]

Far from the body-loving yogic descendants of Pierre Bernard who emphasized the role of yoga in enhancing health and beauty, Vivekananda's most influential successors, such as Paramahansa Yogananda (1893–1952), kept their alternative sexual value systems alive by initiating followers into close-knit monastic families often unified under a single roof and protected there from public scrutiny. Many of them disseminated forms of bhakti or "devotional" yoga focused on the worship of God and gurus as representatives or embodiments of divinity. They offered ascetic challenges to the centrality of marriage and family life in American religion and deemed the pleasures and even reproductive aims of sex undesirable obstacles to union with God. Like Vivekananda, these celibate gurus encouraged disciples to cultivate divine love in place of worldly love, marriage, and sexual desire.

FROM SUBVERSION TO NORMATIVITY IN THE LATTER TWENTIETH CENTURY

By the 1960s the United States experienced an influx of gurus who successfully disseminated yoga to members of the emergent counterculture. A former Mormon woman from Utah, Daya Mata (born Faye Wright), encapsulates the dramatic extent to which yoga served as a sexually subversive mode of life for many twentieth-century Americans. Wright acted as president and spiritual leader of the Self-Realization Fellowship from 1955 to 2010.[42] The fellowship was established in 1920 by Yogananda, a missionary from India who attracted a large following of Americans interested in his universalizing rendition of devotional yoga called Kriya Yoga, which he described as the scientific path to the experience of God. A member of a prestigious Mormon family in Salt Lake City, Wright was seventeen when she first heard Yogananda speak, and she knew immediately that she wanted to follow him as her spiritual guide. Abandoning Mormon norms, including the domestic expectations of her gender and the sacralization of biological reproduction, she moved to Los Angeles, joined his Self-Realization Fellowship, donned the ocher robes of a yogic renouncer, and became one of the first nuns in his monastic order.

Rather than fulfill the traditional Mormon ideal for women of motherhood as described in Neil J. Young's chapter in this volume, Daya Mata was instead a spiritual mother to thousands of members who affectionately referred to her as Sanghamata, "Mother of the Society."[43] Daya Mata emphasized love as the ultimate religious emotion, but it was not the procreative, sexual love believed by Bernard or Craddock to go hand in hand with divine love. This was a love that was believed to transcend and ideally replace worldly love or sexual desire. In other words, Daya Mata represented the yogic idealization of celibacy over marriage.

As the second half of the twentieth century progressed, yoga continued to be envisioned as a subversive mode for pursuing spiritual perfection through ascetic, meditative, and devotional techniques. It began to serve more frequently, however, as a normative mode for pursuing a different kind of self-control, one put in service of physical perfection and beauty. In fact, by the end of the twentieth century, devotion to these aims would become the centerpiece of most American yoga systems. Many instructors valorized yoga as a physical discipline and, in part, even as a means to improving sexual prowess and physical pleasure in ways reflective of cultural norms.

Teaching yoga in the second half of the twentieth century, Blanche DeVries (1891–1984) serves as a model of this approach to yoga as well as a bridge between the early decades of yoga's American career and its broad popularization in the later twentieth century. After teaching yoga with her husband, Pierre Bernard, for many years at their controversial Clarkstown Country Club in Nyack, DeVries became one of the first yoga advocates to teach an exoteric, physical yoga offered especially to women as a wholesome form of fitness. At her Living Arts Center, which she opened in 1945 in New York City, DeVries translated Bernard's esoteric tantric celebration of sex as the divine essence of all religions into an accessible practice aimed at immediately enhancing the body and mind for the sake of a life lived well. DeVries sanitized modern tantra by eliding the secretive, overtly transgressive sexual rituals that had come to be associated with it in the popular imagination and instead emphasizing the benefits of yoga for health and beauty, pursuits of increasing importance around the country. Yoga was a holistic spirituality, according to DeVries, a "profound science for integrating body, mind and spirit into a harmonious whole."[44]

In New York, DeVries taught yoga to many influential students, including the philanthropist and Standard Oil heiress Rebekah Harkness. Harkness, in turn, was responsible for bringing Indian yoga guru B. K. S. Iyengar (1918–2014) in 1956 to Rhode Island for his first visit to the United States. Iyengar, sometimes styled the "father of modern yoga," was among the handful of practitioners responsible for popularizing yoga as an accessible fitness option for urban women. Having suffered through an agonizing childhood in which he lost his father and siblings to various illnesses and afflicted himself with tuberculosis, typhoid, and malaria, Iyengar had gone to the Karnataka city of Mysore at sixteen to study yoga with his brother-in-law, Tirumalai Krishnamacharya (1888–1989). Krishnamacharya was said to have constructed a yoga system meant to strengthen the body through sequences of onerous postures and breathing exercises. The sickly young Iyengar not only recovered his health but also went on to become the most famous among the yoga prodigies and teachers to have studied under Krishnamacharya.

Iyengar constructed his own idiosyncratic system of postural yoga that was a rigorous and disciplined form of body maintenance that required the use of fitness tools, such as belts, bricks, and ropes, but was also capable of being personalized to fit individual needs. He published his *Light on Yoga* in 1966, and it instantly became the global standard reference on modern yoga as a body practice.[45] Iyengar's book was particularly attractive to a consumer audience insofar as it included step-by-step instructions so that individuals could choose yoga as one part of their self-development regimen without having to give up other lifestyle commitments. They could even do yoga in the privacy of their own homes. Furthermore, the book provided detailed biomedical explanations of each posture and its fitness and health benefits. Iyengar, himself a husband and father, represented a very different kind of yoga guru from those idealizing celibacy, such as Vivekananda or Yogananada. Increasingly, he and DeVries, among others, chiseled out a yogic mode of physical fitness and spirituality conducive to U.S. cultural norms.

When the Beatles began practicing yoga in the 1960s, yoga became even more accessible among the counterculture as a tool for challenging everything from gender to sexual norms. In February 1968, accompanied by a retinue of reporters and photographers, the Beatles traveled to Maharishi Mahesh Yogi's Chaurasi Kutia ashram near Rishikesh, India, for a Transcendental Meditation training session. Maharishi was an Indian guru who brought his Transcendental Meditation in 1959 to the United States, promoting it as a simple technique of changing a mantra (a sacred sound repeated as a meditative tool) and as a universal technique for a variety of lofty aims, including reducing stress, drug use, and crime as well as potentially bringing about world peace. The visit, which ended up being one of the band's most fruitful periods in terms of creative productivity, received widespread media attention. Images of the longhaired musicians in white and ocher kurtas and seated in the lotus posture at the feet of an Indian guru were seen far and wide. Maharishi, in turn, was publicized as "The Beatles' Guru."

Unsurprisingly, the media frenzy over the Beatles' yoga experiments triggered further interest in yoga, that mysterious and exotic mind-body-spirit practice from India.[46] The 1960s hippies' experiments with yoga and especially the high-profile experiments of the Beatles were momentous in the history of popular spirituality and especially prolific for American yoga. Furthermore, although twentieth-century emigration from India to the United States had been rare due to U.S. legal restrictions largely preventing the immigration of people of color, those restrictions were lifted in the 1960s, leading to an influx of migrants from various regions, including India, and making cross-cultural exchange between Indian and American yoga proponents more possible. The United States became a hotbed for new religious movements featuring yoga as a centerpiece. Several gurus exploited countercultural trends by introducing tantric, meditational, and devotional yoga systems.

Serious, long-term commitment to these yoga systems frequently required adherents to replicate their gurus' self-control by becoming celibate, to learn Sanskrit or other Indian languages in order to systematically study large bodies of sacred literature, and to adopt an inferior position to a glorified and sometimes worshipped guru. Furthermore, some of these gurus required serious adherents to privilege particular worldviews over others, despite their claims to universal or nonsectarian spirituality. For example, Maharishi's rejection of an entirely individual, preference-oriented approach to spiritual and body practices in favor of particularized Hindu philosophical and devotional commitments situated him in the folds of Hindu traditions.[47]

By the 1970s, postural yoga was familiar to most Americans and could even be seen on mainstream television. The rigorous nature of postural yoga served not to control sexual desire or subvert sexual or gender norms but to improve sexual prowess. This was at a time when, on a larger social level, ascetic regimens of abstinence from sex (unless for the sake of reproduction) or celibacy shifted to ascetic regimens of diet and exercise aimed at the enhancement of sexual prowess.[48] In popular yoga advertisements and publications, practitioners, especially women, were continuously and explicitly invited to embrace a rigorous postural yoga regimen for the sake of attaining the envied "sexy yoga butt." And yoga was prescribed as a means not just to a sexier body but also to better sexual skills. In a lecture by celebrity yoga teacher Bikram Choudhury (b. 1944), for example, the self-proclaimed guru of Bikram Yoga proclaimed the eagle pose as the best for "good sex," explaining, "With this one you are fucking until you are 90! You have seven orgasms in a row!"[49]

From the early 1970s, yoga advocates worked toward popularizing yoga as a method of physical discipline for enhancing sexual prowess. In 1972, Cincinnati's PBS station debuted *Lilias, Yoga and You!* Within the year, the show was on PBS stations across the United States. Featuring Lilias Folan, *Lilias, Yoga and You!* instructed audiences in a thoroughly therapeutic form of modern postural yoga. The show was popular primarily among women viewers interested in yoga as a means to improving their health and physical appearance according to normative standards of the time. Thanks to *Lilias, Yoga and You!*, a person could choose yoga as a body-maintenance regimen without ever challenging normative sexual ethics by abandoning marriage for life in a monastic community or by engaging in transgressive sexual rituals as a part of a countercultural movement.

Publicity efforts for *Lilias, Yoga and You!* led to a re-visioning of yoga as an embodiment of American cultural norms, since Lilias herself embodied the gender and sexual ideals of a married woman. Yoga was the stuff not of longhaired hippies but of longhaired suburban housewives. The biggest challenge, according to Folan, "was convincing Public Television that yoga wasn't peculiar, strange and un-American, that it *isn't* a religion—that was the big one."[50] Having come to yoga through her local YMCA, Lilias prescribed yoga as physical fitness. Though she did don an exotic om symbol across the front of her leotard and used the Sanskrit titles for yoga postures, Folan largely represented the norms of femininity represented in the mass media who, according to Susan J. Douglas, were "young, perfectly groomed, always smiling, never complaining, demure, eager to please, eager to consume."[51] These women starkly contrasted with those representing the emergent women's liberation movement that "violated the nation's most sacred conceits about love, marriage, the family, and femininity," arguing that "motherhood, marriage, sexual behavior, and dress codes all had to be considered symptoms of a broader political and social system that kept women down."⁵² Folan represented the mass media's ideal of feminine beauty and health with her trim body, outfitted in a red or pink leotard and tights; her long, dark hair; and a tasteful gold wedding band. As she moved through a postural sequence, she paused to explain the physiological benefits of each posture. Yoga was not about retreat from society, prolonged meditation, and monastic celibacy, nor was it about sexual experimentation, liberation, and tantric transgression. Rather, yoga was a wholesome physical fitness regimen compatible with the heteronormative standards of sexuality and femininity.

Folan represents a major shift in popular assumptions about yoga. Yoga increasingly became associated with a rigorous fitness regimen for the sake of attaining a desirable body. This embrace of "power yoga" and "hot yoga" systems even produced an entirely new fashion genre, "athleisure," in the first decade of the twenty-first century.⁵³ By that time, yoga had largely shifted away from its subversive beginnings on U.S. soil and become one more tool for replicating the feminine gender and sexual ideals represented in popular media.

In conclusion, the multiple forms of twentieth-century yoga in the United States have taken many positions on the relationship between sex and spirituality, more recently largely normative but historically radically subversive. The ways in which yoga violated sexual and gender norms serve to explain some of the well-vented anxieties of contemporary Christian and Hindu conservative institutions and individuals who have opposed certain yoga systems since the nineteenth century.⁵⁴ Twentieth-century high-profile Christians and Hindus have stoked fear of pop culture yoga in the United States.⁵⁵ The president of the Southern Baptist Theological Seminary, Albert Mohler, for example, became the dominant voice for contemporary Christian "yogaphobia" in 2010 when a blog post in which he warned Christians against yoga made headlines.⁵⁶ Echoing nineteenth- and twentieth-century prejudices against tantra, Mohler insisted that yoga cannot be separated from Hinduism and especially from the nondualist Hindu (and tantric) notion that the body can be a tool for experiencing the divine.⁵⁷

Yet Christians had Hindu bedfellows in opposition to pop culture yoga in the United States. The Hindu American Foundation, a Minneapolis-based organization that advocates for Hindus living in the United States, introduced the "Take Back Yoga" campaign in 2010, which echoed Vivekananda's arguments in favor of a singular authentic and essentially Hindu system of yoga and in opposition to so-called corruptions that focus on yoga postures.⁵⁸ In its most extreme forms, Hindu opposition to pop culture yoga included accusations that U.S. yoga amounted to the "rape" and "theft" of yoga.[59] Though such Christian and Hindu voices are wrong about the historical narratives on which their arguments are based, perhaps they should be nervous about American yoga, given the subversive nature of so many chapters in its history.

NOTES

I am appreciative of the editors of this volume and the anonymous readers. They all provided extensive comments and suggestions. Their close readings of my initial drafts and my consideration of their careful responses greatly enhanced the final product.

1. On Protestant liberalism, see William R. Hutchison, *The Modernist Impulse in American Protestantism* (New York: Oxford University Press, 1992), and the essays in Leigh E. Schmidt and Sally M. Promey, eds., *American Religious Liberalism* (Bloomington: Indiana University Press, 2012).

2. By the start of the twentieth century, gurus such as Swami Paramananda (1884–1940) had attracted large numbers of Americans to yoga, drawing former Christians away from their religious upbringings and home churches. Some American adherents to yoga, including Ida Craddock and Pierre Bernard (discussed below), openly challenged arguments that private and public life should be in accord with Protestant Christian norms. Challenges occurred in public spaces, including courtrooms and widely distributed publications. See, for example, Beryl Satter, *Each Mind a Kingdom: American Women, Sexual Purity, and the New Thought Movement, 1875–1920* (Berkeley: University of California Press, 2001); Catherine L. Albanese, *A Republic of Mind and Spirit: A Cultural History of American Metaphysical Religion* (New Haven: Yale University Press, 2007); Robert Love, *The Great Oom: The Improbable Birth of Yoga in America* (New York: Viking, 2010); Leigh Eric Schmidt, *Heaven's Bride: The Unprintable Life of Ida C. Craddock, American Mystic, Scholar, Sexologist, Martyr, and Madwoman* (New York: Basic Books, 2010); and Andrea R. Jain, "From Counterculture to Counterculture," in *Selling Yoga: From Counterculture to Pop Culture* (New York: Oxford University Press, 2014): 20–41.

3. Andrea R. Jain, "Continuity with Consumer Culture," in *Selling Yoga: From Counterculture to Pop Culture* (New York: Oxford University Press, 2014), 42–72.

4. Although some studies have appeared concerning U.S. unchurched spiritualities—e.g., Wade Clark Roof, *Spiritual Marketplace: Baby Boomers and the Remaking of American Religion* (Princeton: Princeton University Press, 1999); Kimberly J. Lau, *New Age Capitalism: Making Money East of Eden* (Philadelphia: University of Pennsylvania Press, 2000); Satter, *Each Mind a Kingdom*; Jeremy Carrette and Richard King, *Selling Spirituality: The Silent Takeover of Religion* (New York: Routledge, 2005); Albanese, *Republic of Mind and Spirit*; Linda Mercadante, *Belief without Borders: Inside the Minds of the Spiritual but Not Religious* (New York: Oxford University Press, 2014); Schmidt and Promey, *American Religious Liberalism*; Christopher White, *Unsettled Minds: Psychology and the American Search for Spiritual Assurance* (Berkeley: University of California Press, 2009); Matthew S. Hedstrom, *The Rise of Liberal Religion: Book Culture and American Spirituality in the Twentieth Century* (New York: Oxford University Press, 2015); Elizabeth

Drescher, *Choosing Our Religion: The Spiritual Lives of America's Nones* (New York: Oxford University Press, 2016)—it is time for a deeper exploration of what characterizes them in their past manifestations and in their relationships to larger social forces, in this case, sexual and gender norms.

5. David Sehat offers this term to denote the "religiously derived morality, enforceable by law," and the institutional bases of its support that he finds characterized the United States from the late eighteenth century until the mid-twentieth century, when the protections of the Bill of Rights began to be applied to state and municipal as well as federal powers. For much of U.S. history, he argues, a Protestant moral establishment exercised state-level political power to punish free thinkers and social and sexual dissidents via moral laws based on religious orthodoxy. David Sehat, *The Myth of American Religious Freedom* (New York: Oxford University Press, 2011), 5–7. See also Steven Green, *Inventing a Christian America: The Myth of the Religious Founding* (New York: Oxford University Press, 2015).

6. The turn-of-the-century United States provided a broad range of sexual attitudes and ideas, ranging from evangelical prohibitions and prosecutions for obscenity to calls for free love and the embrace of sexual deviants. Anthony Comstock, who succeeded in banning sexual materials from the U.S. mail, is an example of the former. His New York Society for the Suppression of Vice (created in 1873) was dedicated to supervising morality in public life and successfully influenced the U.S. Congress to pass the Comstock Law, which illegalized the delivery by U.S. mail of sexual materials as well as the production and publication of information about abortion and methods of birth control and preventing venereal disease. See Anna Louise Bates, *Weeder in the Garden of the Lord: Anthony Comstock's Life and Career* (Lanham, Md.: University Press of America, 1995); Nicola Kay Beisel, *Imperiled Innocents: Anthony Comstock and Family Reproduction in Victorian America* (Princeton: Princeton University Press, 1997); and Helen Lefkowitz Horowitz, *Rereading Sex: Battles over Sexual Knowledge and Suppression in Nineteenth-Century America* (New York: Vintage Books, 2003).

7. See Bates, *Weeder in the Garden*; and Beisel, *Imperiled Innocents*. Comstock and other members of his organization also harassed Pierre Bernard and members of the Theosophical Society (both discussed below).

8. On the life of Ida Craddock, see Vere Chappell, *Sexual Outlaw, Erotic Mystic: The Essential Ida Craddock* (San Francisco: Weiser Books, 2010); Schmidt, *Heaven's Bride*; and Jain, "From Counterculture to Counterculture," 22–25.

9. Schmidt, *Heaven's Bride*, xi.

10. See Robert W. Rydell, *All the World's a Fair: Visions of Empire at American International Exhibitions, 1876–1916* (Chicago: University of Chicago Press, 1984).

11. David Gordon White, *The Alchemical Body: Siddha Traditions in Medieval India* (Chicago: University of Chicago Press, 1996), 72.

12. On the topic of seminal emission retention as a mode of birth control, Craddock also wrote in support of the Oneida Community, a religious group founded by John Humphrey Noyes in 1848 in Oneida, New York. The founder's son, Theodore R. Noyes, advocated for restricted seminal emission as a mode of birth control, and at least some members of the community embraced the practice; see Ida C. Craddock, "The Danse du Ventre (Dance of the Abdomen) as performed in the Cairo Street Theatre, Midway

Plaisance, Chicago: Its Value as an Educator in Marital Duties (1893)," in Chappell, *Sexual Outlaw*, 14–16.

13. Ida C. Craddock, "Heavenly Bridegrooms (1894)," in Chappell, *Sexual Outlaw*, 83.

14. Ida C. Craddock, "The Wedding Night," in Chappell, *Sexual Outlaw*, 213.

15. Schmidt, *Heaven's Bride*, 147–48; Spencer Klaw, *Without Sin: The Life and Death of the Oneida Community* (New York: Penguin Books, 1993), 58; Janet Farrell Brodie, *Contraception and Abortion in Nineteenth-Century America* (Cornell: Cornell University Press, 1994), 204–5.

16. "Mrs. Craddock in Court," *The Washington Times*, April 26, 1901.

17. On the life of Pierre Bernard, see Hugh Urban, *Tantra: Sex, Secrecy, Politics, and Power in the Study of Religion* (Berkeley: University of California Press, 2003), 214–16; Love, *Great Oom*; and Jain, "From Counterculture to Counterculture," 25–26.

18. "Tantrik Worship: The Basis of Religion," *International Journal of the Tantrik Order* 5, no. 1 (1906): 71–73.

19. See Love, *Great Oom*. According to some tantric traditions, the yoga practitioner can instantly and directly experience the divine but only by intentionally transgressing normative ethical and purity standards. Esoteric practices have included the symbolic or real consumption of forbidden substances, such as semen and menstrual blood, and ritual sex with conventionally forbidden women, often from outcaste social groups.

20. Mark Singleton, *Yoga Body: The Origins of Modern Posture Practice* (New York: Oxford University Press, 2010), 84, 89–94, 119.

21. Ibid., 57–59.

22. Ibid., 64–66.

23. Urban, *Tantra*, 215.

24. Singleton, *Yoga Body*, 56.

25. For examples of pop culture narratives about modern yoga's history that ignore Craddock while highlighting and often exaggerating Vivekananda's role, see the following: Holly Hammond, "Yoga's Trip to America," *Yoga Journal*, August 29, 2007, http://www.yogajournal.com/article/history-of-yoga/yogas-trip-america/; Ann Louise Bardach, "How Yoga Won the West," *New York Times*, October 1, 2011, http://www.nytimes.com/2011/10/02/opinion/sunday/how-yoga-won-the-west.html?_r=3&partner=rss&emc=rss%3E; and Stefanie Syman, *The Subtle Body: The Story of Yoga in America* (New York: Farrar, Straus and Giroux, 2010).

26. Vivekananda's *raja yoga* referred only to what he considered authentic yoga according to his selective reading of what has been popularly identified as the "classical" source on yoga, the Yoga Sutras (circa 350–450 BCE).

27. This was such a momentous occasion for the U.S. reception of Hinduism that, as Vasudha Narayanan states, "most people trace the history of Hinduism in America to this famous address" ("Hinduism in America," in *Cambridge History of Religions in America*, ed. Stephen J. Stein, vol. 3 [New York: Cambridge University Press, 2012], 335).

28. On the role of self-realization in the emergent therapeutic culture, see T. J. Jackson Lears, "From Salvation to Self-Realization: Advertising and the Therapeutic Roots of the Consumer Culture, 1880–1930," in *The Culture of Consumption: Critical Essays in American History, 1880–1980*, ed. Richard Wightman Fox and T. J. Jackson Lears (New York: Pantheon Books, 1983), 1–38. On the emergence of a therapeutic ethos, see Philip Rieff,

The Triumph of the Therapeutic (New York: Harper and Row, 1966); Christopher Lasch, *The Culture of Narcissism: American Life in an Age of Diminishing Expectations* (New York: W. W. Norton, 1978); Donald Meyer, *The Positive Thinkers: Religion as Pop Psychology from Mary Baker Eddy to Oral Roberts*, 2nd ed. (New York: Pantheon, 1980); and T. J. Jackson Lears, *No Place of Grace: Antimodernism and the Transformation of American Culture, 1880–1920* (New York: Pantheon, 1981).

29. Jain, "From Counterculture to Counterculture," 28–36.

30. See ibid. "Yoga from the neck up" as a descriptor for Vivekananda's approach was borrowed from Love, *Great Oom*, 72.

31. See Elizabeth de Michelis, *A History of Modern Yoga: Patanjali and Western Esotericism* (New York: Continuum, 2004).

32. On mythologizing modern yoga, see Andrea R. Jain, *Selling Yoga: From Counterculture to Pop Culture* (New York: Oxford University Press, 2014), 114–15.

33. Love, *Great Oom*, 72.

34. Sister Christine, "Memories of Swami Vivekananda," in *Vedanta for Modern Man*, ed. Christopher Isherwood (New York: Harper, 1945), 134–52.

35. Swami Vivekananda, *Karma Yoga*, first published 1896, http://www.vivekananda.net/PDFBooks/KarmaYoga.pdf.

36. Ibid.

37. Albanese, *Republic of Mind and Spirit*, 331.

38. Ibid., 352.

39. "Yoga Followers Shut Out of Hall," *Chicago Daily Tribune*, September 20, 1909, 8; see also "Yoga Divides Theosophy Ranks," *Chicago Daily Tribune*, September 19, 1909, 3.

40. "This Soul Destroying Poison of the East: The Tragic Flood of Broken Homes and Hearts, Disgrace and Suicide That Follows the Broadening Stream of Morbidly Alluring Oriental 'Philosophies' into Our Country," *Washington Post*, May 28, 1911, M6.

41. "The Heathen Invasion of America," *Current Literature* 51, no. 5 (November 1911): 538; "A Hindu Apple for Modern Eve," *Los Angeles Times*, October 22, 1911, III, 20.

42. Although an American man by the name of Rajarsi Janakananda first succeeded Yogananda, his leadership lasted only three years as he died in 1955.

43. According to David Ritz, Daya Mata's influence reached even Elvis Presley, who met her in the 1960s, meditated with her, and sought her spiritual guidance on several occasions. David Ritz, *Elvis by the Presleys* (New York: Crown Archetype, 2005).

44. Bill Vlasic, "Blanche DeVries Bernard, 92, Dies," *Rockland County (N.Y.) Journal-News*, September 5, 1984.

45. De Michelis, *History of Modern Yoga*, 198.

46. Philip Goldberg, *American Veda: From Emerson and the Beatles to Yoga and Meditation: How Indian Spirituality Changed the West* (New York: Harmony, 2013), 7.

47. On Maharishi's ethnic and religious metanarrative, see Cynthia Ann Humes, "Maharishi Mahesh Yogi: Beyond the TM Technique," in *Gurus in America*, ed. Thomas A. Forsthoefel and Cynthia Ann Humes (New York: State University of New York Press, 2005), 55–80.

48. Mike Featherstone, "The Body in Consumer Culture," in *The Body: Social Process and Cultural Theory*, ed. Mike Featherstone, Mike Hepworth, and Bryan S. Turner (London: Sage, 1991), 182.

49. Clancy Martin, "The Overheated, Oversexed Cult of Bikram Choudhury," *GQ*, February 1, 2011, http://www.gq.com/story/yoga-guru-bikram-choudhury.

50. Quoted in Stephanie Syman, *The Subtle Body: The Story of Yoga in America* (New York: Farrar, Straus and Giroux, 2010), 247.

51. Susan J. Douglas, *Where the Girls Are: Growing Up Female with the Mass Media* (New York: Times Books, 1994), 166. Douglas cites Judith Hole and Ellen Levine, *Rebirth of Feminism* (New York: Russell Sage Foundation, 1974), 32–33.

52. Douglas, *Where the Girls Are*, 166.

53. Anne D'Innocenzio, "Jeans Face Uncertain Future amid Yoga Wear Rage," *USA Today*, September 6, 2014, http://www.usatoday.com/story/money/business/2014/09/06/jeans-face-an-uncertain-future-amid-yoga-wear-rage/15146265/.

54. See, for example, Andrea R. Jain, "Is Downward Dog the Path to Hell? Evangelicals and Fundamentalist Hindus Come Together in Their Denunciation of Yoga's Popularity in the U.S.," *Religion Dispatches*, October 27, 2010, http://www.religiondispatches.org/archive/3616/is_downward_dog_the_path_to_hell/; Jain, *Selling Yoga*; Andrea R. Jain, "Who Is to Say Modern Yoga Practitioners Have It All Wrong? On Hindu Origins and Yogaphobia," *Journal of the American Academy of Religion* 82, no. 2 (June 2014): 427–71; and Andrea R. Jain, "Is Pope Francis Yogaphobic?," *Religion Dispatches*, February 24, 2015.

55. On U.S.-based Christian yogaphobia, see Jain, "Is Downward Dog the Path to Hell?"; Andrea R. Jain, "The Malleability of Yoga: A Response to Christian and Hindu Opponents of the Popularization of Yoga," *Journal of Hindu-Christian Studies* 25 (2012): 3–10; Jain, "Who Is to Say Modern Yoga Practitioners Have It All Wrong?"; Andrea R. Jain, "Yogaphobia and Hindu Origins," in *Selling Yoga: From Counterculture to Pop Culture* (New York: Oxford University Press, 2014), 130–57; and Andrea R. Jain, "Pat Robertson Warns Yoga Will Have You Speaking Hindu," *Religion Dispatches*, February 26, 2015, http://religiondispatches.org/pat-robertson-warns-yoga-will-have-you-speaking-hindu/.

56. Albert Mohler, "The Subtle Body—Should Christians Practice Yoga?," AlbertMohler.com, September 20, 2010, http://www.albertmohler.com/2010/09/20/the-subtle-body-should-christians-practice-yoga/.

57. Ibid. See also Albert Mohler, "The Meaning of Yoga: A Conversation with Stephanie Syman and Doug Groothuis," on the interview forum *Thinking in Public*, AlbertMohler.com, September 20, 2010, http://www.albertmohler.com/2010/09/20/the-meaning-of-yoga-a-conversation-with-stephanie-syman-and-doug-groothius/.

58. Hindu American Foundation, "Yoga Beyond Asana," 2009, Hindu American Foundation, http://www.hafsite.org/media/pr/yoga-hindu-origins.

59. See Aseem Shukla, "The Theft of Yoga," *Newsweek*, April 18, 2010, http://newsweek.washingtonpost.com/onfaith/panelists/aseem_shukla/2010/04/nearly_twenty_million_people_in.html; and Aseem Shukla and Sheetal Shah, "The Rape of Yoga," *The Pioneer*, June 21, 2011, http://www.dailypioneer.com/252823/The-rape-of-Yoga.html.

PURITY AND POPULATION
American Jews, Marriage, and Sexuality
REBECCA L. DAVIS

Speaking before a gathering of Reform rabbis and Jewish educators in 1954, Rabbi Stanley R. Brav encouraged them to reimagine premarital counseling as an opportunity to demonstrate to young people the salience of religion—and the value of clergy—in their lives: "The premarital interview is a supreme occasion for establishing a lasting friendship between a young couple and a religious teacher who shows an intense concern for their welfare. . . . I've been impressed that I've come upon few teaching situations that are ever so promising, few pupils who are ever more receptive than those who take part in a premarital interview."[1] Brav was one of countless religious leaders during the twentieth century who reasserted the value of religiously based premarital and marital counseling in response to the growth of secular marriage counseling and education programs. The cumulative result was an unprecedented religious investment in marriage.

During the twentieth century, religion became more important to American marriages, while marriage assumed a more central place among the activities and priorities of religious organizations. The history of marriage generally—and this chapter's discussion of Jewish marriage in particular—shows that far from being antagonistic, religion and sexuality have shaped one another, often very profoundly. Jewish investment in marriage in the twentieth century affected the ways in which Jewish Americans practiced and valued their faith. In turn, the religious investment in marriage, by Jews and other people of faith, contributed to national conversations about the sanctity and value of marital stability. Until the very recent national movement for marriage equality transformed the legal landscape, investing in marriage necessarily entailed investing in heteronormative sexualities. Religious individuals and institutions therefore played central roles in the promotion of the modern categories of heterosexuality and homosexuality through their efforts to promote and sustain marriage. The history of religious investment in heterosexuality has featured Protestant and Catholic actors most prominently; American Jews articulated and acted upon their ideas about marital sexuality within this predominantly Christian context.

American Jewish religious leaders put concerns about marriage and the family at the center of their communal and spiritual work throughout the twentieth century. That emphasis is largely due to the religiously and ethnically specific preoccupations of American Jews. The twentieth-century American Jewish concern with Jewish survival, most often expressed as a fear of interfaith marriage, shaped the Jewish community's investment in marriage as a site for procreation. This essay examines two branches of the American Jewish experience, Orthodox and Reform, to suggest ways in which the theological and cultural particularities of American Jewry influenced Jewish leaders' approach to modern marriage. Orthodox Judaism, the branch of Judaism that teaches strict adherence to Jewish law (*halakhah*) and ritual, linked the observance of the laws of "family purity" (concerning sexual intercourse and the wife's menstrual cycle) to marital success. Reform Jews, who reject the authority of Jewish law, observe ritual selectively, and embrace an outward-facing social justice mandate, became preoccupied by the mid-twentieth century with a perceived crisis of rising interfaith marriage rates. For all their considerable differences, both Orthodox and Reform Jews highlighted the reproductive aspects of marital sexuality.

This desire to preserve Jewish traditions and Jewish peoplehood did not produce continuity or stasis, however, but instead became a vehicle for cultural and sexual change. The preoccupation with generational survival and family size has shaped the American Jewish politics of marriage to focus more on a couple's reproductive outcomes (will the children be Jewish?) than on sexual orientation. While homophobia and antigay interpretations of Jewish law continue to affect American Orthodox Judaism, the Reform movement was among the first in the United States to ordain openly gay clergy and permit its clergy to officiate at marriages of same-sex couples. Secular cultural and political commitments intersected with religious investments to influence the Jewish approach to marital sexuality. This essay's brief excursion into twentieth-century Jewish attitudes toward marriage and sexuality should function as a reminder to historians not to substitute "religious" for "Christian" when describing the hotly contested terrain of marriage politics. Jewish efforts to promote cultural continuity through marriage became agents of significant shifts in Jewish attitudes toward sexuality.

The twentieth-century religious investment in marriage was a marked change from nineteenth-century attitudes. Prior to the twentieth century, when American Protestants wrote and talked about sexuality, they highlighted the (sinful) alternatives to marital monogamy. Extolling the spiritual and sexual merits of marriage was not part of mainstream American religious conversation. American religions valued marriage, the family, and even marital sexuality, but these were neither foremost priorities nor passionately defended principles of religious life. Protestants circulated spurious tales of lascivious priests and nuns; health reformers warned against masturbation; and sexual scandals involving Protestant clergy, amply covered in the popular press, highlighted the sinfulness of adultery and the weakness of human will when confronted by sexual temptation.[2] Indeed, some of the only people rhapsodizing about the spiritual heights of erotically fulfilling conjugal relations were spiritualists and free lovers. They contrasted the sexually gratifying marriage between equals to the oppressive, even violent marriages in which many women felt trapped and situated marriage reform as essential for women's emancipation.[3] Such alternatives to male-female monogamous, lifelong marriage as Mormon polygamy, "complex marriage" among the Oneidans, and spiritualist "free love" provoked controversy, but far more Americans talked about these radical alternatives than joined them.[4] Protestant American conversations about sexuality in the nineteenth century thus were more often concerned with limiting sexuality within marriage—and protesting against experiments with marriage—than with celebrating the particular erotic configuration of what today might be called heterosexual marriage.

Unlike the Protestant majority, nineteenth-century Jewish Americans worried more about maintaining their small, dispersed population than about sexual sin. Even Jews who settled in areas far from the major Jewish settlements on the East Coast sustained "a cultural tradition that virtually required marriage and child rearing." Jewish survival, rather than strict compliance with Jewish rituals related to marital sexuality, dominated their strategies and priorities. In urban and frontier environments, Jewish men and women overwhelmingly sought out Jewish marriage partners, while women's observance of family purity laws (*nidah*) that required monthly visits to the *mikvah* (ritual bath) fell out of custom.[5] For American Jews as for American Protestants and Catholics, monogamous marriage and its sexual aspects were not unimportant, but neither were they given pride of place in most religious conversations or observances.

American Jews differed from the majority, but they were also participants in the mainstream culture and felt the effects of major transformations in American sexual ideals and practices. From the 1860s onward, the scientific study of sexuality ("sexology") and psychiatry created new categories of sexual desire and pathology, of which heterosexuality and homosexuality were but two.[6] In addition to new ways of speaking about sex, Americans experimented with new modes of sociability. In the early twentieth century, Americans increasingly embraced mixed-gender (heterosocial) leisure practices, such as amusement parks, vaudeville theaters, and nickelodeons, expanding what had been a gender-stratified, male-dominated leisure culture that admitted women only at the cost of their respectability.[7] Americans also began to pay more attention to female sexual pleasure within marriage.[8] Influenced by the women's rights, birth control, and eugenics movements, sociologists, journalists, social workers, clergy, and cultural critics of all stripes began to comment on the strengths and weaknesses of marriage and on ways of improving it.[9] By the early twentieth century, sex within marriage had assumed greater importance in the United States as a principle of mental health and as a requirement for marital happiness.

The same scientific impulse that produced taxonomies of sexual desire likewise resulted in new theories of racial hierarchy, another form of naming and sorting people into distinct categories.[10] Antimiscegenation laws prohibiting marriages between whites and African Americans, Native Americans, and Asians proliferated in Western states in the late nineteenth and early twentieth centuries. (Laws prohibiting marriages between whites and African Americans had long been common throughout the South.)[11] Anti-immigrant movements defended the exclusion of Chinese, Japanese, and other peoples arriving on the West Coast and of southern and eastern Europeans on the East Coast as necessary precautions to preserve "Anglo-Saxon" and "Caucasian" racial identities in the United States.[12] Throughout the twentieth century, Americans deepened their investment in heterosexual marriage and whiteness, attaching legal, economic, and political privileges to marriage, demarcating the boundaries of normal (white) heterosexual relationships, and stigmatizing desires and relationships that either were not heterosexual or were not normatively heterosexual.

Ideas about whiteness were troubling and ambivalent for American Jews because of the ambiguity surrounding whether Judaism represented a faith, an ethnicity, a race, a nation, or some combination of the above. In many respects, Jews benefited from the politics of whiteness; able to change their names and assimilate, Jews by the 1920s had gained meaningful footholds in the professions, public education, and business. Within the American Jewish community, however, the question of whether Judaism survived via biological descent, "in the blood" of the Jewish people, or was a cultural inheritance continued to incite debate and dissent. Prominent Reform rabbis supported the eugenics movement, for example, while protesting against restrictive immigration legislation.[13] Increasingly wary of being identified as a racial subgroup, Jews in the United States did not immediately relinquish their claims to an inherited, biologically based peoplehood.[14]

These ethnic concerns intensified at the same time that the observance of religious laws about "family purity" declined among Orthodox Jewish women. Orthodox Jews follow strict observance of the Talmud, an extensive collection of fifth- and sixth-century-CE commentaries on the Torah (comprising the first five books of the Hebrew Bible). Orthodox Jews view the Talmud as a set of divinely ordained laws that govern all aspects of their lives. According to Orthodox interpretations of the Talmud, family purity laws, or *nidah*, prohibit marital sexual relations during and for a few days following the wife's menstruation and require the woman to immerse herself at the *mikvah* before resuming sexual relations with her husband. Observance of these laws, however, was more difficult in the United States than it had been in Europe, where Jews had been living in larger and longer-established communities. The allure of non-Orthodox views of sexuality may have also been a factor: although there were dozens of *mikvot* on the Lower East Side, their use declined steadily between the 1880s and 1910s.[15] Trying to reverse this trend, during the 1920s Orthodox rabbis published dozens of books and articles extolling "the medical benefits of family purity," integrating emerging scientific evidence about observant women's health and hygiene, some even claiming a eugenic advantage for the children of women who followed the law of *nidah*. Literature targeted to assimilated yet observant Jews highlighted the health benefits of *nidah* while also promoting its ties to Jewish survival. Rabbi Mordecai Aaron Kaplan wrote a book about the health benefits of *nidah* in which he "went so far as to attribute the survival of the Jewish people solely to the faithful adherence to the precepts of *nidah*."[16] These efforts failed; by 1942, an Orthodox rabbinic association declared the observance of *nidah* to be "on the verge of extinction."[17] At the same time, Jewish leaders worried about interfaith marriage, which, while relatively rare during the first half of the twentieth century, symbolized to its critics the end point of assimilation and the threat of the Jewish people's extinction.[18]

The American Jewish investment in marriage intensified alongside a growing secular investment in marital sexuality between the 1930s and 1950s. During these decades, judges, policy makers, legislators, mental health professionals, and bureaucrats created a "straight state." They defined heterosexuality as a psychological, economic, and political ideal, embedded in ideas of citizenship and mental health.[19] The valorization of heterosexuality occurred in tandem with stepped up efforts to demonize same-sex desires. A wave of "sex crime panics" after World War II targeted gay men as supposedly lecherous predators. Arrests for public lewdness rose, and police raids of gay and lesbian bars increased. The first *Diagnostic and Statistical Manual, Mental Disorders* (1952) of the American Psychiatric Association formalized associations between homosexuality and mental instability by describing homosexuality as a sociopathic personality disorder.[20] The straight state privileged marriage and heterosexuality while anathematizing homosexuality. Reform and Orthodox rabbis, like other religious leaders, participated in this emerging cultural emphasis on marital heterosexuality.

Religious leaders learned to view heterosexuality as the expression of "normal" erotic desires (heteronormativity). Starting in the 1930s, a small group of clergy attained recognition as "marriage experts," and they promoted the idea, which was gaining credence among psychologists and social workers, that heterosexuality was a precondition for a happy marriage. By the late 1930s, marriage counselors (who came from the ranks of social workers, social hygiene experts, psychiatrists, physicians, eugenicists, and clergy) began to describe a goal of "heterosexual adjustment" for their clients. Heterosexual adjustment suggested not simply an erotic capacity for different-sex desires but also conformity to normative gender roles. For women, an adequate heterosexual adjustment might require that they embrace the performance of menial household chores or subordinate their career ambitions. For men, heterosexual adjustment demanded that they assume household leadership.[21] Marriage counselors premised mutually fulfilling and happy marriages on the successful adoption of these gendered roles, which they argued would establish a basis for a satisfying heterosexual relationship.

Reform Jewish rabbis modified this emphasis on heterosexuality when they began to practice marriage counseling; they viewed marriage counseling as yet another means to promote family cohesion and thus ensure the survival of the Jewish people. Reform Jews, in contrast to Orthodox Jews, were especially receptive to social scientific methods of marriage counseling. The Reform movement within Judaism had originated in Germany in the nineteenth century and flourished among the German Jewish immigrants who arrived in the United States. While Orthodox Jews considered the Talmud to comprise a set of timeless laws, Reform Jews viewed the Talmud as antiquated and even irrelevant for modern living. Instead, Reform Jews offered new interpretations of the five books of the Torah, shortened and modified the traditional liturgy, and incorporated other modifications to their style of worship. Yet while Reform Jews did not concern themselves with observing *nidah*, they continued to value Jewish continuity and family creation.

The Reform Jewish appreciation for "modern" knowledge meant that Reform rabbis were often eager to incorporate new forms of expertise into their efforts to encourage and sustain marriages within the faith. By the 1930s and 1940s, a growing number of Reform rabbis considered sociology, social work, and psychology to be useful complements to their training in liturgy and exegesis, and this was especially true of rabbis who were involved with premarital and marital counseling.[22] Rabbi Sidney E. Goldstein, who served as the associate rabbi at Stephen Wise's Free Synagogue in New York City, used his pulpit to conduct a mental health and social science laboratory. In 1935, in the midst of the Great Depression, he urged the Central Conference of American Rabbis (CCAR), the organization of the Reform rabbinate, to create a committee on marriage to address a national crisis of marital dissolution. Goldstein became the first chairman of the Committee on Marriage, Family, and the Home.[23] A passionate supporter of the New Deal, Goldstein called for expansive government programs to provide employment and vocational training to more young people so that they could marry and sustain their families without the burden of financial stress.[24] He also wanted Reform synagogues to establish internal or support external "Consultation Centers" that would provide counseling and supportive services to families.[25] Like many progressive Jews of the 1930s, Goldstein was both a eugenicist and a supporter of Margaret Sanger's birth control movement. He thus described marriage as a spiritual relationship, exemplified by an idea from the Torah of *kiddushin*, or sanctification (the name given to the engagement or betrothal ceremony), and an opportunity for eugenic mate selection. Speaking before a synagogue gathering, "he deplored the fact that persons contemplating marriage do not make a careful investigation of their respective physical and mental fitness."[26] A left-leaning Reform Jew, Goldstein understood Jewish marriage as a relationship with profound economic, spiritual, and eugenic consequences. In 1954, one year before his death at age seventy-seven, Goldstein looked back upon his efforts to establish the social justice programs at the Free Synagogue and to create marriage and family counseling programs as equally important legacies: "They are of course closely related."[27]

Goldstein was not alone in seeing the promotion and preservation of Jewish marriage as a social justice issue. His ideas resonated with Rabbi Stanley R. Brav, who became the chairman of the CCAR Committee on Marriage, Family, and the Home in 1940 and whose words opened this essay.

Brav earned a doctoral degree in sociology (from Webster University in Atlanta through correspondence courses).[28] At some point he also took a correspondence course, "The Principles, Techniques and Materials of Counseling," from Paul Popenoe's American Institute of Family Relations in Los Angeles, the largest marriage counseling clinic in the United States.[29] A career pacifist, even throughout World War II, and a civil rights activist from pulpits in Dallas, Texas, and Vicksburg, Mississippi, Brav understood his concern with premarital counseling to be consonant with his other political commitments. Premarital counseling, in other words, was to Brav not a distraction from the "real" work of social justice but an integral component of achieving a peaceful world. He believed that premarital "interviews" afforded an opportunity for a religious official to influence social relations.

Reform rabbis participated in a post–World War II American celebration of marriage that simultaneously exalted the merits of heterosexuality and portrayed homosexuality as a serious psychiatric problem. In Brav's 1959 sexual advice guide, *Since Eve*, he wrote, "Where excessive masturbation, or the incidence of homosexuality, or other sexual deviation is evident, resort to physicians, psychiatrists or marriage counselors is imperative."[30] Like most secular psychiatrists, some religious leaders viewed homosexuality as an impediment to "mature" heterosexual marriage. Reverend Norman Vincent Peale, the famous expositor of positive thinking, authored a regular advice column in *Look* magazine during the 1950s, which on December 11, 1956, included Peale's advice to an anonymous nineteen-year-old who described himself as "homosexually inclined" and desperate to have a wife and children. Peale urged the young man to seek help from a psychiatrist in order to become capable of "normal" sexual attraction. (In his advice column in *Ebony* magazine, Reverend Martin Luther King Jr. offered nearly identical advice to a young gay man in 1957—that he should see a "good psychiatrist" to "solve" his problem.)[31] For Peale and other liberal Protestant pastoral counselors, marriage was the apex of social and spiritual maturity. They thus worried that homosexuality constituted a stubborn obstacle to both psychological health and moral progress. As Roy A. Burkhart, a liberal Protestant minister and well-regarded marriage counseling expert, explained in a premarital counseling pamphlet, "When two people are mature, they are heterosexual."[32] This postwar celebration of heterosexual marriage reached across denominational and sectarian divides, from the Southern Baptist Billy Graham to Peale to Reform rabbis like Brav to Orthodox rabbis, as we will soon see. While Reform rabbis seem to have discussed homosexuality less passionately than their Protestant peers did, they did not critique the Protestant approach and may have broadly agreed with Brav that same-sex desires were serious psychiatric impediments to marital happiness.

The overriding issue for Reform rabbis, however, soon became the uptick in rates of interfaith marriage. American Jewish leaders fretted publicly about the problems of interfaith marriage years before it became widespread. In the first half of the twentieth century, American Jewish leaders had adopted sociological language and concepts to explain the American Jewish propensity for "endogamy," or marrying within the group. The topic of marriage more than any other forced Jewish leaders to explain religious and ethnic solidarity to a broader culture that sought to assimilate immigrants in the ethnic "melting pot." Sociological studies that correlated similarity of family and class background to marital happiness became fodder for Jewish leaders, including rabbis, who began teaching their congregants that interfaith marriage increased the likelihood of divorce. Progressive and liberal rabbis in particular relied on sociological language, rather than religious texts, to explain the risks of interfaith marriage. Rabbis and other Jewish leaders worried simultaneously about Jewish survival via the birth of children within a Jewish family structure and the perceptions among non-Jews that Jewish endogamy was antidemocratic and narrow-minded. Social scientific literatures depicted the children of interfaith marriages as the emotional victims of their parents' selfishness. Psychologically damaged by a lack of clear religious identity and even perhaps the victims of their parents' eventual divorce, these real and imagined children became source material for sermons against marrying outside the faith.[33] One upshot of this preoccupation was that American leaders of liberal and progressive Judaism spent much less time talking about sex than about its reproductive consequences. Reform rabbis who were deeply invested in premarital counseling and marriage education, in other words, had less to say about sex than did secular marriage counselors, Protestant clergy, or Orthodox rabbis.

Modern Orthodox Jewish leaders who spoke and wrote about sexuality, meanwhile, continued to emphasize the salience of family purity laws for the creation of stable Jewish homes. Leading voices of Orthodox Judaism in the postwar United States underlined the centrality of procreation to the Jewish marital ideal. Rabbi Leo Jung, professor of ethics at Yeshiva University from 1931 to 1968, was born in Moravia (now Slovakia) in 1892, grew up in London, and moved to the United States in 1920.[34] When Jung described the Jewish essence of marriage, he echoed the communal emphasis of his Reform peers but, true to his Orthodox immersion in Jewish law, stressed the importance of teaching married couples to observe the family purity laws, *nidah*. In a studio recording of one of his popular lectures, Jung called to his audience, "Let me talk to you this evening about the three factors in marriage: husband, wife and children." Jung, in other words, taught that marriage involved a network of relationships, an ecology of affections and responsibilities. Whereas Reform rabbis turned to sociology for authoritative descriptions of how best to attain marital stability, Jung praised Jewish tradition as the source of wisdom for familial harmony: "All the customs and laws and admonitions and suggestions of Judaism have gone towards one exclusive purpose: that of creating and maintaining the right attitude between husband and wife, between parents and children." Just as Orthodox rabbis earlier in the century had praised *nidah* for its health benefits, so too Jung, speaking as psychotherapy and therapeutic ideals were ascendant in American culture, valorized Jewish tradition for enabling marital mutuality and emotional well-being. Other faiths might treat sexual intimacy "as of the devil," he explained, but "not in Judaism.... We are body and soul, and we love with body and soul, and that is perfectly right." More to the point, Jung argued that *nidah* preserved women's dignity and emancipated them sexually within their marriages.[35] Jung reiterated this sex-positive message in interviews and lectures. He sounded every inch the progressive sex educator and marriage counselor when he explained in the *New York World-Telegram and Sun*, "A good marriage requires intelligent sex preparation."[36] The idea that Judaism was especially good for (married) women's sexual self-determination persisted among American Jewish leaders and educators, despite a growing chorus of complaints from married women about neglectful and even abusive behavior by their husbands.[37]

By the early 1970s, a sense of crisis pervaded American Jewish conversations about sexuality and the family. The American Jewish panic about Jewish "survival" reflected post-Holocaust calls to repopulate world Jewry following the deaths of six million European Jews. This linkage between birth rates and ethnic survival contrasted starkly with the attitudes of liberal Protestants, who increasingly embraced the idea of "zero population growth" and encouraged the use of contraception (a story Samira K. Mehta explores in her essay in this volume).[38] Indeed, national opinion polls showed widespread support for contraception and abortion among American Jews, but Jewish leaders were critical. Stanley Brav bemoaned the widespread use of birth control and frequency of premarital sex, comparing the sexually active unmarried Jewish woman to a prostitute, a gendered assessment of sexual liberalism that suggested the endurance of premodern ideas that correlated women's worth with their "virtue" and excused men's nonmarital sexual behaviors as the inevitable consequences of their carnal natures.[39] Indeed, across the spectrum of Jewish organizational life and institutions, from the most progressive to the most observant, Jewish leaders identified a crisis in Jewish fertility rates and urged Jewish women to marry at younger ages and bear more children. Reform and Orthodox leaders invoked the horrors of the Holocaust to drive home their pleas to Jewish women to bear more than two children. Numerous Jewish commentators suggested that Jews should be exempt from calls for zero population growth. As Rachel Kranson's essay in this volume illustrates, Conservative Jews (who follow Orthodox Jews in valuing Talmudic law but view its interpretation as an ongoing process) likewise viewed the topics of abortion and contraception through the lens of Jewish survival. Antipathy toward homosexuals within organized Judaism derived at least in part from this institutional prioritization of monogamous, procreative marriage.[40]

Jewish feminists and Jewish LGBT activists challenged these stereotypes about the imperative for Jewish women to be fruitful and multiply and the reduction of the Jewish community to the nuclear, heterosexual family. Jewish feminist study groups, spirituality retreats, and institutionally minded action committees fundamentally transformed all but the most tradition-bound expressions of Judaism in the United States. Jewish feminists crafted new rituals for the naming of Jewish girls (to parallel the male circumcision rite, the bris, which welcomes Jewish males into the covenant of Israel), rewrote prayer books, demanded that women be fully integrated into the ritual aspects of Jewish practice, and contested male-dominated communal leadership. Feminist theologians questioned conventional narratives of patrimony and descent, and scholars reinterpreted Jewish law to encompass the experiences of women. Lesbian feminists particularly challenged the gender conventions of Judaism, arguing for radical inclusivity and gender-neutral liturgies.[41]

We know far too little about how mid-twentieth-century American Jews responded to homosexuality within a religious context. For observant Jews, Leviticus 18:22, which describes sex between men as *to'evah*, an abomination, was paramount, but the refusal of Jewish congregations to legitimize or welcome gay men and lesbians derived equally from "the central position of the family in Jewish society and its ethos of reproduction." Because Judaism viewed same-sex sexuality as nonreproductive, it considered gay men and lesbians to be individuals who "challenge the basic unit of the Jewish social fabric, often considered far more important than most other communal institutions, including the synagogue."[42] By 1977 the politics of gay rights mapped onto the Orthodox-Reform divide: Orthodox Jews in Miami joined forces with the evangelical spokeswoman Anita Bryant to oppose a nondiscrimination ordinance that included gays and lesbians, while gay rights activists who organized in opposition to Bryant understood that "liberal Jews" were among their potential allies.[43] Future research will need to explore these tensions, coalitions, and shifting theological perspectives in greater detail.

Jewish organizations were quicker to assert formal equality for gays and lesbians than to welcome them into the familial fabric of Jewish life. By the 1970s the major Jewish movements, with the exception of the Orthodox, had issued statements supporting LGBT civil rights. The Reform movement supported the human rights bill for gays and lesbians in 1977, accepted openly lesbian and gay people as synagogue members in 1987, and welcomed the ordination of openly gay and lesbian rabbis in 1990.[44] Change in policy did not always mean changes in culture, however, as Rebecca T. Alpert and Jacob J. Staub demonstrate in their essay for this volume about efforts to promote LGBT inclusivity at the Reconstructionist Rabbinical College. Just as the college's 1984 policy statement permitting the admission of openly gay or lesbian students to the seminary noted that "the Jewish ideal for man and woman is heterosexuality," the 1990 statement of the Reform movement's CCAR permitting openly gay rabbis included the caveat, "In Jewish tradition heterosexual, monogamous, procreative marriage is the ideal human relationship for the perpetuation of the species, covenantal fulfillment and the preservation of the Jewish people.... To the extent that sexual orientation is a matter of choice, the majority of the committee affirms that heterosexuality is the only appropriate Jewish choice for fulfilling one's obligations."[45] By 1996, however, the CCAR officially supported marriage equality, and in 2000 it became the first major organization of American clergy to permit its members to officiate at the weddings of same-sex couples.[46]

Some Jewish liberals and progressives took the side of LGBT activists in the culture wars of the 1970s, and they often did so by enlarging their investment in marriage to include LGBT people. Since the 1970s, American Jews have supported LGBT rights and same-sex marriage (as well as access to birth control and abortion rights) at among the highest rates of any group in the country. By the 1990s, Reform Judaism in particular became a more welcoming space for openly gay and lesbian congregants and clergy. Reform Jews have tended to be Democrats, and as the Democratic Party and its members increasingly embraced LGBT rights and the broader culture grew more tolerant, Reform congregations faced pressure both from congregants and from their leadership to adopt more tolerant attitudes toward LGBT members. Several prominent Reform Jews helped lead campaigns for marriage equality. In 1998, Reform rabbi Devon Lerner of Boston founded the Religious Coalition for the Freedom to Marry. The group contributed an amicus brief in the 2003 *Goodridge v. Massachusetts* case that resulted in legalizing marriage for same-sex couples in that state.[47] In a 2014 survey of attitudes toward marriage equality, the percentage of American Jews who supported it (77 percent) was second only to Buddhists (84 percent).[48] Yet as Alpert and Staub's essay about the Reconstructionist Rabbinical College suggests, acceptance of marriage equality in many ways sustained Jewish preoccupations with survival by framing LGBT rights as another route to the formation of Jewish families.

Rigorous historical studies of the intersections between religion and sexuality in the United States are relatively recent, and they have overwhelmingly focused on Protestants and Catholics, the majority faiths. This essay has attempted to map the implications of putting a different religious tradition—in this instance, Judaism—at the center of the story. The contrast between Reform and Orthodox Jews further illustrates the significance of cultural and spiritual variety to how religious leaders and laity have articulated their sexual and gendered values and responded to shifting sexual politics in the culture at large. A distinctly pronatalist emphasis on the rituals of "family purity" and the perils of interfaith marriage shaped the American Jewish investment in marriage from the nineteenth century into the early twenty-first. The Holocaust sharpened but did not create the argument in favor of larger families. The American Jewish approach to marriage and sexuality reflects the influence of secular and non-Jewish (Protestant and Catholic) ideas, but it also emerged out of the particularity of Jewish ritual, ethnic priorities, and history. Like his Protestant colleagues, Rabbi Stanley Brav succeeded in privileging marriage as a unique site for Jewish communal engagement and ritual instruction. The consequences of that investment continue to unfold.

NOTES

Many individuals read or commented on earlier versions of this article, especially Gillian Frank, Bethany Moreton, and Heather White. I received valuable feedback on an early version of this essay as part of a panel on religious histories/sexual binaries at the Annual Meeting of the American Academy of Religion in 2013. Emily Johnson's invitation to address a graduate student conference at the John C. Danforth Center on Religion and Politics in May 2014 provided another opportunity to formulate these ideas. For feedback then and since, I thank Wallace Best, Samira Mehta, Anthony Petro, R. Marie Griffith, Leigh Eric Schmidt, Lerone Martin, and Mark D. Jordan. Alison Greene was an engaged conversation partner as this essay developed. Alison Kreitzer provided essential research assistance. Kimberly Blockett was an invaluable writing companion and sounding board. My thanks to all of them.

1. "Family Life," Institute on Marriage, Family, and the Home sponsored by the Department of Human Relations at Hebrew Union College–Jewish Institute of Religion, April 20 and 21, 1954, Cassette #457, Jacob Rader Marcus Center of the American Jewish Archives, Cincinnati, Ohio (hereafter AJA).

2. Robert H. Abzug, *Cosmos Crumbling: American Reform and the Religious Imagination* (New York: Oxford University Press, 1994), 163–66; Helen Lefkowitz Horowitz, "Victoria Woodhull, Anthony Comstock, and Conflict over Sex in the United States in the 1870s," *Journal of American History* 87, no. 2 (September 2000): 403–34; Patricia Cline Cohen, "Ministerial Misdeeds," *Journal of Women's History* 7, no. 3 (Fall 1995): 34–57. On Protestant rumors about sexual misdeeds among Catholic women religious, see Tracy Fessenden, "The Convent, the Brothel, and the Protestant Woman's Sphere," *Signs* 25, no. 2 (Winter 2000): 451–78; and Jenny Franchot, *Roads to Rome: The Antebellum Protestant Encounter with Catholicism* (Berkeley: University of California Press, 1994), 120–26.

3. Helen Lefkowitz Horowitz, *Rereading Sex: Battles over Sexual Knowledge and Suppression in Nineteenth-Century America* (New York: Alfred A. Knopf, 2002), 263–69; Joanne Ellen Passet, *Sex Radicals and the Quest for Women's Equality* (Urbana: University of Illinois Press, 2003), 114–31; Ann Braude, *Radical Spirits: Spiritualism and Women's Rights in Nineteenth-Century America* (Boston: Beacon Press, 1989), chap. 5.

4. Horowitz, *Rereading Sex*, 347–57; Sarah Barringer Gordon, *The Mormon Question: Polygamy and Constitutional Conflict in Nineteenth-Century America* (Chapel Hill: University of North Carolina Press, 2002).

5. Karla Goldman, *Beyond the Synagogue Gallery: Finding a Place for Women in American Judaism* (Cambridge, Mass.: Harvard University Press, 2000), 69–75; William Toll, "From Domestic Judaism to Public Ritual: Women and Religious Identity in the American West," in *Women and American Judaism: Historical Perspectives*, ed. Pamela Nadell and Jonathan Sarna (Hanover: Brandeis University Press, 2001), 129.

6. See, for example, Jennifer Terry, *An American Obsession: Science, Medicine, and Homosexuality in Modern Society* (Chicago: University of Chicago Press, 1999); Lisa Duggan, "The Trials of Alice Mitchell: Sensationalism, Sexology, and the Lesbian Subject in Turn-of-the-Century America," *Signs: Journal of Women in Culture and Society* 18, no. 4 (Summer 1993): 791–814; and Jonathan Ned Katz, *The Invention of Heterosexuality*, with a new preface (1995; repr., Chicago: University of Chicago Press, 2007), chap. 2.

7. David Nasaw, *Going Out: The Rise and Fall of Public Amusements* (New York: Basic Books, 1993), chap. 9; Kathy Lee Peiss, *Cheap Amusements: Working Women and Leisure in Turn-of-the-Century New York* (Philadelphia: Temple University Press, 1986); Elizabeth Alice Clement, *Love for Sale: Courting, Treating, and Prostitution in New York City, 1900–1945* (Chapel Hill: University of North Carolina Press, 2006), 43–44, 52–56, 173–93.

8. Rebecca L. Davis, "'Not Marriage at All, but Simple Harlotry': The Companionate Marriage Controversy," *Journal of American History* 94, no. 4 (March 2008): 1141; Christina Simmons, *Making Marriage Modern: Women's Sexuality from the Progressive Era to World War II* (New York: Oxford University Press, 2009), chap. 3; Jessamyn Neuhaus, "The Importance of Being Orgasmic: Sexuality, Gender, and Marital Sex Manuals in the United States, 1920–1963," *Journal of the History of Sexuality* 9, no. 4 (October 2000): 447–73.

9. Christina Simmons, "Companionate Marriage and the Lesbian Threat," *Frontiers* 4, no. 3 (Autumn 1979): 54–59; Simmons, *Making Marriage Modern*, chap. 5; Davis,

"Companionate Marriage Controversy," 1158–61; Clare Virginia Eby, *Until Choice Do Us Part: Marriage Reform in the Progressive Era* (Chicago: University of Chicago Press, 2014), chap. 2; William Kuby, "Till Disinterest Do Us Part: Trial Marriage, Public Policy, and the Fear of Familial Decay in the United States, 1900–1930," *Journal of the History of Sexuality* 23, no. 3 (2014): 383–414.

10. Julian Carter, *The Heart of Whiteness: Normal Sexuality and Race in America, 1880–1940* (Durham: Duke University Press, 2007), chap. 2.

11. Peggy Pascoe, *What Comes Naturally: Miscegenation Law and the Making of Race in America* (Oxford: Oxford University Press, 2009), chap. 3.

12. See, for example, Matthew Frye Jacobson, *Whiteness of a Different Color: European Immigrants and the Alchemy of Race* (Cambridge, Mass.: Harvard University Press, 1998); and Gail Bederman, *Manliness and Civilization: A Cultural History of Gender and Race in the United States, 1880–1917* (Chicago: University of Chicago Press, 1995).

13. Christine Rosen, *Preaching Eugenics: Religious Leaders and the American Eugenics Movement* (New York: Oxford University Press, 2004).

14. Susan Glenn, "In the Blood? Consent, Descent, and the Ironies of Jewish Identity," *Jewish Social Studies* 8, no. 2/3 (2002): 139–52; Eric L. Goldstein, *The Price of Whiteness: Jews, Race, and American Identity* (Princeton: Princeton University Press, 2006).

15. Hasia R. Diner and Beryl Lieff Benderly, *Her Works Praise Her: A History of Jewish Women in America from Colonial Times to the Present* (New York: Basic Books, 2002), 228.

16. Beth Wenger, "Mitzvah and Medicine: Gender, Assimilation, and the Scientific Defense of 'Family Purity,'" *Jewish Social Studies* 5, no. 1–2 (1998–99): 177–202.

17. Diner and Benderly, *Her Works Praise Her*, 360.

18. Riv-Ellen Prell, *Fighting to Become Americans: Jews, Gender, and the Anxiety of Assimilation* (Boston: Beacon Press, 1999), 67–77.

19. Margot Canaday, *The Straight State: Sexuality and Citizenship in Twentieth-Century America* (Princeton: Princeton University Press, 2009).

20. Ronald Bayer, *Homosexuality and American Psychiatry: The Politics of Diagnosis* (Princeton: Princeton University Press, 1987), 39–40.

21. Rebecca L. Davis, *More Perfect Unions: The American Search for Marital Bliss* (Cambridge, Mass.: Harvard University Press, 2010), chap. 2.

22. For example, Robert Jacobs, a rabbi who chaired the CCAR Commission on Marriage and the Home from 1958 into the 1960s, had a degree in social work and practiced as a marriage counselor. See Robert P. Jacobs, "Call It an Ethical Will" (1996): 2; and Robert P. Jacobs, Resume [undated; ca. 1984], Nearprint file, Jacobs, Robert Paul, AJA.

23. Sidney E. Goldstein, "Report of Committee on Marriage, the Family and the Home," *CCAR Yearbook* 47 (1937): 84, AJA.

24. Ibid., 88.

25. [Sidney E. Goldstein], "Outline Report of Commission on Social Justice, Central Conference of American Rabbis, June 1935," 1, box 15, folder 4, Robert P. Goldman Papers, AJA.

26. On *kiddushin*, see Sidney E. Goldstein, "Report of Committee on Marriage, the Family and the Home," *CCAR Yearbook* 48 (1938): 105, AJA. On hereditary fitness, see Jewish Institute of Religion Records, MS 19, box 16, folder 16, "Goldstein, Sidney. Corr.; Clippings. 1930–1947," AJA.

27. Sidney E. Goldstein to Mrs. Dorothy Millstone (Public Relations Department, Hebrew Union College–Jewish Institute of Religion), November 23, 1954, folder 9, Sidney Goldstein Papers, Stephen Wise Free Synagogue, New York.

28. Stanley R. Brav, "Days of My Life," typescript (1970), 182–83, box 1, folder 5, Papers of Stanley R. Brav, AJA.

29. Ibid., 312. For more on Popenoe and the American Institute of Family Relations, see Davis, *More Perfect Unions*, 32–38, 121–31, 157–58; and Alexandra Minna Stern, *Eugenic Nation: Faults and Frontiers of Better Breeding in Modern America* (Berkeley: University of California Press, 2005), chap. 5.

30. Stanley R. Brav, *Since Eve: A Bible-Inspired Sex Ethic for Today* (New York: Pageant Press, 1959), 5.

31. "Norman Vincent Peale Answers Your Questions," *Look*, December 11, 1956, 132; Rebecca L. Davis, "'My Homosexuality Is Getting Worse Every Day': Norman Vincent Peale, Psychiatry, and the Liberal Protestant Response to Same-Sex Desires in Mid-Twentieth-Century America," in *American Christianities: A History of Dominance and Diversity*, ed. Catherine A. Brekus and W. Clark Gilpin (Chapel Hill: University of North Carolina Press, 2011), 347–65; Thaddeus Russell, "The Color of Discipline: Civil Rights and Black Sexuality," *American Quarterly* 60, no. 1 (March 2008): 17.

32. Roy A. Burkhart, *A Church's Program of Education in Marriage and the Family* (Columbus, Ohio: First Community Church, n.d.), 2.

33. Lila Corwin Berman, *Speaking of Jews: Rabbis, Intellectuals, and the Creation of an American Public Identity* (Berkeley: University of California Press, 2008), chaps. 3 and 7; Davis, *More Perfect Unions*, 104–21. See also Lila Corwin Berman, "Sociology, Jews, and Intermarriage in Twentieth-Century America," *Jewish Social Studies*, n.s., 14, no. 2 (January 2008): 32–60.

34. "Biographical Note," *Guide to the Rabbi Doctor Leo Jung Collection, 1878–1989*, 1994, Yeshiva University Archives, New York.

35. Rabbi Leo Jung, "The Jewish View of Marriage," studio recording, June 11, 1956, dual track audio reel. See also Leo Jung, *What Is Judaism?* (New York: Union of Orthodox Jewish Congregations of America, 1944), 16; and Leo Jung, *The Jewish Way to Married Happiness: A Radio Address*, 2nd ed. (New York, 1933), 9. All located in box 44, folder 3, Leo Jung Collection, Yeshiva University Archives, New York.

36. Hope Johnson, "Atmosphere of Marriage Should Train Child," *New York World-Telegram and Sun*, April 30, 1959, 14.

37. Michael E. Staub, *Torn at the Roots: The Crisis of Jewish Liberalism in Postwar America* (New York: Columbia University Press, 2002), 244–47.

38. Staub, *Torn at the Roots*, 242, 259–65.

39. "Brides Rarely Virgins," *Jewish Post and Opinion*, February 19, 1971, 11, quoted in ibid., 242.

40. Staub, *Torn at the Roots*, chap. 7.

41. See, for example, Jewish Women's Archive, "Feminism," http://jwa.org/feminism (accessed May 18, 2015); Judith Plaskow, *Standing Again at Sinai: Judaism from a Feminist Perspective* (New York: HarperSanFrancisco, 1991); Rebecca T. Alpert, Sue Levi Elwell, and Shirley Idelson, eds., *Lesbian Rabbis: The First Generation* (New Brunswick: Rutgers University Press, 2001); Rachel Adler, *Engendering Judaism: An Inclusive Theology and*

Ethics (Philadelphia: Jewish Publication Society, 1998); Rebecca T. Alpert, *Like Bread on the Seder Plate: Jewish Lesbians and the Transformation of Tradition* (New York: Columbia University Press, 1997); and Elyse Goldstein, *New Jewish Feminism: Probing the Past, Forging the Future* (Woodstock: Jewish Lights, 2009).

42. Moshe Shokeid, *A Gay Synagogue in New York* (New York: Columbia University Press, 1995), 18.

43. Gillian Frank, "'The Rights of Parents': Race and Conservative Politics in Anita Bryant's Campaign against Gay Rights in 1970s Florida," *Journal of the History of Sexuality* 22, no. 1 (January 2013): 145, 149.

44. Shokeid, *Gay Synagogue in New York*, 19. See also Alpert, Elwell, and Idelson, *Lesbian Rabbis*.

45. Staub, *Torn at the Roots*, 251; Jack Wertheimer, *A People Divided: Judaism in Contemporary America* (New York: Basic Books, 1993), 106.

46. "LGBT Rights and the Position of the Reform Movement," Religious Action Center of Reform Judaism, www.rac.org (accessed May 18, 2015); "On Gay and Lesbian Marriage," Resolution Adopted by the 107th Annual Convention of the Central Conference of American Rabbis, March 1996, ccarnet.org. According to a recent study, 35 percent of respondents identified as Reform, 18 percent as Conservative, 10 percent as Orthodox, 6 percent as members of smaller groups (including the Reconstructionist movement), and 30 percent as not affiliated with a denomination. See "A Portrait of Jewish Americans," Pew Research Center, www.pewforum.org, first posted October 1, 2013.

47. Sarah Barringer Gordon, *The Spirit of the Law: Religious Voices and the Constitution in Modern America* (Cambridge, Mass.: Belknap Press of Harvard University Press, 2010), 172, 205, and chap. 6.

48. Robert P. Jones, "Attitudes on Same-Sex Marriage by Religious Affiliation and Denominational Family," April 22, 2015, PRRI, www.publicreligion.org; Public Religion Research Institute, *American Values Atlas*, 2014, PRRI, ava.publicreligion.org.

SEX IS HOLY AND MYSTERIOUS

The Vision of Early Twentieth-Century Catholic Sex Education Reformers

JAMES P. MCCARTIN

"Parents insist that children brush their teeth, clean their nails, comb their hair and wash their hands," lamented Catholic priest and high school instructor Matthew Michel in 1929. "Yet ever so many, even among modern mothers, cannot be brought to the point of relating to their children the simplest facts of sex." Too many youngsters consequently suffered from "complete ignorance, even upon the threshold of marriage." Worse still, too many more drew the full extent of their sexual knowledge from "the movies, the theatre, modern dress, servants, the automobile, the crowded tenement, the magazine, the scandal sheet, the dance floor, [and] the street corner." Parents' aversion to instructing their children about sex led Michel to advocate a straightforward, if daunting, solution: the church's official representatives must transcend their reticence about addressing sexuality and commit themselves to "compete with other agencies offering sex knowledge wherein religion has no part." According to Michel, the urgent task of reversing adolescents' misconception that "sex is unclean and vulgar" while affirming that "the body is good and sacred in all its parts" and instilling a "simple and truthful narrative of the sacred story of life" thus fell to an army of professional Catholic educators comprised overwhelmingly of sisters, brothers, and priests who were solemnly vowed to the spiritual discipline of perpetual celibacy.[1]

The dual emphasis on reticence and urgency in this 1929 proposal underscores a key tension that shaped U.S. Catholic leaders' engagement with sexuality in the early twentieth century. On the one hand, a keen sense of restraint had long characterized Catholics' approach to sex. No less than their Protestant counterparts, Catholic clergy and vowed religious affirmed Victorian ideals that emphasized public discretion and delicacy about sexual matters. Such reticence was bolstered on the one hand by a long history of anti-Catholic polemics that scorned the Catholic spiritual discipline of lifelong sexual abstinence, painting its practitioners as deviant threats to the American public. On the other hand, a vanguard of alarmed Catholic educators, determined to counter the effects of rapid societal and cultural transformation, argued for a new regime of forthright instruction for their youthful charges. Amid a purported upsurge in adolescent promiscuity, those venues where Catholics had previously transmitted sexual mores to younger generations—the family home and the confessional box in the parish church—appeared increasingly inadequate to the task of cultivating modesty and sexual continence.[2] Changed circumstances demanded nothing less than a full-scale commitment from the church's most visible representatives among Catholic youth—teachers and administrators in the vast network of U.S. Catholic schools—to speak openly about sex and thereby breach a silence that helped underwrite the youthful descent into sexual sin.

Father Michel's insistence that school instructors take responsibility for this critical element in youth formation—an insistence echoed by many of his contemporaries—also highlights a larger effort among early twentieth-century Catholic educators to develop an approach to sex that was both theologically sound and firmly grounded in up-to-date physiological and social scientific research. Aiming to make age-appropriate sex instruction standard in Catholic schools, these educators hoped to instill a clear sense of moral boundaries and spotlight health threats that could befall sexually active youth. But they also aspired to impart an enduring moral sensibility, capable of aiding students through their lives, of which sexuality was an integrated part. Opting for an affirmative approach, they emphasized that sex was both "natural" and "sacred"—at once impelled by strong biological and emotional drives and bound to the spiritual nature and destiny of the human person. Rather than prescribing restrictive moralism designed merely to suppress sexual desire, these educators promoted an elevated sense of human sexuality and encouraged a heightened capacity for thoughtful reflection on the topic. In the process, they indicated a capacity for fluid engagement with a range of perspectives on sexuality but also demonstrated that Catholic approaches to sex were not universally condemnatory and routinely outdated, as critics have frequently asserted.

Narratives of sex education's emergence and development in the twentieth-century United States invariably spotlight secular progressive activists and relegate religious figures to minor roles as conservatives bent upon stifling sexual liberation and, in the process, endangering the public health.[3] Specifically in the history of sex education and, more broadly, in the history of sexuality, historians have consistently portrayed U.S. Catholics in such negative terms: regardless of the particular period under investigation, Catholics tend to appear as agents of denunciation and repression, intransigently opposed to the advance of "modern" sexual values and practices. The result of such portrayals is to make Catholics into *ahistorical* actors, entering the narrative only to give voice to their church's purportedly unchanging views on sexual morality.[4]

Yet U.S. Catholic educators' effort to promote sex education suggests an alternate narrative in which Catholics operate as true historical actors undertaking complex analysis and executing nuanced judgments about sexuality. The story of these educators highlights how their approach was shaped by multiple contingencies, from the lingering effects of Catholics' long-standing status as a religious minority to changing patterns of formal education to shifting ideas about human development. Though they advocated views distinct from those of non-Catholic counterparts, these educators were far from simple reactionaries intent upon prohibiting access to sexual knowledge. Instead, they were reformers who, in the words of Matthew Michel, aimed to overcome the "bane of absolute silence" about sex in Catholic schools and promote in their students "respect for self and high reverence for others" as cornerstones of sexual morality.[5] The movement for Catholic sex education thus highlights how a careful investigation that integrates religious history and the history of sexuality has the potential to bring to light new narratives and uncover rich—even surprising—possibilities within two historical subfields that, until now, have seldom intersected in more than a cursory fashion.

Catholics in the United States have long borne the mark of sexual difference. Amid successive waves of nineteenth-century European Catholic immigration, non-Catholic observers continually remarked on the newcomers' peculiar attachment both to the papacy and to the practice of vowed celibacy, a spiritual discipline carried down from Christianity's first centuries. According to Protestant critics, obedience to papal authority and lifelong commitment to sexual abstinence represented dangerous perversions of Christianity: in the case of the papacy, it usurped authority rightly held by scripture alone and spawned a full complement of theological and spiritual errors; in the case of celibacy, it was an abnormal discipline that drew practitioners away from family life and, more alarmingly, made them susceptible to all manner of sexual temptation and deviance. Such views prompted spikes of anxiety and anti-Catholic attacks, which placed the immigrant church on the defensive. As representatives of religious and ethnic minorities, most Catholic spokesmen carefully responded to their critics in temperate fashion, even as the experience of interreligious controversy sharpened their sense of Catholicism as a distinctive presence in the United States. Though church officials downplayed the criticism that Catholic difference made their flock an unassimilable mass within the American nation, they nevertheless advanced distinctively Catholic viewpoints, voicing perspectives they regarded as vital to the broader public welfare, including perspectives on sex.[6]

A proliferation of published works, churned out from the 1830s onward, made sexual peculiarity and a propensity to deviance central themes in their treatment of Catholics, coloring both how non-Catholics viewed their immigrant neighbors and how Catholics themselves publicly approached the topic of sex over a long haul. Most memorable in this regard was a wildly successful, sensationalistic 1836 volume titled *The Awful Disclosures of the Hotel Dieu Nunnery*. Marketed as the first-person narrative of nineteen-year-old Maria Monk—an escapee from a Montreal convent where priests repeatedly raped resident nuns who, in turn, suffocated and secretly buried their newborn offspring—the book sold some three hundred thousand copies over the next quarter century. An investigation immediately after its release revealed *Awful Disclosures* to be a work of fiction orchestrated by a New York–based evangelical preacher, publisher, and anti-Catholic, anti-immigrant activist.[7] Nevertheless, the book hit a public nerve, sparking a large and lucrative genre that included scores of subsequent publications—some novelistic, others presented as "real life" narratives, all lingering on pornographic images and details—that starred duplicitous Catholics who employed the mask of sexual purity to hide habitual depravity.[8]

Such works found a less sensationalist, though still alarmed, parallel among post–Civil War medical researchers who fixated on dangers associated with Catholics' practice of prolonged sexual abstinence. By the late nineteenth century, physicians increasingly agreed that sexual desire and its physical articulation in marital sexual intercourse was a "natural" element of human physiology and psychology and that its suppression, especially over extended periods, wrought harmful effects, ranging from acne and nervous exhaustion to early death or suicide.[9] Beyond medicine, scholars and popular writers alike viewed vowed celibacy as merely a tool for extending papal control: by isolating practitioners from the commitments of family life and funneling their energies entirely into the church's service, Vatican officials built an "efficient instrument in creating and consolidating both the temporal and spiritual power of the Roman hierarchy."[10] Critics thus branded celibacy not only a "device of inhuman absolutism" that was merely "fostered in the interest of power" but also one that threatened the sacred institution of marriage by attaching an irrational "stigma" to sexual relations and relegating marital partners to an "inferior condition of sanctity."[11]

Compared to their non-Catholic neighbors who continually reinforced Catholic sexual difference, the immigrant church's leaders said relatively little about sex. True, church authorities made known the Council of Trent's three-hundred-year-old teaching that vowed celibacy was spiritually preferable to the married state.[12] Partially to encourage idealistic youth to choose a life in ministry, they also extolled the renunciation of carnal pleasure as an unparalleled means of conforming to the model of Jesus Christ, "*par excellence* the Virgin."[13] But among Catholic leaders, their interest in sex was far surpassed by their attention to the practical concerns of tending to a burgeoning flock within a hostile environment: establishing a baseline of devotional practice among newcomers, many with a tenuous connection to their faith; founding social service organizations to support parishioners subject to the vicissitudes of rapid urbanization and industrialization; developing parochial schools to ensure a vital future for U.S. Catholicism; nourishing a shared sense of Catholic identity among a diversity of ethnic groups jostling for jobs and housing—among nineteenth-century church leaders, these concerns, amid others, consumed the bulk of their energy.[14]

Yet as post–Civil War era courts and legislatures tightened the secular state's regulatory oversight of the nuptial bond and unprecedented numbers sued for divorce, church officials offered a full-throated defense of marriage's indissolubility and sacramental essence.[15] Writing in 1884 as a unified body, seventy-eight Catholic U.S. bishops drew a clear distinction between a misguided secular approach, which cast marriage as a civil contract, and the proper sacramental approach, which acknowledged that marriage "had God for its Founder" and was therefore tied to humanity's "eternal welfare." They further insisted that marriage, "once consummated, can never be dissolved save by death" and that, even after a martial partner committed the grave offense of adultery, "legal divorce" was mere fiction without even "the slightest power, before God, to loose the bond of marriage and make a subsequent marriage valid."[16] Arguing that the "looseness of Protestant teaching and practice" regarding marriage—that is, Protestants' historic refusal to affirm marriage's sacramental nature—wrought a "fatal result to morality," Catholic authorities projected themselves as the foremost moral guides on these questions.[17] In doing so, the church's representatives left no room for doubt: those who failed to oppose the increasingly lax attitude toward divorce were abetting "a consummate act of rebellion" against the divine Creator, and those who violated the sanctity of marriage through adultery or remarriage after civil divorce may well turn out to be "entirely rejected by God Himself."[18]

Already marked as sexually different due to celibacy, the church's highest authorities in the United States took a noteworthy step and forthrightly raised their voices on a sexual matter. Consequently, they set the stage for future interventions, laying the foundations for a reputation—one that would grow substantially after 1930—for outspoken involvement in matters of sexual morality. (Aiko Takeuchi-Demirci's chapter on Catholic opposition to population control in U.S.-occupied Japan highlights one noteworthy example of such intervention.) Nevertheless, early twentieth-century U.S. Catholic leaders still bore a substantial degree of reticence when it came to engaging publicly about sex. That reticence would ultimately be challenged by a range of developments that prompted calls for a specifically Catholic brand of sex education.

In 1928, Chicago-based educator Ellamay Horan, worried about the quality of the instruction for Catholic adolescents, polled graduates from scores of midwestern Catholic girls' high schools about how well their education prepared them for the challenges of adulthood. Knowing these alumnae would never again be subject to formal religious instruction, Horan was particularly concerned about teachers' effectiveness at imparting an enduring sense of theological and spiritual wisdom during high school. Her concerns were borne out by the survey data: 86 percent of respondents—all between twenty and thirty years old—said they had been imbued with sufficient understanding about their "financial obligation to the Church," while only 29 percent attested to obtaining an appropriate sense of the "nature and purpose of marriage," and a mere 9 percent said they received "adequate information" about the "origin, meaning, [and] reproduction of life." Such figures, Horan concluded, revealed a major flaw: if Catholic educators wished to make religion "primarily a way of living" rather than an abstract collection of formulas and commands, then they must train young Catholics to give religious principles "concrete" application in everyday circumstances, bringing theological principles to bear in all areas of their lives, including the most intimate of relationships.[19]

Advocating a practice-oriented form of religious instruction, Horan allied herself with a vocal, reform-minded segment of U.S. Catholic educators who, since the first decade of the twentieth century, challenged pedagogical methods of the past as unfit for the dynamic social and cultural context of the present. Especially rueful to these educators was their colleagues' reliance on the *Baltimore Catechism*—a four-volume doctrinal compendium, composed in didactic question-and-answer format, from which parochial school students were compelled to memorize since publication in the 1880s.[20] Given that busy teachers inevitably measured students' progress through accuracy in recitation rather than through genuine understanding, critics branded this approach "practically useless" and called on religion instructors to embrace "the work of *inspiration*," appealing to youthful "hearts and wills" and thereby providing necessary resources for living "useful, upright, holy lives."[21] "I might be able to recite the Commandments of God [and] the entire catechism," concluded one such critic in 1918, "but as long as I don't live the knowledge, and incorporate it into my conduct, my religion is vain, for I do not even know rightly and truly until I act my knowledge."[22] Ultimately, the goal of such an education was "to supernaturalize the life endeavors of each student."[23]

Such arguments resonated with trends in secular education advanced by renowned Columbia University philosopher and educational reformer John Dewey. Though church officials deplored Dewey's theological unorthodoxy and his fierce opposition to government-funded parochial schools, Catholic educational reformers saw in his student-centered, practice-oriented methods hope for transforming "arid and lifeless" learning into "sound and healthy" personal development.[24] When Dewey argued that the purpose of education was to "discover what each person was good for, and train him in the mastery of that mode of excellence, because such development would also secure the fulfillment of social needs in the most harmonious way," hearty endorsement issued from reformist Catholic educators whose vision was similarly fixed on life's distant horizons and on the broader good of society.[25] In an age when, as one Catholic commentator complained, the prominence of science ensured that the "objective point of view is extolled over the subjective," Dewey's insistence on forming each individual subject into a moral agent paralleled the vision of Catholic instructors who aimed to train individuals to navigate the ever-more complex "mazes of everyday life" and, provided a student had received proper theological and spiritual formation, also be capable of furthering "the cause of Christ in the work-shop, the council-chamber, the office, the store, as well as the sanctuary."[26]

Amid such developments in the field of education, cultural commentators noted a rapid collapse of genteel avoidance when it came to addressing sexual matters in public. The increasingly explicit and public discussion of sexual matters wrought hand-wringing anxiety about the dangerous consequences for American youth.[27] Critics, both Catholic and non-Catholic, were quick to implicate the entertainment industry, frequently geared toward younger audiences, and they charged the titans of publishing, theater, and the newly developed medium of motion pictures with prosecuting what one concerned educator, writing in 1914, labeled a vast "campaign of pitiless publicity" promoting sexual titillation.[28] At the same time, anti-vice activists' prolonged effort to eradicate "white slavery"—the urban sex trade—focused popular attention on sexuality from another angle, affirming traditional morals while also eroding the notion that sex should be avoided in public discourse.[29] American participation in World War I further energized the cultural shift: venereal disease outbreaks within the U.S. Army not only spurred efforts to educate young soldiers about sexual hygiene but also propelled a diversity of federally funded home-front efforts to broadcast the dangers of sexually transmitted infections and encourage use of prophylactics during intercourse.[30] Together, these developments buoyed a postwar drive, spearheaded by the already seasoned birth control activist Margaret Sanger, to force a candid national debate about contraception. Sanger's willingness to endure vilification by her opponents—including many prominent Catholics—combined with savvy media management that heightened public sympathy allowed her both to claim popular support and to deal a blow to the overbearing "prudery and ignorance" that, she said, had too long plagued the United States.[31]

Waning reticence and shifting morals energized progressive educators concerned about students' deficiency in sexual knowledge and prompted a vigorous, though not always successful, campaign to introduce formal sex education into public schools. Leaders in this effort invoked reports of extensive adolescent sexual activity and blamed parental negligence for what, in 1909, one promoter called a "monstrous brood of disease, misery, and moral degradation" among American youth.[32] Since "normal children" generally received information about sex "not later than the early adolescent years," educators argued that it was crucial for well-informed and responsible adults, "rather than playmates and other unreliable sources," to assume responsibility in this area.[33] Public school instruction in literature, history, math, and science may be vital to ensuring good citizenship, but by focusing on these subjects alone, educators tragically "leave it to the boys and girls to discover for themselves the central facts of life," argued prominent sex education advocate Benjamin Gruenberg, "to make for themselves their own charts in a perilous sea, or drift helplessly at the mercy of every breeze and current."[34] Already by 1913, such arguments bore initial fruit in Chicago, where officials approved the nation's first school-district-wide high school sex education program—a program that was short-lived, due in part to local Catholics who stirred opposition.[35]

By 1920, however, some 2,638 of the nation's public high schools—out of a total of 6,488 whose leadership responded to a federal government survey—provided sex education.[36] Thereafter, the number of participating schools fluctuated depending on funding and the depth of local support. Nevertheless, the rapid spread of public high school sex education programs after 1913 allowed proponents to claim definitive victory for their cause.[37]

Advocacy by proponents of Catholic sex education grew quickly amid these broader cultural and educational shifts. The first step came with the simple acknowledgment of past failures: if young Catholics did not grasp the truth that "sex is holy and mysterious" and that sexual relations are therefore reserved for marriage, it was because parents and church officials sidestepped these issues and thus deprived youth of access to an appropriate and compelling vision of sexuality.[38] Such negligence, Catholic reformers insisted, was nothing short of a "fatal blunder," often exacerbated by a reflexive "exaggeration or rigorism" about sexual matters, which caused young people to develop a "false conscience" that viewed all sexual desire and activity as sinful by nature.[39] Catholic advocates likewise faulted educational reformers in the public schools whose approach, they said, unduly emphasized biological processes and "physical sanitation," downplaying moral questions and entirely neglecting the relationship of sex to the "eternal destiny of man [and] the fate of his immortal soul."[40] When secular reformers announced their intention to combat the youth "sex problem" and the "social evil" attendant to it, they generally understood these things to refer to practical challenges such as the spread of venereal diseases. But among Catholic educators, reference to the "sex problem" implied a broader framework that included the "inter-relation of the soul to the senses," and when they spoke of "social evil," they generally envisioned the commercialization of sex and the concurrent separation of sex from "what is most sacred in life . . . home, parenthood, domestic affection and sacrifice, childhood, and the future race."[41]

Making a case for sex education in U.S. Catholic schools meant overcoming a variety of obstacles within the Catholic community, each significant in its own right. Proponents certainly faced a tendency toward "prudery" among fellow Catholics—a characteristic hardly limited by religious affiliation.[42] But compounding this challenge was the fact that the vast majority of Catholic school instructors were young religious sisters—often with minimal higher education and limited sexual knowledge—who not only were vowed to perpetual celibacy but also were members of hierarchical religious communities that observed stolid silence about sex. Even within their own ranks, advocates of Catholic sex education had to overcome a stubborn sense that it was parents' duty—not educators' or school officials'—to address the sensitive topic of sex. Further, despite incremental moves toward greater coordination, the highly localized organization of parochial schools in the early twentieth century vastly complicated efforts to enlighten students: educational standards and expectations varied from diocese to diocese, even school to school, and local pastors and principals were often loath to cede authority to outside experts.[43]

Yet the most serious challenge was an unrelentingly conservative mindset, propounded by early twentieth-century Vatican authorities and adopted by high-ranking churchmen throughout the world, that caused many ecclesiastical officials to blanch at even the slightest hint of intellectual innovation in the realm of doctrine and religious education. Spurred by Pope Pius X's unsparing 1907 rebuke of Catholic intellectuals whom he labeled "Modernists"—many of them scholars who simply aimed to integrate insights from contemporary science and philosophy into theology and pastoral ministry—vigilant papal partisans denounced writers and educators they perceived as dangerous harbingers of heresy. A palpable chill thus settled in among Catholic intellectuals across Europe and North America, and, lest they leave themselves open to the taint of accusation, many elected to stay well within traditional intellectual boundaries laid down by medieval philosophers and favored in Rome. Though Pius X's reign gave way to that of a more lenient Pope Benedict XV in 1914, an atmosphere of suspicion and caution prevailed, and those who gleaned wisdom from extra-ecclesiastical sources—including educators who drew upon biology, sociology, and psychology to formulate a vision for Catholic sex education—did so knowing they risked association with grave error and the possibility of censure.[44]

Despite the obstacles, an array of vocal reformers, convinced of the urgency of their cause, provoked a robust and prolonged conversation aiming to introduce young people to this topic of crucial importance. Among the early voices in the conversation was that of John Montgomery Cooper, a priest and respected anthropologist at Catholic University of America in Washington, D.C., who noted deficient sexual knowledge in his adolescent male students and began covering sexuality in his college courses already by 1910.[45] Another was the previously mentioned Ellamay Horan, a laywoman with a doctoral degree in education and graduate training in sociology, who emerged as a leading force within the National Catholic Educational Association and became founding editor of the reformist *Journal of Religious Education*.[46] By the late 1920s, Fulgence Meyer, a Franciscan priest and popular devotional writer, was known as the foremost expert in this area thanks to a series of well-regarded books on the "sacred mysteries" of human sexuality pitched to youth, parents, and high school instructors.[47] Linking as it did traditional theological and moral teachings with new research findings, the collaboration that emerged among such educators was remarkable, not least because of their shared openness to insights drawn from a full range of sources susceptible to papal disapproval.

Catholic reformers certainly differed on details like the appropriate age and format for education, but they invariably agreed that all sexual activity had profound implications. Writing in 1922, Joseph Husslein, a prominent Jesuit author and teacher, admitted that adolescents were prone to "sweep aside the Church's wisdom of twenty centuries," and yet echoing a sustained refrain among his colleagues, he insisted that teachers must promote the sense that one's sexual choices were intimately tied up with the "temporal as well as the spiritual welfare of all mankind, and of themselves in particular."[48] Since the meaning of sex was disastrously distorted by a consumer culture that sought to "liberate sex life from all inhibitions, to surrender it completely to individual whim and fancy," as one Philadelphia priest and seminary professor put it, only an unwavering emphasis on "the metaphysical approach" could allow sexuality to assume its proper place in human life and experience.[49] To give the metaphysical approach a practical foundation, Catholic authorities elevated the idea of "training the will" or "training of character": though readily acknowledging the "sex drive" as a natural product of physical maturation, its potential to overwhelm uninformed, inexperienced adolescents necessitated a program of moral and mental formation that could prepare them to approach sex with emotional and spiritual maturity. The overall aim in such training was to "cultivate the personal initiative and spiritual energy of the student" in the service of morally upright "ideals, habits, and activities," affirming that "the body is the abode and the instrument of the immortal soul" and thereby underscoring the link between sexual activity and the eternal destiny of the human person.[50]

Above all, what distinguished Catholic reformers' approach was their underlying vision of sex as sacramental—the idea, just then developing in Catholic theological reflection, that sexual activity was a vehicle through which women and men could grow in their relationship to the divine Creator. Thus, the aim of sex instruction was "detraining the unwholesome sex tendencies" increasingly prevalent among American youth and in their place instilling a sense that while "in animals love and courtship is [sic] only physical; in man it is psychic." Because "the body of the good Christian is the temple of the Holy Ghost," sexual activity, properly understood and practiced, was a privileged experience for humans—a physical, emotional, and spiritual sign of God's enduring presence and creative power within the temporal order.⁵¹ Properly cultivating this sacramental sense demanded a pedagogy that eschewed chiding recitations of "irksome prohibitions of wrong-doing" and instead multiplied the "temptations to right-doing." Catholic educators who drew on this sacramental approach therefore viewed sex education as having less of an emphasis on the biological and hygienic dimensions favored by their counterparts in public education and more of an emphasis on encouraging the fulfillment of the "high ideals" proper to the Christian life. By urging young charges, for example, not to do "anything that would let you forfeit your self-respect" and to "let every woman be sacred in your eyes," advocates of Catholic sex education sought to bring about the result of "fewer sins, more mutual consideration and protection, less liberties, and more of ennobling and purifying love on its highest levels."⁵² In short, they aimed to form young adults capable of controlling those impulses directed toward the "violation of the human body and its sexual powers" and ultimately to prepare them to serve as fitting heterosexual marital partners who took it as their responsibility to "minister to the spiritual and psychic side of love" through their sex lives.⁵³

Despite the better part of two decades of substantive deliberation and collaboration, when it came to implementing sex education in U.S. Catholic schools, the reformers' vision never took off. Determined advocates had long pressed forward despite multiple challenges, carefully cultivating an approach that could muster broad appeal and be introduced in Catholic schools across the nation. But the effect of two major interventions by Pope Pius XI definitively undermined their prospects. In the first, an encyclical letter on modern education titled, in Latin, *Divine Illius Magistri* and released in 1930, the pope began by affirming reformers' general approach and criticizing the proliferation of pedagogical methods designed to prepare the pupil merely for "earthly happiness" rather than "the sublime end for which he was created"—the soul's reward of eternal life with God. Yet he went on to take aim at the entire notion of "so-called sex education," concluding that, by addressing the "most delicate matter of purity of morals" in schools, educators erroneously removed it from its rightful location within the home. The pope further instructed parents to execute their sacred duty of educating their children about sex by emphasizing sin and vice and maintaining silence about the "infernal hydra" of sexual desire and how it "destroys with its poison."⁵⁴ With this pronouncement, Pius XI hit at the very heart of Catholic sex education: from promoters' positive approach and their insistence on forthright instruction to their advocacy for the crucial role of formal classroom instruction, the vision of reformist U.S.

Catholic educators and the view coming forth from Rome could not have been more disparate.

Addressing marriage in *Casti Connubii*, another encyclical letter that was released in 1931 to an unprecedented onslaught of press coverage, Pius XI only further stifled realization of the reformers' vision. Ironically, as he highlighted the sacramental character of the lifelong relationship between those joined in the "sacred partnership" of heterosexual marriage, the pope affirmed the positive spiritual significance of sex and thereby took the historic step of lending papal approval to an idea that, when educators had previously integrated it in their plans for Catholic sex education, was only an emerging strain in Catholic theological reflection. But in the outpouring of commentary, both religious and secular, after *Casti Connubii*, the theological notion that marital sex was sacramental was almost universally neglected. Papal boosters and critics alike instead focused on Pius XI's unambiguous denunciation of birth control, a practice he labeled a "criminal abuse" and a "foul stain" on civilization that was not only "shameful" in intent and "vicious" in effect but also "intrinsically against nature." Such invective—along with the pope's equally sharp denunciations of abortion, sterilization, and divorce—determined how the encyclical would be interpreted the world over. It also projected an official tone—particularly notable since this papal statement was the first to address sexual morality in so prolonged and direct a fashion—that cascaded downward to U.S. church officials entrusted with cultivating morals in the face of a modern culture that, in the words of the pope, veered toward the "extremes of unbridled lust."[55] In the years following *Casti Connubii*, many church representatives who were previously reluctant to speak publicly about sex not only followed the pope's lead in taking up the topic but also replicated his denunciatory tone and his air of vigilant defiance in the face of changing popular attitudes about sexual morality.[56]

With the interventions of Pius XI and the developing crisis of the Great Depression, reformers were forced to admit defeat and accept the imperatives of a new era. Thus, their efforts to equip Catholic youth to affirm the connection between sexuality and spirituality came to an abrupt conclusion.

While proponents were convinced of the necessity of Catholic sex education, they always knew their project could ultimately collapse. Reformers not only met deep resistance but also faced the considerable challenge of integrating a distinctly Catholic approach to sex with up-to-date knowledge drawn from contemporary research in the natural and social sciences. In terms of weaving sacred and secular perspectives into a coherent and affirmative vision that could be readily communicated to Catholic youth, these educators attained a substantial measure of success. Yet when it came to implementation, they faced the heavy weight of papal pronouncements that challenged reformers' candid approach, disparaged the very suggestion of sex instruction outside the home, and modeled a denunciatory style that frequently prevailed among the church's official representatives who proved to be more clearly united and outspoken about matters of sexual morality than their counterparts in any previous era. In the wake of *Casti Connubii*, the reticence that reformers labored to overcome was definitively breached and the desired sense of urgency certainly achieved. But their chief goal—an expansive population of Catholic youth educated to regard the sexual life as intimately entwined with the spiritual life—proved elusive.

In spite of failure, reformers' efforts to shape young Catholics' understanding of sex represent a noteworthy story line within the longer history of U.S. Catholicism and sex. Through most of the nineteenth century, nativists branded immigrant Catholics as sexual deviants and, in doing so, aimed to marginalize them and minimize their influence in American life. After *Casti Connubii*, latter-day opponents also sought to diminish the church's influence by labeling Catholic attitudes and morals regarding sex as untenable and unsuitable in a modern context.[57]

Yet the story of reformers who sought to cultivate a vision of sex appropriate for a new era highlights an alternate narrative and challenges the assumption that U.S. Catholics formed a unified bloc on sexual matters. In the 1940s, the affirmative vision earlier advanced by reformist educators took on new life in two successful initiatives—the Cana Movement and the Christian Family Movement—which, by the 1960s, directly influenced how hundreds of thousands of lay Catholics from every region of the United States would understand their sex lives. The Cana Movement accomplished this through its widely implemented program of preparing engaged couples for marriage, while the Christian Family Movement did so through a network of local study groups that gathered married couples committed to cultivating the spiritual dimensions of married life.[58] In part because of the success of these initiatives, when Pope Paul VI issued *Humanae Vitae*, a 1968 encyclical letter reaffirming the position in *Casti Connubii* against birth control, an army of ordinary U.S. Catholics, along with a chorus of trained theologians, felt empowered to argue that the spiritual value of marital sex was at least equal to its procreative value.[59] Indeed, by the 1970s, lesbian and gay Catholics in the United States also drew upon this approach to articulate the view that sexual relations between committed same-sex partners could have a positive spiritual value equal to that of heterosexual marriage.[60] (In contrast to these Catholics, Whitney Strub's chapter in this volume explores how conservative U.S. Catholics after World War II tactically embraced aspects of "sexual liberalism" for different reasons in an effort to give their cultural and political program broader appeal.)

In the end, the story of early twentieth-century Catholic sex education suggests that the depiction of Catholics as predictable reactionaries in the history of U.S. sexuality is at least inadequate if we seek to construct a complex and truthful narrative. Despite their failure, Catholic sex education reformers articulated a particular vision of sex that attained substantial adherence as the century progressed—a vision that has yet to be fully understood for its enduring significance.

NOTES

I wish to thank Gillian Frank, Bethany Moreton, and Heather White, as well as the anonymous readers assigned by UNC Press, for their careful reading of this chapter and their insightful recommendations

1. Rev. Matthew Michel, "The Role of the Catholic High School in the Matter of Sex Education" (MA thesis, Catholic University of America, 1929), 8, 3, 37, 4–5.

2. On sacramental confession and sex, see Leslie Woodcock Tentler, *Catholics and Contraception: An American History* (Ithaca: Cornell University Press, 2004), 24–25, 58–59.

3. Noteworthy works include Jeffrey P. Moran, *Teaching Sex: The Shaping of Adolescence in the Twentieth Century* (Cambridge, Mass.: Harvard University Press, 2000); Janice M. Irvine, *Talk about Sex: The Battles over Sex Education in the United States* (Berkeley: University of California Press, 2002); Kristin M. Luker, *When Sex Goes to School: Warring Views on Sex—and Sex Education—since the 1960s* (New York: W. W. Norton, 2004); Alexandra M. Lord, *Condom Nation: The U.S. Government's Sex Education Campaign from World War I to the Internet* (Baltimore: Johns Hopkins University Press, 2010); Jennifer Burek Pierce, *What Adolescents Ought to Know: Sexual Health Texts in Early Twentieth-Century America* (Amherst: University of Massachusetts Press, 2011); Jeffrey P. Moran, "'Modernism Gone Mad': Sex Education Comes to Chicago, 1913," *Journal of American History* 83 (September 1996): 481–513; Susan B. Carter, "Birds, Bees, and Venereal Disease: Toward an Intellectual History of Sex Education," *Journal of the History of Sexuality* 19 (April 2001): 213–49; and Alexandra M. Lord, "Models of Masculinity: Sex Education, the U.S. Public Health Service, and the YMCA, 1919–1924," *Journal of the History of Medicine and Allied Sciences* 58 (2003): 123–52.

One exception to the norm regarding its treatment of religion is Kristy L. Slominski, "An American Religious History of Sex Education" (PhD diss., University of California, Santa Barbara, 2015).

4. An outstanding exception for its subtle and sophisticated treatment of Catholics' engagement with sexuality is Tentler's *Catholics and Contraception*.

5. Rev. Matthew Michel, "Some Practical Aspects of Moral Education in the Catholic High School" (PhD diss., Catholic University of America, 1931), 12, 101.

6. Ray Allen Billington, *The Protestant Crusade, 1830–1860: A Study of the Origins of American Nativism* (New York: Macmillan, 1938); John T. McGreevy, *Catholicism and American Freedom: A History* (New York: W. W. Norton, 2002); Jon Gjerde, *Catholicism and the Shaping of Nineteenth-Century America*, ed. S. Deborah Kang (New York: Cambridge University Press, 2012).

7. Susan M. Griffin, "Awful Disclosures: Women's Evidence in the Escaped Nun's Tale," *PMLA* 111 (January 1996): 93–107.

8. Susan M. Griffin, *Anti-Catholicism and Nineteenth-Century Fiction* (New York: Cambridge University Press, 2004), 27–61; Tracy Fessenden, "The Convent, the Brothel, and the Protestant Woman's Sphere," *Signs* 25, no. 2 (Winter 2000): 451–78; and Marie Anne Pagliarini, "The Pure American Woman and the Wicked Catholic Priest: An Analysis of Anti-Catholic Literature in Antebellum America," *Religion and American Culture* 9 (Winter 1999): 97–128.

9. "The Psychology of Celibacy," *Quarterly Journal of Psychological Medicine and Medical Jurisprudence* 1 (October 1867): 324; Faneuil D. Weisse, "Folliculitis Sebacea," *Archives of Dermatology* 2 (January 1876): 108; Thomas Addis Emmet, *The Principles and Practice of Gynaecology* (Philadelphia: Henry C. Lea, 1880), 84; Maria M. King, *The Principles of Nature* (Hammonton: A. J. King, 1880), 141–43; and Henry Morselli, *Suicide: An Essay on Comparative Moral Statistics* (New York: D. Appleton, 1882), 227–32. Specific reference to Catholic celibates include "Occupation and Death Rate in England," *Scientific American* 25 (September 1876): 169; George H. Napheys, *The Transmission of Life: Counsels on the Nature and Hygiene of the Masculine Function* (Philadelphia: H. C. Watts, 1882), 62–68; "The Expectation of Life," *New York Times*, January 8, 1893, 17; and "The Power of Marriage to Prolong Life," *Literary Digest* 21 (December 22, 1900): 771.

10. Henry Charles Lea, *An Historical Sketch of Sacerdotal Celibacy in the Christian Church* (Philadelphia: J. B. Lippincott, 1867), 20.

11. Rev. L. W. Hart, "Married Priests: Or Hildebrand's Victims," *The Independent*, January 23, 1868, 2; John Lalor, ed., *Cyclopedia of Political Science, Political Economy, and the Political History of the United States, Vol. 1* (New York: Charles E. Merrill, 1890), s.v. "Celibacy, Political Aspects of"; and Rev. George P. Fisher, "Protestantism, Romanism, and Modern Civilization," in *History, Essays, Orations, and Other Documents of the Sixth General Conference of the Evangelical Alliance*, ed. Rev. Philip Schaff and Rev. S. Irenaeus Prime (New York: Harper and Bros., 1874), 464.

12. Rev. Michael Müller, *God, the Teacher of Mankind: A Plain, Comprehensive Explanation of Christian Doctrine* (New York: Benziger Bros., 1882), 549; "On the Celibacy of the Clergy," in *The Glories of the Catholic Church: The Catholic Christian Instructed in Defence of His Faith*, vol. 2 (New York: John Duffy, 1895), 148–53; "Celibacy," in *The Catholic Dictionary; or, The Universal Christian Educator and Popular Encyclopedia of Religious Information*, ed. William E. Addis and Thomas Arnold (New York: Christian Press Association, 1896), 132–34. On Trent, see William P. Roberts, "Christian Marriage," in *From Trent to Vatican II: Historical and Theological Investigations*, ed. Raymond F. Bulman and Frederick Perella (New York: Oxford University Press, 2006), 209–11.

13. Rev. William Stang, "Clerical Celibacy," *American Ecclesiastical Review* 19 (August 1898): 141.

14. Jay P. Dolan, *The American Catholic Experience: A History from Colonial Times to the Present* (New York: Doubleday, 1985), 127–293.

15. Hendrik Hartog, *Man and Wife in America: A History* (Cambridge, Mass.: Harvard University Press, 2000), 242–49.

16. *Pastoral Letter of the Archbishops and Bishops of the United States Assembled in the Third Plenary Council of Baltimore to the Clergy and Laity in Their Charge* (Baltimore: Baltimore Publishing, 1885), 18.

17. "The Catholic Doctrine on Marriage," *American Catholic Quarterly Review* 8 (July 1883): 388; "The Catholic Law of Marriage," *Catholic World* 39 (May 1884): 149–50.

18. "Two Difficulties," *Donohoe's Magazine* 36 (September 1896): 320; Rev. Joseph Deharbe, *A Full Catechism of the Catholic Church*, trans. Rev. John Fander (New York: Catholic Publication Society, 1890), 303.

19. Ellamay Horan, "Religious Needs of the Catholic High-School Girl," *Thought* 3 (December 1928): 378, 381, 395.

20. Mary Charles Bryce, *Pride of Place: The Role of Bishops in the Development of Catechesis in the United States* (Washington: Catholic University of America Press, 1984); Berard Marthaler, *The Catechism Yesterday and Today: The Evolution of a Genre* (Collegeville: Liturgical Press, 1995).

21. Scholasticus, "The Form of Our Catechism," *American Ecclesiastical Review* 38 (January 1908): 71; Rev. Michael J. Larkin, "Discussion," *Catholic Educational Association Bulletin* 13 (November 1916): 329–30. Emphasis in original.

22. Rev. John Gavin, "The Tests of a Teacher's Efficiency," *Catholic Educational Association Bulletin* 15 (November 1918): 385.

23. Rev. William H. Russell, "Character Formation in High School," *Catholic Educational Review* 25 (March 1927): 137.

24. Review of *Schools of Tomorrow*, by John Dewey, *Catholic World* 111 (April 1920): 105. On Catholic critiques of Dewey, see Alan Ryan, *John Dewey and the High Tide of American Liberalism* (New York: W. W. Norton, 1995), 339–41; and Patrick Kennedy, "'A Native Sturdy Plant': The American Catholic Education System, the American Catholic Philosophy of Education, and American Catholic Identity, 1919–1972" (PhD diss., University of Illinois at Urbana-Champaign, 1994), 72–74.

25. Dewey quoted in Mary Jeanette, *Vocational Preparation of Youth in Catholic Schools* (Washington: Catholic University of America Press, 1918), 26.

26. George Johnson, *The Curriculum of the Catholic Elementary School* (Washington: Catholic University of America, 1919), 37, 115.

27. Moran, *Teaching Sex*, 68–97.

28. William Trufant Foster, "The Social Emergency," in *The Social Emergency: Studies in Sex Hygiene and Morals*, ed. William Trufant Foster (Boston: Houghton Mifflin, 1914), 7.

29. Christopher Diffee, "Sex and the City: The White Slavery Scare and Social Governance in the Progressive Era," *American Quarterly* 57 (June 2005): 411–37.

30. Allan M. Brandt, *No Magic Bullet: A Social History of Venereal Disease in the United States since 1880* (New York: Oxford University Press, 1987), 52–95; Moran, *Teaching Sex*, 73–76.

31. Margaret Sanger, "Morality and Birth Control," *Birth Control Review* 2 (February–March 1918): 11.

32. Charles Richmond Henderson, *The Eighth Yearbook of the National Society for the Scientific Study of Education—Part I: Education with Reference to Sex* (Bloomington: Public School Publishing, 1909), 7.

33. Maurice A. Bigelow, *Sex Education: A Series of Lectures Concerning Knowledge of Sex and Its Relations to Human Life* (New York: Macmillan, 1916), 14.

34. Benjamin C. Gruenberg, ed., *High Schools and Sex Education: A Manual of Suggestions on Education Related to Sex* (Washington: United States Public Health Service, 1922), 5.

35. Moran, "'Modernism Gone Mad.'"

36. *The Status of Sex Education in High Schools* (Washington: United States Public Health Service, 1922), 3. Also see Moran, *Teaching Sex*, 105.

37. Moran, *Teaching Sex*, 98–117.

38. Rev. Thomas J. Gerrard, *Marriage and Parenthood: The Catholic Ideal* (New York: Joseph F. Wagner, 1911), 144, 139.

39. Rev. Michael Gutterer and Rev. Francis Krus, *Educating to Purity: Thoughts on Sexual Teaching and Education Proposed to Clergymen, Parents, and Other Educators*, trans. Rev. C. van der Donckt (New York: Frederick Pustet, 1912), 14, 63.

40. Rev. John W. Melody, "Instruction in Sex Hygiene," *Catholic University Bulletin* 19 (June 1913): 473; Rev. Richard H. Tierney, "The Catholic Church and the Sex Problem," *Journal of Education* 78 (September 1913): 285.

41. Rev. Henry J. Spalding, *Talks to Nurses: The Ethics of Nursing* (New York: Benziger Bros., 1920), 171; Rev. John M. Cooper, "The Next Steps in Social Hygiene," in *Proceedings of the National Conference of Social Work at the 48th Annual Session* (Chicago: University of Chicago Press, 1921), 116.

42. P. C. Kemeny, "'Banned in Boston': Moral Reform Politics and the New England Society for the Suppression of Vice," *Church History* 78 (December 2009): 814–46.

43. John T. McGreevy, *Parish Boundaries: The Catholic Encounter with Race in the Twentieth-Century Urban North* (Chicago: University of Chicago Press, 1996), 7–28; David John Peters, "The History of the Catholic Elementary Schools in Omaha, Nebraska, 1858–1999" (PhD diss., University of Nebraska–Lincoln, 2002); Mary Anne Lindskog, "'Not One Whit Inferior': Theory and Practice of Catholic Teacher Education in Homestead, Pennsylvania, 1884–1920" (PhD diss., Pennsylvania State University, 1995).

44. William L. Portier, *Divided Friends: Portraits of the Roman Catholic Modernist Crisis in the United States* (Washington: Catholic University of America Press, 2013); Philip Gleason, *Contending with Modernity: Catholic Higher Education in the Twentieth Century* (New York: Oxford University Press, 1995), 12–17; Gary Lease, "Denunciation as a Tool of Ecclesiastical Control: The Case of Roman Catholic Modernism," *Journal of Modern History* 68 (December 1996): 819–30.

45. Rev. John M. Cooper to M. J. Exnor, April 1, 1920, box 51, folder 1, John Montgomery Cooper Papers, Catholic University of America Archives. On Cooper, see Regina Flannery, "John Montgomery Cooper, 1881–1949," *American Anthropologist* 52 (January 1950): 64–74. Examples of Cooper's early writings on sex education include "Human Welfare and the Monogamous Ideal," *Journal of Social Hygiene* 6 (October 1920):

457–67; and *Sex Education in the Home* (Washington: National Conference of Catholic Charities, 1921).

46. Mary Lou Putrow, "Ellamay Horan and the Journal of Religious Instruction," *Living Light* 40 (Fall 2003): 74–82.

47. Rev. Fulgence Meyer, *Helps to Purity: A Frank, yet Reverent Instruction on the Intimate Matters of Personal Life for Adolescent Girls* (Cincinnati: St. Francis Book Shop, 1929), 1. Also see his *Plain Talks on Marriage* (Cincinnati: St. Francis Book Shop, 1927); *Youth's Pathfinder: Heart to Heart Chats with Catholic Young Men and Women* (Cincinnati: St. Francis Book Shop, 1927); and *Helps to Purity: A Frank, yet Reverent Instruction on the Intimate Matters of Personal Life for Adolescent Boys* (Cincinnati: St. Francis Book Shop, 1929).

48. Rev. Joseph Husslein, "Courtship," in *Courtship and Marriage: Practical Instructions by Priests of the Society of Jesus* (New York: America Press, 1922), 3.

49. Rev. Charles Bruehl, foreword to Rev. Rudolph Geis, *Principles of Catholic Sex Morality*, trans. Rev. Charles Bruehl (New York: Joseph F. Wagner, 1930), vii, xiv.

50. Rev. Edward Garesché, *Training for Life* (New York: P. J. Kennedy and Sons, 1926), 25; Rev. Leigh Hubbell, "Teaching Religion to Adolescents," *National Catholic Educational Association Bulletin* 22 (November 1925): 197; Rev. John Laux, *A Course in Religion for Catholic High Schools and Academies: Part III—Christian Moral, Second Edition* (New York: Benziger Bros., 1928), 71.

51. Cooper, "Next Steps in Social Hygiene," 117; and Michel, "The Role of the Catholic High School," 60.

52. Rev. Felix M. Kirsch, *Sex Education and Training Chastity* (New York: Benziger Bros., 1930), 404, 405, 446–47.

53. Meyer, *Helps to Purity: A Frank, yet Reverent Instruction on the Intimate Matters of Personal Life for Adolescent Girls*, 7; Rev. Edgar Schmiedeler, *An Introductory Study of the Family* (New York: Century, 1930), 334.

54. Pope Pius XI, "Rappresentanti in Terra [Divini Illius Magistri]," in *The Papal Encyclicals, 1903–1939*, ed. Claudia Carlen (Raleigh, N.C.: McGrath, 1981), 354, 363.

55. Pope Pius XI, "Casti Connubii," in *The Papal Encyclicals, 1903–1939*, ed. Claudia Carlen (Raleigh, N.C.: McGrath, 1981), 392, 399, 400–402, 404–7, 398.

56. John T. Noonan, *Contraception: A History of Its Treatment by Catholic Theologians and Canonists* (1965; repr., Cambridge, Mass.: Harvard University Press, 1986), 424–32; Tentler, *Catholics and Contraception*, 73–129.

57. John T. McGreevy, *Catholicism and American Freedom: A History* (New York: W. W. Norton, 2003), 217–81.

58. Jeffrey M. Burns, *Disturbing the Peace: A History of the Christian Family Movement, 1949–1974* (Notre Dame: University of Notre Dame Press, 1999); Tentler, *Catholics and Contraception*, 189–203.

59. Tentler, *Catholics and Contraception*, 264–79.

60. James P. McCartin, "The Church and Gay Liberation: The Case of John McNeill," *U.S. Catholic Historian* 34, no. 1 (Winter 2016): 125–41.

REAL TRUE BUDS

Celibacy and Same-Sex Desire across the Color Line in Father Divine's Peace Mission Movement

JUDITH WEISENFELD

In February 1954, *Ebony* magazine featured a photograph of the African American religious leader known as Father Divine seated at a table in his Peace Mission Movement's Philadelphia headquarters and surrounded by a group of black and white women who, the caption informed readers, were his "young, attractive secretaries."[1] The brief accompanying article outlined the movement's theology, which centers on the belief that Father Divine was God in a body. The item's main focus, however, was sexuality in this group in which the fully committed followers lived celibate lives in sex-segregated communal residences. Capitalizing on the recent publication of white sociologist Sara Harris's sensationalist study titled *Father Divine: Holy Husband*, the *Ebony* article, "Why Father Divine Outlawed Sex," informed readers that Divine's proscription derived from his "overwhelming need to be not only supreme with all of his followers but also 'the one and only' with them." Quoting Harris's work, the brief piece concluded, "It rests in Father's recognition that if he did permit his followers to have normal sex lives, their lovers would be bound to gain some of the affection he wants to keep entirely to himself."[2] For Harris and the authors of the *Ebony* piece, a "normal" sex life stemmed from "natural urges" manifested in heterosexual marriage rather than in a sex-segregated, celibate structure such as the Peace Mission with Divine as the object of devotion.

Harris's book and media interpretations of her findings consolidated a set of interrelated concerns that Father Divine's movement had generated since the group emerged on the public scene in the early 1930s. That thousands of people, white and black, could believe in the divinity of this unimposing man, who had probably been born George Baker in Maryland in the late 1870s, preoccupied observers.[3] Speculation about manipulation and control on

Divine's part and racialized theories about the sources of his mostly African American followers' susceptibility to charisma appear throughout commentaries on the movement, linking observers' varied assessments of the negative religious, sociological, psychological, and economic impact on followers.[4] Concern about Divine's excessive control of his devotees extended to the curiosity that outsiders expressed about sex within the Peace Mission and about Father Divine's sex life in particular.[5] Such criticism resonated with American Protestant discourses about papal control of Roman Catholics and the sexual deviance and social dangers of celibacy, about which James P. McCartin writes in his chapter on early twentieth-century Catholics and sex education.

Most of the critical assessments of sexuality in the Peace Mission focused on the fact that Divine married twice even while requiring his followers to give up sexual relations, relinquish all ties to family members, and embrace their status as children of God as the only relationship of consequence. The first Mother Divine, Penninah, an African American woman older than he, was an early adherent who had met Divine in the South and helped him build the movement in New York in the 1920s and 1930s.[6] The second Mother Divine, whom he presented as containing the spirits of the Virgin Mary and the first Mother Divine, who died in 1943, was Edna Rose Ritchings, a white Canadian who was twenty-one when they married in 1946.[7] The second Mother Divine served as the spiritual head of the movement from Father Divine's death in 1965 until her death in 2017. Divine contended that the union consecrated Ritchings as "his Virgin Spotless Bride." He preached that the marriage represented the uniting of heaven and earth, the Lamb and his church, and that it would "produce the virginity of honesty and competence and truth and ... give this whole nation a new birth of freedom, of virtue, of unity."[8] Divine's followers accepted both marriages as integral to his broader work to purify the world, and they embraced this promise of a life of purity in the Kingdom of God on earth.

Opening a box in an archival collection in which I expected to find copies of the Peace Mission periodicals featuring Father Divine's sermons but instead finding a cache of what read like love letters from two of Divine's black female followers—Wonderful Joy and Happy S. Love—to Dorothy L. Moore, a white visitor, raised significant questions that scholars have not addressed about the relation of theology to sexuality for members of the movement. The sensationalist focus on Father Divine's sexual life in press coverage and scholarly analyses of the Peace Mission Movement has made it difficult to discern the contours of the lived theology of sexuality among his thousands of

Father Divine and the second Mother Divine, late 1940s. *From the author's collection.*

followers, the majority of whom were black women, both African American and Caribbean immigrants. How did they understand and experience the transformation of self that being one of Father Divine's children required: abandonment of family attachments, the taking of a new spiritual name, rejection of racial categories and racialized identity, and commitment to living a communal, sex-segregated, celibate life? The lack of sources about the movement other than accounts by disillusioned former members, salacious newspaper coverage, and police, court, and psychiatric records makes pursuing this question especially challenging. The Peace Mission's own textual record contains primarily published transcripts of Divine's sermons and followers' devotional testimonials, neither offering much information about the daily lives and experiences of those within the movement. This unique archival collection of correspondence between insiders and an outsider to the Peace Mission, which also includes letters from Divine directly engaging and policing the women's relationships, opens up the possibility of exploring more broadly how the movement's particular understandings of divinity and theology of the body, gender, race, and social relations framed members' practice of celibacy.

It might be tempting to use this archive of letters as evidence to describe the women as lesbians, to interpret their relationships as sexual and in violation of the religious commitment that the two Peace Mission members had made to celibacy, and thereby find confirmation of the sensationalist approaches that have long characterized discussions of Divine's movement. This archive calls for analysis that resists situating the women within "preconceived historical categories" of sexual identity, however, and that highlights the ways in which Father Divine's followers navigated broader social constructions of race and sexuality as well as those produced and supported within the movement's theological framework.[9] The archival record does not provide evidence that would allow us to draw conclusions about sexual activity between women in the movement or to gain a clear sense of how they understood their sexual identities. But, as Amy Sueyoshi argues in her study of Yone Noguchi's intimate relationships, "sexual intercourse . . . might have little to do with the most intimate exchanges between people. An identical sexual act might hold varied [meanings] depending on geography, history, and culture. . . . Ultimately genital or any physical contact, even if available, might prove to be a faulty determiner of the true nature of relationships."[10] Framing the questions we bring to the correspondence as a search for proof of a particular sexual practice or orientation obscures the rich evidence the archive provides of religious constructions of same-sex desire in a celibate community situated in a broader social context saturated with discourses about black women as hypersexual and that located "normal" sexuality solely in heterosexual marriage.[11]

Although this essay focuses on a small religious movement that saw its peak of membership and influence during the 1930s and early 1940s and whose members set strong boundaries between their utopian kingdom of Father Divine and the social world around them, the case nevertheless suggests broader possibilities for examining the erotics of celibacy in twentieth-century American religious history. This case of relationships within the Peace Mission underscores for historians of sexuality and of religion the need to understand religious celibacy as a complex practice and identity, shaped and inflected by the particular theological frameworks and institutions that support it as well as by the broader social context in which its practitioners are located. The contours of celibacy within the Peace Mission are not identical to those within twentieth-century Roman Catholic convents, for example, and discerning the differences requires careful attention to context.[12] Similarly, attending to the varieties of sexual expressions that a given religious orientation can produce lends nuance to our understanding of religion and sexuality in twentieth-century America. Kathi Kern's essay in this volume explores how Christian faith affirmed YWCA worker Winnifred Wygal's polyamorous desire for women, and she situates Wygal's sexuality in the context of her belief that "personal relationships were intimately 'related to our sense of God.'" This belief also held true for Peace Mission members who sought intimate connection to God in the person of Father Divine and to the divine within, but they saw celibacy as the necessary sexual expression derived from their sense of God. Cultivating this ongoing connection to God within themselves and within a communal sex-segregated environment produced a queer celibacy, at odds with mid-twentieth-century American norms in a variety of ways, including in its interracial character in racialized and segregated America, and provided a theological vernacular for some women to express same-sex desire.[13]

I use the framework of same-sex desire in two senses to explore what the epistolary record may tell us about religion and sexuality and the erotics of celibacy in this particular social and theological context. Characterizing the archival letters I examined as containing expressions of desire highlights the intimacy and affection so evident in the correspondence and the yearning for personal and emotional contact it reveals. Unlike the lifelong intense communications between nineteenth-century American women that scholars have examined, these were short-term relationships that seem to have lasted about a year, from 1948 to 1949. Nevertheless, it is useful to think of these letters, in which longing for emotional connection is evident, in relation to earlier histories of passionate relationships developed among women and fostered through writing.[14] The highly structured, ritualized, and rule-bound nature of life within Peace Mission residences also calls to mind early to mid-twentieth-century prisons where relationships between working-class women across the color line were common and exchanges of letters and notes also served as avenues to express desire.[15] Of course, women in the Peace Mission chose to join the sex-segregated, celibate communities seeking salvation, while incarcerated women were consigned to prisons as punishment. In both cases, however, the particular institutional cultures and modes of regulating daily life and interpersonal interactions helped to structure expressions of affection.

In addition to using the term "desire" to characterize the affection and longing evident in the letters, I deploy it because of its particular religious meaning for the correspondents in this case. Desire, not limited to the interpersonal or erotic, was a potent theological category in the Peace Mission Movement and, therefore, a critical framework for understanding relationships among Divine's followers. The religious significance of desire for members of the Peace Mission derived from the influence on Father Divine of the New Thought movement's focus on channeling God's spirit to promote health and well-being. Divine preached that emotional desire for or attachment to anyone but him limited spiritual development, and he taught that eternal life and residence in the kingdom on earth could be achieved only by sacrifice of ego and mortal connections in favor of a constant focus on God in their midst.[16] At the same time, Divine insisted that his followers not be focused exclusively on his embodiment. In the tradition of New Thought, he encouraged them to align their consciousness with that of God, the Universal Mind, in order to allow God to be expressed in them and through them. The Peace Mission's religious imperative to control ego and desire in favor of God working in the individual shaped the interactions between the women in significant ways. The sex-segregation and celibacy required of members may have paradoxically facilitated forms of desire prohibited in Divine's theology, but the correspondence makes clear that Happy S. Love and Wonderful Joy interpreted their attachment to Dorothy Moore through the lens of the movement's theology, employing its religious vernacular to communicate affection, longing, and desire.

A ROSEBUD'S LIFE

As was the case with so many of Father Divine's followers, it is difficult to recover information about Wonderful Joy and Happy S. Love before they joined the movement and changed their names. We know from photographic evidence that Happy S. Love, who lived in the Sorority Peace Mission Democratic Apartment House in Newark, was a young African American woman. Wonderful Joy, who lived at the Circle Mission Church Home and Training School in the movement's Philadelphia headquarters in the late 1940s, was most likely also of African descent and could have been one of the various black women with that name who earlier in the decade had resided in one of the numerous Peace Mission residences in Harlem. That there remains no record of their past identities would probably have pleased Wonderful Joy and Happy S. Love. Ultimately for believers, it did not matter whom they had been before joining Divine's movement. Everything about members' lives prior to accepting the divinity of Father Divine had to be left behind because these things tied them to what he characterized as mortal negativity and prevented them from aligning their minds with his spirit and consciousness. He told his followers, "I have stressed for your sakes, so often, that God is your Father and you never had another. Now if you say, or think, or act, in any other way from henceforth, you are disputing what I have said in words in deeds, and in actions, that God is your Mother and you never had another.

God is your Sister and your Brother, your Relatives and your Kin, and all of your Friends, and every other thing, and you never had another."[17] Members told of experiencing new birth—out of the flesh and into the Spirit—through their acceptance of the divinity of Father Divine and, in taking names that encapsulated the positive spiritual qualities they hoped to embody, began their lives anew.

Divine's followers believed that letting go of attachment to family members and reconceiving themselves as children of God helped release them from the bonds of mortality and put them on a path to health, agelessness, and eternal life. It was such faith in Divine's promises that led Madeline Green, an African American migrant from South Carolina to Harlem who was married and had seven children, to leave her family for "an angelical life" as Sister of Sweetness in a nearby Peace Mission residence. She told a family court judge that "I've been living a life of sacrifice. I couldn't live with my husband. That wouldn't be angelical." She further justified her abandonment of the children as a requirement in giving her life to God. "I have no more children," she told the judge. "All belongs to God now."[18] There are many other similar cases of family courts, divorce attorneys, insurance companies, and worried family members pursuing Divine's followers into their new lives, trying to understand how they could leave their old ones behind.

Many members eagerly embraced the promise of life in God's kingdom free from disease, aging, and economic worry and seemed not to find the requirement to sever ties to "so-called family" a hardship, focusing instead on the work of ongoing sacrifice of the self and desire for mortal things and turning their minds to God. For others, the transformation was difficult, and many struggled with how to relate to their families of birth. Mary Justice, a twenty-six-year-old South Carolinian, had left home to join the Peace Mission and wrote Divine for advice for dealing with her "so-called father" who wanted to maintain contact and was angry that she no longer acknowledged their relationship. Mobilizing the movement's theological vernacular derived from Divine's sermons, she wrote, "I said the Bible said call no man on Earth your Father and mother and God is my Father and Mother and I never had another."[19] In some cases, Divine's followers understood that they must cut ties with "the mortal family of men" but, because of circumstance or genuine affection, could not put the theology into practice. Another Mary Justice, this one in California, wrote to Divine because she had found it necessary to help care for the father of her children but insisted that neither he nor the children meant anything to her. Divine responded with a sharp and chastising letter rejecting her claim and countering, "If you did not care for him and them, you would not have gone. Truly it is written, 'You cannot serve two masters.'"[20] He suggested that she would do well to confess her sins of attachment and desire if she wanted to continue to receive his blessings. We do not know if Wonderful Joy or Happy S. Love struggled with the decision to submit to Divine's teaching to "surrender all in all to God."[21] But regardless of whether their entries were difficult, the fact that they cut family ties, changed their names, and moved into Peace Mission residences indicates an investment in his promise that "God in reality, in you, will be All and in All, and therefore nothing else will have dominion over you saving God Himself within you."[22]

The focus on Father Divine fulfilling all roles for followers may account for the affectionate and romantic terms that male and female followers used to describe their connection to him, rejoicing in his "sweetness" and often casting him as husband or boyfriend. As one woman wrote, "There really is no love to compare with the love one feels for Father. Praise His Holy Name. He really is the sweetest most lovable boyfriend a girl could ever have."[23] Members produced devotional items that reflected this combination of romantic and spiritual devotion, as in one hand-crafted collage that features a charcoal drawing of an eye with a cut-out image of Divine's face pasted in and a handwritten caption, "I have eyes only for you!"[24] Divine's dual focus on disciplining oneself in order to surrender to God (that is, to him) *and* to surrender to "God Himself within you" is of particular importance and shaped members' self-understandings and their interactions with others. Even though the movement was focused primarily on the power of God embodied in their midst, Divine insisted repeatedly that his followers' transformations were not dependent on his physical presence but on their ability to connect to his consciousness and have it work in and through them.[25] Thus, the image in the devotional collage of Divine within the female follower's eye could represent both her vision of God and God's vision through her.

In coming into Father Divine's kingdom, Wonderful Joy and Happy S. Love pledged to live out the movement's doctrine that race did not truly exist but was a product of the negative mind under the devil's influence. Following Divine's command to reject racial identity, members refused to use conventional racial language, opting instead to speak of people as "dark complected" and "light complected," thus distinguishing skin color from the American system of race in order to embrace the former and reject the latter.[26] People of different complexions ate, worked, and lived together. Even the shared rooms and beds in the sex-segregated residences were integrated when possible, and the visual record

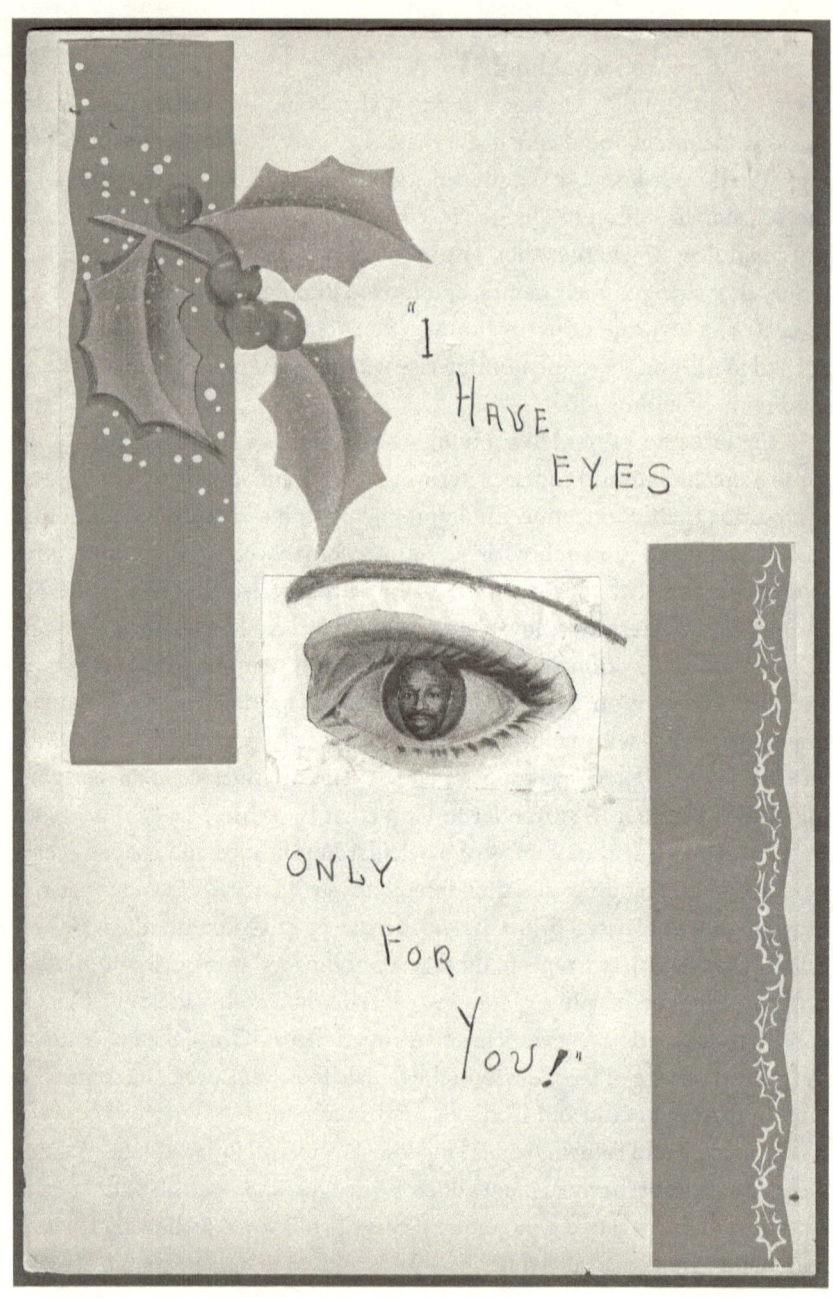

A devotional collage made by a follower of Father Divine, n.d. Father Divine Papers, Stuart A. Rose Manuscript, Archives, and Rare Books Library, Emory University.

of life in the movement shows members' commitment to integration or, in their words, "enacting the Bill of Rights" in daily life.[27] Divine preached of this commitment, "In our method of the cooperative system; in our Religious and Spiritual; in our social and economic activities; whatsoever we represent; you can plainly see the abolition of all segregation and discrimination is established among us."[28] One white follower spoke of the impact of the practice on her, telling a reporter, "The flesh is nothing.... It was not intended that we should all look alike, it would have been too monotonous and much of nature's beauty would have been lost. When you become spiritualized—win the victory over the flesh—you will see men with a spiritual eye and cease to be a respecter of persons."[29] The archival record does not indicate how Wonderful Joy and Happy S. Love experienced their relationships with "light complected" sisters in the movement. It is safe to say, however, that the Peace Mission opened up new possibilities for interactions across the color line that differed from those in the largely racially segregated outside world.

At the same time that members of the movement embraced a new understanding of themselves as race-less children of God, they also learned that with acceptance of Father Divine as God came an affirmation of sex differences. Divine endorsed sex segregation as natural and part of the divine order of creation, preaching, "We will not tolerate but one discrimination and that is between the males and the females. That is all the segregation we shall have. But we shall have segregation to that degree, for that is the way GOD Created them in the beginning. Now isn't that Wonderful! We shall endorse the degree of segregation to the degree of the Scripture as it was in the beginning. God Created he-male and female, two distinct expressions."[30] Even as Divine endorsed an essentialized approach to maleness and femaleness, his counsel that members strive to overcome the limitations of embodiment and materiality and focus on the power of mind over body opened up additional possibilities for experiencing gender. Divine called on followers, quoting and expanding on Romans 12:1, to "give up your body for the Spirit's sake and recognize the Spirit and the Life as Supreme. And when you do that, ... you are looking to the Heavenly state of consciousness and not to the material or mortal state."[31] Moreover, Father Divine sometimes spoke of his followers as being "in the likeness of women" and "in the likeness of men."[32] Followers' spiritual names also sometimes served to erase gender distinctions, as names like Obey Love, Peaceful Mind, or Hope Faith might be adopted just as easily by male or female members, and women sometimes took masculine spiritual names, as in the case of David Faithful, John Revelator, and Isaac Isaiah, among others, a practice also common among Roman Catholic women religious, for example.

The structure of life in the communal residences helped Divine's "Angels" sacrifice their mortal bodies to a spiritual purpose, a goal they sometimes spoke of as "living the evangelical life." Like the "gay men on the land" about whom Daniel Rivers writes in this volume, the Peace Mission's Rosebuds—a cadre of women committed beyond the general membership who also functioned as a choir and were pledged to virginity—understood their community as radically distinct from the world outside and saw themselves as liberated from its norms. In this case, sexual freedom took the form of freedom from sex. Residents were to abide by Divine's "International Modesty Code" that forbade smoking, drinking, obscenity, vulgarity, and profanity and prohibited members from receiving gifts or taking bribes. Finally, the code cautioned against "undue mixing of the sexes," which supported the sex segregation of the residences, some of which were buildings owned by Peace Mission members or the movement's incorporated churches and others simply apartments rented and inhabited by groups of followers.[33]

Celibacy was a core theological commitment in this sex-segregated environment and, in the New Thought tradition, meant to assist followers in their endeavor to overcome materiality and discover the workings of divinity within themselves.[34] Divine preached, "If you live in fleshly affections, tendencies, pleasures, desires and fancies, it is then an impossibility for you to dwell with ME in Peace!"[35] Divine also explained his theology of celibacy and procreation as grounded in and consonant with Christianity, writing, "After the similitude of the Christ, or of the Man Jesus, those in the likeness of men live as Jesus lived, and those in the likeness of women, live as Mary, the Mother of Jesus, lived before Jesus was born."[36] As participants in the Peace Mission, Wonderful Joy and Happy S. Love dedicated themselves to celibacy and became Rosebuds. Through acceptance of the creed written for them by Father Divine, each Rosebud declared her heart "a heart for GOD" and proclaimed to others, "You should all have a Rosebud's heart, / that is PURE, MEEK and SWEET; / A heart as the fertile VIRGIN ground of Salvation / Where CHRIST will take His Seat."[37]

Wonderful Joy's and Happy S. Love's membership in the sex-segregated Peace Mission movement and their commitment to virginity and celibacy placed them largely in a world of women. Published photographs of the Rosebuds show them in groups of alternating light- and dark-skinned members engaged in work, play, and choir performances. The archival record also contains snapshots taken by members (and not intended for public viewing) showing women in dresses or in their uniforms—consisting of a red jacket with *V* for "virtue" above the heart, a white blouse, a blue skirt, a blue beret, and white gloves—standing in pairs, perhaps representing bedmates. The second Mother Divine was often photographed, both informally and for publicity, with Peaceful Love, the African American member who was her roommate and companion.[38] Wonderful Joy's and Happy S. Love's daily lives would have revolved around work, perhaps in one of the movement's many cooperative businesses, participation in Peace Mission worship services, and Rosebud choir activities. Because she lived at the movement headquarters in Philadelphia, Wonderful Joy sometimes traveled with Father Divine as part of the Rosebuds' contingent, riding in cars following his as he made the weekly rounds to various communities in New York and New Jersey.[39] Some Rosebuds expressed pleasure in their experiences, even though their schedules were often highly regulated and they may have missed family connections, noting the joy of riding in elegant cars, the fun of picnics and swimming, and the opportunity to aid in Father Divine's work. As one woman wrote, the "diversified activities" helped her to put her past far away: "For those of us who are Rosebuds we have the most fun."[40]

Observers of the movement often characterized the practice of celibacy and the homosocial character of the movement as unnatural and "contrary to all biological laws," in the words of one sociologist.[41] Indeed, Father Divine himself expressed concern about the potential negative impact of the intensity of women's sociality in the movement on his followers' quest for detachment from mortal desire. In his 1936 Christmas address, he cautioned followers against "indulging in the appearance of human affection, human devotion or love for one another or one for the other." He had a specific message for the women in his movement, however, declaring that "they will not even so much as ride in automobiles correspondingly together as couples. They will not walk together nor have any special communication for such is a violation to My spiritual rule and regulation." The *Baltimore Afro-American*'s report about Divine's warning conjectured that the statement came in response to "the growing menace of sexual perversion which has developed out of the taboo on sex mixing."[42] Some fifteen years later, Divine warned his followers about behavior within the sex-segregated dormitories, preaching that "it has been definitely, stressfully emphasized, over and over again, not any of you should go in the other's rooms, unless you are the roommate or roommates to those with whom you are accompanying or associating with in the rooms; I mean, in the bedrooms! Some of you so-called sisters and some of you so-called Believers and Followers, some may even have the audacity to call themselves Rosebuds, will not stay away from others' rooms." Such violation of the Modesty Code, Divine warned, would result in excommunication. Divine issued the same caution to the men in the movement, but women, who outnumbered men and set the culture of the residences, received special attention in this sermon that sociologist Sara Harris says followers "interpreted to be aimed at stamping out overt homosexuality."⁴³

While Divine emphasized that he considered special communication and affection between women in the movement contrary to his teaching, Faithful Mary, his former right hand, charged that his theology fostered homosexual relationships and made the movement attractive to "abnormal" women. In her treatise on the movement's theological, social, and economic errors, the apostate Peace Mission member intent on undermining the movement charged that "by attempting to have the followers refrain from sexual cohabitation with the opposite sex—he is responsible for many becoming homosexual perverts."⁴⁴ Harris also reported overt expressions of sexual desire "in the hungry way in which women sometimes stare at other women, at their breasts and hips and legs."⁴⁵ Given the limited archival record, it is difficult to determine the precise connection between the perception that this sex-segregated religious world fostered lesbian relationships and the actual experiences and practices of women in the movement. It is safe to say, however, that in their respective communal residences, Wonderful Joy and Happy S. Love understood themselves to be Father Divine's children and focused their spiritual energies on him at the same time that, on a daily basis, their lives revolved in large measure around community and communion with their spiritual sisters.

FROM FATHER IN ME

In 1948 Dorothy L. (Dot) Moore, a twenty-year-old white student at Bemidji State Teachers College in Minnesota who had discovered the movement through white middle-class friends who had joined and moved to Philadelphia, entered the world of Divine's followers. Moore grew up in Minneapolis and graduated from Edison High School in June 1946. In the school yearbook, which noted her membership in the National Honor Society, the school orchestra, and the Pan American League, she declared her intention to become a teacher, and she was majoring in English and vocal and instrumental music at Bemidji State when she encountered Divine and his devotees.⁴⁶ Curious about her friends' life choice, Moore decided to spend her 1948 summer and Christmas vacations visiting them and met Wonderful Joy and the other Rosebuds who lived at various Peace Mission residences in Philadelphia and Newark. She found her stay in Philadelphia to be fun and

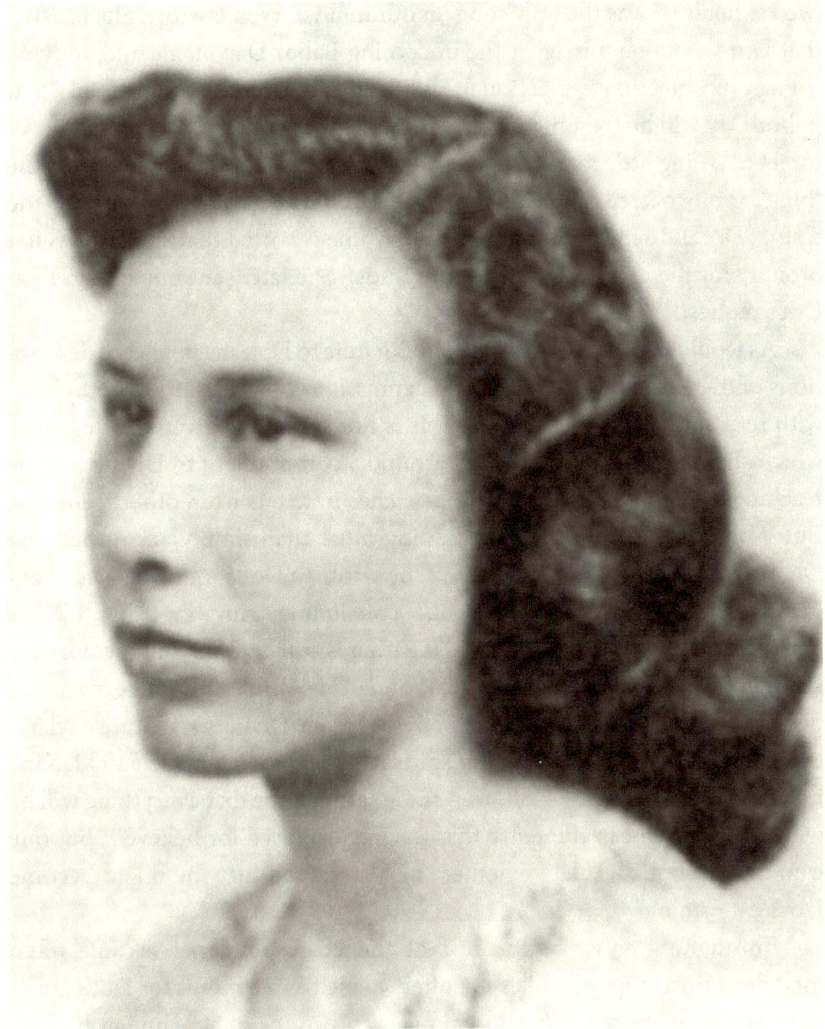

Dorothy L. Moore in 1946. From the *Wizard*, Thomas Edison high school yearbook, 1946, Minneapolis. Courtesy Hennepin County Library.

exciting and, even though the racially integrated beds initially shocked her, came to appreciate the movement's enactment of "the Bill of Rights."⁴⁷

When Dot returned to school in September 1948, Wonderful Joy, or Wonie as she called herself, initiated a correspondence that reveals something of the depth of attachment and affection that could develop between women in the movement, even in the context of a theology of sexual restraint and emotional detachment. "I betcha your little ears were burning like everything because Dorothy was the only subject while going home from the station and, 'we are floating' was the only song on our minds," Wonie wrote. She insisted that Dot would be missed at the upcoming Labor Day picnic and, moving from group affection to individual desire, wrote that Dot shouldn't think "that Labor Day will be the only time I will remember you because I could never forget a darling little girl like you. Therefore, a picture of you will be just the thing for me to keep on my dresser so that you'll also be remembered by the rest."[48] Dot did send a photograph and Wonie reported that she displayed it proudly for the admiration of "all the Buds." She later sent one of herself at Dot's request.[49]

As would become typical of Wonie's letters to Dot, she peppered descriptions of the Rosebuds' activities and expressions of interest in Dorothy's life with references to Father Divine. This is not surprising given the degree to which she had reorganized her life around a commitment to Divine and his teachings, and one finds similar approaches in letters from other members. But Wonderful Joy appears to be doing more than simply acknowledging Divine's significance. In one instance she wrote to Dot about what she imagined were the pressures of college life, concluding, "Anyway, babes, I know you will still make the best of it and if Father is still deep in your memories, I know everything will be Wonderful, Wonderful, Wonderful! (I like my name, don't I?)"[50] Here Wonie mobilizes one of Father Divine's signature declarations, and one that influenced her spiritual name, to link herself and Divine in Dot's mind. As Divine's follower, she asserts a hope that everything will be wonderful for Dot in the sense that Divine promised for believers, but one cannot help but speculate whether she also hoped that she might become Dot's everything.

Throughout most of the rest of the correspondence, Wonie often includes a postscript in which she offers herself as a conduit for Dot's greetings to Divine, bringing her individual expressions of attachment back to the movement's theological world. At other points she includes comments on Divine's behalf but often in a way that makes it possible to interpret his words or sentiments as her own. In one letter Wonie reported that she had delivered "a Sweet Peace" (their substitute for hello) to Divine on Dot's behalf, which pleased him. She continued, "He also said that you were—oh, maybe I better not say. Anyhow, it was very good and it sounded sweet to my ears. Imagine, dear, having someone who thinks of you daily to make you happy all the time."[51] This final sentiment might apply equally to Wonie as to Divine. The archive reveals that Wonie's affection for Dot grew over the course of the brief correspondence. She wrote that the sight of a letter from Dot on her bed would produce "a happy spell" and reveled in details in

Dot's letters such as a description of "how cute [she] looked... in that drum major outfit," a disclosure that generated a self-described "greedy" request for another photograph.[52] Wonie was careful along the way to give Dot the opportunity to modulate the level of contact and worried that the volume of letters she sent might be overwhelming. But it appears that Dot was eager to participate in the correspondence and Wonie was thrilled that she received such quick responses.

The correspondence also makes clear Wonie's awareness that her affection for Dot violated the theological requirements of the Peace Mission Movement to reject human attachments and affection. An encounter with Father Divine one day caused Wonie to reflect on the religious implications of her feelings for Dot. It is unclear precisely what transpired between Wonderful Joy and Divine, but it seems that in the course of the conversation she became aware that Dorothy and Divine had exchanged letters. This realization caused Wonderful Joy concern about the impact of their relationship on Dot's spiritual development, particularly because Dot had not committed herself to the movement. Underscoring her belief that perfection could be reached only through communion with Father Divine's spirit, she wrote, "For just that reason, Dottie, I feel that if you would only correspond with Him, and if I didn't interfere so much, that you would come to be closer in his heart."[53] In fact, Divine himself responded to a query from Dorothy about the suitability of her correspondence with Wonderful Joy in a similar way, writing, "So far as you and Wonderful Joy continuing to correspond, that would be entirely up to you two; however, it has been somewhat of a ritual between MY Real True Buds that they would correspond only with the ONE they so greatly admire and therefore, put no one between their LORD and SAVIOR."[54]

Father Divine's reminder that the individual's relationship with him was central to her or his spiritual development effectively ended the easygoing and affectionate correspondence between Wonderful Joy and Dorothy, although the record contains a few scattered exchanges and a poignant farewell from Wonie. In one of Wonie's late letters she once again connects her feelings for Dot to Father Divine's, writing, "So you see, Dotty, Father nor I would ever forget you (How could we anyway!)."[55] Before their correspondence ended, however, Wonderful Joy pursued an approach to continuing her contact with Dot that was grounded fully in Father Divine's theology. Recall Divine's teaching that his embodiment brought salvation but that followers should also recognize that God is in them and works through them. In the earlier letter in which Wonderful Joy acknowledged that she might be interfering with Dot's spiritual development, she wondered briefly about whether this notion of "God in her" might help locate her affection for Dorothy within the movement's theological boundaries. She suggested hesitantly that "every time I write, it could perhaps be a letter from Him instead; I'm sure you would enjoy that more."[56]

Happy S. Love, who met Dorothy at the Newark Peace Mission in 1948, would pursue this approach in letters that express an even more intense level of emotional attachment and desire than did Wonderful Joy's and in language that relies explicitly on the movement's theology and religious vernacular. Their correspondence appears to have been less extensive than that between Wonie and Dot, but what is preserved in the records is noteworthy. Like Wonie, Happy S. began her correspondence focusing on her sorrow at Dot's departure after a visit: "I was feeling bad nearing the end, especially when I saw the last of you.... But Dot how happy will I be again when you come home to stay forever.... I miss you. I don't know if you miss my crazy way and action."[57] As did Wonie and Dot, Happy S. and Dot exchanged photographs, letters, and small gifts. But from the start, Happy S. appears to have interpreted her emotional connection to Dot through the movement's theology as one between "Father in you" and "Father in me." Elaborating in her first letter on why she was so affected by Dot's visit, Happy S. wrote, "You—I mean Father in you— are a very nice person to keep company with." Happy S. used this formulation repeatedly, framing expressions of affection, longing, and desire in terms of Father Divine's teaching about God manifesting himself in his followers and followers' common casting of their relationship with Divine in amorous terms.

This approach is clearest in a poem that Happy S. wrote for Dorothy combining the movement's theology, language of the Rosebud's creed, and desire for emotional connection:

> To stay sweet and meek
> Right at your Savior's feet
> For He will make a way to keep
> "Your Dorothy" as His very heart beat
> Then why not stay soft, tender and sweet
> You have no other to seek
> Cause He will forever be
> The very one you need
> So come and see
> When He calls You Dorothy
> "Please come and see me"
> Because, I cause you to fall in love with me
> And I want You solely for my very heart beat

Happy S. Love sent this photograph of herself to Dorothy in 1949. Dorothy L. Moore Papers, Stuart A. Rose Manuscript, Archives, and Rare Books Library, Emory University.

Happy S. Love added a postscript to the poem to underscore how her desires—unacceptable in the normal course of things within the Peace Mission—were situated within her religious commitments: "P.S. How do you like that? Dedicated to your Dot from Father in me."[58] Happy S.'s belief that God was in her and that Father Divine could work through her reveals the complex religious contours of her celibate same-sex desire. At the same time that Father Divine's theology was intended to limit the development of emotional attachments and sexual contact between members, the movement's theology, practices, and spiritual vocabulary made it possible for Happy S. to form a connection to Dot that remained true to her belief in the divinity of Father Divine and adherence to the "evangelical life."

Although Moore did not join the Peace Mission, the archive contains evidence that, over time, she became increasingly interested in the movement. She subscribed to the *New Day*, the movement's official magazine, and expressed interest in becoming a Rosebud.[59] It also seems that she told her roommates and others about Father Divine.[60] But she remained conflicted about her relationship to the Peace Mission. In an undated, handwritten draft of an article, Moore expressed her hope to "present the facts as I personally saw them of a religion about which relatively little is known but about which much is negatively discussed." She tells her readers that they will not be able to discern her opinion about the movement from reading the piece "for the very reason that I have not come to any definite conclusions myself." She notes that she first visited the movement wondering how someone "of the Afro-American race" could have so many white followers but was soon convinced that, contrary to the common image of the group in the press, white and black followers were neither uneducated nor crazy. "I can honestly say I've never met so many friendly, honest, and pleasant people in my life. I made many good friends among the girls or Rosebuds as they are called. They are intelligent and active just like anyone outside the movement." At one point she indicated an interest in the physical appearance of the members, writing but crossing out, "They are good looking people too, and it is impossible not to like them."[61] Thus, although she remained uncertain about committing to the movement and was clear that she did not believe Divine was God, her admiration for the women she met is evident in the unpublished manuscript. Moreover, her account of Divine's theology and of the workings of the movement gives a strong sense of her deep understanding of both.

In addition to developing respect for the movement's principles and its members, it is clear that Moore felt a connection not only to Rosebuds Wonderful Joy and Happy S. Love but also to Father Divine himself. She wrote to LaVere Belstrom, her friend from home in the movement, that she missed Divine when she was away at school, and judging by the number of letters Divine sent to her, she was a fairly frequent correspondent. In fact, at one point Moore wrote to ask Divine whether he would like her to write more often than she did. He replied, "I AM always pleased to hear from you whensoever you have the time to write and although the Personal contact is not necessary I believe you might find it to be beneficial."[62] Belstrom expressed pleasure at the signs of Moore's growing interest in Father Divine and wrote, "You say He has lightened your burden, so I am sure that you are well-substantiated in your Faith. You say that Father fixed up the male situation for you, too. It is Wonderful! Tell me more if you get around to it." It is difficult to know what "the male situation" was, but it is possible that, while at college, Moore was able to mobilize a commitment to Father Divine and the Rosebuds' pledge to virginity as a way of avoiding dating men.[63]

This limited body of correspondence does not reveal what became of Wonderful Joy or Happy S. Love or whether either maintained their relationship with Dorothy. That Moore, who never married, saved the letters, photographs, and cards indicates that they were important to her.[64] The surviving record provides no evidence of physical expressions of affection between these women, nor did Wonderful Joy or Happy S. Love discuss their sense of sexual identity in ways that differed explicitly from the commitment to virginity entailed in their status as Rosebuds. Called to abandon their bodies, they nevertheless drew on the movement's theology and religious vernacular to convey desire, longing, and love for Dot. In the context of a theological emphasis on sex as spiritually destructive, celibacy nevertheless became an arena for these women to experience and express same-sex desire cast in spiritual terms. Moreover, the fact that this desire crossed the color line located it even more firmly within the religious habits of the Peace Mission Movement as an enactment of "the Bill of Rights" of racial integration and harmony. This small archive provides a window into the lived theology of the movement and allows us to consider more broadly how an individual might attempt to make sense of human desire and sexuality in the context of a particular set of religious habits, practices, and spiritual vocabulary. Similarly, this epistolary record underscores that religiously based celibacy is not a uniform sexual practice but is inflected by the social and theological contexts in which it takes shape. In this case, the Peace Mission's theology, with its emphasis on emotional detachment and sexual restraint on the one hand and romantic devotional culture directed at Father Divine on the other, produced a particular mode of celibacy that reveals complex interactions among religion, desire, intimacy, and celibacy.

NOTES

I am grateful to participants in Princeton's Religion, Gender, and Sexuality Working Group and the Religion in the Americas Workshop and to Rebecca Alpert, Bruce Dorsey, Gill Frank, Marie Griffith, Kathi Kern, Leslie Ribovich, Amy Sueyoshi, Timea Széll, Heather White, and Melissa Wilcox for comments on earlier versions of this article.

1. "Why Father Divine Outlawed Sex," *Ebony*, February 1, 1954, 25.

2. Sara Harris, with the assistance of Harriet Crittendon, *Father Divine: Holy Husband* (New York: Doubleday, 1953), 97.

3. Jill Watts, *God, Harlem, USA: The Father Divine Story* (Berkeley: University of California Press, 1995), 1, 130, 142; Robert Weisbrot, *Father Divine and the Struggle for Racial Equality* (Urbana: University of Illinois Press, 1983), 69.

4. Lauretta Bender and Zuleika Yarrell, "Psychoses among Followers of Father Divine," *Journal of Nervous and Mental Disease* 87, no. 4 (April 1938): 418–49; James A. Brussel, "Father Divine: Holy Precipitator of Psychoses," *American Journal of Psychiatry* 92, no. 1 (July 1, 1935): 215–23.

5. A few former members charged that Divine promoted sexual contact with him as part of their spiritual development. Faithful Mary, *"God," He's Just a Natural Man* (New York: Universal Light Publishing, 1937); "Divine Is Accused by Widow," *Baltimore Afro-American*, April 17, 1937; Ruth Boaz, "My Thirty Years with Father Divine," *Ebony*, May 1965, 88–98; Carol Sweet Hunt, "I Was One of Father Divine's Angels," *Confidential*, May 1956, 34–36, 64.

6. Watts, *God, Harlem, USA*, 45–48.

7. Ibid., 167; "Father Divine Wed to White Woman," *New York Herald Tribune*, August 8, 1946, "Joyous Shouts Greet Father Divine and Pretty Wife at Marriage," *Philadelphia Tribune*, August 10, 1946.

8. "Father Divine Says His Marriage to Give Nation New Freedom," *Daily Boston Globe*, August 9, 1946; "Father Divine and White Girl Wed in Secret," *Chicago Daily Tribune*, August 8, 1946.

9. Estelle B. Freedman, "'The Burning of Letters Continues': Elusive Identities and the Historical Construction of Sexuality," *Journal of Women's History* 9, no. 4 (Winter 1998), 182.

10. Amy Sueyoshi, "Finding Fellatio: Friendship, History, and Yone Noguchi," in *Embodying Asian/American Sexualities*, ed. Gina Masequesmay and Sean Metzger (Lanham, Md.: Lexington Books, 2009), 166.

11. Patricia Hill Collins, *Black Feminist Thought: Knowledge, Consciousness, and the Politics of Empowerment* (Boston: Unwin Hyman, 1990).

12. Rosemary Curb and Nancy Manahan, eds., *Lesbian Nuns: Breaking Silence* (Tallahassee: Naiad Press, 1985).

13. Benjamin Kahan, "The Other Harlem Renaissance: Father Divine, Celibate Economics and the Making of Black Sexuality," *Arizona Quarterly* 65, no. 4 (Winter 2009): 37–61.

14. Carroll Smith-Rosenberg, "The Female World of Love and Ritual: Relations between Women in Nineteenth-Century America," *Signs* 1, no. 1 (Autumn 1975): 1–29; Karen V. Hansen, "'No *Kisses* Is Like Youres': An Erotic Friendship between Two African-American Women during the Mid-Nineteenth Century," *Gender and History* 7, no. 2 (August 1995): 153–82. See also the preface to Carolyn De Swarte Gifford, ed., *Writing Out My Heart: Selections from the Journal of Frances E. Willard, 1855–1896* (Urbana: University of Illinois Press, 1995), xi–xvi.

15. Cheryl D. Hicks, "'Bright and Good Looking Colored Girl': Black Women's Sexuality and 'Harmful Intimacy' in Early-Twentieth-Century New York," *Journal of the History of Sexuality* 18, no. 3 (September 2009): 418–56; Sarah Potter, "'Undesirable Relations': Same-Sex Relationships and the Meaning of Sexual Desire at a Women's Reformatory during

the Progressive Era," *Feminist Studies* 30, no. 2 (Summer 2004): 394–415; Regina Kunzel, "Situating Sex: Prison Sexual Culture in the Mid-Twentieth-Century United States," *GLQ: A Journal of Lesbian and Gay Studies* 8, no. 3 (2002): 253–70; Estelle B. Freedman, "The Prison Lesbian: Race, Class, and the Construction of the Aggressive Female Homosexual, 1915–1965," *Feminist Studies* 22, no. 2 (Summer 1996): 397–423; Margaret Otis, "A Perversion Not Commonly Noted," *Journal of Abnormal Psychology* 8, no. 2 (June–July 1913): 113–16.

16. Watts, *God, Harlem, USA*, chap. 2; R. Marie Griffith, "Body Salvation: New Thought, Father Divine, and the Feast of Material Pleasures," *Religion and American Culture* 11, no. 2 (Summer 2001): 119–53.

17. Father Divine's Message, verbatim transcriptions, 1932, box 1, folder 10, Father Divine Collection, Manuscripts, Archives and Rare Books Division, Schomburg Center for Research in Black Culture, New York Public Library (hereafter FD Collection).

18. "Ma Leaves Pa and Seven Children; Divine Blamed," *Baltimore Afro-American*, July 27, 1935; "Divine 'Angel' Disowns Family," *New York Amsterdam News*, July 27, 1935; "Cult Breaks Family Ties," *Los Angeles Times*, August 5, 1935.

19. Mary Justice to Father Divine, n.d., Father Divine Papers, Stuart A. Rose Manuscript, Archives, and Rare Book Library, Emory University (hereafter FD Papers).

20. Rev. M. J. Divine to Miss Mary Justice, October 26, 1946, FD Papers.

21. Father Divine's Message, verbatim transcriptions, June 1, 1934, box 1, folder 12, FD Collection.

22. Ibid.

23. Anita to Lillian, January 3, 1949, folder 3, Dorothy L. Moore Papers, Stuart A. Rose Manuscript, Archives, and Rare Book Library, Emory University (hereafter DLM Papers).

24. Collages of Father Divine, FD Papers.

25. See, for example, Banquet Table Sermon, June 1, 1934, 3, box 1, folder 12, FD Papers.

26. *The New Day*, June 18, 1936, 3; Judith Weisenfeld, *New World a-Coming: Black Religion and Racial Identity during the Great Migration* (New York: New York University Press, 2016).

27. Boaz, "My Thirty Years with Father Divine," 96.

28. *The New Day*, September 1, 1938, 26.

29. *Norfolk (Va.) New Journal and Guide*, July 22, 1933.

30. *Spoken Word*, September 8, 1936, 20.

31. Father Divine's Message, verbatim transcriptions, 1932, box 1, folder 10, FD Collection.

32. See, for example, *Baltimore Afro-American*, January 9, 1937.

33. Kenneth E. Burnham, *God Comes to America: Father Divine and the Peace Mission Movement* (Boston: Lambeth Press, 1979), chap. 7; Harris and Crittenden, *Father Divine*, 211–13.

34. On New Thought debates about sexual restraint, see R. Marie Griffith, *Born Again Bodies: Flesh and Spirit in American Protestantism* (Berkeley: University of California Press, 2004).

35. "Light and Shadow (and) the Impersonal," Father Divine's Message, Sayville, L.I., 1931, FD Papers.

36. Rev. M. J. Divine to Helen E. Chisholm, June 1940, box 2, folder 1, FD Collection.
37. Burnham, *God Comes to America*, 87.
38. Photographs of Rosebuds, photos of Mother Divine, FD Papers.
39. Wonderful Joy to Dorothy L. Moore, September 18, 1948, DLM Papers.
40. Heavenly Rest to Dorothy L. Moore, February 9, 1949, DLM Papers.
41. F. Blair Mayne, "Beliefs and Practices of the Cult of Father Divine," *Journal of Educational Sociology* 10, no. 5 (January 1937): 305.
42. *Baltimore Afro-American*, January 9, 1937.
43. Holy Communion Table, Circle Mission Church, August 7–8, 1952, http://www.libertynet.org/fdipmm/word7/52080802.html; Harris and Crittenden, *Father Divine*, 307.
44. Faithful Mary, *"God" He's Just a Natural Man*, 105.
45. Harris and Crittenden, *Father Divine*, 307.
46. 1930 U.S. Federal Census, Minneapolis City, Hennepin County, Minnesota, Enumeration District 27–100, Family Number 317; *Wizard*, Thomas Edison high school yearbook, 1946, 56, 70, 74; "Outstanding Alumni Awards," *Horizons: A Publication for Alumni & Friends of Bemidji State University* 17, no. 2 (Winter 2001–2), 4. I am grateful to Bailey Diers at the Hennepin County Library for providing me with copies of the Edison high school yearbook.
47. "Father Divine," DLM Papers.
48. Wonderful Joy to Dorothy L. Moore, September 3, 1948, DLM Papers.
49. Ibid., September 18, 1948, and October 15, 1948.
50. Ibid., September 3, 1948.
51. Ibid., October 15, 1948.
52. Ibid.
53. Ibid.
54. Rev. M. J. Divine to Dorothy L. Moore, October 26, 1948, DLM Papers.
55. Wonderful Joy to Dorothy L. Moore, June 17, 1949, DLM Papers.
56. Ibid., October 15, 1948.
57. Happy S. Love to Dorothy L. Moore, January 8, 1949, DLM Papers.
58. Ibid.
59. *The New Day* subscription card, folder 15; Rev. M. J. Divine to Dorothy L. Moore, November 17, 1948; Joan Joy to Dorothy L. Moore, December 31, 1948; Rev. M. J. Divine to Dorothy L. Moore, January 25, 1949; Happy S. Love to Dorothy L. Moore, February 15, 1949; Heavenly Rest to Dorothy L. Moore, February 17, 1949, all in DLM Papers.
60. LaVere Belstrom to Dorothy L. Moore, December 11, 1947, DLM Papers.
61. "Father Divine," n.d., DLM Papers.
62. Rev. M. J. Divine to Dorothy L. Moore, June 22, 1949, DLM Papers.
63. LaVere Belstrom to Dorothy L. Moore, December 11, 1948, DLM Papers.
64. Dorothy L. Moore obituary, *Minneapolis Star Tribune*, April 19, 2009.

SEXUAL DIPLOMACY

U.S. Catholics' Transnational Anti–Birth Control Activism in Postwar Japan

AIKO TAKEUCHI-DEMIRCI

In the years immediately following World War II, U.S. intellectuals and political leaders feared that an overpopulated Japan posed a racial and ideological threat to global stability. Attributing Japan's military expansionism during World War II to its high fertility, U.S. officials and scholars in Occupied Japan considered population control—primarily through the use of contraceptives—as vital to Japan's peaceful recovery and transformation into a democratized ally. As Cold War tensions intensified, they found it imperative to secure Japan as a bulwark against communism in Asia.

From the beginning of the Occupation of Japan, U.S. officials in the Occupation government—commonly referred to as the GHQ (General Headquarters) or SCAP (the Supreme Commander of the Allied Powers)—discussed how to deal with the "big question": overpopulation.[1] They maintained that their interference into Japan's population problem was a matter of "an historical significance of the first magnitude" in order to develop "a sound economy for a free, noncolonial, democratic Japan" that would "neither need nor want to wage war again."[2] American political leaders feared that overpopulation would cause poverty and social instability in Asia, making it vulnerable to Communist infiltration. They saw Japan in particular as a strategically important "workshop" for democracy in Asia and the "balance of power" in the region.[3] Japan's increasing birth rates—from 27 percent before the war to an all-time high of 34 percent in 1947—thus became a matter of concern for the Occupation government.[4] It also set SCAP on a collision course with American Catholics living in Japan.

As a rising world power and an occupying force in the wake of World War II, the United States needed to distinguish itself from other hegemonic systems: colonialism, totalitarianism, and communism. This need made the

United States especially sensitive to Catholic critiques of U.S. population policies in Japan. The Occupation government feared the fallout should Catholics accuse it of attempting to reduce the population of a conquered race. American Catholics had an increasingly prominent role at the dawn of the Cold War. With growing numbers and political and economic power, the backing of American Catholics became vital for the U.S. fight against communism abroad in the 1950s.[5] Against the backdrop of the Cold War and a growing Holocaust consciousness, American Catholic protesters raised the specters of genocide and imperialism to call attention to the eugenic ideas infiltrating the Anglo-Protestant mission to fight "overpopulation" in Japan and other parts of the developing world. Western nations had invented these racialized discourses to justify their continued rule over poor countries and to blame the depletion of the world's resources on the "excessive sexuality and fertility" of women in these countries.[6] The Nazis' wartime eugenics programs, however, made any foreign imposed policies on another population or race an especially delicate matter. American officials in the Occupation government acceded to Catholic objections to population programs in Japan because they were wary of the negative repercussions such programs might have on America's image as the moral leader of the world in their fight against the Soviets.

This chapter demonstrates how transnational religious networks, racial tensions, and competing sexual norms affected official policies during social and political changes in postwar Japan and the United States. Transnationalism—the movements of people, ideas, and practices that extend beyond national borders but are still defined by the framework of the nation-state—is a useful concept in analyzing the intertwined histories of religion and sexuality.[7] Both religions and sexuality have crossed national boundaries and have been shaped by overlapping forces including globalization, nationalism, colonialism, and war. Religious actors, as part of a "transnational civil society," have actively challenged, resisted, and co-opted the power of the nation-state and the empire over the morals and practices of sexuality.[8]

American Catholic priests, Catholic organizations, and the Catholic press in Japan effectively used transnational networks to stymie what they saw as the rapid degeneration of sexual morals caused by the spread of contraceptives. As José Casanova illustrated, Catholicism—with the church's mission to propagandize "universal" moral norms—has always been transnational in scope.[9] The media—both Catholic and secular—were integral to their efforts. Catholic opponents of SCAP's population policies raised awareness of population policies through Catholic newspapers in Japan even as they used

American newspapers to broadcast their efforts to the Vatican and the United Nations. These transnational Catholic networks played a key role in taking personal matters of marital sexuality and procreation beyond the bedroom and connecting them to international politics.

While their activism was transnational in scope and approach, the American Catholics' anti–birth control campaigns in Japan were deeply rooted in American identity and nationalism. They were primarily concerned about protecting the image of the United States in the world as well as with promoting Catholic doctrine regarding sexuality and human life in the United States. As Americans and as Catholics, these activists believed that they had the moral obligation to protect young men and women of a defeated, non-Christian nation from moral and sexual confusion. Yet even as they provided a powerful critique against eugenics and Anglo-Protestant imperialism, the American Catholics' relationship with the Japanese remained based on the colonial, hierarchal structure. The religious-inspired controversy over birth control policies in Japan was, for American Catholics, ultimately an interreligious American battle over the politics of procreation, sexual morality, and a national-racial future.

Beginning in the 1920s, an increasing number of white Americans promoted birth control for "colored races" in the name of world peace, even as they opposed the use of contraceptives among their own women. This practice of attempting to control reproduction based on racial origin—eugenics—had links to domestic and international policies. Domestic eugenic policies aimed to improve the quality of the "white" race, which many contemporary elites believed was deteriorating as a result of the influx of southern and eastern European immigrants. Eugenicists also directed their attention abroad, warning of the "threat to world white supremacy" represented by the "rising tide of color."[10] Against this backdrop, the supposed high fecundity of the Japanese race evoked the threat of the "yellow peril," anxieties about the racial Other rooted in earlier Western encounters with Asian peoples.[11] Japan's belligerent pronatalism, they asserted, led the Japanese to invade China as well as the U.S. West Coast through immigration and colonialism.

In the postwar years, the issue of birth control became for many American Catholics a central battleground—domestically and abroad—to defend their own Christian theology and identity. Until the 1920s and 1930s, most U.S. Protestant and Jewish leaders also opposed contraception, but they remained silent on the issue in the public arena. But the global depression in the 1930s, as well as the spread of eugenic theories that preached the improvement of quality—rather than the quantity—of offspring, prompted a number of

Protestant denominations to provide cautious public endorsement of marital contraception. Partly in response to the "apostasy" of Protestant denominations, Pope Pius XI plainly and vigorously reaffirmed Catholic teaching against contraception in *Casti Connubii*, his encyclical on Christian marriage issued in 1930. The official ban on birth control provided an authoritative boost for American Catholic priests and bishops, who were already alarmed by the falling birth rates and by what they saw as the deterioration of sexual morality among the younger generation of Catholics, to enunciate the evil of contraception in their teaching.[12] Meanwhile, as Samira K. Mehta demonstrates in her chapter in this volume, most Protestant and Jewish leaders by the postwar years came to approve of marital contraceptive use as a practice of "responsible parenthood" among the white middle-class laity and as a social good for the overpopulated areas in the world.

In tandem with their anti–birth control stance, Catholics had long represented a major dissenting voice against the eugenics movement, which was sweeping the world during the first half of the twentieth century. Even though they found themselves in agreement with the pronatalist—and usually antifeminist—aspect of eugenics for the purpose of building a strong and healthy population, Catholics strongly opposed negative measures that sought to restrict reproduction among the poor, the disabled, immigrants, and minority races through sterilization or birth control. Backed by the official condemnation of sterilization by Pope Pius XI, U.S. Catholics openly expressed their opposition to sterilization laws and policies in Germany and Puerto Rico as encroachments on the sanctity of life.[13]

From early in the Occupation, American Catholics in Japan were suspicious that American officials were behind the eugenics/population programs carried out by the Japanese government. In October 1945, Japanese bureaucrats started to set up population control initiatives and programs to solve postwar food and housing shortages, poverty, and racial degeneration. The following year, Crawford Sams, chief of the Public Health and Welfare Section of SCAP, gave a statement to the press in which he endorsed Japanese initiatives for birth control promotion as part of a broader plan to rebuild a democratic Japan.[14] Sams's statement provoked immediate criticism from American priests and Catholic groups in Japan, forcing American officials to refrain from any public reference to the subject of birth control.

American Catholic leaders also denounced the 1948 passage and enactment of the Eugenic Protection Law, a national measure and the first of its kind in the world to legalize abortion, sterilization, and birth control for "eugenic" reasons. They described the law as "worse than the Nazis' evil law" and "against the spirit of the [new Japanese] constitution which stressed the fundamental right" of human life.[15] Because all legislative reforms had to obtain SCAP approval, these critics asserted that SCAP should have prevented the Japanese legislature from passing such a drastic—and immoral—law. Father Patrick O'Connor, one of the most vociferous critics of birth control promotion in Japan, pointed out that even some SCAP officials admitted that the list of "genetic diseases" for sterilization had no medical basis.[16] SCAP, however, had approved the Eugenic Protection Bill, offering "no objection" except for some minor changes.[17] Another Catholic reporter suspected that Americans had more active roles in the conception and passage of the law, as a group of American experts visited Japan to investigate public health and population issues just before the enactment of the law. The writer asserted that the American leaders were using the Japanese as "guinea pigs in a laboratory dissected by American experts."[18]

If American Catholics had any lingering doubts about SCAP's active interest in Japan's reproductive policies, they were dispelled when the Allied powers invited prominent American experts in demography and public health to serve as consultants. In early 1949, leading American demographer Warren Thompson, new to his post at SCAP's Natural Resources Section, publicly declared that nationwide adoption of birth control was the only solution to Japan's overpopulation problem.[19] Later that year, SCAP announced its plans to publish a report prepared by another consultant, Harvard professor Edward Ackerman. The report, titled "Japanese Natural Resources," starkly concluded that if "control of the birth rate [was] not achieved," Japan would be left to reduce its population through "death control"—from natural or man-made disasters such as poverty, food shortage, and even war.[20]

SCAP consultants' public endorsement of birth control triggered a series of protests from American Catholics in Japan, which resonated across global religious and news networks. Even as local protests took place, American Catholics in Japan used transnational Catholic networks to sound the alarm worldwide about the Anglo-Protestant attempts to spread birth control in Japan. An editorial by Father William Kaschmitter, chief of the Information Department of the National Catholic Committee in Japan, which denounced Thompson, was transmitted to news media both in Japan and abroad.[21] Soon after, the National Catholic Welfare Conference (NCWC) in the United States issued a statement to Catholics worldwide clarifying the church's official position against all forms of "artificial birth control."[22] The NCWC, which established an office at the United Nations in 1946, was the hub of American Catholics' worldwide activities.[23] The NCWC News Service was syndicated to all Catholic newspapers in the United States as well as to many foreign news services. Patrick O'Connor used his role as correspondent of NCWC News Service to spread his anti–birth control messages worldwide to lay and religious audiences. When the Allied Catholic Women's Club of Tokyo published an open letter condemning Japan's birth control policy, the mainstream press covered the story and sensitized Americans to the U.S. government's involvement in Japan's sexual practices.[24] Catholic leaders in Rome soon weighed in on the issue, and a Vatican newspaper deplored the fact that "a victor nation, which on the one hand made efforts to spread Christian moral spirits in Japan," was "on the other hand sending experts who advocate latest methods [of birth control] that contradict the immutable natural law mandated by the Creator."[25]

The efficacy of Catholic activism was due to the growing cultural prominence of Catholics in the United States. The 1950s represented the Catholic Church's "triumphant era in America."[26] The number of Catholics in the United States doubled between 1940 and 1960, representing more than 20 percent of the population by the 1950s.[27] The postwar economic boom and GI bill opened wide the doors of higher education and higher-paid jobs for hundreds of thousands of Catholic youths. With the drastic reduction of southern and eastern European immigrants following the 1924 Immigration Act, the Catholic "races" in the United States had gradually been integrating into the white, "Caucasian" majority.[28] Many had left their seclusion in urban immigrant enclaves and flocked to new suburban homes to embrace a solid middle-class lifestyle. In Washington and on Wall Street as well as in Hollywood films, Catholics enjoyed prominent positions in American society and culture.[29] The Supreme Commander, General Douglas MacArthur, had ambitions to run for the Republican presidential nomination after his tour of duty in Japan and therefore did not want to alienate this increasingly powerful constituency.

Catholicism figured prominently in the Occupation government in Japan. It was well known that MacArthur publicly endorsed Christianity in the country. In a personal conversation with O'Connor, MacArthur stressed the need to implant Christianity in Japan as "the most powerful bastion of democracy."[30] As a governing body, SCAP promoted religious freedom and diversity in Japan with the intent of eliminating ultranationalism and militarism. After wartime suppression, the Christian population in Japan, even though still a small minority, grew rapidly under SCAP's ordinance for "religious freedom." The number of Catholics nearly doubled within ten years after the war, from 108,324 in 1946 to 212,318 in 1955.[31] SCAP welcomed

Catholic clergy from abroad and supported them in rebuilding churches and spreading membership throughout the nation.[32] American Catholic chaplain groups and Catholic women's clubs were formed under the auspices of the GHQ and cast a strong influence on SCAP's population policy in Japan.[33]

U.S. Catholics yielded their influence further on international politics. By the 1950s, Catholic opinion aligned with the American mainstream in its diplomatic stance against communism. Popular media personalities, such as Bishop Fulton Sheen, helped spread Catholics' anticommunist views widely to the American public. At a time when Catholics were still associated with authoritarian regimes in Italy, Spain, Portugal, and Austria, anticommunism, according to John McGreevy, "eas[ed] Catholic acceptance in liberal circles."[34] American Catholics, now united with Protestant and Jewish leaders, emphasized the religious character of the United States—a country of democracy and religious freedom—in contrast to the "bolshevistic and atheistic Communism."[35] As Whitney Strub in this volume also illustrates in his essay on antipornography activism, the concept of a "Judeo-Christian heritage" brought together a loose coalition of reformers across the three faiths in the name of American social justice and religious freedom against the backdrop of the Cold War.[36] Catholics, in particular, projected themselves as the archetypal Americans, representing the most loyal and vigilant of the nation's citizens.

In their opposition against eugenic sterilization and birth control targeting nonwhite races, American Catholics tacitly critiqued Anglo-Protestant nationalism and imperialism.[37] Domestically in the United States, Catholic leaders were more forward-looking than many contemporary white Christians in their rejection of racial discrimination and segregation in the South. The topic of eugenic birth control—sterilization and contraceptive use to limit the fecundity of nonwhite races—was one major area where the Anglo-Protestant faith in individual autonomy faltered and the Catholics' argument against eugenics sounded racially progressive.[38] The Tokyo Catholic Women's Club's letter of protest expressed concern for what that group considered SCAP's imperial abuse of power: "As American citizens we protest when any individual or section of any Government department uses the channels and influence of the United States to promote birth control."[39]

The transnational debates over Japan's birth control policies placed American domestic battles over sexual politics on an international stage. This was especially evident in the controversy over birth control activist and luminary Margaret Sanger's visit to Japan. In 1949, a Japanese newspaper company invited Sanger to discuss the benefits of birth control in Japan. Sanger was already well known there, as she had visited the country a couple of times since 1922 and had many friends and followers. The Japanese government had initially denied Sanger's visa application for her first visit, alarmed by her association with radicalism, but eventually allowed her entry thanks to the support of some elite Japanese liberals who espoused neo-Malthusianism.[40] The birth control philosophy attracted the attention of these intellectuals during the 1920s, who saw it a useful tool to build a stronger Japanese race that could compete with Western powers. After wartime suppression under the pronatalist regime, the idea and practice of birth control regained nationwide attention as a key to economic, social, and racial recovery.[41]

In February 1950, General MacArthur denied Sanger's entrance to Japan, sparking a heated debate among Americans about international, sexual, and religious politics. Sanger applied for a visa to Japan at the very moment SCAP was dealing with the controversies over Thompson and Ackerman. While SCAP vigorously defended its own policy experts against Catholic attacks, it did not want to overextend itself to protect Sanger.[42] The news made national headlines, including front-page coverage by the *New York Times* and a cover story in *Newsweek*.[43] As a result, letters of both approval and dissent flooded into MacArthur's office. Many letters voiced concern about Catholic activism. Some wrote to "applaud and thank [MacArthur] for [his] firm stand against immorality." Others questioned MacArthur's "undemocratic" decision to yield to an opinion that denied birth control to the Japanese people—"practiced by many American mothers," including many Roman Catholics—when the world was "rapidly being over-populated" bringing "all the future hazards."[44] Supporters of Sanger's cause could not understand how a minority religious group in the United States—a group "virtually non-existent in Japan"—could have such powerful political impact as to block Sanger's invitation.[45] They asserted that Sanger, already a popular figure in Japan, had more right to be heard by the Japanese than "some 350 American women in a Roman Catholic club in Tokyo" who allegedly excluded Japanese from membership.[46] The English-language newspaper in Japan, the *Nippon Times*, reproduced these American letters to MacArthur discussing the pros and cons of birth control in its column headed "Readers in Council." So "ill-tempered and extreme" had the debate become, according to MacArthur's description, that the editor decided to close the column.[47]

Resentment toward Catholic contraceptive activism had already been brought to a boiling point in the United States in 1948, when Catholic bishops had helped defeat a proposal to legalize birth control clinics in Massachusetts.

Since the 1930s, courts, legislatures, and medical professionals repudiated the Catholic Church's stance on birth control. In 1936, in *United States v. One Package of Japanese Pessaries*, a federal appeals court ruled that the government could not prevent physicians from dispensing contraceptive information or devices. This decision essentially nullified part of the Comstock Law that had forbidden the distribution of "obscene" material since 1873 by establishing that birth control instruction was a legitimate medical practice. The following year, the American Medical Association officially endorsed contraception under medical advisement. Against this tide of sexual liberalism, Catholic influence on foreign policy stoked anger in the United States.[48]

It would be a mistake, however, to view Catholic opposition to birth control as stemming from conservative impulses and to view this history as one that pits liberalism against conservatism. Rather, Catholic perspectives on birth control were inextricable from other social justice causes. Catholic activists highlighted the racism and violation of human rights in some of the controversial acts committed by the U.S. government against other races or nations—such as immigration restriction and the use of the atomic bomb. Proposing emigration and increased food production as a moral solution to Japan's population problem, Catholic leaders called for the relaxation of the racist immigration law in the United States. Kaschmitter, in particular, presented a proposal to lend "unused land" in the United States and other parts of the world to Japanese farmers abroad to harvest enough food needed to support the growing population.[49] Referring to the pope's teaching that God had created land for the use of all people, the Catholic priest sharply criticized "nationalistic sentiments" that hampered such spirit.[50] With Kaschmitter's plans in mind, an NCWC representative at a Senate committee on legal issues expressed his support for a bill to relax immigration restriction.[51] The Catholic leaders, through the NCWC, further urged the UN to accord more territory or immigration rights "to forestall a Third World War waged by 'hungry nations' against the 'aggression' of selfish, wealthy powers."[52] As a result of the NCWC's activism, the Vatican at the World Catholic Press Congress adopted a resolution, introduced by Patrick O'Connor, for the opening up of underpopulated areas to emigration.[53] O'Connor also submitted an article through the NCWC to the Vatican newspaper, *Osservatore Romano*, describing the legalization of birth control as "a greater disaster to Japan than the atomic bomb" and warned that it would enable the Communists, who forbade such knowledge and practice, to "take over the country in 20 years." In the end, the reverend declared, "the Communists will laugh maliciously and will congratulate themselves on the easy victory" while the rest of the world's population declined.[54] By comparing American officials' promotion of birth control to the act of dropping an atomic bomb, the Catholic activists questioned the morality of some American leaders in the context of the Cold War.[55]

Although American Catholic activists claimed to save the Japanese from the imperial, racist, and morally corrupt doctrine of birth control, they seemed to care little about the actual opinion and responses of the Japanese themselves, Catholic or non-Catholic. Their reporting on SCAP's active involvement in Japan's sexual politics appeared everywhere, translated into Japanese, in the Catholic media—especially *Catholic Shinbun* (Catholic news), the official news organ for Catholics in Japan. Yet, there is no record of them actually working together alongside their Japanese counterparts on these issues despite the fact that Japanese Catholics expressed their own concerns for SCAP's and the Japanese government's population policies. The Population Problem Committee in the Tokyo Catholic Students' Federation, for example, sent some one hundred copies of letters to Catholic organizations and individual clerical leaders across the world in order to bring attention to the birth control issue in Japan.[56] Other Japanese opponents of birth control, through the Catholic media, also called out for support from the world, especially the UN, to help ease Japanese immigration and population problems.[57] An American Catholic writer noted, however, that such clamor from a small religious minority in a defeated country would hardly have any effect on the policy decision of the conquerors. In the end, therefore, American Catholic activists believed that *they* needed to carry out the transnational campaigns to protest SCAP actions on behalf of a nation that had "surrendered unconditionally."[58] Americans, they asserted, had a moral obligation to help the young men and women of a non-Christian nation who had lost their anchorage after a disastrous war.[59] Preoccupied with protecting the United States' preeminent position in the world, which in fact was based on the legacy of colonialism, they fell short of forming a transnational bond with the Japanese people.

American Catholics therefore did not probe further into the matter when they could not prove that Americans were involved. For example, after learning that the Institute of Public Health of Tokyo had newly added a department that dealt with research on family planning, Catholic reporters furiously questioned its Japanese director whether MacArthur, Sams, or any other American official was behind the creation of this department. Upon learning from him that it was exclusively his idea, the director recalled, the Catholics immediately relaxed their tone, apologized to him, and left.[60] The incident shows how the American Catholic leaders in Japan failed to see the Japanese as independent people capable of carrying out their own discussions and decisions about the fate of the nation.[61]

Another issue that American Catholic agitators did not pursue was abortion. Patrick O'Connor did voice opposition to the "wholesale killing" by abortion as legalized in the Eugenic Protection Law.[62] SCAP officials were indeed apprehensive about the possible publicity over the rapid increase in legal abortion in Occupied Japan.[63] But despite their concern, they received no official protest from American Catholics over the issue. Chief of the Public Welfare Section Crawford Sams recalled that a Catholic priest-correspondent—likely O'Connor—came to see him to obtain evidence to show that the maternal death rate was rising as a result of increased abortions in Japan. He proudly wrote that the priest went home "disappointed" because he could not find such evidence.[64] Abortion generated less controversy at this time, compared with birth control and sterilization, and even birth control advocates, including Margaret Sanger and her supporters, were "steadfastly opposed to abortion."[65]

American Catholics' tactic to frame their transnational anti–birth control activism as part of a broader humanitarian fight against totalitarianism, communism, and imperialism ultimately proved effective in shaping SCAP's sexual policy in Japan. MacArthur responded to Catholic protests by disavowing population control views expressed by Thompson and other SCAP consultants as "individual opinions alone" rather than as the "authoritative consideration or views of the Occupation."[66] He fully accepted the request by the Catholic Women's Club to expurgate the objectionable parts in Edward Ackerman's report on Japanese resources and published it for internal rather than public consumption.[67] And finally, he flatly rejected Margaret Sanger's request to visit Japan—an unpopular decision for many Americans as well as Japanese.[68]

Against the backdrops of the Holocaust and the Cold War, American leaders in the Occupation government were indeed apprehensive about the negative diplomatic attention that they might receive from a Catholic campaign against state-run contraceptive programs in Japan. Sams confessed that he was more concerned about "the issues of genocides and communists" than about "the attitude of U.S. Catholicism" itself.[69] MacArthur elaborated these ideas in his letter to protesters regarding Sanger's attempts to visit Japan: "The entrance of Mrs. Sanger for the purpose indicated could not fail to invite propaganda attributing responsibility to the Allied Powers that which had already been done by the Japanese themselves toward birth control and with it the charge that the Allied Powers in the exercise of their supreme authority through coercion had imposed measures upon the conquered Japanese People leading to genocide."[70] MacArthur's explanation of SCAP's stance against genocide proved effective in quelling the suspicion among ACLU and Planned Parenthood groups that it was simply privileging the views of Catholics. Prominent birth control supporters such as Eleanor Roosevelt and Marie Stopes wrote back to MacArthur expressing their appreciation for his "wise decision" to forestall an international scandal.[71]

By the 1940s, American leaders had become sensitized to the negative optics of eugenics programs, especially those targeting another race or nation. Scientists and national leaders of the Allied countries strongly denounced the Nazis' eugenics programs against the Jews during World War II.[72] After the UN's Genocide Convention went into effect in 1951, the U.S. Department of State ordered all American diplomatic and consular offices to alert it of any Communist charges of American "genocide" against domestic or foreign racial groups.[73] Given the UN announcement, Sams advised that "it would be most unwise for the occupying powers to come into a conquered country and attempt to force on these people limitation of families."[74] Similarly, another SCAP officer expressed his concern in a private letter to Ackerman that, after the UN convention, "anyone who practice[d] contraception and, possibly, celibacy, etc. [might] end up next door for practicing genocide."[75]

As it became increasingly difficult to avoid publicity in their involvement in Japan's fertility control, SCAP instead started to send Japanese demographers and health officials to the United States. SCAP not only approved their travels but also helped arrange and monitored their personal meetings with American individuals. There, the Japanese met and freely discussed reproductive policies with American leaders in the field, including Thompson and Sanger, without attracting any public attention. Clarence Gamble, a wealthy birth control supporter whom SCAP also denied a visit to Japan, sarcastically wrote to Sanger, "Though MacArthur won't let us go to Japan, I am gradually seeing some of the Japanese notables whom he is sending to this country."[76] Based on the guidance of American population experts, field observations of American "public health" programs, and the financial backup of American philanthropists, these Japanese leaders eventually carried out their own birth control programs in Japan. The Japanese experiments, in turn, set the precedent for similar programs in other "overpopulated" Asian countries, namely India and China, which were intended to serve as important defense strategies against communism.[77] The continuing involvement of Americans and other Westerners in population programs in so-called third world countries would stoke religious backlash decades later.

By exposing the racist and imperialist nature of America's mission to fight "overpopulation" abroad, American Catholics effectively galvanized worldwide support for their mission to protect the sacredness of human life across the world. In order to maintain the diplomatic image of the United States as the moral leader of the world, American political leaders in postwar Occupied Japan ultimately gave in to their demands to disassociate themselves from Japan's population issues.

This specific episode in United States–Japan relations illustrates how our bodies, especially women's bodies, are gendered, sexualized, and racialized to conform to national interests, moral doctrines, or future visions of the race. They are constantly subjected to public scrutiny and outside forces that frequently extend beyond national borders. A transnational analysis helps illuminate these intricate forces that affect a nation's sexual and reproductive practices and the negotiations that religious and secular actors make to articulate their beliefs about human sexuality and procreation amid changing social norms and dynamic international relations.

NOTES

1. Crawford F. Sams, *"Medic": The Mission of an American Military Doctor in Occupied Japan and Wartorn Korea* (Armonk, N.Y.: M. E. Sharpe, 1998), 183–85.

2. Lieutenant Colonel Hubert G. Schenck, "Natural Resources Problem in Japan," *Science*, October 8, 1948, 367, 72.

3. John W. Dower, *Japan in War and Peace: Selected Essays* (New York: W. W. Norton, 1993), 155–76, 179; John W. Dower, *Embracing Defeat: Japan in the Wake of World War II* (New York: W. W. Norton, 1999), 526.

4. Statistics and Information Department, Ministry of Health, Labour and Welfare, "Table 2–24: Number of Births and Birth Rates, by Sex," 2015, http://www.stat.go.jp/data/chouki/02.htm. After 1947, birth rates in Japan decreased rapidly, falling below 20 percent by 1955. Meanwhile in the United States, birth rates similarly increased from 19 percent in 1939 to 27 percent in 1947. By the mid-1950s, U.S. birth rates were higher than those of Japan. For historical data of U.S. vital statistics, see Centers for Disease Control and Prevention, "Table 1–1 Live Births, Birth Rates, and Fertility Rates, by Race: United States, 1909–2003," *Vital Statistics of the United States, 2003, Volume I, Natality*, http://www.cdc.gov/nchs/products/vsus/vsus_1980_2003.htm.

5. For the influence of Catholicism on U.S. foreign policy and Cold War strategy, see, for example, Seth Jacobs, *America's Miracle Man in Vietnam: Ngo Dinh Diem, Religion, Race, and U.S. Intervention in Southeast Asia, 1950–1957* (Durham: Duke University Press, 2004). For Catholic influence on domestic anticommunist policies, namely McCarthyism, see, for example, Patrick H. McNamara, *A Catholic Cold War: Edmund A. Walsh, S.J., and the Politics of American Anticommunism* (New York: Fordham University Press, 2005).

6. For critical examination of the concept of "overpopulation," see Laura Briggs, *Reproducing Empire: Race, Sex, Science, and U.S. Imperialism in Puerto Rico* (Berkeley: University of California Press, 2002), 81–89; Timothy Mitchell, "America's Egypt: Discourse of the Development Industry," *Middle East Report* 169 (1991): 18–21; and Susan George, *How the Other Half Dies: The Real Reasons for World Hunger* (New York: Penguin Books, 1976), 58–60.

7. For the intellectual genealogy of the "transnational turn" in American history/ American studies, which started around the 1990s and became prominent in the 2000s, see Akira Iriye, "The Internationalization of History," *American Historical Review* 94, no. 1 (1989): 1–10; Shelley Fisher Fishkin, "Crossroads of Cultures: The Transnational Turn in American Studies," *American Quarterly* 57, no. 1 (2005): 17–57; Ian Tyrrell, "Reflections on the Transnational Turn in United States History: Theory and Practice," *Journal of Global History* 4 (2009): 453–74; and Donald E. Pease, "Introduction: Re-mapping the Transnational Turn," in *Re-framing the Transnational Turn in American Studies*, ed. Winfried Fluck, Donald E. Pease, and John Carlos Rowe (Hanover: Dartmouth College Press, 2011), 1–48. On the scholarly intersection between the history of sexuality and transnational studies, as well as some specific examples of work that use transnationalism in their study of sexuality, see Margot Canaday, "Thinking Sex in the Transnational Turn: An Introduction," *American Historical Review* 114, no. 5 (2009): 1250–57; and Joanne Meyerowitz, "Transnational Sex and U.S. History," *American Historical Review* 114, no. 5 (2009): 1273–86.

8. The relationship between transnational religion, transnational civil society, and the state is theorized in Susanne Hoeber Rudolph, "Introduction: Religion, States, and Transnational Civil Society," in *Transnational Religion and Fading States*, ed. Susanne Hoeber Rudolph and James Piscatori (Boulder: Westview Press, 1997), 1–26.

9. José Casanova, "Globalizing Catholicism and the Return to a 'Universal' Church," in *Transnational Religion and Fading States*, ed. Susanne Hoeber Rudolph and James Piscatori (Boulder: Westview Press, 1997), 121–43. For other studies that illuminate American Catholics' internationalism in their relationship with the Vatican in the prewar period and with the United Nations after World War II, respectively, see Peter R. D'Agostino, *Rome in America: Transnational Catholic Ideology from the Risorgimento to Fascism* (Chapel Hill: University of North Carolina Press, 2004); and Joseph S. Rossi, *Uncharted Territory: The American Catholic Church at the United Nations, 1946–1972* (Washington: Catholic University of America Press, 2006).

10. Harvard-educated historian and eugenicist Lothrop Stoddard helped popularize the idea of an impending "yellow peril" in his influential book *The Rising Tide of Color against White World-Supremacy* (New York: Scribner, 1920). For early twentieth-century discussions among U.S. eugenicists on the fertility of the colored races, see Briggs, *Reproducing Empire*,

74–108; Laura L. Lovett, *Conceiving the Future: Pronatalism, Reproduction, and the Family in the United States, 1890–1938* (Chapel Hill: University of North Carolina Press, 2007), 77–108; Matthew James Connelly, *Fatal Misconception: The Struggle to Control World Population* (Cambridge, Mass.: Belknap Press of Harvard University Press, 2008), 53–59; and Alexandra Minna Stern, *Eugenic Nation: Faults and Frontiers of Better Breeding in Modern America* (Berkeley: University of California Press, 2005), 86–92.

11. Historian John Dower traces the imaginary of apes, lesser men, children, and madmen that characterize the yellow peril to Aristotle as well as earliest encounters of Europeans with African peoples and Native Americans. Gina Marchetti finds the psycho-cultural perception of a menace from Asians rooted in medieval fears of Genghis Khan and the Mongolian invasions of Europe. The term "yellow peril" itself was coined by Kaiser Wilhelm II of Germany in 1895 to express the perils the European colonists faced in their invasions of China and later to evoke racial fear among Western nations in response to the Japanese military victory over Russia in 1905. For the definitions and applications of the yellow peril in American political discourses and popular culture, see Dower, *Embracing Defeat*, 10; and Gina Marchetti, *Romance and the "Yellow Peril": Race, Sex, and Discursive Strategies in Hollywood Fiction* (Berkeley: University of California Press, 1993), 2.

12. Leslie Woodcock Tentler, *Catholics and Contraception: An American History* (Ithaca: Cornell University Press, 2004), 45–46, 73–75.

13. For details of U.S. Catholics' crusade against the eugenics movement during the first half of the twentieth century, see Sharon M. Leon, *An Image of God: The Catholic Struggle with Eugenics* (Chicago: University of Chicago Press, 2013); and Christine Rosen, *Preaching Eugenics: Religious Leaders and the American Eugenics Movement* (New York: Oxford University Press, 2004), 10–21, 139–64. For U.S. Catholics' opposition to eugenic policies in Germany and Puerto Rico, see Leon, *Image of God*, 101–13.

14. Sams, *"Medic,"* 185–86; Deborah Jane Hacker Oakley, "The Development of Population Policy in Japan, 1945–1952, and American Participation" (PhD diss., University of Michigan, 1977), 173, 359.

15. Patrick O'Connor, "Danshu kyōsei wa Nachi no akuhō ijō" [Forced sterilization is worse than the Nazis' evil law], *Catholic Shinbun*, October 23, 1949, 1.

16. Patrick O'Connor, "Sanji seigen ni hantai suru" [I oppose birth control], *Catholic Digest* 3, no. 9 (1950): 36. In fact, a SCAP official had expressed "utmost alarm" when he learned about the Japanese plan to "control population through eugenics" and "earnestly recommend[ed] that SCAP forbid the Japanese government from undertaking or entertaining such a program." Herbert Passin, check sheet from Public Opinion and Sociological Research, J. A. Greene, November 7, 1946, file: "Eugenics," PHW 04824, GHQ/SCAP Records, National Diet Library, Tokyo, Japan (hereafter NDL).

17. Crawford F. Sams, "Bill for Eugenic Protection Law," June 25, 1948, file: "Eugenic Protection Law," PHW 01178, GHQ/SCAP Records, NDL.

18. Originally published in *Sunday Visitor*, reprinted in Japanese in "Beikoku kara mita sanjiseigensaku: Nihonjin wa jikkenshitsu no morumotto" [Birth control policies as seen by Americans: The Japanese are guinea pigs in a laboratory], *Catholic Shinbun*, August 28, 1949.

19. Warren Thompson directed the Scripps Foundation for Research in Population Problems at Miami University in Ohio and had a reputation as "America's best-known

Malthusian." He established his career by presenting a demographic model that later became known as the "demographic transition theory" in his influential book *Danger Spots in World Population* (New York: Knopf, 1929). In the book, he argued that nations with rapidly growing fertility, declining mortality, and a low prevalence of birth control presented a danger to world politics by resorting to force in order to obtain land and resources abroad. Japan, according to Thompson, was a prime example of such a "danger spot."

20. Catholics' objection to the Ackerman report and SCAP's response to it summarized by Rutherford Poasts, Natural Resources Section, SCAP, February 7, 1950, folder 17, box 1, Daniel B. Luten Jr. Papers, Hoover Institution Archives, Stanford University, (hereafter Luten Papers).

21. The Japanese report on Thompson's statement in *Mainichi Shinbun*, March 2, 1949; William Kaschmitter's editorial reproduced in "Priest Supports Migration Issue: Emigration of Japanese to Underdeveloped Parts of World Is Emphasized," *Nippon Times*, April 16, 1949.

22. "Nihon no jinkō mondai: Zensekai katorikku ga chūshi" [Japan's population problem: Catholics worldwide take notice], *Catholic Shinbun*, April 17, 1949. This statement was made in response to Thompson's misleading comment that Catholics were only against "birth control for immoral purposes." With the inevitable spread of birth control among American women since the 1930s, most Catholic clergy and the laity had come to accept the use of the rhythm method, or periodic abstinence. Thompson might have been alluding to this so-called Catholic birth control. For the Catholic position on the "rhythm method," see Tentler, *Catholics and Contraception*, 104–22.

23. Since its establishment by progressive American bishops as an outgrowth of the church's activities during World War I, the NCWC had been the national base to dispatch Catholic teaching on birth control and eugenics. See Rossi, *Uncharted Territory*, 73–83; and Leon, *Image of God*, 69, 122, 132.

24. The Catholic Women's Club of Tokyo to Douglas MacArthur, January 7, 1950, folder 17, box 1, Luten Papers.

25. "Sekai no shinto wa sakebu: Nihon no sanji seigen ni hantai" [Catholics worldwide call out: Oppose Japan's birth control], *Catholic Shinbun*, January 1, 1950.

26. Charles R. Morris, *American Catholic: The Saints and Sinners Who Built America's Most Powerful Church* (New York: Times Books, 1997), 227.

27. U.S. Bureau of the Census, *Historical Statistics of the United States, Colonial Times to 1970* (Washington: U.S. Government Printing Office, 1975), 8, 389.

28. Matthew Frye Jacobson, *Whiteness of a Different Color: European Immigrants and the Alchemy of Race* (Cambridge, Mass.: Harvard University Press, 1999), 91–96; John T. McGreevy, *Parish Boundaries: The Catholic Encounter with Race in the Twentieth-Century Urban North* (Chicago: University of Chicago Press, 1996), 78–79.

29. For the development of the American Catholic Church in the mid-1940s and 1950s, see James P. McCartin, *Prayers of the Faithful: The Shifting Spiritual Life of American Catholics* (Cambridge, Mass.: Harvard University Press, 2010), 42–70.

30. Patrick O'Connor, "Nihon no makkāsā gensui" [Japan's General MacArthur], *Catholic Digest* 1, no. 3 (1948): 2–4. For General MacArthur's and SCAP's positions on Christianity in Japan, see William P. Woodard, *The Allied Occupation of Japan 1945–1952 and Japanese Religions* (Leiden: E. J. Brill, 1972), 210–17, 243–28.

31. Takashi Gonoi, *Nihon kirisutokyōshi* [The history of Christianity in Japan] (Tokyo: Yoshikawa kōbunkan, 1990), 303–7.

32. Letter from Douglas MacArthur to Paul Taguchi (bishop of Osaka), January 23, 1946, reproduced in Paul Taguchi, *The Catholic Church in Japan* (Kyoto: Mainichi Shimbun, 1946).

33. These included the Tokyo Catholic Women's Club, Grand Heights Catholic Women's Club, Washington Heights Catholic Women's Club, Yokohama Rosary Club, and the Catholic Chaplains of the Tokyo-Yokohama Area.

34. John T. McGreevy, *Catholicism and American Freedom: A History* (New York: W. W. Norton, 2003), 194, 211.

35. McGreevy, *Parish Boundaries*, 64. For more on American Catholics' new focus on democracy and freedom in the context of anticommunism, see Kevin M. Schultz, *Tri-faith America: How Catholics and Jews Held Postwar America to Its Protestant Promise* (New York: Oxford University Press, 2011), 73–74; McNamara, *Catholic Cold War*, 167.

36. Schultz, *Tri-faith America*, 77–81.

37. During the early twentieth century, American Catholics also took part in the Anglo-Protestant imperial project of taming land and uplifting its people through missionary work in former Spanish colonies, namely Mexico, Puerto Rico, and the Philippines. See Anne M. Martínez, *Catholic Borderlands: Mapping Catholicism onto American Empire, 1905–1935* (Lincoln: University of Nebraska Press, 2014).

38. McGreevy, *Catholicism and American Freedom*, 208–11, 221–28.

39. Catholic Women's Club to MacArthur, January 7, 1950.

40. For details on Sanger's 1922 visit to Japan, see Malia Sedgewick Johnson, "Margaret Sanger and the Birth Control Movement in Japan, 1921–1955" (PhD diss., University of Hawaii, 1987), 31–50; and Aiko Takeuchi-Demirci, "Birth Control and Socialism: The Frustration of Margaret Sanger and Ishimoto Shizue's Mission," *Journal of American–East Asian Relations* 17, no. 3 (2010): 257–80.

41. For the prewar social and legal status of birth control and abortion in Japan, see Sabine Frühstück, *Colonizing Sex: Sexology and Social Control in Modern Japan* (Berkeley: University of California Press, 2003), 116–51; Elise K. Tipton, "Birth Control and the Population Problem in Prewar and Wartime Japan," *Japanese Studies* 14, no. 1 (1994): 54–64; and Tiana Norgren, *Abortion before Birth Control: The Politics of Reproduction in Postwar Japan* (Princeton: Princeton University Press, 2001), 22–35.

42. MacArthur's defense of SCAP position in regard to Thompson's statement carried in "SCAP on Birth Control," *Nippon Times*, July 2, 1949.

43. "Mrs. Sanger Barred by MacArthur from Birth Control Talks in Japan," *New York Times*, February 13, 1950; "Too Many Babies? Japan Tried All Out Birth Control," *Newsweek*, May 8, 1950. See also "Mrs. Sanger's Visa," *Washington Post*, February 15, 1950; and "MacArthur Aides Ban Birth Control," *Los Angeles Times*, February 13, 1950.

44. Edith Swason to Douglas MacArthur, May 26, 1950; Lucille K. MacDonald to MacArthur, May 28, 1950; Kingsland Camp to MacArthur, March 18, 1950, file: "Birth Control," GS(B) 01272–01276, GHQ/SCAP Records, NDL.

45. Johnson, "Margaret Sanger and the Birth Control Movement," 104.

46. Camp to MacArthur, March 18, 1950.

47. Douglas MacArthur to Reverend LeRoy J. Hess, June 17, 1950, file: "Birth Control," GS(B) 01272–01276, GHQ/SCAP Records, NDL.

48. Sarah C. Hill to Douglas MacArthur, May 2, 1950, ibid. For the battles over birth control legislation in Massachusetts, see McGreevy, *Catholicism and American Freedom*, 229–31. Kevin Schultz illustrates the continuing tension between Protestants and Catholics in the postwar years, the former seeing the rapid growth and vigor of the church in the United States as a threat. Birth control was one of the areas where such tension played out. Schultz, *Tri-faith America*, 94–95.

49. Many articles appeared in Catholic newspapers refuting the Malthusian theory that food production could not match the rate of population growth and introducing multiple methods to increase the production of farm products. "Shin-Marusasu setsu wa ayamari: Shokuryō daizōsan wa kanou" [Neo-Malthusianism is wrong: Increasing food production is possible], *Catholic Shinbun*, April 17, 1949; "Kakute Marusasu wa ayamareri" [This is how Malthus was wrong], *Catholic Digest* 6, no. 2 (1949), 61–77. The idea of using America's latest science and technology for horticultural innovation to feed "hungry nations" became the foundation of the Green Revolution in the 1950s and 1960s. For the American battle to "conquer hunger" in Asia during the Cold War, see Nick Cullather, *The Hungry World: America's Cold War Battle against Poverty in Asia* (Cambridge, Mass.: Harvard University Press, 2010). Catholic leaders also considered Argentina, a Catholic nation, as a destination for Japanese farmers. "Imin keikaku susumu: Aruzenchin de beisaku" [Progress in immigration plan: Growing rice in Argentina], *Catholic Shinbun*, January 22, 1950.

50. W. A. Kaschmitter, "Nihon no tochi mondai wo dou kaiketsu suruka" [How to solve Japan's land problem], *Catholic Digest* 3, no. 9 (1950): 76–79; W. A. Kaschmitter, "Katorikku kyōkai to imin" [The Catholic Church and immigration], *Koe* 897 (1952): 5–8. Kaschmitter also urged Western nations to reconsider the so-called right of discovery, which had served as the basis of Western claims on land, pointing out that Native Americans had already "discovered" the Americas before Columbus. "Priest Supports Migration Issue," *Nippon Times*, April 16, 1949.

51. "Beikoku no imin seigen, kanwa ka" [The United States may relax immigration restriction], *Catholic Shinbun*, August 28, 1949.

52. "Catholic Church Organ Urges UN Members to Give Japan Land or Emigration Rights," *Nippon Times*, December 3, 1949.

53. "Vatican Meet Adopts Move for Emigration: Resolution Introduced by Rev. Patrick O'Connor," *Nippon Times*, March 13, 1950.

54. "Vatican Paper Scores Japan Birth Control," *Nippon Times*, August 6, 1949.

55. There were in fact some Catholic theologians who denounced America's use of atomic bombs after the war. McGreevy, *Catholicism and American Freedom*, 228.

56. "Sekai ni uttau: Sansei mondai tou wo gakusei yūshi houkoku" [Appeal to the world: Student volunteers report birth control problem], *Catholic Shinbun*, February 26, 1950.

57. Yōichi Toshimitsu, "Jinkō mondai to imin" [Population problem and emigration], *Catholic Shinbun*, August 28, 1949.

58. "Sekai no shinto wa sakebu."

59. O'Connor, "Sanji seigen ni hantai suru," 35.

60. Yoshio Koya, *Kōgakukyū no techō kara* [From an old scholar's diary] (Tokyo: Japanese Planned Parenthood Federation, 1970), 75–77.

61. Emory Stevens Bucks to Douglas MacArthur, April 7, 1950, file: "Birth Control," GS(B) 01272–01276, GHQ/SCAP Records, NDL.

62. Patrick O'Connor, "Wholesale Killing by Abortion Worse Than Atomic Bombings," *Hawaii Catholic Herald*, October 13, 1949.

63. Oliver R. McCoy to Marshall C. Balfour, May 28, 1951, folder 3629, box 543, series 609, RG 2, Rockefeller Foundation Archives (hereafter RFA), Rockefeller Archive Center, Sleepy Hollow, New York (hereafter RAC); Crawford F. Sams to Marshall C. Balfour, January 26, 1951, ibid. SCAP fears were not necessarily unfounded, as later in the first UN World Population Conference in 1954, delegates from Communist nations criticized Japanese leaders for the legalization of abortion as a solution to overpopulation. Koya, *Kōgakukyū no techō kara*, 197–98.

64. Sams, *"Medic,"* 187.

65. McGreevy, *Catholicism and American Freedom*, 226.

66. "SCAP on Birth Control," *Nippon Times*, July 2, 1949.

67. SCAP allowed the Japanese press to publish the Japanese translation of the original report later that year. Daniel B. Luten to K. Miyashita, March 15, 1950, folder 8, box 1, Luten Papers.

68. Japanese birth control supporters wrote a petition, approached SCAP officials, and gained support from some Japanese high officials to overturn the decision to deny Sanger's entry, to no avail. Sanji seigen fukyūkai [Birth control popularization society], petition to General MacArthur, May 1951, in *Sei to seishoku no jinken mondai shiryō shūsei* [Collection of material related to sex, reproduction, and human rights], ed. Miho Ogino, Yōko Matsubara, and Hikaru Saito, vol. 11 (Tokyo: Fuji Shuppan, 2000), 209.

69. Roger F. Evans, "Rough Notes on RF Mission Conference with General Sams," October 1, 1948, folder 6, box 1, series 600, RG 1.2, RFA, RAC.

70. MacArthur to Hess, June 17, 1950.

71. Eleanor Roosevelt to Douglas MacArthur, March 23, 1950; Marie C. Stopes to MacArthur, April 13, 1950, file: "Birth Control," GS(B) 01272–01276, GHQ/SCAP Records, NDL.

72. Leading Anglo-American scientists publicly denounced Nazi eugenics in the so-called Geneticists' Manifesto, written primarily by Nobel laureate H. J. Muller and issued at the Seventh International Congress of Genetics at Edinburgh in 1939. For the full text of the Geneticists' Manifesto, see "Plan for Improving Population Drawn by Famed Geneticists," *Science News Letter*, August 26, 1939, 131–33. Many studies, however, have complicated the straightforward narrative of the demise of eugenics after World War II and illuminated the continuation of eugenics programs, using semiforced sterilization and contraceptives, across the world. See, for example, Briggs, *Reproducing Empire*; Stern, *Eugenic Nation*; Johanna Schoen, *Choice and Coercion: Birth Control, Sterilization, and Abortion in Public Health and Welfare* (Chapel Hill: University of North Carolina Press, 2005); and Nancy Ordover, *American Eugenics: Race, Queer Anatomy, and the Science of Nationalism* (Minneapolis: University of Minnesota Press, 2003).

73. "Circular Airgram to All American Diplomatic and Consular Offices," January 31, 1952, file: "People, Race, Problems, Programs, Racial Disturbances," FSP 1983, Records of the Foreign Service Posts of the State Department, NDL.

74. Crawford Sams to Kenneth Colegrove, February 20, 1950, file: "Eugenics," PHW 04821, GHQ/SCAP Records, NDL.

75. Daniel Luten to Edward Ackerman, February 23, 1950, folder 2, box 1, Luten Papers.

76. Clarence Gamble to Margaret Sanger, February 20, 1951, folder 3097, box 196, Clarence James Gamble Papers, Francis A. Countway Library of Medicine, Boston.

77. For the significance of birth control experiments in Japan to population control projects in other parts of Asia, see, for example, Connelly, *Fatal Misconception*, 134–41; and Aiko Takeuchi-Demirci, "From Race Biology to Population Control: The Rockefeller Foundation's 'Public Health' Projects in Japan, 1920s–1950s," in *Science, Public Health and the State in Modern Asia*, ed. Liping Bu, Darwin Stapleton, and Ka-che Yip (New York: Routledge, 2011), 113–28.

MODERNIZING DECENCY

Citizens for Decent Literature and Covert Catholic Activism in Cold War America

WHITNEY STRUB

Citizens for Decent Literature (CDL) despised the influx of pornography washing over American society in the 1960s, but its leaders sought to be clear on one thing. "I don't think I am a prude," declared executive director Raymond Gauer at the group's 1962 convention in Chicago; "I think sex is great!" Quickly he added, "But I think it's being abused and I think it's this abuse that should concern all decent people."[1]

This emphatic proclamation bespoke a comfort with modernity jarringly at odds with midcentury public perceptions of antismut activists—a very productive modernism that CDL harnessed to great effect over the course of the late 1950s and 1960s. Even as CDL pioneered new discursive formations, which often emanated directly out of obsolete earlier movements, it adopted the tropes and trappings of evolving social mores to reposition activism against obscenity and pornography not as retrograde but rather as an integral part of red-blooded, decent American citizenship.

By the mid-twentieth century, moral reformers focused on pornography faced significant hurdles. Two legacies haunted them: first, that of Anthony Comstock, pioneer of American obscenity enforcement from the 1870s to his death in 1915 but now regarded as a puritanical Victorian with an unhealthy obsession, and second, that of Catholic pressure groups such as the Legion of Decency and the National Organization for Decent Literature (NODL) whose advocacy of boycotts and censorship had fallen out of public favor with the rise of what historian Andrea Friedman calls "democratic moral authority" in the 1940s, as the broader public increasingly insisted on its right of access to diverse reading materials and films.[2] Even as national anxieties over comics and then pornography circulated throughout the 1950s, no significant activist group was able to mobilize around these issues until Charles

Keating, an ambitious young Cincinnati lawyer, founded Citizens for Decent Literature in 1955.

Though the social origins of CDL were transparently rooted in Cincinnati's conservative Catholic politics, Keating was able to recast antipornography politics for a national audience.[3] Divesting antiporn sentiment of its unsavory cultural baggage, Keating reinvented it as a newly modern endeavor. The language of obscenity law, recently upheld by the Supreme Court in *Roth v. U.S.* (1957), created distance from *censorship*, more closely associated with the Catholic pressure groups. A broadly ecumenical approach, too, secured CDL's nonsectarian stance, as the group engaged in successful outreach to Protestant and Jewish supporters by frequently alluding to such concepts as a shared "Judeo-Christian heritage," which hovered in the background of CDL's insistently nonreligious arguments and resonated with Eisenhower-era national sentiment. Catholic efforts to join in what one historian calls a "tri-faith America" of the mid-twentieth century would successfully culminate in the 1960 election of John F. Kennedy as the first Catholic president. But while earlier Catholic censorship efforts had often been seized upon to justify long-standing anti-Catholic prejudice, CDL helped provide access to the emerging multireligious mainstream—without sacrificing the goals of earlier Catholic censorship and pressure groups.[4]

Bolstering the claim to midcentury ideas of modernism, the discourses of the social sciences that Keating constantly cited resonated with the skillfully calibrated modern administrative state, where much public policy was driven by "expert" analysis. Much of this was surface sheen, a new gloss on what remained a fundamentally Comstockian framework of sexual containment, one that distrusted sexuality as a socially destabilizing force when not channeled into its proper institutional expressions. CDL articulated its moral positions through tropes of psychology, statistics, and history, bestowing upon its arguments the imprimatur of the expert.

Keating's true masterstroke, however, was the implicit endorsement of sexual liberalism, the twentieth-century framework that increasingly celebrated desire and pleasure, at least when contained within heteronormative marital arrangements. The large-scale changes of the early twentieth century, such as increasing urbanization, the rise of advertising and motion pictures, and a new leisure culture, as well as young women's increased employment and thus independence and a burgeoning urban gay culture, all resulted in shifting social mores that highlighted sexuality and pleasure in newly public ways. This shift was already underway in consumer culture, advice manuals, and several branches of theology, but bringing it to antiporn activism was an innovation that helped sever CDL from the legacy of Comstock, who was perceived as repressed and antisex by an American society eager to distance itself from an imagined Victorian past.[5] Thus CDL, though without question a direct extension of midcentury Catholic censorship groups, was able to attain national prominence in the 1960s in part because its ostensibly secular framework played on an emerging American national imaginary that Keating perfectly gauged and exploited and adjusted civic religious sentiment to accommodate both sexual liberalism and the dominant tropes of scholarly and scientific experts. While the group faded from view during the 1970s as Keating turned his attention to the financial sector, CDL set an important precedent for conservative groups in forwarding a sexually conservative, religiously motivated politics through modern, secular language as well as a model for future religious efforts at mainstreaming activism, such as the antiabortion movement. Over a decade before abortion became a fulcrum for the hybrid movement known as the religious (or Christian) right, CDL helped shape a template for using sexual politics to forge Catholic-Protestant political alliances.

THE GHOSTS OF CENSORS PAST

As Charles Keating surveyed the social landscape of the mid-1950s, no figure cast a greater shadow over the politics of pornography and censorship than Anthony Comstock. Comstock had first fused an antipornography moral politics to modern American state-formation in the wake of the Civil War during what historian Gaines Foster calls the "moral Reconstruction."[6] The 1873 Comstock Act that was passed largely at his behest was the first meaningful federal measure against obscenity, and along with the often literal war against polygamy, the banning of lotteries through the mails (upheld by the U.S. Supreme Court in an important 1879 decision), and the lengthy struggle for national Prohibition, the Comstock Act marked a new era in federal moral regulation.

Comstock's rise to power, from local New York City do-gooder to federally appointed enforcer of his own law, signified the ascent of a new regime of sexual politics, spearheaded by bourgeois white Protestants. While the early nineteenth century had seen public, visible prostitution and a bachelor culture that eagerly read erotic "flash press" newspapers in urban America, Comstock's New York Society for the Suppression of Vice, building on and often financed by earlier groups such as the Children's Aid Society and the Young Men's Christian Association, dramatically reshaped American sexual culture, first in New York City and then more widely.[7] Smut was burned, dealers were imprisoned, and a good portion of the distributional pipeline dried up in the face of Comstock's aggressive tactics—which bore the official weight of the federal government, after Comstock was deputized.

Comstock's prose and speech burned with a naked evangelical zeal; obscene material was literally satanic, as Comstock announced in the opening sentence of his chapter on obscene "death traps by mail." Lust, to Comstock, was like "a frightful monster" that "stands peering over the sleeping child, to catch its first thoughts on awakening." Once ensnared in smut's clutches, a child or even adult would undergo "a succession of sickening, offensive, and disgusting scenes" until life itself was "made up of disease, wounds, and putrefying sores." From there, "the peace of the family is wrecked, homes desolated, and society degraded." Clearly pornography was no idle moral trifle.[8] Importantly, Comstock explicitly included contraception and abortion in the legal definition of obscenity, reflecting a commitment to keeping sexuality linked to procreation by suppressing devices that might incite or allow their disentangling; to him, condoms or abortifacients were as obscene as smut.

Though Comstock never wavered or adjusted his beliefs during his four-decade moral reign, the culture around him shifted dramatically in the early twentieth century. The rise of leisure culture, burgeoning independence for young urban women, nascent queer subcultures, the sexual emphases of Freudian psychoanalysis, and an increasingly sexualized mass culture all undermined the rigid Comstockian framework. At the time of his death in 1915, he still commanded a decisive legal, but only a depleted cultural, authority; two decades later, he would be remembered by no less than *Time* magazine as "the late gorilla-like prude," while feminist birth control activist Margaret Sanger, one of his final targets for prosecution, would successfully chip away at his legacy—and his commitment to chaining sex perpetually to procreation—by successfully facilitating the importation of Japanese contraceptives for use by married couples in 1936.[9]

By this point, "Comstockery" had become a term of derision, alongside "bluestockings," "Victorians," and "bowdlerization." Smut publisher Samuel Roth, for instance, openly mocked vice-busting successor John Saxton Sumner by framing his fervid commitment as itself pathological in the parodic 1930 *Diary of a Smut-Hound*.[10] Yet, buoyed by conservative gender politics emanating out of the familial anxieties of the Great Depression, resurgent pro-censorship activism emerged in the 1930s. This time the source was organized Catholicism, in the form of the Legion of Decency, established in 1933 to monitor films, and the National Organization for Decent Literature, which closely followed it and tracked books and magazines. Employing ban lists and boycotts, these groups exercised national power, also reflected in the 1933 adoption of the Hollywood Production Code by the major film studios—a gesture emanating out of several sources but distinctly Catholic in origin and enforced by the Catholic Joseph Breen, Hollywood's chief censor for most of the period between the 1930s and early 1950s.[11]

Despite the cultural power of Catholic suasion, public response to these efforts was frequently negative. Censorship itself took on newly fraught qualities when set against a backdrop of rising European fascism. New York City mayor Fiorello La Guardia, for instance, had amassed broad-based ethnic support from Catholics and Jews, partly by positioning himself against the nightlife-friendly demeanor of predecessor Jimmy Walker. Even as he strong-armed local magazine dealers into abandoning overtly sexualized publications, though, La Guardia hastened to add that there was "not even the remotest suggestion of censorship here" in his ostensible "request" to "kindly conform to the requirements of decency." A wary *New York Times*, meanwhile, cautioned, "We do not want to set up a precedent in suppressing smut that will afterward be used to suppress any ideas that some other Mayor does not like." More pointedly, one local man sent the mayor an irate note, labeling him "prudish" and demanding that he "call off your Gestapo hounds."[12] Catholics in the lay public did not always personally embrace the top-down edicts of church leaders, as James P. McCartin shows in his essay on efforts at progressive Catholic sex education in the early twentieth century, but the papacy remained the public face of Catholicism for most Americans.

Meanwhile, the sectarian nature of the Legion of Decency and the NODL became liabilities as the myth of the American melting pot reached its midcentury zenith. The legion's demand that "the state declare Catholic theology as official dogma," as historian Gregory Black writes, struck a dissonant note with the tenor of the times.[13] And indeed, even the theological underpinnings of the legion and the NODL ran back to the *Index Librorum Prohibitorum*, or "Index of Forbidden Books," which had begun in 1564 "in the heat of Counter-Reformation anxiety about the spread of Protestantism by means of the newly-invented printing press"—hardly a convincing claim to modernity.[14] It was possible to hear echoes of long-standing, and still-prevalent, anti-Catholic xenophobia in an essay like John Fischer's October 1956 *Harper's* article "The Harm Good People Do," with its denunciation of a "little band of Catholics" dictating American culture, but it was equally possible to situate this in a broader imperative toward generic American identity that transcended ethnic or sectarian affiliation. Like Jews and various white ethnic groups such as Italians, Poles, and Germans, Catholics felt a pressure to join in an idealized Americanness—an identity whose unblemished generic quality rarely came to pass but that nonetheless remained a dominant national narrative, particularly in these middle decades.[15] For such Catholic celebrities as radio and television host Fulton Sheen, fame and influence were possible but existed in an ironic state of tension wherein expression that read as too aggressively Catholic often needed to be downplayed.[16] Yet even amid these convoluted social and cultural negotiations, Catholics did often take discernibly more conservative stances on sexual politics than many mainline Protestants, on issues ranging from birth control (increasingly accepted, if only tacitly, in the latter camp) to the controversial Kinsey reports. As well, before the 1970s, opposition to abortion emanated most vocally out of the formal positions of the Catholic Church, with Protestants yet to show great organized interest in the matter.[17]

By the mid-1950s, Catholics were effectively entering the American mainstream, but organized Catholic censorship groups were on the decline, with the backlash against NODL-style tactics well underway and the Hollywood Production Code withering in the face of more openly sexual foreign films and the financial pressures generated by competition from television.[18] Yet even as Catholic censorship joined evangelical Protestant censorship in public disfavor, the emerging geopolitics of the Cold War ensured new religious formations. As American freedom and democracy were contrasted against Soviet totalitarianism and "godlessness," the United States constructed what Jonathan Herzog has called "the spiritual-industrial complex," a massive reassertion of national religiosity, albeit a nondenominational one predicated on an imagined sharing of a "Judeo-Christian" heritage, linked as well through the presumptive whiteness that subsumed ethnic identity in the normative national narrative.[19] Thus came a wave of state-sanctioned religious sentiment: Congress requiring the president to declare a National Day of Prayer in 1952, the insertion of "under God" to the Pledge of Allegiance in 1954, and the adoption of "In God We Trust" as the national motto in 1956, among other measures.[20]

These, then, were the religious frameworks into which the young Charles Keating launched his activism for decent literature. Avoiding being smeared with the brush of sectarian Catholic pressure tactics of the Legion of Decency or the NODL or of neurotic Comstockian antisex prudery while still tapping into the powerful national religiosity that undergirded Cold War policies at home and abroad required delicate rhetorical positioning, much like the Catholic reformers who embraced the languages of democracy and human rights to skirt over their tensions with Protestants and Jews concerning birth control and authoritarianism, as Aiko Takeuchi-Demirci notes in her chapter in this volume. By harnessing ecumenical religious sentiment while adopting the attitudes of sexual liberalism but emphasizing its tight parameters, Keating was able to push Citizens for Decent Literature to the forefront of national debates over obscenity, pornography, and the limits of social toleration.

ECUMENICAL ANTISMUT ACTIVISM

Though Keating gave varied, inconsistent versions of the founding of Citizens for Decent Literature, it most likely began in 1955 among a group of middle-class Catholic men, friends all disturbed by the seemingly unstoppable proliferation of smutty books, comics, magazines, and films in the greater Cincinnati—and broader national—cultural landscape. From the start, it was Keating's project; fervent, articulate, and blandly attractive, the ambitious young lawyer had clearly studied the mistakes of the past as well as the discursive contours of the present.

From the start, Keating was careful to keep CDL free from overt Catholic associations. As the group grew locally in Cincinnati, subtle hints occasionally came through, as when the group mobilized "high school girls" at local St. Mary in early 1958.[21] The next year, a local civil libertarian made the news by accusing CDL of being subject to covert Catholic control and "sectarian censorship," but Keating managed to contain the coverage, in part because of a sympathetic local press.[22] As framed by the Cincinnati newspapers, CDL "embraces a broad representation of civic, business, religious, labor, and medical leaders."[23]

Recurring allegations would continue to haunt CDL throughout its early years, as new chapters formed, often out of the ashes of declining Catholic groups. Some of CDL's early national coverage came from the Catholic magazine *America*, which promoted the group as it grew in the late 1950s.[24] Longtime CDL opponent Hugh Hefner used his *Playboy* magazine as a venue to highlight CDL's Catholic ties in Chicago and elsewhere, calling it "only a front group" for the National Organization for Decent Literature in 1963. This charge had merit, as numerous monitors at the American Civil Liberties Union noted. In one particularly flagrant episode, an observer in Illinois showed how local CDL chapters developed when branch units of Americans for Moral Decency, "avowedly an arm of the NODL in the organizational sense," were able to attract a nominally interfaith membership and then change their name.[25]

Only rarely did Keating himself slip up. In a local Cincinnati missive of 1962, he launched an attack on the ACLU as "fellow travelers" of the "filth merchants" and ended with an uncharacteristic "God is good! Pray!"[26] This attack on the ACLU resulted in serious blowback from several local Catholic leaders who had allowed their names to be used on CDL letterhead; David Thornberry, archdeacon of the Diocese of Southern Ohio, expressed "considerable embarrassment" at being associated with the "not very responsible" letter, while a fellow bishop of Thornberry's called the statement untrue and threatened to withdraw from CDL.[27] While Keating's overwrought letter constituted a rare misstep on his part, the local response reflected the broader Catholic mainstreaming within which CDL calibrated its rhetoric. "I value the work of the A.C.L.U. and agree thoroughly with its basic concerns," Thornberry added, though he hastened to distance himself from the group's positions on obscenity and pornography. Once more, Keating contained damage to CDL's image by keeping the slip out of the press, but the disciplinary message to him from the Catholic leaders was clear and showed the need to carefully tailor CDL's language.

Ultimately more useful than informal press-massaging was Keating's impressive ability to couch CDL in terms that matched the tenor of the times. Psychiatry was on the rise in America, its tropes becoming widely adopted by, and adapted to, the white middle class. "We've gone psychiatric," wrote one observer of American culture already by the 1930s, and indeed, the language of psychiatry resonated deeply with midcentury liberal Protestant theology in particular.[28] From the widely read magazine *Christian Century* to the inspirational lectures and books of *Power of Positive Thinking* author Norman Vincent Peale, the language of psychology became an effective venue to adjust some of the "theological language of morality and grace," as Keith Meador writes, to modern twentieth-century life.[29] CDL carried this language into its own work, pioneering the use of "expert testimony" in local obscenity prosecutions and coordinating such interventions as testimony by University of Cincinnati psychology professor Arthur Bills at a December 1958 obscenity trial. "The tendency to play up and magnify" such acts as "adultery, sadism, masochism, cannibalism, voyeurism (peeping tom), incest, and nymphomania," explained Bills, was "an invitation to the reader to do likewise." Though on cross-examination, Bills conceded that he had neither medical nor legal training, his words nonetheless carried the weight of a certified expert. The trial resulted in the conviction of a local newsstand operator.[30]

This modern approach to the psychological impact of pornography built on the work of other recognized experts: J. Edgar Hoover, director of the FBI, who had asserted links between pornography and perversion since the 1930s; psychiatrist Fredric Wertham, whose arguments against violent, sexualized comics in his 1954 magnum opus, *Seduction of the Innocent*, lent themselves to extrapolation and application to smut; and Senator Estes Kefauver, whose 1955 hearings on pornography had helped spark a national crisis when his commission concluded that smut threatened to pervert American youth. Though the preponderance of medical and psychological experts had great qualms with all three of these figures, the mass media generally highlighted them as the collective voice of truth.[31] Thus Keating could rest his new activist tactics upon a foundation of knowledge claims supported by a reputable consensus of authority figures—and, in contrast to the NODL's reliance on the Vatican as the source of ultimate authority, for CDL, unimpeachably American figures.

In doing so, he comfortably invoked "the Judeo-Christian aspects of our society," an interfaith formulation that emerged in the 1930s as a particularly American counterpart to European fascism. While the phrasing could carry tinges of anti-Catholicism, as historian John McGreevy notes, it could also displace sectarian connotations, and Keating expertly deployed the phrase time and again to register CDL's broad ecumenical character.[32] Yet he never hinged CDL's primary arguments directly upon religion per se, rather relying on this ambient backdrop to build secular arguments based on social science, law, and other powerful discourses of the era. This gave CDL not only a modern hue but a moderate one as well; Keating was quick to note in 1959 that "inroads made by pornography and obscenity in our society" were in danger of pushing the public to "overstep" in response. As he warned, "We could end up with an overpowering return to Victorianism and fantastic Puritanism which would be repulsive to our democratic society."[33] By fighting smut through rational, modern means, then, CDL positioned itself as both a bulwark of decency but also as a preventive measure against extremists. Even the tactics—a perpetually "aroused" citizenry maintaining steady pressure on local prosecutors to pursue obscenity cases instead of the more moblike actions of the past—were routed through state bureaucracies rather than vigilante action.

For these purposes, the 1957 Supreme Court decision in *Roth v. United States* proved a godsend. In the decades since Comstock's reign, the Supreme Court had almost completely dodged the legal question of obscenity, offering no substantive comment after the 1890s. By the mid-1950s, as Senator Kefauver's antiporn crusade resonated with larger Cold War domestic sexual politics, structural tension mounted, with lower courts applying pressure for the Supreme Court to resolve the widely divergent doctrines then circulating. *Roth* was the result, with a convoluted majority opinion by William Brennan that undertook two doctrinal feats: first, removing obscenity from the realm of First Amendment protection, and second, restricting the category to material that, taken as a whole, lacked redeeming social merit and appealed to "prurient interest."[34]

Though Brennan fashioned himself a liberal justice, and indeed *Roth*'s tight restrictions on obscenity law played a formative role in the textual side of the sexual revolution by allowing increasingly graphic sexual content, *Roth* also allowed CDL to distinguish obscenity prosecutions, which pertained to material that, by definition, lacked free-speech claims, from censorship, still a loaded and negative term in the 1950s. Justice Brennan's own Catholic faith had been prominently noted upon his appointment but rarely carried over into public discussions of *Roth*, thus severing it from the legacy of Legion of Decency tactics.[35] Meanwhile, Keating was "vehement" in denying that CDL's platform was censorial in a 1959 interview.[36] As CDL grew from a local Cincinnati group to a sprawling series of local chapters and finally to a formal national organization over the course of 1959, a member of the executive committee described it as "the first national organization of American communities and cities united in a legal effort to regain a standard of decency in literature and the arts."[37] Speaking before Congress the next year, Keating explained, "We do not use lists. We make no attempt to tell retailers what they can or can't sell.... We make no effort to tell our fellow citizens what they can or can't read." Rather, CDL's agenda was to "bring to their attention the obscenity and expect that against this awakened public" the police and prosecutors "will act."[38]

This framework insulated CDL from some of the unsavory connotations of past antismut and pro-censorship groups. Yet in and of itself, it hardly provided a surging rallying cry for Americans anxious about dirty books and magazines infiltrating their homes or the minds of their children. After all, other groups had arisen alongside CDL, paralleling some of Keating's innovations. Crusaders for Decency in Literature formed in 1953, headed by Rabbi Moshay Mann and emphasizing a broadly interfaith membership of Catholics, Protestants, and Jews.[39] The Churchmen's Commission for Decent Publications followed a few years later, also striving for a broad, albeit largely Protestant, base. Both the ACLU and Keating seemed to observe these groups closely; when CDL formed, internal ACLU correspondence suggested that it was explicitly modeled on the Churchmen's Commission.[40]

But these competing groups, while all self-consciously moving beyond sectarian constraints, lacked engaging new methods of confronting smut in the Cold War era. Successful antismut activism had to not only move beyond Comstockian fervor and heavy-handed NODL suppression but also navigate the convoluted currents of American sexual politics, where the advances of sexual liberalism had made it imperative that a group's agenda not be perceived as neurotically anti*sex*. Most Americans voiced no objection to the violent state suppression of queer sexuality. But they had read, or at least read accounts of, Alfred Kinsey and his work, and within the middle class at least, references to Kinsey and Freud served as a form of sexual capital, establishing one's modern sensibilities.[41] Sexual expression that hovered around marriage, sometimes exceeded its borders, and operated for nonprocreative ends had found widespread acceptance, and any antipornography group that wanted to gain traction within the dominant white middle class needed to make clear its acceptance of this new status quo, perhaps best represented in the enormous success of Hugh Hefner's *Playboy*, which debuted in 1953 and found immediate favor among white professional men (and often women).[42]

The secular discourses of law and social science provided the structural framework for CDL's modernized antismut work, a necessary but not sufficient quality to capture public sentiment. For that, Keating delivered the touch that set CDL apart from its competition. While the Crusaders for Decency in Literature encouraged parents to actively guide children's reading as a means of circumventing the appeal of smut and the Churchmen's Commission offered a newsstand "guide-list" that looked dubiously similar to the NODL ban lists of old, CDL instead focused its attention on "perverse" sexuality, thereby targeting an easy mark in Cold War America but also securing the gains made by sexual liberalism in the twentieth century.

SECURING SEXUAL LIBERALISM THROUGH PERVERSION

"But why (I suspect you will ask) dwell upon perversion," Keating posed rhetorically in his stock speech of the early 1960s. After all, "sex deviation has always been with mankind and might well always be." His answer fused Cold War heteronormativity and premonitions of a dark side to what Marshall McLuhan had recently termed "the global village": "never before has there been available to the disseminators of these aberrated, perverted philosophies the system of distribution afforded by our mass media, which acts as a catalytic agent in bringing the utmost depravity within reach of every man, woman, and child within the nation."[43]

If echoes of Comstock undeniably reverberated in the overwrought phrasing, modernism was nonetheless the consistent chord Keating struck. As always, statistics abounded, including citations from Dr. Pitrim Sorokin, Harvard sociologist and CDL member, whose recent *American Sex Revolution* was an apotheosis of Cold War sexual politics, linking "sexual anarchy" at home to the Communist ploys of Soviet Russia.[44] Indeed, linkages between foreign threats and sexual menaces pervaded conservative rhetoric of the era. The American national project was explicitly pinned to procreative heterosexuality, as seen in the Nixon/Khrushchev "kitchen debate" of 1959. In this framework, queer sexuality and other destabilizing forces such as pornography posed a threat to national security, and from the start, Keating's real target was "the world of lesbians, homosexuals, sadists, masochists, and other deviates," which could be reached "the crook of an elbow away from the counter stool" of the average malt shop.[45]

Everywhere in Keating's stock speech, perversion contrasted against "our Judeo-Christian heritage." Physique magazines with erotic pictures of scantily clad men posed a "terribly sad indictment of our society," with their "perfidious footsteps" that might be followed by "poor young lads." *Sexual Problems of a Masochist*, *Strange Flagellation Cults*, and *Famous Transvestites* were just three of the titles singled out, but all of them reflected some form of nonnormative sexuality. While Keating offered little positive vision of what he called "the God-given gift of sex," the space carved out by the glaring contrast to perversion left tacitly clear that CDL had adjusted to the realities of sexual liberalism; Keating might read an extended passage about heterosexual rape from an unnamed pulp novel, but more banal versions of heterosexuality were rarely targeted.

Keating thus secured an expansive space for modern heterosexuality by consistently highlighting its opposite, using perversion as a form of boundary-policing against permissible, if unarticulated, pleasures. Absent from the CDL agenda were the contraceptive devices and information that helped constitute the original Comstock Act, premarital sexual exploration, and nonprocreative marital sexuality—exactly the parameters of sexual liberalism.

This helps explain why, for instance, Keating struck a particularly vindictive note toward "a homosexual group called the Mattachine Society" while testifying in 1963 before a congressional committee on "protecting postal patrons from obscene and obnoxious mail and communist propaganda," the very composition of which reflected the Cold War interlacing of sexual and international politics. While the original Mattachine had indeed been founded by leftist activists with roots in the Communist Party (from which, however, founder Harry Hay had been banished on account of his homosexuality—the Communists being every bit as homophobic as the American mainstream consensus of the era), the group that spearheaded the homophile movement in the 1950s had quickly adopted an assimilationist, patriotic, mainstream approach to gay rights.[46] Keating emphasized its perversity, accusing "these homosexuals" of "saturating America with their propaganda and making wild and bizarre statements." Linking homosexuality and smut, he explained, "If they cannot seduce the youngsters one way or another, they often will tell the readers to get the kids who are intended victims to become interested in obscenity and pornography." In perhaps his most outlandish claim, he also noted, "Every homosexual is a potential homicidal."[47] While this claim resonated with some of the more lurid scare tactics of antigay propaganda, such as the short film *Boys Beware* (1961), it contrasted with the gentler, more therapeutic heteronormativity of liberal Protestants such as author Norman Vincent Peale, who "gravitated toward psychiatry's definition of homosexuality as a psychological disorder rather than a sin or criminal proclivity," as historian Rebecca Davis notes.[48]

These various queer specters—homosexuality, sadism, masochism, fetishism, and more—haunted the speeches and publications of CDL. They saturated the propaganda films CDL produced, with male physique magazines, lesbian pulp novels, and even unerotic homophile periodicals playing central visual roles in *Perversion for Profit* (1962) and *Printed Poison* (1965). In the former film, which grew to become CDL's signature work, narrator George Putnam lingers on gay erotica, using it to reveal "the evil of the breed" of "these misfits, these homosexuals." Again arguing from secular authority, he explains the "terrifyingly sad indictment of our society" that physique magazines pose: "psychiatrists believe that prolonged exposure of even the normal male adult" will irreparably "pervert" him. Youths stood even less of a chance. Rather than a comment on the precariousness of heterosexual normalcy, this signified the destabilizing threat of the queer. That it also represented a clear ceding of moral legitimacy to modern sexual liberalism went continuously unarticulated but tacitly allowed; precisely through the bogeyman of perversion was "normalcy" quietly adjusted.[49]

This antiperversion rhetoric proved enormously successful in the 1960s, as CDL units and membership expanded rapidly, drawing on constituencies that ranged from suburban New Jersey to the rural Bible Belt. Denominational differences mattered little in CDL's discourse of decency; over a decade before the antiabortion backlash to the 1973 *Roe v. Wade* decision would begin formally fusing Catholic and Protestant activism, CDL derived its support from an eclectic membership that included Catholics, mainline Protestants, Southern Baptists, and others. A more important commonality was race, as CDL participated in the broad white racial identity that subsumed ethnic difference, at least in the national imagination.[50] The early anti-Catholic critiques from its opponents, written off as smear campaigns, did nothing to impede its ascent, and by the end of the 1960s, CDL had played a central role in blocking President Lyndon Johnson's attempt to name liberal justice Abe Fortas chief justice of the Supreme Court. Shortly thereafter, Charles Keating was named to the President's Commission on Obscenity and Pornography by Richard Nixon and almost single-handedly undermined the body's three-year investigation by supplanting its social-scientific approach and liberal conclusions with his anecdote-driven minority report that again emphasized the dangers of perversion.[51]

The very cautiousness CDL showed in exercising restraint against displays of religiosity helped secure the group's power, but its origins in mid-century Catholic assimilation showed as new evangelical Christian groups more openly reveled in often flamboyant rhetorical excesses in the late 1960s. Sex education in the public schools proved one fertile site for conservative mobilization, and such pamphlets as Gordon Drake's *Is the Schoolhouse the Proper Place to Teach Raw Sex?* pointed toward a growing evangelical discourse, winning approval and distribution from such groups as the Christian Crusade and the John Birch Society's MOTOREDE (Movement to Restore Decency). While Keating had walked a careful tightrope to avoid charges of extremism, these activists felt no such compunction, as MOTOREDE called sex education a "filthy Communist plot" upon its emergence in 1969.[52] Though CDL had capitalized on its particular historical moment to bring Catholic antismut activism into the mainstream, the social conditions of its origins were rapidly giving way to new religious frameworks.

Charles Keating shifted his attention in the 1970s to finance, capitalizing on the birth of what would later become known as "junk bonds," a fraudulent endeavor that proved catastrophic in the savings and loan scandals of the 1980s and ultimately landed him briefly in federal prison in the 1990s.[53] Without his hands-on leadership, CDL declined in national visibility, surpassed by new groups for sexual conservatism such as the National Federation for Decency, Morality in Media, and the Moral Majority. But while those groups earned credit in the 1980s for forging a new "Christian right" that transcended, if often tenuously, traditional divisions between Catholics and Protestants, much of their work in the Reagan era carried on a legacy set by CDL's earlier work. Some of Keating's carefully positioned legal and social scientific arguments would revert in the hands of the Christian right to a more aggressively evangelical language. But the "Judeo-Christian" coalition that CDL helped forge would prove foundational, if under-recognized, in the coalescence of the new Christian right. By the 1990s, the fiery moralism of Jerry Falwell gave way to the more sophisticated strategies of Ralph Reed, under whose guidance the Christian right returned to secular social-scientific discourse that linked abortion to breast cancer and depression, homosexuality to mental illness, and pornography to the exact same social ills Keating had diagnosed decades earlier.[54] Far from backward-looking Comstockians or retrograde book-burners, CDL in fact helped pave the road for one of the most powerful and significant modern political movements in the United States.[55]

NOTES

My thanks to the editors of this volume and to the participants of the History of Sexuality and Religion writing workshop at Princeton University in 2014, especially Samira Mehta, for sharpening and clarifying my ideas in this piece.

1. "A Typical Talk Delivered by Ray P. Gauer to Those Attending the National Organization Meeting in Chicago, on September 14, 1962," box 2, file: Misc., Youth Protection Committee Records, Utah Historical Society, Salt Lake City.

2. Andrea Friedman, *Prurient Interests: Gender, Democracy, and Obscenity in New York City, 1909–1945* (New York: Columbia, 2000).

3. On Catholic power and prevalence in Cincinnati history, see Roger Antonio Fortin, *Faith and Action: A History of the Catholic Archdiocese of Cincinnati, 1821–1996* (Columbus: Ohio State University Press, 2002).

4. Kevin Schultz, *Tri-faith America: How Catholics and Jews Held Postwar America to Its Protestant Promise* (New York: Oxford University Press, 2011). Schultz covers topics from race relations to education but has very little to say about censorship, decency campaigns, or pornography.

5. Sexual liberalism was a concept pioneered by John D'Emilio and Estelle B. Freedman in *Intimate Matters: A History of Sexuality in America* (New York: Harper and Row, 1988) and further developed in such works as Sharon Ullman, *Sex Seen: The Emergence of Modern Sexuality in America* (Berkeley: University of California Press, 1997), and Kevin White, *The First Sexual Revolution: The Emergence of Male Heterosexuality in Modern America* (New York: New York University Press, 1993), among numerous others.

6. Gaines Foster, *Moral Reconstruction: Christian Lobbyists and the Federal Legislation of Morality, 1865–1920* (Chapel Hill: University of North Carolina Press, 2002).

7. Donna Dennis, *Licentious Gotham: Erotic Publishing and Its Prosecution in Nineteenth-Century New York* (Cambridge, Mass.: Harvard University Press, 2009); Patricia Cline Cohen, Timothy Gilfoyle, and Helen Lefkowitz Horowitz, *The Flash Press: Sporting Male Weeklies in 1840s New York* (Chicago: University of Chicago Press, 2008).

8. Anthony Comstock, *Traps for the Young* (New York: Funk and Wagnalls, 1883), 131–32.

9. "Medicine: Sanger Milestone," *Time*, December 21, 1936; see also Kathy Peiss, *Cheap Amusements: Working Women and Leisure in Turn-of-the-Century New York* (Philadelphia: Temple University Press, 1986).

10. Hugh Wakem, *Diary of a Smut-Hound* (Philadelphia: William Hodgson, 1930).

11. Gregory Black, *The Catholic Crusade against the Movies, 1940–1975* (Cambridge: Cambridge University Press, 1997); Frank Walsh, *Sin and Censorship: The Catholic Church and the Motion Picture Industry* (New Haven: Yale University Press, 1996); Thomas O'Connor, "The National Organization for Decent Literature: A Phase in American Catholic Censorship," *Library Quarterly* 65 (1995): 386–414; Stephen Vaughn, "Morality and Entertainment: The Origins of the Motion Picture Production Code," *Journal of American History* 77 (1990): 39–65; Thomas Doherty, *Hollywood's Censor: Joseph I. Breen and the Production Code Administration* (New York: Columbia University Press, 2009).

12. Letter to mayor, August 20, 1940, Fiorella LaGuardia Papers, New York Municipal Archives; "Decency on the Stands," *New York Times*, August 21, 1940.

13. Black, *Catholic Crusade against the Movies*, 101.

14. Una Cadegan, *All Good Books Are Catholic Books: Print Culture, Censorship, and Modernity in Twentieth-Century America* (Ithaca: Cornell University Press, 2013), 86.

15. John Fischer, "The Harm Good People Do," *Harper's*, October 1956, 14, 16–18, 20; Matthew Frye Jacobson, *Roots Too: White Ethnic Revival in Post–Civil Rights America* (Cambridge, Mass.: Harvard University Press, 2006).

16. On these tensions, see Mark Massa, *Catholics and American Culture: Fulton Sheen, Dorothy Day, and the Notre Dame Football Team* (New York: Crossroad Publishing, 1999).

17. R. Marie Griffith, "The Religious Encounters of Alfred C. Kinsey," *Journal of American History* 95, no. 2 (2008): 349–77; Leslie Woodcock Tentler, *Catholics and Contraception: An American History* (Ithaca: Cornell University Press, 2004).

18. Frank Walsh titles his chapter on this period "Waning Powers" in *Sin and Censorship*, 262–81.

19. Jonathan Herzog, *The Spiritual-Industrial Complex: America's Religious Battle against Communism in the Early Cold War* (New York: Oxford University Press, 2011).

20. As Bruce Dierenfield notes, these were also reactions to internal domestic politics, especially the Supreme Court's growing wall between church and state heralded by the 1947 *Everson v. Board of Education* decision, a landmark in Establishment Clause jurisprudence. Dierenfield, *The Battle over School Prayer: How* Engel v. Vitale *Changed America* (Lawrence: University Press of Kansas, 2007).

21. "They Fight for Decent Literature," *Cincinnati Post*, March 5, 1958.

22. "'Smut Foes' Are Given Scolding," *Cincinnati Enquirer*, March 5, 1959.

23. Alfred Roller, "Cincinnatian Sparked Crusade against Filth," *Cincinnati Post and Times-Star*, June 16, 1959.

24. "Bad Day for Dirty Books," *America*, January 24, 1959, 488.

25. Hugh Hefner, "Playboy Philosophy," *Playboy*, November 1963, 56; Roland Burke to Sidney Kramer, June 16, 1960, box 342, file 2, American Civil Liberties Union Papers, Princeton University.

26. Charles Keating to Citizens for Decent Literature, September 8, 1962, box 2, file: CDL, American Civil Liberties Union of Cincinnati Papers, University of Cincinnati.

27. David Thornberry to Charles Keating, December 12, 1962, and Roger Blanchard to Keating, October 15, 1962, both in ibid.

28. S. H. Kohs, quoted in Elizabeth Lunbeck, *The Psychiatric Persuasion: Knowledge, Gender, and Power in Modern America* (Princeton: Princeton University Press, 1994), 1.

29. Keith Meador, "'My Own Salvation': The *Christian Century* and Psychology's Secularizing of American Protestantism," in *The Secular Revolution: Power, Interests, and Conflict in the Secularization of American Public Life*, ed. Christian Smith (Berkeley: University of California Press, 2003), 69. See also Matthew S. Hedstrom, *The Rise of Liberal Religion: Book Culture and American Spirituality in the Twentieth Century* (New York: Oxford University Press, 2013), 176–213; Rebecca L. Davis, "'My Homosexuality Is Getting Worse Every Day': Norman Vincent Peale, Psychiatry, and the Liberal Protestant Response to Same-Sex Desires in Mid-Twentieth-Century America," in *American Christianities: A History of Dominance and Diversity*, ed. Catherine A. Brekus and W. Clark Gilpin (Chapel Hill: University of North Carolina Press, 2011), 347–65.

30. "Psychologists Give Testimony at Marshall Obscenity Trial," *Cincinnati Enquirer*, December 2, 1958; Joseph Sagmaster, "The Caves of Obscenity," *Cincinnati Enquirer*, December 6, 1958. The conviction was subsequently overturned by the Ohio Supreme Court; "Obscene Literature Law Ruled Invalid," *Cincinnati Post and Times-Star*, May 25, 1961.

31. Whitney Strub, *Perversion for Profit: The Politics of Pornography and the Rise of the New Right* (New York: Columbia University Press, 2011).

32. John McGreevy, *Catholicism and American Freedom: A History* (New York: W. W. Norton, 2003). On the history and historiography of "Judeo-Christian" America, see K. Healan Gaston, "Interpreting Judeo-Christianity in America," *Relegere: Studies in Religion and Reception* 2, no. 2 (2012): 291–304. Also see Schultz, *Tri-faith America*.

33. "Revolt against Smut Due, Cincinnati Man Warns," *Cincinnati Enquirer*, August 29, 1959.

34. Whitney Strub, *Obscenity Rules: Roth v. United States and the Long Struggle over Sexual Expression* (Lawrence: University Press of Kansas, 2013).

35. This link was drawn privately at times, however; as one man wrote to Justice John Marshall Harlan, "I am particularly uneasy about Justice Brennan, a Catholic, who seems to be intent on doing what he thinks is right regardless of what the Constitution says. I hold no prejudice against Catholics as such, but history strongly indicates that in general they are inclined toward an authoritarianism that is incompatible with democracy." A. A Van Petten to Harlan, July 1, 1957, John Marshall Harlan Papers, Princeton University.

36. Alfred Roller, "Cincinnatian Sparked Crusade against Filth," *Cincinnati Post and Times-Star*, June 16, 1959.

37. "War on Smut," *Cincinnati Enquirer*, October 30, 1959.

38. Charles Keating testimony in *Control of Obscene Material: Hearings before Subcommittee on Constitutional Amendments and Subcommittee to Investigate Juvenile Delinquency*, U.S. Senate Committee on Judiciary (Washington: Government Printing Office, 1960), 55.

39. "Children's Welfare Cited in Message to Comics Head," *Albuquerque Journal*, February 23, 1954; "Three Faiths Join Fight on Indecent Literature," clipping, n.d., box 769, folder 16, ACLU Papers.

40. Alan Reitman to Martha Thomas, July 23, 1958, box 778, file 21, ACLU Papers.

41. On reactions to Kinsey, see Elaine Tyler May, *Homeward Bound: American Families in the Cold War Era* (New York: Basic Books, 1988); and Miriam Reumann, *The American Sexual Character: Sex, Gender, and National Identity in the Kinsey Reports* (Berkeley: University of California Press, 2005).

42. On *Playboy*, see Elizabeth Fraterrigo, *Playboy and the Making of the Good Life in Modern America* (New York: Oxford University Press, 2009); and Carrie Pitzulo, *Bachelors and Bunnies: The Sexual Politics of Playboy* (Chicago: University of Chicago Press, 2011).

43. Charles Keating, "Typical CDL Talk," n.d. (ca. 1962), box 2, file: Published Material, Youth Protection Committee Records, Utah Historical Society, Salt Lake City.

44. Pitrim Sorokin, *The American Sexual Revolution* (Boston: Porter Sargent, 1956), 81.

45. For more on the interweaving of antiporn and anticommunist rhetoric, see Strub, *Perversion for Profit*, 30–33.

46. On the Mattachine, see John D'Emilio, *Sexual Politics, Sexual Communities: The Making of a Homosexual Minority in the United States, 1940–1970* (Chicago: University of Chicago Press, 1983); Martin Meeker, "Behind the Mask of Respectability: Reconsidering the Mattachine Society and Male Homophile Practice, 1950s and 1960s," *Journal of the History of Sexuality* 10, no. 1 (2001): 78–116.

47. Charles Keating testimony in *Protecting Postal Patrons from Obscene and Obnoxious Mail and Communist Propaganda*, Hearings before the Committee on Post Office and Civil Service, House of Representatives (Washington: Government Printing Office, 1963), 10, 16, 15. On the Mattachine, see D'Emilio, *Sexual Politics, Sexual Communities*; and Meeker, "Behind the Mask of Respectability."

48. Davis, "'My Homosexuality Is Getting Worse Every Day,'" 347. Sid Davis's notorious *Boys Beware* can be viewed online at https://archive.org/details/boys_beware.

49. *Perversion for Profit* (Citizens for Decent Literature, 1962). This film can be seen at https://archive.org/details/PerversionForProfit.

50. In 1969 a sociologist attended CDL's annual conference and noted the almost entirely all-white nature of the attendees. W. Cody Wilson, memorandum, n.d. (1969), box 42B, folder: Citizen Action Groups, Records of the President's Commission on Obscenity and Pornography, Lyndon B. Johnson Library, Austin, Tex.

51. On the later career of Keating and CDL, see Strub, *Perversion for Profit*.

52. MOTOREDE quote from Luther Baker Jr., "The Rising Furor over Sex Education," *Family Coordinator* 18, no. 3 (1969): 210–17, quoted at 214. While MOTOREDE and Gordon Drake have yet to receive sustained scholarly attention, on sex ed battles involving them see Janice M. Irvine, *Talk about Sex: The Battles over Sex Education in the United States* (Berkeley: University of California Press, 2002); and Natalia Mehlman Petrzela, *Classroom Wars: Language, Sex, and the Making of Modern Political Culture* (New York: Oxford University Press, 2015), esp. 131–57.

53. On this aspect of Keating's career, see Michael Binstein and Charles Bowden, *Trust Me: Charles Keating and the Missing Billions* (New York: Random House, 1993).

54. On the extension of these techniques into the twenty-first century, see Esther Kaplan, *With God on Their Side: George W. Bush and the Christian Right* (New York: New Press, 2005).

55. The historical literature on the Christian right is enormous. A reasonable overview might consist of Steve Bruce, *The Rise and Fall of the New Christian Right* (Oxford: Clarendon Press, 1988); Michael Lienesch, *Redeeming America: Piety and Politics in the New Christian Right* (Chapel Hill: University of North Carolina Press, 1993); Clyde Wilcox, *God's Warriors: The Christian Right in Twentieth-Century America* (Baltimore: Johns Hopkins University Press, 1992); William Martin, *With God on Our Side: The Rise of the Religious Right in America* (New York: Broadway Books, 1996); Daniel K. Williams, *God's Own Party: The Making of the Christian Right* (New York: Oxford University Press, 2011); and Neil J. Young, *We Gather Together: The Religious Right and the Problem of Interfaith Politics* (New York: Oxford University Press, 2015).

FAMILY PLANNING IS A CHRISTIAN DUTY

Religion, Population Control, and the Pill in the 1960s

SAMIRA K. MEHTA

When Alan Guttmacher, president of the Planned Parenthood Federation of America, delivered the 1970 commencement address at Smith College, he closed with a clarion call: "I started this discourse like a historian; I conclude it like a preacher, not a preacher of religion, but a preacher of social behavior."[1] With this comparison, Guttmacher—a secular leader in the birth control movement—borrowed from the power of religious authority to underscore the moral implications of the choice to use birth control. Despite larger societal anxieties that the availability of birth control promoted sexual promiscuity, Guttmacher was not railing against contraception. Instead, he preached the value of fertility control, continuing, "You have been given a singular gift, the gift to control your fertility. It presents a challenge: meet it and use the gift well."[2] Guttmacher was not the only one to frame his work in religious terms. Indeed, the year before, the *New York Times* had referred to him as the "evangelist" of birth control.[3] While both the *New York Times* and Guttmacher were likely speaking metaphorically, the religious implications of the birth control debate were in fact numerous. Throughout the 1960s, the Protestant mainline developed a theology of "responsible parenthood," grounded in scripture and Christian thought that turned the use of contraception within marriage into a site of Christian moral agency.

Responsible parenthood language offered religious responses to scientific advances and scientifically articulated social problems like population explosion. Protestant clergy, nationally and locally, deployed it to encourage birth control among married couples. These leaders were often members of what is called "mainline" Protestantism, encompassing such moderate, non-evangelical denominations such as the United Methodist Church, the

United Church of Christ, the Presbyterian Church (USA), the American Baptist Church, and the Episcopal Church. They eschewed fundamentalism and valued ecumenical cooperation, particularly among liberal white Protestants, building alliances through groups such as the National Council of Churches (NCC). While the number of mainline Protestants has declined since the middle of the twentieth century, in the 1960s mainline Protestants constituted a prominent voice in public conversations. Their influence was so great that much of what historians tend to see as secular was actually deeply inflected with liberal Protestant values.[4] The conversations in these circles were religious and motivated by a certain set of values that were Christian but distinct from the Catholic debates detailed in the chapter by James P. McCartin in this volume.

Specifically, the liberal values that advanced the cause of birth control in the United States seem to exemplify the secular and scientific forces that clashed spectacularly with both Protestant and Catholic values in the twentieth century. But in the years after World War II, individual decision-making about how many children to have and when to have them became a part of being a "good Christian." To justify the need for reproductive control, leading clergy drew from religious tradition and texts, couching support for birth control firmly within existing white middle-class Protestant discourses and creating a new ecumenical position on fertility control and the Christian family. While scholars have largely painted support for birth control and moves toward sexual liberalism as secular, an examination of these responses demonstrates that the so-called secular support for the Pill was, in fact, deeply rooted in Protestant theology.[5]

From interdenominational leadership to laity, mainline Protestants came to frame birth control as the Christian obligation of responsible parenthood. In this model, contraception allowed married couples to control conception and therefore prayerfully make "responsible" decisions about how many children to have, based on societal concerns about the health of the planet, their ability to provide for those children without burdening society, and the number of children they had the emotional capacity to nurture. While teaching about responsible parenthood did not entirely defuse anxieties about sexual promiscuity, important publications like the *Christian Century* and organizations like the NCC provided strong religious support for the use of birth control within marriage. Liberal Protestant support for contraception was not simply, then, a caving to a "practical" fear but a carefully considered understanding of how couples might use science and technology to enact their faith.

This chapter uncovers the religious history of responsible parenthood through four examples. First, Richard Fagley's text *The Population Explosion and Christian Responsibility* provided the first book-length Protestant response to the growing worry that the world population would soon outstrip its resources. While rooted in part in demographic realities, the concept was also highly political—the U.S. interest in population control came at a moment when its own use of resources was skyrocketing.[6] Published in 1960, the same year that the Food and Drug Administration approved the birth control pill, this book presented a Protestant theology of responsible parenthood as a practice for "the stewardship of the earth," thus tying Christian couples' reproductive decisions to global concerns. Second, this chapter examines the treatment of responsible parenthood in the influential interdenominational publications the *Christian Century* and *Christianity and Crisis*, two magazines that captured a series of debates about birth control and responsible parenthood taking place within the Protestant mainline. Third, the work of William and Elizabeth Genné elucidates the NCC's theological support for responsible parenthood and its translation into educational endeavors for clergy and congregations. Finally, private letters to John Rock, one of the doctors who developed the Pill, demonstrate how often Christian laity adopted the language of moral obligation and Christian values in support of birth control.[7] In each of these settings, responsible parenthood provided the underpinnings for Christian education on sexuality and the family.

HISTORICIZING THE CONTRACEPTION DEBATE: MORALITY AND DEFINITIONS OF "SOCIETAL GOOD"

The historiography on both contraception generally and the early years of the Pill specifically has focused on how the principal actors framed the debate in terms of competing anxieties about population control on the one hand and promiscuity on the other. Historians Elaine Tyler May and Beth Bailey have provided rich cultural histories of the development and dissemination of the birth control pill.[8] Their work explains how concerns about women's ability to control their own reproduction were almost entirely absent from early debates surrounding the Pill. Rather, arguments about the availability of the Pill were largely positioned between the practical need to limit population growth and moral concerns about the Pill's potential to increase sex outside of marriage, particularly with respect to middle-class white women.

While scholars reject a causal link between the development of the Pill and changes to sexual behavior, the media made the connection immediately and framed the birth control method within a broader conversation about religion and morality. Advocates for the Pill, including Dr. John Rock, one of its developers and primary spokesmen, argued that "nice girls" would not seek out the Pill and "naughty girls" would have sex anyway, so society might as well mitigate the effects.[9] Skeptics, however, abounded. In 1966, *U.S. News and World Report* asked, "What is the pill doing to the moral patterns of the nation?" The article quoted a wide range of community leaders, including clergy and educators, who believed that the profound severing of sex from reproduction by the Pill was changing sexual morality in the United States for the worse. John Alexander, general director of the evangelical InterVarsity Christian Fellowship, worried, "I think it is certain that the pill will tear down the barriers for more than a few young people hitherto restrained by fear of pregnancy. . . . I am very much afraid that sexual anarchy could develop."[10] Members of the Protestant mainline voiced concerns around sexual permissiveness as well. In 1966, the General Assembly of the Presbyterian Church (USA) worried that the birth control pill could lead to "confusion about the meaning of sex." If the Pill were to become widely available outside of marriage, some religious leaders and university and civic authorities fretted that it would erode the boundaries that confined sex to marriage.[11]

Moral language, however, was not deployed only around fear of promiscuity. Religious liberals applied a very different moral matrix to assess contraception application within marriage. Liberal Protestant leaders advocated for birth control within marriage through the language of population control, morality, and a newly articulated theology of responsible parenthood. They grouped their debates around the questions of who should have access to birth control and to what ends. These leaders therefore used religious logic to illuminate what they saw as a broader social and societal concern. As early as the 1954 annual meeting of the Planned Parenthood Association—six years before the FDA approved oral contraception in the United States—the Reverend Harry Emerson Fosdick, one of the most prominent Protestant voices of the age, framed overpopulation as one of the world's "basic problems," which could be relieved by knowledge of and access to contraception. Fosdick, one of that year's recipients of the Albert and Mary Lasker Foundation Awards in Planned Parenthood, asserted that "the liberty to use contraceptive control [to build] thoughtfully planned, wisely planned homes" was essential to proper family life.[12] In this instance, leading voices in religion and science were hand in hand. Harvard Medical School's John Rock said at the same meeting that if such a pill could be developed, "we could be virtually assured of obtaining the greatest aid ever discovered to the happiness and security of individual families . . . help[ing] to avert man's self-destruction through starvation and war."[13]

Fosdick's remarks, covered alongside Rock's in the *New York Times*, demonstrate that both religion and science offered moral arguments around the end of starvation and war and the promotion of happy and healthy families as among the benefits of the Pill. For Fosdick and other Protestant clergy, the moral obligation of birth control was clear: proper use of contraception had global implications—implications that American Protestants, as part of a nation rich in resources, were obligated to abide by.

In addition to the global good, family planning offered a new scope for maintaining healthy Christian families. Since the early decades of the twentieth century, mainline and liberal Protestant denominations issued statements on ideal Christian family life. These statements held that for the contemporary Protestant with the medical means to do so, family planning was vital because it allowed for the more thoughtful and deliberate creation of Christian families. In 1931, the Committee on Marriage and Home of the United States Federal Council of Churches declared "the careful and restrained use of contraceptives by married people" to be "valid and moral" if used to "safeguard the health of the mother and child" and protect "the livelihood and stability of the family." No direct action came from this statement, but it prompted much public debate and represented a shift from commonly held Protestant condemnation of contraception. That same year, the Congregational Christian General Council announced its support of "voluntary child bearing" to "safeguard the well-being of family and society." In 1954, the Augustana Evangelical Lutheran Churches in America adopted a statement advocating for the spacing of children so as to ensure their proper care and the health of the mother. While the Anglican Communion's Lambeth Conference had condemned birth control in 1908 and 1920, by 1958 it stated that it was a "primary obligation of Christian marriage . . . that children may be born within the supporting framework of parental love and family concern, with a right to an opportunity for a full and spiritually wholesome life."[14] Taking into account factors such as the cost of education, the Lambeth Conference chastised parents "who carelessly and improvidently bring children into the world, trusting in an unknown future or a generous society to care for them."[15] These Protestant denominations connected the freedom to make one's own decisions about reproduction with the responsibility to create and maintain a healthy family.

These statements around contraception were, by and large, policy statements from various denominations, not carefully fleshed-out theologies.

They were intended for the guidance of their own clergy, not an attempt at a pan-Protestant approach to birth control. The synthesis of these movements into a Protestant position on birth control would come in the 1960s, with a monograph by a Congregationalist minister and a statement from the National Council of Churches.

THE POPULATION EXPLOSION AND CHRISTIAN RESPONSIBILITY

While many Protestant voices had deemed birth control moral, either out of concern for population explosion or from a desire to shape the Christian home, Richard Fagley was the first to synthesize these statements into a unified theology of "responsible parenthood," a term that he preferred to either "family planning" or "contraception." A Congregational minister, Fagley served as the representative of the Commission of the Churches on International Affairs at the United Nations, a commission sponsored by the World Council of Churches and the International Missionary Council. His position as an institutional leader in the Christian ecumenical movement allowed him to speak about broad trends in Protestantism in his 1960 monograph, *The Population Explosion and Christian Responsibility*.[16] Through his scholarship, he became one of the most vocal and explicitly Christian advocates for population control.

Responsible parenthood synthesized the appropriate relationship between religion and science, the religiously mandated responsibility to be good stewards of the earth, the responsibilities that Christian parents had for their children, and the autonomy of the Protestant couple in making their own decisions about child rearing into a theologically rooted approach to contraception. In many ways, responsible parenthood was a direct response to Catholic objections to birth control. Responsible parenthood also served as a counterweight to conservative Protestant voices. In responsible parenthood, contraception became both marital and moral, shoring up rather than eroding traditional Christian values.

For Fagley and other liberal Protestants, birth control was not merely tolerated; it was a spiritually conscious act that drew upon medical innovations in order to improve the resources and well-being of the world. Responsible parenthood merged scientific knowledge with religious understanding. Medical knowledge, Fagley wrote, is "a liberating gift from God, to be used to the glory of God, in accordance with his will for men." He continued that this knowledge "affects deeply the size of the family and the rate of population growth, and has therefore created a new area for responsible decision." By linking birth control technology to other widely accepted medical advances, Fagley attempted to undercut the Catholic Church's arguments that birth control was unnatural and immoral. He further equated birth control with other medical advances that lowered the infant mortality rate. The innovation of responsible parenthood was to extend this logic to the more contested idea of birth control, a move that was echoed even by some of the movement's Catholic supporters, including Father John A. O'Brien, a theologian at Notre Dame University. For Fagley, to reproduce without a conscience was not merely ignorant or irresponsible—it was perhaps even "un-Christian."

Responsible parenthood balanced global concerns with individual decision-making by Christian couples. Fagley and others responded to what they believed was a global crisis of exploding population and decreasing food supplies and recommended contraception as a necessary form of population control. While the individual Protestant was to make decisions in a global context of population growth, proponents of responsible parenthood were careful not to dictate individual family choices in a stringent fashion. Fagley noted that no council or commission had the right to dictate to individual churches; to do so was counter to the "ethos of the Reformation and to the nature of the present fellowship of Churches." The ecumenical statements should be read as recommendations—not mandates—to church leaders. The Protestant consensus around responsible parenthood rested on the fact that no religious leader or institution framed it as a "substitute for the responsibility of husband and wife to make their own prayerful and conscious decisions in this area." The potential parents needed to determine the nature of their "vocation," and this was a conclusion over which "no court of the church has comparable jurisdiction."[17] A Protestant theological consensus, in other words, could not be used to compel individual Christians.

Fagley's defense of individual decision-making had implications for how he viewed the role of the state. Christians, he argued, can only "condemn" any state "coercion" around family planning. This criticism denounced state-run eugenics programs that still operated in the 1960s.[18] In addition to these secular concerns, Fagley's strong opposition to state-mandated birth control was also an implicit criticism of the Catholic Church. Fagley, like other Protestant critics of the Catholic Church, objected to a religious institution's dictating moral choices either to a congregation or to an individual Christian. Thus the argument that the ecumenical Protestant consensus could not compel congregations to take particular stances around contraception, any more than clergy could dictate to a couple how to enact their vocation as parents, functioned as a critique of the Catholic Church's stand—both on birth control and on religious authority.

Despite these concerns about coerced forms of birth control, Fagley's theology of responsible parenthood still retained a subtle eugenic cast. To be sure, explicit racialized language was strikingly absent from the theological arguments that mainline Protestant clergy presented to their flocks about the need to control reproduction. However, by framing birth control in terms that advocated for the "moral good" of society as a whole, Fagley and others implicitly privileged a certain type of family. This family—middle class, typically white, and residents of North America and Europe—was the focus of this Protestant ethic of responsible family planning. At the margins of this discourse was another type of family—one located in Latin America, Africa, or Asia, all places that birth control advocates named as most vulnerable to global shortages. These references implied a racialized dynamic that authors like Fagley seem to have carefully avoided stating directly, perhaps out of sensitivity to the postwar links between birth control and eugenics (like the ones that Aiko Takeuchi-Demirci analyzes in this volume). But the coded message belied the supposed neutrality and race-blind rhetoric: population control was supposed to be for everyone, but the problem was located in the nonwhite developing world while the answer was found in the prudent choices of white American families. Thus, the flipside of the religiously inflected language of birth control, population control, and morality reiterated an idealized family that was implicitly both white and middle class.[19]

THE *CHRISTIAN CENTURY* AND THE NATIONAL COUNCIL OF CHURCHES

Protestant readers likely encountered the concept of responsible parenthood in the *Christian Century* (*CC*), the most prominent publication of the Protestant mainline. Its centrality to postwar liberal Protestant conversations can hardly be overstated, with *Newsweek* calling it "the most important organ of Protestant opinion today" in 1947 and *Time* referring to it as "Protestantism's most vigorous voice."[20] The multiple iterations of the conversation in the *CC* demonstrate how widely support for birth control circulated. While these opinions reflected the religious elites, the *CC* could also be found in public libraries and in homes and churches affiliated with liberal and moderate expressions of Protestantism. While *Christianity and Crisis* never achieved the circulation or establishment support enjoyed by the *CC*, it also served liberal Protestants across the denominations. Although its coverage of the population crisis and birth control came later and was less extensive, its pages also demonstrated clear support for the Christian responsibility to use contraception and concern about the expanding population.

The Protestant mainline's primary print venue strongly promoted a "pan-Protestant" theology of population control through birth control. In 1960, the year the Pill received FDA approval, the *CC* offered a number of commentaries on birth control, including descriptions of the "Roman Catholic View" against contraception and the "Protestant Views" in favor of the birth control movement.[21] It also printed an article titled "Family Planning Is a Christian Duty," reporting on a World Council of Churches' call to systematically address the relationship between family planning, population explosion, and starvation. When Fagley published his treatise on responsible parenthood, the *CC* was happy to endorse his work, saying that "his treatment of responsible Christian parenthood—'A Christian doctrine whose time has come and which calls for church and personal support'—should rally the Protestant conscience and greatly hasten the achievement of a Protestant Consensus."[22] The *CC*'s coverage joined with the Protestant views and likewise endorsed the use of birth control by married couples. The *CC* not only offered editorials praising Fagley's work but also published a piece by theologian Paul King Jewett arguing that "if we believe that the decrease of infant mortality and the higher valuation of a woman's life are pleasing to God, then we cannot also believe it is pleasing to God that natural fecundity should run its unimpeded course, with its wretched train of poverty, suffering, and degradation." It is, he argued, "one thing to replenish the earth" but quite another to "burden the earth with an irresponsible prodigality."[23]

The *CC* often gave coverage to the Catholic Church's views on birth control and the Catholic laity's dissent with church doctrines in order to highlight that "good" and "socially responsible" Catholics shared Protestant hopes that birth control could curb population control. A 1960 article noted that 29 percent of Catholic physicians in a recent poll "disagree with their church's stand and will recommend and fit contraceptive devices when requested to do so by patients," with another 24 percent agreeing with the church's opposition but either providing contraceptives to patients anyway or sending them to other doctors without an objection and 47 percent refusing to help women obtain contraception in any form.[24] The same article noted that the Catholic Church applied a great deal of pressure on its physicians to act in accordance with church teachings. A 1961 article suggested that Catholic clergy and laity were trying to find ways for the church to "adjust itself to the population problem."[25] In support of those efforts, the magazine lent its pages to Catholic theologians writing to persuade the church to accept birth control within marriage, at least in some cases. For instance, in 1963, the CC printed an article by Father John O'Brien calling for Catholics to practice religious tolerance toward Protestants and to cease attempts to block birth control legally. O'Brien argued that the "revolution in Protestant ethical and religious thought" meant that Catholics could no longer assume that their objections to birth control reflected dominant Christian thought.[26] Finally, the CC covered Catholic debates over contraception through the Second Vatican Council (which did not resolve the question of the Pill) and beyond. Overall, the CC aimed to solidify its own distinctly Protestant approach while drawing both support from sympathetic Catholic voices and distinctions from the institutional Catholic position.

The progressive ecumenical journal *Christianity and Crisis* circulated similar views, and its coverage suggested that these opinions had widespread appeal among white liberal Protestants. *Christianity and Crisis* published a piece by Fagley in its Winter 1960 issue and continued in subsequent years to cover issues of population explosion, responsible parenthood, and contraception.[27] Where the articles in the CC offered an expository tone, authors in *Christianity and Crisis* seemed to speak instead from consensus opinion. In the mid-1960s, the magazine published a handful of such pieces, including critiques of the Catholic Church's stance on birth control. Such articles argued that the church's position was at odds with its antipoverty work and that the anti-contraception stance would be damaging to Catholic-Protestant collaboration.[28] All of the articles, however, assumed an audience that supports family planning—the articles focused, rather, on how to achieve it and how to understand Catholic failure to support contraception and therefore population control.

This emergent understanding of population control, responsible parenthood, and Christian values was solidified in a statement by the NCC on birth control titled "Responsible Parenthood," which appeared in the CC's March 29, 1961, edition. In the 1950s and early 1960s, the NCC served as a leading Christian ecumenical organization, reaching beyond the Protestant mainline to include evangelical, Orthodox, and Peace churches, though its often left-leaning views politically aligned it most closely with its mainline members. Because the organization took public policy and Christian social engagement as a central concern, population explosion became a key focus. The two-page statement that was adopted by its general board established the contemporary need for population control and warned that increased life expectancy and lower child mortality would combine to strain the planet's resources. The NCC then spotlighted as a solution the newly available birth control pill, which gave couples the ability to control their childbearing.[29]

Birth control, the NCC argued, enabled contemporary Christians to strike an appropriate balance between sexual desire, the desire for children, and fulfillment of their vocational work beyond the home. In a language of morals and rights, the statement then articulated clearly the reasons for family planning, citing both scripture and the teachings of various member churches. The organization included the right of the child to be wanted, loved, educated, and given a Christian education.[30] The NCC statement reflected its limited gendered assumptions about the place of women; it imagined women only as the "mother-wife" and offered no other image of them. More, the NCC did not entertain that women might want birth control in contexts other than marriage. Like Fagley and others, the NCC advanced concerns that linked sexuality with marriage while promoting population control.

Birth control, moreover, served the moral purpose of preventing abortion. While the NCC endorsed birth control via methods like the Pill, it did not go so far as to condone abortion. In fact, in the 1961 NCC Statement on Birth Control, it explicitly noted that "the destruction of life already begun cannot be condoned as a method of family limitation."[31] The NCC hoped that underscoring the Christian responsibility to use contraception would decrease the possibility of an accidental pregnancy and the need for an abortion.

Responsible parenthood reached beyond the elite leadership of the Protestant mainline. William Genné, director of family ministries for the NCC from 1957 to 1975, conducted outreach and training based on the principles of the NCC statement on responsible parenthood. In 1961, the Canadian and National (USA) Councils of Churches sponsored a conference that was attended by more than five hundred administrators and opinion shapers in thirty-three denominations across fifty-seven states and provinces. The conference had a two-pronged mission: to face failures, confusion, and ambiguity in Christian practices around sex and family life and to bring the resources of science to bear on that discussion. Both of these conversations were to be framed within the context of biblical thought. The NCC's statement of responsible parenthood was axiomatic for attendees. Participants opened each day with a reading from scripture, participated in three-hour-long work groups, and formulated "positive proposals" to the participating churches that would structure their own policies and outreach programs around sex and family life.[32] The conference covered a range of topics, such as "factors in the formation of marriage," "contemporary sexual behavior," and "facts and issues in family planning." Family planning was treated as central to the conversation, on a par with the nature of marriage and Christian responses to sexual behaviors like infidelity. Genné and his wife, Elizabeth, published highlights from the conference in *Christians and the Crisis in Sex Morality*, a "faithful reflection of the spirit of the North American Conference on Church and Family."[33]

Protestant conversations about contraceptive use veered into discussions about sex education. The Gennés compiled information arguing that low income and a low level of education were the strongest detriments to use of contraception and that the use of medical birth control among Protestants rose in tandem with level of education. They pointed to reports about the prevalence of unwanted children in low-income families and drew from research that warned of young people who were raised in contexts where adults demonstrated limited control over their own reproduction.[34] These reports understood working-class (and often nonwhite) families as in particular need of birth control and sex education. The authors argued that Christians who had "managed to learn how to combine, in [their] thinking hearts and spirits and actions, all the functions and meanings of sex" were best equipped to teach youth about healthy sexuality.[35]

To undertake the teaching of sexuality and family planning within a Christian context, the NCC (through the Gennés) began to develop a program disseminated through churches and chaplains. This program held that couples should be encouraged to wait two years after marriage before having their first child, so as to ensure that the marriage was stable and that they were ready for parenthood. To counter the fear that the presence of birth control might result in declining moral standards, the NCC's sex education programs emphasized to young people that sex is a privilege reserved for marriage. These ideas were disseminated through a variety of means. The Gennés called for ministers to remind their congregations of the obligation to plan their families and encouraged congregations to offer information and support to congregants. Also, Protestant hospital chaplains were instructed to make sure that all non-Catholic patients had contraceptive information available to them on a par with other medical services. They advised that Protestant chaplains in the armed services should aid military wives in obtaining contraceptive services.[36] Protestant missionary services, they believed, should include contraceptive services in their offerings to "suppressed minority migrants and American Indian groups."[37] As director of family ministry, Genné traveled to churches and other community groups, particularly in the Northeast, giving them tools to implement these agenda items.

Family Planning Is a Christian Duty

RESPONSIBLE PARENTHOOD AND CHRISTIAN
LAITY: RESPONSES AND PERSPECTIVES

Even as leaders in American Protestantism articulated nuanced understandings of responsible parenthood in light of the burgeoning population, lay Christians also joined the debate. When Catholic physician and Harvard Medical School professor John Rock became a public spokesman for the birth control pill, dispensing advice about its role as a central weapon in the battle against population explosion, he received both fan mail and sharp criticism. Often, the critical letters were from Catholics who referenced Rock's own Catholicism. One typical response came from a woman who wrote to chastise Rock for his association with Planned Parenthood. She argued, "As a Catholic—how could you believe that you have a right over life [and] death? God alone has this right [and] by cooperating with an organization that recommends murder through Birth Control you advocate murdering of babies God wills in the world."[38]

Letters like this, though, were in a distinct minority. Most correspondents commented on the Pill as a tool of social good or on its impact in their own lives. Rock's laudatory letters often came from people who wrote about their Christian faith. Protestant clergy wrote to Rock, seeking advice for their flocks on the practice of "voluntary parenthood."[39] Other letters came from laity who worried about unchecked population growth and emphasized that religious groups could promote contraceptive use to solve this problem. One man commented, "I hope you will continue your vigorous program and campaign on birth control. The world today has the problem of an exploding population. This is a problem educated men and all religious groups must solve and solve soon."[40] Other correspondents believed that Catholic proscriptions against birth control were fueling the world's population problem.

Although a couple shared the Christian responsibility to practice contraception, women, more than men, wrote to Rock thanking him for the role that the Pill played in their lives. These letters of gratitude did not necessarily address responsible parenthood directly but implicitly spoke to its tenets. For example, one thankful mother wrote, "As the mother of two boys, thirteen months apart, I wish to express my gratitude to you and your staff for making the oral contraceptive pill. I am not Catholic, but my husband is, and so naturally we used the rhythm method. After the birth of our second child, who was five weeks premature, my husband consulted the priest who married us. He told my husband that by all means we should use the pill and that we should use it until we wanted another child." For this couple, contraception meant relief. She continued, "The joy and peace that is in our home now is wonderful. Thank you again and may God Bless you and your work."[41] This young mother's appreciation begins to point us in the direction of contraception as transformative of personal life—a message that was strikingly absent from early Protestant documents in favor of contraception but that would become increasingly prominent in future conversations.

These letters present birth control in radically different terms than are traditionally considered. Contraception here is not merely acceptable; instead, it is divinely given and presented as a necessary and wholly Christian obligation. By explicitly divorcing birth control from the language of women's rights, these women make contraception a religious right. While the assertion that birth control was antithetical to a divine concept of the creation of human life was certainly present, it was a remarkable—and perhaps even radical—reformulation that cast contraception as a Christian concept on its own and as one to which the laity, as much as clergy and theologians, laid claim.

CONCLUSION

Focusing on the language of responsible parenthood shows that, as much as the Pill caused moral anxiety in some quarters, it also provided a new landscape for Protestant moral agency. Leaders at the highest levels of mainline Protestant ecumenical cooperation encouraged making deliberate and prayerful decisions about when to have children, decisions that took into account the health of one's own marriage and finances, the rights of children and one's capacity to fulfill those rights, and broader social issues, particularly population explosion, as a central responsibility of Christian marriage. Protestant leadership argued that technological advances, including vaccinations, antibiotics, and birth control, created the obligation to use them for social good. They then justified the use of contraception as a social good based on scientific evidence of the dangers posed by a rapidly expanding population and on doctrine from various denominations and scriptural interpretation of both family life and "stewardship of the earth."

These elite voices spread this new theology of responsible parenthood through the pages of publications such as the *Christian Century* and through the efforts of the National Council of Churches. In these venues, leadership spelled out responsible parenthood, tracked developments around birth control availability, and, perhaps most important, made suggestions for how churches, parish ministers, and chaplains might advance access to birth control while disseminating the understanding of sexuality supported by the NCC's broader teaching.

While responsible parenthood resulted in strong mainline support for birth control, Protestant elites, in order to create a particular form of "desirable" American family, were trying to create middle-class families who would be able to use fertility control for upward mobility. While race was rarely explicitly mentioned (and when it was, authors often decried using eugenics against racial minorities), race was implicit in the conversation—Africans and Asians were depicted as the people most likely to be hurt by an expanding population and therefore were implied to be most in need of birth control. While the responsible parenthood discourse sought to distance itself from racially motivated eugenics, the distance was not as great as might have been hoped for: arguments about social class in the United States often noted the high percentage of African Americans among the "lower class" of people whom responsible parenthood advocates hoped to reach. The goal of responsible parenthood was, notably, care of children and the earth, not egalitarianism or increased sexual freedom for women. Protecting the health of wives and mothers was important. Giving women more control over their fertility for their professional advancement was not.

As the letters that average Americans sent to John Rock demonstrate, the ideas of responsible parenthood did inform the moral choices of some American Protestants. While not all Americans supported the use of contraception, many wrote to Rock noting their faith and their concern for the expanding population on God's earth. Women, in particular, also expressed gratitude for the ability to delay their families until their households were financially stable. Notably, these letters reveal that the logic and values of responsible parenthood had become part of the theological and reproductive worldview of American believers. By connecting their intimate actions and familial decisions to broader social concerns, sexual relationships gained a new moral agency in which birth control was a moral and social good. The letters to Rock, however, also started to hint at what birth control pills would mean in the lives of American women. The ability to disconnect sex and procreation provided immense psychological relief to the women who wrote to Rock. That relief, however, was not the ultimate goal of the responsible parenthood movement.

Understanding responsible parenthood changes the way that historians view the role of religion in the early days of birth control. Clergy support for the birth control pill and the tenets of responsible parenthood provide a far more nuanced view of the impact of the Pill on American society. Similarly, demonstrating that responsible parenthood was part of a larger social mission with far-reaching social implications uncovers a previously unexplored arena of Christian social agency made possible by the advent of the Pill. In theory, any form of contraception might have provided this opportunity, but the birth control pill is unique in its ability to separate the act of contraception from the act of sex, making it a more appealing type of contraception. This view highlights the importance of sex within marriage outside of the context of parenthood in mainline Protestantism and gives us a clearer understanding of the intersections between religion, science, and sex in the mid-twentieth century.

NOTES

I conducted much of the research for this project with support from the New England Regional Fellowship Consortium. I would like to thank the group and its member institutions, particularly the Sophia Smith Collection and Smith College Archives; the Schlesinger Library at the Radcliffe Institute for Advanced Study, Harvard University; and the Center for the History of Medicine, Harvard University. I completed the article as a David B. Larson Fellow at the John W. Kluge Center of the Library of Congress. I appreciate the space to think and write that the Kluge Center afforded. I would also like to thank Gillian Frank, Heather White, Bethany Morton, Whitney Strub, Natalia Mehlman Petrzela, Rebecca Davis, Wallace Best, Judith Weisenfeld, and Anthony Petro for feedback at various points in the writing process.

1. Alan F. Guttmacher, "1970 Commencement Address to Smith College," May 31, 1970, 80. Cla, Smith College Archives.

2. Ibid.

3. David Dempsey, "Dr. Guttmacher Is the Evangelist of Birth Control: Dr. Guttmacher Is Gambling that Planning and Freedom Are Not Incompatible," *New York Times Magazine*, February 9, 1969.

4. For more information on the Protestant shaping of the American secular, see Steven M. Tipton, *Public Pulpits: Methodists and Mainline Churches in the Moral Argument of Public Life* (Chicago: University of Chicago Press, 2008), 34–67, 146–85; Janet Jakobsen, "Sex + Freedom = Regulation: Why?," *Social Text* 84–85 vol. 23, no. 3–4 (Fall–Winter 2005): 285–308; Janet R. Jakobsen and Ann Pellegrini, *Love the Sin: Sexual Regulation and the Limits of Religious Tolerance* (Boston: Beacon Press, 2004); Matthew S. Hedstrom, *The Rise of Liberal Religion: Book Culture and American Spirituality in the Twentieth Century*, repr. ed. (New York: Oxford University Press, 2015).

5. For a nuanced view of Catholic responses to contraception, see Leslie Woodcock Tentler, *Catholics and Contraception: An American History* (Ithaca: Cornell University Press, 2009).

6. For more on the concept of population explosion and its political ramifications, see Matthew James Connelly, *Fatal Misconception: The Struggle to Control World Population* (Cambridge, Mass.: Belknap Press of Harvard University Press, 2008); and Betsy Hartmann, *Reproductive Rights and Wrongs: The Global Politics of Population Control*, rev. ed. (Boston: South End Press, 1995).

7. For work on John Rock's navigation of his Catholicism and his work on the birth control pill, see *The Time Has Come: A Catholic Doctor's Proposals to End the Battle over Birth Control* (New York: Knopf, 1963); and Margaret Marsh and Wanda Ronner, *The*

Fertility Doctor: John Rock and the Reproductive Revolution (Baltimore: Johns Hopkins University Press, 2008).

8. Elaine Tyler May, *America and the Pill: A History of Promise, Peril, and Liberation* (New York: Basic Books, 2010); Beth Bailey, *Sex in the Heartland* (Cambridge, Mass.: Harvard University Press, 2002).

9. May, *America and the Pill*, 81.

10. "The Pill: How It Is Affecting U.S. Morals, Family Life," *U.S. News and World Report*, July 11, 1966, http://www.pbs.org/wgbh/amex/pill/filmmore/ps_revolution.html.

11. May, *America and the Pill*; Bailey, *Sex in the Heartland*.

12. "Bar to War Seen in Birth Control: Harvard Professor, Fosdick View Simple Contraceptive as Ending H-Bomb Fears," *New York Times*, May 7, 1954.

13. Ibid.

14. Richard M. Fagley, *The Population Explosion and Christian Responsibility* (Oxford: Oxford University Press, 1960), 194–96.

15. Ibid., 203–5.

16. Fagley, *Population Explosion and Christian Responsibility*; Richard M. Fagley, "A Protestant View of Population Control," *Law and Contemporary Problems* 25, no. 3 (1960): 470–89.

17. Fagley, "Protestant View of Population Control."

18. Kevin Begos et al., *Against Their Will: North Carolina's Sterilization Program and the Campaign for Reparations*, paperback ed. (Apalachicola, Fla.: Gray Oak Books, 2012). According to Begos, thirty states had eugenics-based sterilization laws for much of the twentieth century, with two-thirds of them in effect until the 1970s.

19. The debates around contraception in Fagley's writings, in the pages of the *Christian Century* and *Christianity in Crisis*, and in the National Council of Churches focused on the need for "responsible parenthood" among their perceived demographic of their readers and members, which was white, Protestant, and middle or upper class. For more on the racial implications of population explosion and the reproductive realities of black and brown women who were not trusted to be "responsible parents," see Laura Briggs, *Reproducing Empire: Race, Sex, Science, and U.S. Imperialism in Puerto Rico* (Berkeley: University of California Press, 2002); Dorothy Roberts, *Killing the Black Body: Race, Reproduction, and the Meaning of Liberty* (New York: Vintage, 1998); Alexandra Minna Stern, *Eugenic Nation: Faults and Frontiers of Better Breeding in Modern America* (Berkeley: University of California Press, 2005); Alondra Nelson, *Body and Soul: The Black Panther Party and the Fight against Medical Discrimination*, repr. ed. (Minneapolis: University of Minnesota Press, 2013); Begos et al., *Against Their Will*; and Rebecca M. Kluchin, *Fit to Be Tied: Sterilization and Reproductive Rights in America, 1950–1980*, paperback ed. (New Brunswick: Rutgers University Press, 2011).

20. Elesha J. Coffman, *The Christian Century and the Rise of the Protestant Mainline* (New York: Oxford University Press, 2013), 6. For more on the circulation and distribution of the *Christian Century*, see Coffman's work, particularly her introduction.

21. John R. Von Rohr, "Christianity and Birth Control," *Christian Century* 77, no. 42 (October 1960): 1209–12.

22. Ibid.

23. Paul King Jewett, "A Case for Birth Control," *Christian Century* 78, no. 21 (May 1961): 651–52.

24. "Catholic Physicians and Birth Control," *Christian Century* 77, no. 4 (January 1960): 110, 112.

25. "Catholics Seek Birth Controls within Church's Teachings," *Christian Century* 78, no. 2 (January 1961): 36–37.

26. John A. O'Brien, "Let's End the War over Birth Control," *Christian Century* 80, no. 45 (November 1963): 1362.

27. Richard M. Fagley, "Christian Approaches to Responsible Parenthood," *Christianity and Crisis* 19, no. 24 (January 25, 1960): 211–15.

28. John Leo, "Rethinking Birth Control," *Christianity and Crisis* 25, no. 13 (July 26, 1965): 160–62; John C. Bennet, "Disastrous Encyclical," *Christianity and Crisis*, 28, no. 16 (September 30, 1968): 214–15.

29. "Responsible Parenthood," *Christian Century* 78, no. 13 (March 1961): 396–98.

30. Ibid.

31. Ibid.

32. Elizabeth Genné and William H. Genné, *Christians and the Crisis in Sex Morality: The Church Looks at the Facts about Sex and Marriage Today* (New York: Association Press, 1962), 10.

33. Ibid., 9.

34. Ibid., 86.

35. Ibid.

36. Ibid., 89–90.

37. Ibid., 90.

38. Anonymous Catholic woman, "Letter to John Rock from a Catholic Woman," n.d., HMS c161 22:37, Center for the History of Medicine, Francis A. Countway Library of Medicine, Boston, Mass.

39. "Fan Mail: 1960s" folder, HMS c161 22:28, ibid.

40. Anonymous, "Letter to John Rock from a Man [name redacted]," January 28, 1962, HMS c161 22:28, ibid.

41. Anonymous woman, "Letter to John Rock from a Woman Married to a Catholic Man," March 19, 1965, HMS c161 22:37, ibid.

FROM WOMEN'S RIGHTS TO RELIGIOUS FREEDOM

The Women's League for Conservative Judaism and the Politics of Abortion, 1970–1982

RACHEL KRANSON

While twenty-first-century opponents of reproductive rights have adopted the rhetoric of "religious freedom" to justify their refusal to provide medical coverage for contraceptives, an earlier generation of religious actors leveraged the guarantees of the First Amendment for quite opposite purposes. In 1982, for instance, the Women's League for Conservative Judaism, then the largest organization of religiously identified Jewish women in the United States, declared that "the principle of Separation of Church and State guaranteed by our constitution" made it incumbent upon their constituency to support legal abortion. The decision over whether or not to terminate a pregnancy, they argued, was a matter of "religious values" and the responsibility of the "religious sector." The state, they argued, held no proper authority to restrict the procedure.[1]

This essay traces the Women's League for Conservative Judaism's engagement in the issue of reproductive rights during the 1970s and early 1980s, as the hardened ideological positions that would later come to characterize the national debates over abortion were only just beginning to form. Members of Women's League first championed legal abortion in 1970, defending their position through expressly feminist arguments upholding reproductive autonomy as a woman's civil right. While they never backed down from their support for legal abortion, the political shifts of the late 1970s and early 1980s compelled them to develop a new language through which to discuss the issue. By 1982, they began to justify their stance on abortion through the principal of religious freedom rather than through an endorsement of women's rights.

Reframing access to abortion as a matter of religious freedom offered Women's League members a way to articulate their support for the procedure without publicly endorsing the notion of women's reproductive autonomy, an idea that had become increasingly controversial over the course of the 1970s. The late 1970s saw the "religious right," a coalition of socially conservative activists dominated by evangelical Protestants, emerge as the central religious voice in the national debates over reproductive rights. As much of the American public began to view a particularly right-wing, Christian opposition to abortion as a universal religious principle, the leaders of Women's League struggled to show that their backing of legal abortion did not conflict with their religious commitments. Reconfiguring access to abortion as a religious right enabled them to present their stance on abortion as a component of their spiritual worldview rather than as a capitulation to secular, feminist ideals.[2]

That an organization like Women's League, whose members overwhelmingly favored legal abortion and largely sympathized with the feminist movement, retreated from discussing abortion as a woman's right demonstrates the strong influence that the anti-abortion activism of the Christian right had on less conservative, even non-Christian, religious groups. The story of how this organization negotiated the issue of abortion, therefore, reveals the surprisingly broad impact of late twentieth-century religious conservativism.

Drawing attention to Jewish participation in the debates over abortion also corrects certain distortions that have emerged in the scholarship on reproductive rights in the United States. Much as Rebecca L. Davis cautions us in this volume against using the term "religious" to refer to ideas that are particularly Christian, I have also found that both the scholarly and popular writing on abortion has suffered from the tendency to assume that all religious Americans share conservative Christian views on reproductive rights. With few exceptions, scholars have considered the impact of religion only on the conservative Christians who oppose the procedure. Not only does this erase the strong convictions of pro-choice Protestants and Catholics from the historical record, but it also entirely ignores the involvement of Jews, and indeed all non-Christians, in national discussions over abortion. Including American Jews in this conversation complicates what has too often been presented as a simplistic dichotomy between conservative Christian anti-abortion activists and nonreligious backers of women's reproductive rights. Moreover, showing how some representatives of American Judaism struggled to articulate a religious rationale for legal abortion reveals the continued power of Christian leaders to delimit the public terms of religious discourse, even in a country with no established religion.[3]

The Christian right's outsized influence on all religious groups in the late twentieth century hinged on its leaders' advocacy for renewed legal regulations on sexuality and reproduction. Indeed, the assumption that religious authorities ought to shoulder the responsibility of monitoring sexuality has deep roots in American history. Early attempts to separate religion from the public state placed religion—at least ideologically—within the same private domain in which all sexual activity and, until the twentieth century, all respectable women were supposed to remain. While this configuration diminished the direct influence of religious leaders in certain areas of public life, it increased their cultural authority over sexuality and other presumably private matters. As a result, religious leaders in the United States have long held significant sway over which sorts of sexual acts ought to be considered proper and licit in both social and legal arenas.[4]

In the late 1970s and early 1980s, these assumed linkages between religion and sexuality offered right-wing Christian leaders the chance to secure a powerful voice in American politics through their attempts to restrict sexual and reproductive behavior. This political climate forced representatives of American Judaism to consider carefully their statements on abortion. Because Jewish law does not support the idea of ensoulment at conception, nearly all Jewish legal authorities consider it necessary to terminate a pregnancy in some situations, most consistently in the case when a fetus endangers the life of the mother. On the other hand, few of the traditional Jewish authorities recognize a woman's right to choose an abortion independently, without first securing the permission of a rabbi. Since Jewish law neither prohibits abortion on principle nor allows women the right to curtail their pregnancies autonomously, the leaders of American Judaism have had license to participate in national debates over abortion in ways that reflect their complex political interests as much as their religious convictions. Tracing the ways that Jews discussed reproductive rights, therefore, affords us insight into the parameters of public religious discourse during the rise of the religious right. It offers a sense of the arguments that could, and could not, be made by the spokespeople of American Judaism if they expected their position to be taken seriously by politicians, the judiciary, the media, and the American public.[5]

Since the earliest years of the Jewish migration to America, Jewish leaders worked to convince an overwhelmingly Christian public that the Jewish religion—and by extension, the Jewish people—legitimately belonged in the United States. Beginning in World War II and continuing through the postwar years, these attempts yielded a certain amount of success. In the wake of the genocide of Jews in Europe, referring to the United States as a "Christian nation" seemed increasingly distasteful, even malevolent. During the 1950s, politicians proclaimed that a "Judeo-Christian" tradition, based on the shared values of both Christians and Jews, guided the American nation. "Our form of government has no sense unless it is founded in a deeply-felt religious faith, and I don't care what it is.... With us of course it is the Judeo-Christian concept but it must be a religion that all men are created equal," declared President-elect Dwight Eisenhower in 1952. By 1955, though other non-Christian religions continued to remain outside the parameters of accepted religion in the United States, the public status of Judaism had increased to the point that Will Herberg could argue in *Protestant, Catholic, Jew* that Judaism functioned alongside Catholicism and Protestantism as one of three bona fide American religions.[6]

The new acknowledgment of Judaism as a valid American religion had a crucial impact upon American Jewish politics. In the years after World War II, it had become abundantly clear that most non-Jewish Americans—and a growing number of American Jews, as well—had come to understand Jewish difference in religious, rather than in ethnic or racial, terms. In order to be able to communicate Jewish interests to politicians and to the public, many of the communal Jewish organizations that did not subscribe to a religious worldview would have to learn to express themselves, at least at times, through the language of religion. Moreover, religious organizations sponsored by the Reform, Conservative, and Orthodox denominations of American Judaism found themselves with unprecedented public recognition as the spokespeople of American Jewry.[7]

As representatives of a group that had only recently achieved recognition as a legitimate American religion, the leaders of American Judaism had to be particularly sensitive to the vagaries of public discourse. The political ascendance of socially conservative Christian activists in the late 1970s and early 1980s, and the attention they received from the media and the Reagan administration, narrowed the ways in which representatives of Judaism could engage in reproductive issues and still be considered sufficiently religious by an American public that was rapidly leaning rightward. Prominent voices within the religious right advanced the idea that women's sexual autonomy could not be compatible with a truly religious worldview—a notion with which many secular feminists did not necessarily disagree—and by the late 1970s, it became difficult for representatives of any religious group to declare otherwise. The continued recognition of Judaism as a valid American religion seemed contingent on how American Jewish leaders would respond to women's calls for sexual and reproductive autonomy.[8]

The Women's League for Conservative Judaism's changing rhetoric on abortion reflects not only the group's response to a shifting political climate but also the pressures that faced the Conservative movement of American Judaism. The Conservative movement represented 23 percent of American Jewish households in 1971, making it the largest religious denomination of American Jews at the time. Conservative Judaism achieved this popularity in the middle of the twentieth century by forging a middle ground between the Reform movement's commitment to liberal social values and Orthodoxy's strict adherence to rabbinic Jewish law. Throughout its history, Conservative Jewish leaders endeavored to find a balance between the movement's right wing, whose adherents argued for stricter interpretations of Jewish law, and the movement's left wing, whose members pushed for bolder adaptations of rabbinic traditions to the demands of the modern world. This tension came to a head over the course of the 1950s, when the far-left members of Conservative Judaism broke off and formed the Reconstructionist movement (discussed by Rebecca T. Alpert and Jacob J. Staub in this volume), leaving the more traditional-minded at the helm of the denomination.

While feminism challenged all of the branches of American Judaism in the late 1960s and 1970s, petitions for the full participation of women in Judaic ritual and leadership placed particular strain on the Conservative movement. Generally speaking, over the course of the 1970s the Reform and Reconstructionist movements officially embraced these changes while the Orthodox movement largely resisted them. Within the Conservative movement, however, debates over women's participation and leadership proved drawn-out and acrimonious, with activists on both sides believing that the integrity of the movement hinged on a proper resolution of these issues. The responses of the Women's League for Conservative Judaism to the debate over abortion echoed the movement's larger struggle to find a balance between its commitments to traditional Jewish law and feminist demands for substantive change.[9]

Moreover, members of Women's League entered into these debates not only as representatives of the Conservative movement but also as the most respected female leaders within their denomination. Their organization, originally called the Women's Religious Union of the United Synagogue, was founded in 1918 for the purpose of promoting "traditional Judaism" in the homes, synagogues, and communities of American Jews. Over the course of the 1920s, it expanded into an umbrella organization linking all of the sisterhood groups that served congregations affiliated with the Conservative movement, and by the late 1960s it boasted a membership that included two hundred thousand women belonging to eight hundred sisterhoods. These women also tended to be older and financially secure. According to a demographic poll administered in 1979, the majority of Women's League members enjoyed established, middle-class lives: most were of middle age, 80 percent of them lived in the suburbs, and more than 50 percent accessed an annual family income of $30,000 or more ($97,940 in 2015 dollars).[10] Along with the United Synagogue, which represented the congregations of the Conservative movement; the Rabbinical Assembly, which represented its rabbis; and the much smaller Federation of Jewish Men's Clubs, Women's League had become one of the main constitutive membership organizations within the Conservative movement and served as its strongest and most active lay-led group.[11]

For the members of Women's League, the feminist movement of the late 1960s and 1970s sparked new ways of thinking about what it meant to be a women's organization and how their interests as women might intersect with their priorities as Conservative Jews. During the 1950s and early 1960s, the organization had not expended much effort on what its members would come to call the "civil rights of women," though they had passed resolutions that backed the civil rights of black Americans and religious minorities. By the late 1960s, however, the burgeoning feminist movement encouraged the American public to begin to conceptualize women as a minority group that deserved resources and support in their own struggle for opportunity, autonomy, and power. This newly politicized understanding of womanhood would come to transform how Women's League engaged in issues of public policy.

The late 1960s also marked a moment of increasing political ferment within the Women's League for Conservative Judaism. Though the organization had a long history of involvement in public life, Women's League members established their first social action committee just prior to their 1948 biennial convention. Under the leadership of Ida Krohn, the first national social action chairman, the committee took on the responsibility of preparing statements on public policy. Often in consultation with the social action committee of the United Synagogue, committee members developed resolutions that they distributed to the leaders of Women's League branches around the country. Then, delegates who attended the Women's League's biennial conference discussed, amended, and voted upon these resolutions during plenary sessions devoted to social action. In the early years of the committee, however, issues of public policy did not generate much interest among the delegates. During the 1950s, recalled Helen P. Sussman, who had served as president of the Women's League between 1954 and 1958, "scarcely a quorum" of delegates could be convinced to attend the social action sessions and talk about "the resolutions so painstakingly prepared for their information and approval."[12]

From Women's Rights to Religious Freedom

But by the late 1960s, Women's League members embraced this opportunity for political engagement. Social action workshops quickly filled to capacity, with many attendees placing their bright yellow delegate kits on the floor to use as makeshift seats. Participants prepared diligently for these sessions, sometimes staying up past midnight the evening before to discuss the resolutions with other delegates. The social action plenaries elicited passionate, sometimes heated discussion, as woman after woman approached the microphone to question certain aspects of the prepared resolutions or to propose new resolutions of their own. "People came to convention specifically for these social action sessions—they were so exciting, and dealt with so many topics," recalled Evelyn Seelig, a past president of Women's League who had served as a chair of the social action committee during the 1970s. Interest in public policy issues proved so great, she remembered, "that we were always taking too long . . . and postponing activities after the discussion because we wanted to take more time." Indeed, those who attended the social action plenary at the 1970 conference commented that these sessions were of "prime importance" to the mission of Women's League and suggested that future conferences devote a "full day" to hammering out social policy resolutions. Six years later, participants continued to complain about the "poor discipline of time" in their evaluations of the social action sessions but felt nonetheless that the social action plenary was the "best session of this convention . . . the epitome of democracy in action."[13]

Women's League passed its first resolution in support of abortion access at its 1970 biennial convention, during an especially dynamic social action plenary. The social action committee proposed resolutions on racial unrest, campus activism, the separation of church and state, and Soviet Jews. In spite of the increasing visibility of the feminist movement and the recent decriminalization of abortion in Hawaii and New York, however, they had not prepared a statement on the issue of reproductive rights.[14]

While reproductive rights may not yet have reached the political radar of the social action committee, these matters concerned Women's League members at the grassroots level. When the session moderator invited comments from the floor, delegates from the Midwest branch presented the women who attended the social action plenary with a resolution that they had prepared late the night before. This statement supported women's access to birth control and abortion, and the membership voted unanimously to adopt it. Helen Sussman, for her part, deemed it both remarkable and admirable that the idea had emanated from the delegates themselves and not from the social action committee. "This session was an example of the democratic process," she gushed.[15]

This initial resolution on reproductive rights that Women's League passed unanimously in 1970 utilized the expressly feminist vocabulary of women's rights and women's choice to justify support for abortion and birth control. It proclaimed the "freedom of choice as to birth control and abortion" to be "inherent in the civil rights of women," adding that "all laws infringing on those rights should be repealed."[16]

With this statement, Women's League became the first branch of the Conservative movement to pass a national resolution on reproductive rights. Three years before *Roe v. Wade* made legal access to abortion the law of the land, five years before any other branch of the Conservative movement would declare support for legal abortion, and thirteen years before the Rabbinical Assembly would do so, the Women's League went on record declaring anti-abortion laws an infringement of women's civil rights. This language, in many ways, mirrored their previous resolutions supporting the civil rights of African Americans and religious minorities, but this signified the first time that either the Women's League or any national branch of the Conservative movement had treated women as a political entity with a distinct set of rights that ought to be secured.[17]

Significantly, and in spite of Women's League's identity as an expressly religious organization, this 1970 resolution did not refer to Jewish religious law or Jewish theology in its defense of reproductive rights. Indeed, neither the delegates at the convention nor the members of the social action committee deemed it necessary to consult with the rabbis of the Conservative movement—who, in these years before women's ordination, were by definition all men—before adopting this resolution. In 1970, during the heyday of the feminist movement and prior to the political ascendance of the religious right, Women's League members did not see a woman's legal right to abortion as being in conflict with a religious worldview. Rather, much like the members of the National Association for the Repeal of Abortion Laws, the National Organization for Women, and other advocates of liberal feminism, they conceived of reproductive rights as a cornerstone of women's political, social, and economic independence rather than a spiritual matter to be discussed with rabbinic authorities.

Two years after they passed their initial resolution in support of birth control and abortion, delegates at the 1972 biennial convention reaffirmed their decision to defend reproductive rights as a woman's civil right without referencing religious or theological principles. During that year's plenary session on social action, some members proposed separating the statement on abortion and birth control into two distinct resolutions. Interestingly, they did not suggest modifying the statement on abortion but rather that on contraception, arguing that as a religious organization, Women's League should not advocate for "complete birth control" since Jewish law considers it a religious obligation to procreate. After discussion, members agreed that their resolution did not imply that the organization supported either abortion or complete contraception from a religious or moral perspective but rather asserted a woman's legal right to access either one based on her own religious and moral conscience. After establishing that their stance on behalf of women's reproductive rights did not conflict with their identity as religious Jews, members opted to retain the statement in its original form.[18]

Though Women's League members voted not to amend their resolution in 1972, their discussion reveals the careful deliberations through which they crafted their public response to the abortion controversy. They debated the implications of confronting this issue as a matter of women's rights rather than as a matter of religious law or theological concern. At this point in time, they decided that their support for women's reproductive autonomy did not contradict their religious values.

Women's League's resolution on abortion and contraception represented just one of the ways that members embraced feminism during the early 1970s. The organization passed additional resolutions inspired by the feminist movement, including statements in support of the Equal Rights Amendment and the inclusion of women in Jewish ritual life.

Though Women's League members offered their support to many of the issues that engaged the feminist movement, their response to the struggle for gender equality in the synagogue diverged sharply from how they dealt with the Equal Rights Amendment and reproductive rights. When grappling with matters they understood as being within the purview of religion, such as women's inclusion in a prayer quorum and the right of women to be ordained as rabbis, they looked to the rabbis of the Conservative movement for guidance and discussed these issues through the language of Jewish law and theology. When responding to matters that they recognized as primarily social and political phenomena, such as the ERA and abortion, they drew upon the lexicon of civil rights and felt empowered to act on their own.[19]

The response of Women's League to the controversy over women's ordination and ritual participation is a case in point. Beginning in the early 1970s, the issue of women's equality in the synagogue roiled the Conservative movement. As of the year 1970, the institutions of the Conservative movement not only barred women from being ordained as rabbis and cantors but also did not permit them to join a prayer quorum, to lead synagogue services, or to read publicly from the Torah. That year, members of the Rabbinical Assembly's Committee on Jewish Law and Standards began to contest the notion that only men could be included as full members in a prayer quorum. And after 1972, when the Reform movement ordained Sally Priesand, America's first woman rabbi, the issue of women's ordination became a major point of contention within the Conservative movement's Rabbinical Assembly as well.[20]

At the same time, at the grassroots level, young feminists within the Conservative movement also began to clamor for women's equality. In March 1972, a collective by the name of Ezrat Nashim (the women's section of the synagogue, literally meaning "help of women"), a group of Jewish feminists in their twenties, requested permission to speak at the Rabbinical Assembly's annual conference and present their "call for change." They demanded that women be included as equal members in a prayer quorum, that women be allowed to lead synagogue services and read publicly from the Torah, and that women be permitted to attend rabbinical and cantorial schools and perform rabbinical and cantorial functions. Though individual rabbis supported the group, the Rabbinical Assembly officially denied Ezrat Nashim a place in the conference program. Instead, it offered the group permission to distribute a letter to attendees and to meet informally, on a voluntary basis, with any of the rabbis and rabbis' wives who wished to speak with them.[21]

Leaders of the Women's League for Conservative Judaism took the concerns of the young women of Ezrat Nashim much more seriously than did the members of the Rabbinical Assembly. Selma Rappaport, then the president of Women's League, had attended the conference at which the members of Ezrat Nashim had tried to publicize their call for change and elected to meet with the young feminists. In the pages of *Women's League Outlook*, a magazine distributed to Women's League members, she described the women of Ezrat Nashim as "intelligent, Jewishly well-educated and Jewishly-committed young women ... well-mannered, earnest and honest, reared in our Conservative congregations, graduates of our religious schools, products of our Ramah Camps." Rather than dismissing the activists of Ezrat Nashim as rebels or upstarts, she understood them as consummate insiders within the Conservative movement. By extension, she validated—though she did not go so far as to endorse—their feminist critique.[22]

Later that year, in November 1972, the Women's League of Conservative Judaism held its own biennial convention. Instead of marginalizing Ezrat Nashim, it put the group at the center of the program. The first night of the conference, Women's League organized a keynote session during which Paula Hyman, a founder of Ezrat Nashim on her way to becoming a leading Jewish feminist activist and scholar, participated in a debate along with rabbis and Women's League members over whether "the woman in Judaism should have more rights." After the debate, Women's League polled its constituents to ascertain their views on the roles that women should play within the Jewish tradition. Members voted decisively for greater inclusion. And the next morning, the young feminists of Ezrat Nashim guided conference attendees through their first prayer service led entirely by women.[23]

Still, in spite of strong support for women's ritual inclusion and ordination among the membership, the leaders of Women's League remained quite cautious about passing official resolutions on these matters without the endorsement of their rabbis. Though the 1972 poll proved that Women's League members favored women's ritual inclusion, the organization did not pass a resolution on this issue until November 1974, after the Conservative movement's Committee on Jewish Law and Standards equalized women and men in all matters of Jewish ritual. Similarly, though minutes from the late 1970s show that members desperately wanted to see their movement ordain women, the organization did not make a public statement about this issue until its 1980 convention, after receiving the approval of Rabbi Gerson Cohen, chancellor of the Conservative movement's Jewish Theological Seminary.[24]

The divergent ways in which Women's League handled reproductive rights and women's inclusion in the synagogue demonstrate that in the early 1970s, the members of Women's League considered reproductive rights to be a social and political issue rather than a matter of religious concern. Because they did not think of legal access to abortion as a question relating to Jewish law or theology, they quickly declared their support without consulting with religious authorities. For issues that they deemed religious in nature, they would not publicly respond without rabbinic affirmation.

By the early 1980s, however, Women's League would overhaul its long-standing resolution on abortion in ways that reflected larger shifts in American politics that reframed abortion as a conservative issue associated with religious commitment. In the years before the *Roe* decision, Catholics led the political movement to limit abortion rights and the general public understood their opposition to abortion as a particularly Catholic issue. Anti-abortion sentiment gradually became ensconced in the mainstream of conservative politics over the course of the 1970s as Nixon courted the Catholic vote and sought to draw them into the Republican Party.

By the late 1970s, evangelical Protestants joined and then came to dominate the anti-abortion movement, working with Catholics and Mormons to oppose *Roe v. Wade*. By the 1980 election that pitted Jimmy Carter against

Ronald Reagan, the influence of such politicized religious organizations as Jerry Falwell's Moral Majority and Beverly LaHaye's Concerned Women for America, both established in 1979, deployed the religiously inflected language of "family values" against the vocabulary of "women's rights." Family values functioned as an ecumenical binding that held together the evangelical Protestants, Catholics, and Mormons who worked together for shared political goals despite their theological differences. Together, they sought to restrict access to abortion and contraception in addition to fighting against other proposals, such as state-sponsored childcare, that sought to help working mothers provide economically for their families. Their conception of these matters as assaults against what they saw as the God-given, traditional structure of the family, an institution they imagined as being led by a breadwinning father and nurtured by a full-time, procreative mother, struck a chord with many Americans. Moreover, their vision garnered a great deal of attention from Republican politicians who had been trying to bring these voters into their party for the better part of a decade.

Opposition to abortion emerged as a central component of this new political vision, achieving its primacy due to national anxieties over profound transformations to sexual and gender norms. From the late 1960s, arguments for abortion reform that sought to protect the health of (respectable, married) mothers competed with anti-abortion arguments that described the procedure as a means by which unmarried, sexually active women could escape the consequences of their promiscuity. As the ideas and rhetoric of the religious right gained currency, many politicians and much of the public began to view anti-abortion sentiment as a universal belief shared by all socially conservative people of faith and as a cultural litmus test for traditional religious leadership.[25]

Unsurprisingly, therefore, it was not until the late 1970s that prominent rabbis within the Conservative movement introduced Women's League members to new ways of thinking about the abortion issue that had little to do with women's autonomy. Robert Gordis, a renowned professor of biblical studies at the Conservative movement's Jewish Theological Seminary and a past president of the Rabbinical Assembly, challenged the way that Women's League members discussed reproductive rights. Gordis, by all accounts, was "very beloved" by the leaders of Women's League, who were grateful to him for consistently taking the time to speak at their national conventions. Women's League members, for their part, supported Gordis professionally and financially by regularly sponsoring and publicizing his scholarly work.[26]

Earlier, in the late 1960s, Gordis had become quite interested in the transformation of American sexual mores that occurred in the wake of improved birth control options, youth rebellion, and the feminist movement. He endeavored to write a Jewish response to this "sexual revolution," and the leaders of Women's League actively supported this project. In 1967, they funded the publication of Gordis's *Sex and the Family in the Jewish Tradition*, a thin volume that discussed Jewish texts and legal traditions concerning the sanctity of marriage, the positive value of licit, marital sex, and the permissibility of birth control. Though Gordis briefly mentioned the then-illegal abortion procedure as a tragic phenomenon signifying "danger and death for mothers and for offspring yet unborn," abortion did not appear as a major theme within this book. Nowhere in this volume did Gordis theologize abortion or delve into Jewish legal traditions concerning the procedure. While Gordis certainly did not endorse women's reproductive rights, he nonetheless painted abortion as a matter of social, rather than religious, concern.[27]

Gordis did not begin to discuss abortion through the lens of Jewish religious law until the late 1970s. In honor of Women's League's sixtieth anniversary, leaders of the organization offered their financial backing to Gordis for an updated volume on Jewish sexual ethics. The book was released under the title *Love and Sex: A Modern Jewish Perspective*, which the Women's League published in cooperation with Farrar, Straus and Giroux in 1978 and which won a National Jewish Book award in 1979. In a chapter titled "Abortion: Major Wrong or Basic Right," Gordis addressed abortion within the framework of Jewish religious and legal traditions. Considered in this way, he emphatically rejected the idea that Judaism supported the idea that a woman ought to have "rights over her own body." The notion that a woman was entitled to determine her own reproductive destiny, he insisted, was "a contention which Judaism, and indeed all high religion, must reject on both theological and ethical grounds." The proper way to ensure that abortion would be available to women but not abused by them, he argued, was for abortion to be "legally available but ethically restricted" by religious and moral authorities. Gordis's views became one of four opinions adopted by the Rabbinical Assembly when it officially declared its own support for legal abortion in 1983.[28]

In this work, Gordis praised right-wing Christian opposition to abortion even as he continued to advocate for the procedure to remain legal. "All Americans, even those who did not share the [anti-abortion] position, owe the movement a debt of gratitude for reminding the American people that moral issues cannot be settled merely by a majority in the legislature or by the decisions of judges," wrote Gordis in *Love and Sex*, a statement that posited Jews and the Christian right as joint defenders of sexual and reproductive ethics.[29] Indeed, Gordis's insistence that "Judaism, and indeed all high religion," rejected the idea that a woman held rights to her own body can also be interpreted as an attempt to raise the status of Judaism on the basis of its efforts to control women's sexuality and reproduction. Gordis's notion of "high" religion, implicitly pitted against "low" religion, referenced a colonialist discourse in which non-Christians were thought to engage in spiritual traditions that celebrated the body and encouraged sexual abandon. Gordis's statements show the extent to which the Christian right had surpassed pro-choice mainline Protestants as the standard-bearers of traditional morality and reveal real concern over whether Judaism would continue to be considered a "civilized" religion by the American public because of its relatively lax views on abortion.[30]

As Gordis shared his ideas on abortion, Gerson D. Cohen, the aforementioned chancellor of the Jewish Theological Seminary, also challenged Women's League's conception of reproductive autonomy as a woman's civil right. When he addressed Women's League members at their 1976 conference, he underscored "the inconsistency with tradition of the relatively new idea that a woman's body is her own property." In his address at the 1980 convention, he further specified his conflicted feelings regarding the procedure: "I have no doubt in my mind that the life of the mother comes first," he said. "On the other hand, I am seriously dubious about the freedom with which we use abortion today." Cohen's comments reflected a late-1970s cultural conversation in which abortion was no longer discussed as a therapeutic procedure that could save women's lives but rather as a means through which women could attain the "freedom" to engage in sexual activity without the consequence of bearing children afterward. For Cohen, this feminist ideal of women's sexual autonomy was not a principle that a religious organization could endorse.[31]

Cohen explicitly framed his thoughts on reproductive rights in relation to conservative Christian groups like Jerry Falwell's Moral Majority. "You and I are in agreement with most of the things that the Moral Majority stands for: religious standards, religious community, strict family standards, great concern over the question of abortion, over the moral breakdown of this country in our time," he told Women's League members in 1980. Cohen's words offer a clear sense of how the religious right's conception of sexual morality and "family values" set the standard to which at least some politically liberal and non-Christian religious leaders believed that they needed to adhere.[32]

While neither Gordis nor Cohen misrepresented Jewish legal traditions in their discussions of reproductive rights, not until the late 1970s did either scholar feel the need to address the issue within the framework of Jewish law. Both Gordis's and Cohen's concerns over abortion, therefore, have to be understood within the context of the newly politicized Christian right that framed abortion as a theological issue and women's reproductive autonomy as incompatible with a religious worldview. Arguing that abortion must be "legally available but ethically restricted" allowed these representatives of American Judaism to claim that the Jewish tradition, no less than Christianity, also policed women's sexual and reproductive behavior. However, and in contrast to the solutions offered by conservative Christians, they insisted that Jewish authorities reserved the right to dictate women's sexual and reproductive behaviors according to their own religious traditions, without interference from the state.

In the midst of these shifts, Women's League leaders decided to restructure their social action program. Beginning in the late 1970s, Women's League leaders had come to fear that their public policy efforts had become undisciplined, unwieldy, and out of tune with their identity as a religious organization. In 1978, they hired Bernice Balter as their director of World Affairs, with a mandate to systematize their public policy agenda. Balter, the wife of a Conservative rabbi, felt strongly that all Women's League's social action resolutions needed to reflect members' position as Conservative Jews who were bound by Jewish law. While she had great respect for those Women's League members who had managed the social action program before her arrival, describing them as "very smart, very liberal, forward thinking," she also believed that "halacha [Jewish law] was not where their heads were." Along with the social action committee, Balter combed through past resolutions with the intention of amending those that, in their view, did not adequately reflect the organization's commitment to Jewish religious traditions.[33]

Unsurprisingly, the Women's League's original statement on reproduction, which championed abortion as a women's civil right, stood out as one of the resolutions that did not register as sufficiently religious in tone. By the early 1980s, the principle of women's reproductive autonomy seemed to clash with a conservative point of view that came to be viewed as *the* religious position on abortion. Consequently, in 1982, Balter and the social action committee proposed an amended resolution on abortion that overhauled the language and logic that had guided the committee's earlier statement.[34]

Though the Women's League continued to support legal abortion, its amended 1982 resolution justified this stance through the logic of religious freedom instead of through the principle of women's rights. In this formulation, proposed limits on abortion access did not place a woman's right to reproductive autonomy into jeopardy; rather, they threatened the right of Jews to free exercise of their religion. This resolution effectively erased women as a political entity with rights that ought to be secured and protected.

In addition to changing the central logic behind the organization's support for legal abortion, the amended statement also stressed that Jewish religious traditions did not support women's reproductive autonomy. It quoted Robert Gordis's claim that abortion needed to be "legally available but ethically restricted" and insisted that the members of Women's League deplored the "burgeoning casual use of abortion." With this language, the resolution echoed the Christian right's framing of abortion as a vehicle for sexual promiscuity and admonished the women who chose the procedure for their presumed moral deficiency. This revised resolution placed the issue of reproductive rights within a religious framework and painted women as a group whose sexuality and reproductive capacity needed to be monitored by moral, if not legal, arbiters.

Many of the delegates at the Women's League's biennial convention protested this revision to their abortion resolution and preferred to retain their original statement in support of women's reproductive autonomy. "Our members were very pro-choice," recalled Bernice Balter. "We really had to sell the halachic [Jewish legal] point of view. Some people found this point of view too restrictive. . . . Whenever there was a complaint, I could always bring up the Torah as justification, which is what I did in this case." In spite of the objections, Women's League leaders moved forward with their revised statement on abortion that drew on the language of Jewish law, sexual conservatism, and religious freedom. The sexual politics of the early 1980s had made it unseemly, perhaps even untenable, for many religious organizations to continue to advance the principle of a woman's right to reproductive autonomy, even if they continued to support legal access to abortion.[35]

Those who feel strongly about a woman's right to sexual and reproductive independence might consider the shift in the Women's League's statement disappointing, or even a capitulation to the (then all male) rabbis of the Conservative movement and their susceptibility to the influence of the Christian right. However, this story represents more than a mere tale of co-optation and in fact gives us a sense of the significant, if limited, power that the members of Women's League wielded within their movement. Though Women's League eventually retreated from a stance on abortion that stressed women's autonomy, its early embrace of reproductive rights had a critical impact on the Conservative movement's position on abortion. After all, while all of the constitutive bodies of the Conservative movement joined Women's League in publicly backing legal abortion by 1983, this consensus emerged only after significant debate. As late as 1980, Gerson Cohen still believed the issue of abortion to be so problematic that he refused "to take a stand . . . on the abortion question, even though Conservative Jewish organizations have done so." And yet, despite their reservations, Conservative leaders never made any public resolutions against *Roe v. Wade*. After the Women's League backed legal abortion in 1970, other representatives of Conservative Judaism no longer had the option of officially opposing abortion without causing a rift within the movement. Women's League's original 1970 resolution had real and lasting political effects.[36]

But even though Women's League never shied away from supporting legal abortion—and propelled the larger Conservative movement toward a similar position—the organization's retreat from the language of women's rights and reproductive autonomy is nonetheless significant. Wittingly or unwittingly, its revised statement on abortion contributed to the growing cultural assumption that a religious organization could not advocate for a woman's right to control her own reproductive destiny without compromising its religious principles. This widespread—and patently false—presumption that people of faith invariably oppose women's reproductive autonomy continues to undergird contemporary court decisions that restrict women's access to contraception and reproduction. That a non-Christian, liberal-leaning, and arguably feminist organization like the Women's League did not challenge this misconception also had real and lasting political effects.

In the end, the story of how the Women's League for Conservative Judaism confronted the issue of reproductive rights is more complicated, and far more interesting, than determining whether or not that organization ended up on the "pro-choice" or "pro-life" side of the political divide. Indeed, the responses of many American Jewish organizations to the abortion controversy trouble these very categories, as some of the Jewish groups that endorsed legal abortion did not necessarily support a woman's right to choose it independently, without the approval of rabbinic authorities. Examining how Women's League navigated the debates over abortion disrupts simplistic dichotomies between public and private, religious and secular, liberal and conservative. It shows how difficult it would become for representatives of American Judaism to publicly acknowledge the civil rights of women during the rise of conservative Christian activism and outlines the limits of religious discourse in late twentieth-century America.

NOTES

I gratefully acknowledge Bernice Balter and Evelyn Seelig for sharing their memories of the Women's League for Conservative Judaism, and Lisa Kogen for offering access to the WLCJ Archives. I would also like to thank the 2013–14 cohort of the Frankel Institute for Advanced Judaic Studies at the University of Michigan (especially Deborah Dash Moore and Beth Wenger), Sarah Imhoff, Melissa Klapper, David Koffman, Rebecca Davis, Rebecca Alpert, and the editors of this volume for their insightful suggestions.

1. "Social Action," p. 37, 1982 Convention Proceedings, WLCJ Biennial Convention, November 14–18, 1982, WLCJ Archives, New York, NY http://www.wlcj.org/articlenav.php?id=75 accessed 10/17/2013.

2. In this essay, I will be using the term "religious right" without quotes and treating it as if it were a singular and cohesive movement. I am aware that the movement known as the religious right consisted of a variety of individuals, groups, and organizations with a variety of ideas and agendas. I refrain from giving a more nuanced analysis of the religious right in this piece, not only because it is beyond the scope of this chapter but also because my subjects took their cues from the popular media. Most did not have a sophisticated understanding of the complexities involved in conservative Christian activism, even though they were quite influenced by it.

3. Influential studies that divide the abortion debate between religious pro-life activists and nonreligious supporters of choice include Kristen Luker, *Abortion and the Politics of Motherhood* (Berkeley: University of California Press, 1985); Faye Ginsburg, *The Abortion Debate in an American Community* (Berkeley: University of California Press, 1989); Dallas Blanchard, *The Anti-abortion Movement and the Rise of the Religious Right* (New York: Twayne, 1994); and Kerry Jacoby, *Souls, Bodies, Spirits: The Drive to Abolish Abortion since 1973* (Westport, Conn.: Praeger, 1998). Other studies briefly mention pro-choice religious activists (such as members of the Religious Coalition for Abortion Rights, Catholics for Free Choice, or the Clergy Consultation Service) without considering the ways in which these pro-choice faith communities complicate the abortion controversy. See Simone M. Carron, *Who Chooses? American Reproductive History since 1830* (Gainesville: University Press of Florida, 2008); Linda Gordon, *The Moral Property of Women: A History of Birth Control Politics in America* (Urbana: University of Illinois Press, 2002); Suzanne Staggenborg, *The Pro-choice Movement: Organization and Activism in the Abortion Conflict* (New York: Oxford University Press, 1991); and Rickie Sollinger, *Abortion Wars: A Half Century of Struggle* (Berkeley: University of California Press, 1998). Important exceptions include Tom Davis's *Sacred Work: Planned Parenthood and Its Clergy Alliances* (New Brunswick: Rutgers University Press, 2006); Maureen Muldoon's sourcebook *The Abortion Debate in the United States and Canada* (New York: Garland, 1991); John H. Evans, "Multi-organizational Fields and Social Movement Organization Frame Content: The Religious Pro-choice Movement," *Sociological Inquiry* 7, no. 4 (November 1997): 451–69; Samuel A. Mills, "Abortion and Religious Freedom: The Religious Coalition for Abortion Rights and the Pro-choice Movement, 1973–1989," *Journal of Church and State* 33, no. 3 (Summer 1991): 569–94; and Barbara Ferraro and Patricia Hussey, *No Turning Back* (New York: Poseidon Press, 1990). Rosalind Pollack Petchesky acknowledges the "struggle for moral hegemony that is being waged *within* the major religious groups . . . between their liberal and

sometimes feminist tendencies and their orthodox or fundamentalist tendencies," *Abortion and Woman's Choice* (Boston: Northeastern University Press, 1990), 336; Johanna Schoen's *Abortion after Roe: Abortion after Legalization* (Chapel Hill: University of North Carolina Press, 2015) folds in the history of the Clergy Consultation Service and Catholics for a Free Choice; Mary J. Henold's discussion of pro-life Catholic feminists in *Catholic and Feminist* (Chapel Hill: University of North Carolina Press, 2008) also complicates this discussion.

4. Joan Wallach Scott, "Secularism and Gender Equality," 24–45, and Janet Jacobson and Ann Pellegrini, "Bodies Politics: Christian Secularism and the Gendering of US Policy," 139–74, both in *Religion, the Secular, and the Politics of Sexual Difference*, ed. Linell Elizabeth Cady and Tracy Fessenden (New York: Columbia University Press, 2013). The editors' excellent introduction to this volume also explores the implications of this construction; see 8–9.

5. On the intricacies of Jewish law regarding abortion, see Rachel Biale, *Women and Jewish Law: An Exploration of Women's Issues in Halakhic Sources* (New York: Schocken Books, 1984); David Feldman, *Birth Control in Jewish Law: Marital Relations, Contraception, and Abortion as Set Forth in the Classic Texts of Jewish Law* (New York: New York University Press, 1968); and Daniel Schiff's *Abortion in Judaism* (Cambridge: Cambridge University Press, 2002), which brings a historical approach to rabbinic decisions regarding abortion and shows how the laws developed over time.

6. Mark Silk, "Notes on the Judeo-Christian Tradition in America," *American Quarterly* 36, no. 1 (Spring 1984): 65–86 (quote on page 65); Deborah Dash Moore, "Jewish GIs and the Creation of a Judeo-Christian Tradition," *Religion and American Culture* 8, no. 1 (Winter 1998): 31–53; Kevin Schultz, *Tri-faith America: How Catholics and Jews Held Postwar America to Its Protestant Promise* (New York: Oxford University Press, 2011); Jonathan Sarna, *American Judaism* (New Haven: Yale University Press, 2004), 274–77; Will Herberg, *Protestant, Catholic, Jew* (Chicago: University of Chicago Press, 1955).

7. On the ways that American Jews grappled with issues of self-definition and racial understandings of Jewish difference, see Eric Goldstein, *The Price of Whiteness: Jews, Race, and American Identity* (Princeton: Princeton University Press, 2008).

8. Considering how crucial the issue of abortion was to American Jewish politics by the 1970s, it is surprising how little has been written on the topic by historians of American Jews. Two of the three monographs on postwar American Jewish politics that have been published since the year 2000 do not make any mention of sexual politics, though the periodization of both volumes extends into the 1970s, when the issue became a major area of focus for many American Jewish organizations. See Marc Dollinger, *Quest for Inclusion: Jews and Liberalism in Modern America* (Princeton: Princeton University Press, 2000); and Joshua Zeitz, *White Ethnic New York: Jews, Catholics, and the Shaping of Postwar Politics* (Chapel Hill: University of North Carolina Press, 2007). Michael Staub's *Torn at the Roots: The Crisis of Jewish Liberalism in Postwar America* (New York: Columbia University Press, 2002) is the sole exception, as it includes a chapter on Jews and the sexual revolution, but even this volume devotes fewer than five pages to the discussion of abortion (251–54). Essays that discuss American Jews and reproduction in the years after World War II include Rebecca Alpert, "Sometimes the Law Is Cruel: The Construction of a Jewish Antiabortion Position in the Writings of Immanuel Jakobovits," *Journal of Feminist Studies in Religion* 11, no. 2 (Fall 1995): 27–37; and Sylvia Barack Fishman's sociological study "Public Jews and Private Acts: Family and Personal Choices in the Public Square and in

the Private Realm," in *Jews and the American Public Square*, ed. Alan Mittleman, Robert Licht, and Jonathan Sarna (Lanham, Md.: Rowman and Littlefield, 2002), 265–88. Neither of the most influential synthetic volumes of American Jewish history mentions abortion at all, which reflects the lack of attention this matter has received from practitioners in the field. See Hasia Diner, *The Jews of the United States* (Berkeley: University of California Press, 2004); and Jonathan Sarna, *American Judaism* (New Haven: Yale University Press, 2004). When compared to the many volumes devoted to birth control and reproductive rights in the fields of Protestant and Catholic American history, this lacuna becomes all the more glaring. Unfortunately, this lack of scholarly attention to Jewish responses to the abortion debates distorts Jewish political history, as the issue found its way to the docket of nearly every Jewish communal organization in the 1970s.

9. Pamela Nadell, *Conservative Judaism in America: A Bibliographical Dictionary and Sourcebook* (New York: Greenwood, 1988), 1–24; Abraham J. Karp, "A Century of Conservative Judaism in the United States," *American Jewish Year Book* 86 (1986): 3; Alvin Chenkin, "Demographic Highlights: Facts for Planning," *National Jewish Population Study* (New York: Council of Jewish Federations and Welfare Funds, 1971), 23.

10. The Bureau of Labor Statistics inflation calculator is at http://www.bls.gov/data/inflation_calculator.htm (accessed June 18, 2014).

11. Evelyn Auerbach, "Women's League Profile," *Women's League Outlook* 94, no. 4 (Summer 1979): 8; Shuly Rubin Schwartz, "Women's League of Conservative Judaism," *Jewish Women: A Comprehensive Historical Encyclopedia*, March 1, 2009, Jewish Women's Archive, http://jwa.org/encyclopedia/article/womens-league-of-conservative-judaism; author interviews with Bernice Balter, executive director of the Women's League in the 1980s and 1990s, May 12, 2014, and Evelyn Seelig, president of the Women's League between 1994 and 1998, May 14, 2014.

12. Bernice Balter, "World Affairs," *75 Years of Vision and Voluntarism* (New York: Women's League for Conservative Judaism, 1992), 66–68; Helen Sussman, "Springboard to Social Action," *Women's League Outlook* 41, no. 2 (Winter 1970): 20; Esther Lublin, "Why Social Action Programs?," *Women's League Outlook* 18, no. 4 (May 1948): 15; Seelig interview, May 14, 2014; Balter interview, May 12, 2014.

13. At the 1970 convention, for instance, delegates from the Midwest branch of Women's League stayed up until 1:00 a.m. preparing for the next day's social action session. Minutes of Midwest Branch Board Meeting, November 16, 1970, Concord Hotel, National Programs/Minutes of Meetings Folder, box 181, Midwest Branch of Women's League for Conservative Judaism, Upper Midwest Jewish Archives, Minneapolis, Minn.; Barbara Grau, "Sitting Room Only," *Women's League Outlook* 45, no. 2 (Winter 1974): 20; Sussman, "Springboard to Social Action," 20; "Convention Evaluation Report," National Board Meeting (December 16, 1970), 5, WLCJ Archives; Convention Log 1976, "Evaluation of Wednesday Afternoon Plenary Session," 14, WLCJ Archives; author interview with Evelyn Seelig, November 5, 2014.

14. "Idea Exchange Sessions on Social Action," Convention Proceedings, National Women's League of the United Synagogue of America, Biennial Convention, November 15–19, 1970, 1970 Convention folder, 78–79, WLCJ Archives.

15. Sussman, "Springboard to Social Action," 20; "Social Action," *Hi Lites: Biennial Convention* no. 3 (November 15–19, 1970), 1970 Convention folder, 7, WLCJ Archives.

16. "Resolutions," Convention Proceedings, National Women's League of the United Synagogue of America, Biennial Convention, November 15–19, 1970, 1970 Convention folder, 126, WLCJ Archives.

17. While the United Synagogue did not pass a national resolution on abortion rights until 1975, its New York metropolitan region presented testimony in favor of abortion law reform before the New York State Legislature in 1967 during discussions over whether to liberalize state abortion laws. See "Abortion," *United Synagogue of America, Biennial Convention Proceedings* (New York: United Synagogue of America, November 16–20, 1975), 193–94.

18. Lola Jessel, "Social Action Blueprint," *Women's League Outlook* 43, no. 2 (Winter 1972): 26.

19. "Resolution: Equal Rights Amendment," *Convention Proceedings: 1974 Biennial Convention*, 1974 Convention folder, 110, WLCJ Archives; "Social Action," *Convention Proceedings, Biennial Convention 1978*, 1978 Convention folder, 39, WLCJ Archives; Confidential Executive Meeting Notes (December 3, 1980), 4, WLCJ Archives; Executive Committee Meeting, Wednesday (March 4, 1981), 2, WLCJ Archives.

20. Pamela Nadell, *Women Who Would Be Rabbis: A History of Women's Ordination, 1889–1985* (Boston: Beacon Press, 1998), 191. As early as 1955, the Rabbinical Assembly's Committee on Jewish Law and Standards ruled that women were allowed to receive an *aliyah*, a ritual in which a worshipper is honored by being called to the Torah during the synagogue service and reciting a blessing before the public reading. But in spite of this ruling, it was not until the 1970s that the vast majority of Conservative synagogues began to bestow this honor upon women. See Shuly Rubin Schwartz, "Conservative Judaism in the United States," *Jewish Women: A Comprehensive Historical Encyclopedia*, March 1, 2009, Jewish Women's Archive. http://jwa.org/encyclopedia/article/conservative-judaism-in-united-states (accessed June 20, 2014).

21. Ezrat Nashim's challenge to the Rabbinical Assembly in 1972 has been well documented; there has not been any scholarly mention, however, of the group's subsequent visit to the Women's League biannual convention. See Paula Hyman, "Ezrat Nashim and the Emergence of a New Jewish Feminism," in *The Americanization of the Jews* (New York: New York University Press, 1995), 284–95. Paula Hyman, "Jewish Feminism in the United States," *Jewish Women: A Comprehensive Historical Encyclopedia*, Jewish Women's Archive, March 1, 2009. http://jwa.org/encyclopedia/article/jewish-feminism-in-united-states. See also Deborah Lipstadt, "Feminism and American Judaism," in *Women and American Judaism: Historical Perspectives*, ed. Pamela Nadell and Jonathan Sarna (Hanover: Brandeis University Press, 2001), 291–308; and Pamela Nadell, "Women and American Judaism," in *Women and Judaism: New Insights and Scholarship*, ed. Frederick Greenspahn (New York: New York University Press, 2009), 162. The full text of Ezrat Nashim's call for change can be found at the Jewish Women's Archive: http://jwa.org/feminism/_html/JWA039.htm (accessed February 22, 2012).

22. Selma Rappaport, "Our President Speaks: Two Worlds?," *Women's League Outlook* 42, no. 4 (Summer 1972): 4, 24.

23. Mickey Kaplan, "Joy in Prayer," *Hi-Lites: Biennial Convention 1972* 3, no. 4, 1972 Convention folder, WLCJ Archives; "The Ayes Have it," *Hi-Lites: Biennial Convention 1972* 3, 1972 Convention folder, 2, WLCJ Archives; "Opinion Poll: Women's Rights in Judaism," *1972 Biennial Convention Journal*, 1972 Convention folder, 55, WLCJ Archives.

24. Confidential minutes of executive committee (March 6, 1974), 2, WLCJ Archives; "Resolution on Women (discussed and passed on Monday, November 18, 1974)," *Convention Proceedings*, 1974 Biennial Convention, 1976 Convention Folder, 33, WLCJ Archives; *Seventy-Five Years of Vision and Volunteerism* (New York: Women's League for Conservative Judaism, 1992), 49; Executive Committee Minutes (September 6, 1978), 1, WLCJ Archives; Executive Committee Minutes (November 8, 1978), 1, WLCJ Archives; Confidential Executive Committee Minutes, November 5, 1980, 4, WLCJ Archives. On women's ordination in the Conservative movement, see Beth Wenger, "The Politics of Women's Ordination," in *Tradition Renewed: A History of the Jewish Theological Seminary*, ed. Jack Wertheimer (New York: Jewish Theological Seminary of America, 1997), 485–523; and Nadell, *Women Who Would Be Rabbis*, 170–214. Amy Eilberg became the first woman rabbi in the Conservative movement in 1985.

25. Randall Balmer, *God in the White House: A History* (New York: Harper Collins, 2008), 93–105; Donald Critchlow, *Intended Consequences: Birth Control, Abortion, and the Federal Government in Modern America* (New York: Oxford University Press, 1999), 208–10; Matthew Lassiter, "Inventing Family Values," in *Rightward Bound: Making America Conservative in the 1970s*, ed. Bruce Schulman and Julian Zelizer (Cambridge, Mass.: Harvard University Press, 2008), 13–28; Daniel K. Williams, "The GOP's Abortion Strategy: Why Pro-choice Republicans Became Pro-life in the 1970s," *Journal of Policy History* 23, no. 4 (2011): 513–39; James P. McCartin, *Prayers of the Faithful: The Shifting Spiritual Life of American Catholics* (Cambridge, Mass.: Harvard University Press, 2010).

26. Seelig interview, May 14, 2014.

27. Robert Gordis, *Sex and the Family in the Jewish Tradition* (New York: Burning Book Press, 1967). Acknowledgment of the sponsorship of the Women's League appears on the copyright page. Brief mentions of abortion as a social phenomenon appear on pp. 12, 16, and 25–26.

28. Robert Gordis, *Love and Sex: A Modern Jewish Perspective* (New York: Farrar, Straus and Giroux and Women's League for Conservative Judaism, 1978), 145, 147; "NJBA Winners," http://www.jewishbookcouncil.org/awards/njba-list (accessed June 19, 2014); WLCJ Executive Committee Special Meeting, Confidential Report (July 9, 1975), 1, WLCJ Archives; WLCJ Executive Committee Meeting, Confidential Report (September 10, 1975), 2, WLCJ Archives. The four opinions on abortion adopted by the Rabbinical Assembly included Rabbi Kassel Abelson, "Prenatal Testing and Abortion," http://www.rabbinicalassembly.org/sites/default/files/public/halakhah/teshuvot/20012004/03.pdf (accessed January 3, 2014); Rabbi David Feldman, "Abortion: The Jewish View," http://www.rabbinicalassembly.org/sites/default/files/public/halakhah/teshuvot/19861990/feldman_abortion.pdf (accessed January 3, 2014); Rabbi Robert Gordis, "Abortion: Major Wrong or Basic Right," 25–26, http://www.rabbinicalassembly.org/sites/default/files/public/halakhah/teshuvot/20012004/05.pdf (accessed January 3, 2014)—this opinion was lifted verbatim from his book *Love and Sex*; and Rabbi Isaac Klein, "A Teshuvah on Abortion," http://www.rabbinicalassembly.org/sites/default/files/public/halakhah/teshuvot/20012004/06.pdf (accessed January 3, 2014).

29. Gordis, *Love and Sex*, 39.

30. Ibid., 145.

31. "Torah Study with Dr. Gerson D. Cohen," *Hi-Lites: Women's League for Conservative Judaism Biennial Convention 1976*, Monday, November 15, 1976, 1976 Convention folder, 2,

WLCJ Archives; Torah Study Session with Dr. Gerson Cohen, "Choose Life: What Does This Mean in Jewish Tradition?," Convention Proceedings, WLCJ Biennial Convention, November 16–20, 1980, 1980 Convention folder, 19–20, WLCJ Archives.

32. Torah Study Session with Dr. Gerson Cohen, "Choose Life," 21.

33. Balter interview, May 12, 2014; Seelig interview, May 14, 2014.

34. "Social Action," 1982 Convention Proceedings, WLCJ Biennial Convention, November 14–18, 1982, 37, WLCJ Archives; "Resolutions of the Women's League for Conservative Judaism," http://www.wlcj.org/articlenav.php?id=75 (accessed October 17, 2013). The full text of the resolution reads as follows:

> Reverence for life is the cornerstone of our Jewish heritage. Since abortion in Jewish law is primarily for the mother's physical or mental welfare, we deplore the burgeoning casual use of abortion. Abortion should be "legally available but ethically restricted. Though the abortion of a fetus is not equivalent to taking an actual life, it does represent the destruction of potential life and must not be undertaken lightly."*
>
> However, Women's League for Conservative Judaism also believes that the practice of the principle of separation of Church and State guaranteed by our Constitution has kept our nation strong and preserved full freedom for the individual. Women's League believes that transmitting religious values is the responsibility of the religious sector.
>
> Women's League for Conservative Judaism urges its Sisterhoods to oppose any legislative attempts through Constitutional amendments, the deprivation of Medicaid, family services, and/or other current welfare services, to weaken the force of the Supreme Court's decision permitting abortions. *From *Love and Sex: A Modern Jewish Perspective* by Robert Gordis [citation appears in original]

35. Indeed, the internal dissension over amending this resolution was such that there is some discrepancy in the record over whether it actually passed. Balter, Seelig, and the Women's League record of resolutions indicate that the membership voted to pass the resolution, as did past president Audrey Citak in a 1992 article on reproductive rights. See Audrey Citak, "Tikkun Olam: Women's League's Mandate for Action," *Women's League Outlook* 62, no. 4 (June 30, 1992), 5; Balter interview, May 12, 2014; Seelig interview, May 14, 2014. On the other hand, a 1982 report in *Women's League Outlook* indicates that members voted against amending the resolution. See Norma Mann, "Very Much Part of the World," *Women's League Outlook* 53, no. 2 (Winter 1982): 18.

36. I am comfortable indulging in this counterfactual argument for two reasons. First, considering Gerson Cohen's insistence in 1980 that he would not take a stand on abortion, we cannot assume that the Rabbinical Assembly would have gone on record in support of abortion had the Women's League, and then the United Synagogue, not released their statements first. Second, I note that the Orthodox Union, the main representative body of Modern Orthodoxy and another group that, like Conservative Judaism, sees itself as embracing both traditional Judaism and the modern world, has consistently spoken out against legal abortion except in cases where a mother's life is in danger. I do not think it out of the range of possibility that the Conservative movement might have followed suit. Torah Study Session with Dr. Gerson Cohen, "Choose Life," 19–20.

FASCINATING AND HAPPY

Mormon Women, the LDS Church, and the Politics of Sexual Conservatism

NEIL J. YOUNG

In the late 1960s, Jaquie Davison, an Arizona housewife who struggled to find happiness while raising her seven children, enrolled in a Fascinating Womanhood (FW) workshop at her Mormon church ward led by a fellow Latter-day Saint (LDS) woman, Helen Andelin. Andelin's workshops, and her accompanying best-selling book, *Fascinating Womanhood*, offered LDS women the hope of finding personal fulfillment by accepting their divinely ordained roles and responsibilities, including embracing their sexual gifts as wives. If women followed God's plan of femininity and female submission, Andelin promised their marriages would achieve "Celestial Love," a heavenly notion of perfection drawn from LDS theology that linked women's sexuality to their salvation. While Andelin mostly avoided the brewing controversies of her era, the meetings radicalized Davison, not only transforming her marriage but also awakening her to politics.

Terrified of how the Equal Rights Amendment would impact her daughters' lives, Davison threw herself into organizing against the proposed constitutional amendment that guaranteed equality of rights under the law regardless of sex. Creating the organization Happiness of Womanhood (HOW), Davison's group not only targeted the defeat of the ERA but also opposed abortion, homosexuality, pornography, sex education, busing, and the removal of school prayer. HOW soon claimed ten thousand members in all fifty states. Davison's message built on Andelin's but directed it in a more explicitly political direction, arguing that the women's movement's false promises of liberation and equality and the sexual revolution's assaults on traditional monogamous heterosexuality threatened women's happiness and endangered the family. This chapter examines Andelin and Davison within the context of LDS teachings on sexuality as a way of understanding how Mormon women responded to and helped shape the development of Mormonism's conservative culture of sexuality and gender and its political consequences. Through Fascinating Womanhood, LDS women developed an internal culture that affirmed the social arrangements of the traditional heterosexual family and empowered women to seek happiness through wifely submission and marital sexual pleasure. Yet this was not a contained phenomenon transforming select Mormon homes. Rather, the lessons of FW turned these women's attention outward to the nation and committed them to countering the country's social and sexual developments they believed directly opposed their moral vision and ideological worldview. Through the HOW organization, these women entered the political realm to work against issues—particularly the ERA, abortion reform, and gay rights—they saw as an attack on their families and their way of life.

In order to understand Mormon involvement, it is necessary to understand the theological and cultural underpinnings of the women who led and participated in these campaigns. Other than one recent treatment of Andelin, she and Davison have received little attention from historians.[1] Scholars of modern conservatism have briefly noted Andelin and Davison, mentioning them alongside their more well-known evangelical counterparts, like Marabel Morgan and Beverly LaHaye, but rarely noting their own Mormon backgrounds or how LDS theology shaped their treatments of marriage and sexuality.[2] Indeed, these evangelical authors of marriage and sex guides have received far more attention from scholars, including historians of sexuality, thinking about the rise of conservative women as a backlash to 1960s and 1970s feminism.[3] Yet Andelin, writing *Fascinating Womanhood* in 1965, was a forerunner of the sexual revolution's cottage industry of antifeminist authors and activists. And Andelin and Davison, along with their Mormon sisters, were at the forefront of the era's political battles over sexuality. This activism, notably, predated the LDS Church's critical involvement in preventing the Equal Rights Amendment's ratification and helping build the grassroots ecumenical coalition that formed the basis of the religious right and augmented the rise of modern conservatism.[4]

It might seem odd that these LDS women would become public political actors even before their church organized against the amendment, especially considering they believed their most important work was as wives and mothers in the home. Yet historians have shown how conservative religious women drew upon their identity as moral guardians of the home both to motivate their public engagement and to articulate their politics. Believing that social and political changes in the 1960s and 1970s threatened the "traditional home," by which they meant a monogamous, heterosexual unit led by a male single-breadwinner, these women stepped out to defend their way of life in the public square.[5] Other scholars have noted how women like these became instrumental in the upsurge of political conservatism through the 1970s, culminating in Ronald Reagan's 1980 election that signaled the nation's conservative political and cultural realignment. Organizing against the Equal Rights Amendment, abortion, pornography, and gay rights, these conservative women became powerful political actors, often working together in grassroots organizations like Happiness of Womanhood.[6]

While historians of the Equal Rights Amendment have mentioned Davison's Happiness of Womanhood in studies of the broad anti-ERA grassroots movement, these works still focus their attention on Phyllis Schlafly's STOP ERA group as the primary force behind the amendment's defeat.[7] Yet, as Davison proudly noted, HOW predated STOP ERA by two years; long before Schlafly had heard of the Equal Rights Amendment, Davison was working against it.

For Mormon women, their sexuality and gender linked directly to their most fundamental religious beliefs. LDS theology taught that women's salvation owed to their status as married women who fruitfully procreated both on earth and in the hereafter, but that relationship often came across as burdensome and dutiful in the hands of Mormonism's male theologians and authorities. This chapter first examines how Andelin's writings and workshops recast those teachings, presenting women's sexuality as a privilege and a pleasure—one that could bring earthly fulfillment while also guaranteeing an eternal reward. It then demonstrates how Davison's politicization of Andelin's message importantly built from that sacred notion of sexuality. In doing so, it distinguishes HOW from its peer anti-ERA organizations, particularly STOP ERA, which historians have paid closer attention to. Women in those organizations, on the one hand, showcased more conventional politics, lobbying their legislators and leading public rallies as respectable, traditional, and demure women concerned about the nation's shifting sexual mores. Led by Jaquie Davison's unique example, the women of Happiness of Womanhood, on the other hand, capitalized on their femininity and "proper" sexuality as married women to defend the traditional home and heterosexual marriage against the Equal Rights Amendment they believed would radically alter both. As Mormon women moved from participating in Andelin's marriage workshops into political activism through Davison's organization, they came to understand that they not only could embrace their wifely duties but also could defend God's plan of human sexuality and the traditional family against the threats of women's liberation, sexual freedom, and homosexuality.

FASCINATING WOMANHOOD

In the 1950s, Helen Andelin was a miserable woman. Married to her college sweetheart, Aubrey, whom she had met while attending Brigham Young University, Andelin bristled in her life as a homemaker and mother, stifled by her responsibilities and feeling trapped in a loveless marriage. Andelin was hardly alone. Across the country, the problem of unhappy marriages plagued homes at midcentury. As historians Steven Mintz and Susan Kellogg have argued, the metaphor of marriage as a trap had become routine in feminist circles by the 1960s, but this discontent transcended political boundaries with conservative women also expressing dissatisfaction with their lives.[8]

For many American women, Betty Friedan's *The Feminine Mystique* offered a ray of hope, if not also a bombshell to their perfectly orchestrated but unhappy domestic lives. Friedan's book examined "the problem that has no name."[9] "The problem lay buried, unspoken, for many years in the minds of American women," Friedan wrote in the book's first sentence. As women devoted themselves to their husbands and children, they wondered, Friedan argued, why they were missing out on the fulfillment and contentment their society and culture had promised such devotion would provide them. Inside them, unaware that any other woman felt the same, they asked themselves "the silent question: Is this all?"[10] Friedan advocated women look outside their marriages and home life to a professional career for personal fulfillment. Other feminists promoted more radical legal and political changes, but for millions of conservative women, like Andelin, abandoning marriage and motherhood never seemed a desirable option. As Rebecca L. Davis shows in this volume, religious leaders in the twentieth century emphasized the religious nature of marriage in order to promote and sustain heterosexual marriage, a message Andelin heard constantly as a Mormon woman.

Thus, Andelin looked to a Mormon friend about how she might improve her life and marriage. The friend loaned her a set of booklets published in the 1920s called *The Secret of Fascinating Womanhood* that Andelin devoured immediately. The booklets taught that the key to fixing a marriage came through the wife improving herself. The message resonated with Andelin—by remaking herself, she could rehabilitate her marriage. For Andelin, this was a revelation, like some hidden eternal truth that now had been communicated to her. Andelin determined to spread this message to other women, and she quickly began writing up her own thoughts about how the booklets' lessons might be applied to the modern age.[11]

While writing her book, Andelin also started leading workshops for women at her local LDS Church ward. Andelin instructed her students to focus on fixing themselves into highly feminized, entirely submissive wives as the key to a happy marriage. This involved the requirement, as one of the early lessons in the ten-week workshop instructed, to "Accept a Man at Face Value." Man's needs were basic and unchanging, according to Andelin, but were complicated by his "very sensitive Pride and the peculiar way he acts when it is *wounded*."[12] Wives, therefore, had to understand how men operated and adjust themselves accordingly in order to guarantee his, and thereby their own, happiness.

While she wrote and taught, Andelin recognized that she was envisioning the "Ideal Woman." This Ideal Woman, as Andelin described, was half woman and half angel, and she named her model woman Angela Human to reflect that composition. Andelin also imbued her message with a religious context for which she drew heavily from her Mormon faith. In short, Andelin worked from the premise that neither man nor woman could be happy in life without a marriage relationship. This assumption drew straight from Mormon theology that treated marriage as the highest calling in life and an essential requirement for exaltation, the highest realm of salvation. Marriage was a divinely ordained institution with the purpose of producing children. Husband and wife had separate but complementary tasks that worked together for the good of the individual and the family unit. The man was to be the leader, the breadwinner, and the authoritarian in the house. The woman would submit to her husband in everything, care for the home and the children while spurning any professional career, and always attire herself in the most feminine dresses. For Andelin, pantsuits were verboten. In the workshops, women even learned which dress colors, fabric weaves, hairdos, and shoe styles to use and avoid in order to heighten their femininity. Andelin recommended dresses with ruffles and forbade the wearing of tweed. In her book, *Fascinating Womanhood*, Andelin offered an expanded section, "Introduction to Femininity," teaching that woman should use their feminine appearance to attract their husband's attention and get what they wanted in marriage.[13]

This message of marital responsibility and gender difference resembled LDS teachings directed at Mormon women in the 1960s, but Andelin's workshops and book contained a playful joyfulness often missing in the church's lectures. While church leaders frequently implored LDS women (and men) to conform to strict gender roles, avoid all unchaste behavior outside of wedlock, and commit their marriages to the religious obligation of procreation, Andelin spread a more hopeful and happy message. Femininity was more than a faithful task—it was fun! A woman could delight in how her husband responded to her flirtatious manner and frilly dress, making the home a sexually charged playground rather than a prison of drudgery and oppression. Accenting gender differences in the home was fundamental to a sexually fulfilling marriage because it created an electric frisson that stirred amorous passions. "The *contrast* of your femininity causes him to feel masculine," Andelin explained. "This is a thrilling sensation and arouses within him his highest and noblest sentiments toward womanhood."[14] Yet Andelin's emphasis on the work required to effect these gender differences contrasted from LDS teaching that saw gender and sexuality as inherently determined and divinely ordained. Instead, Andelin seemed to agree with feminists of the time who argued gender was a social construction. Andelin, however, saw this not as a burden for women to relinquish but rather as the key by which they could unlock personal happiness and sexual fulfillment. With detailed instructions about dress and behavior, including hand motions, body postures, facial expressions, and voice tones, Andelin instructed women on how to enhance their femininity as a concerted and deliberate choice. Any woman could achieve it through proper training and personal effort, even the "terribly unfeminine" farmhand Andelin touted who took an FW workshop and "learned to be a woman through willpower."[15]

Among the book's many controversies, Andelin's suggestion that women cultivate a "childlike" nature in their marriage aroused her critics' ire the most. Andelin argued that children, unlike adult women, freely and openly expressed themselves, whereas women concealed their feelings from their husbands or reacted in ugly and manipulative ways. Either response bred resentment in a woman and discontent in the marriage, so Andelin stressed that wives must take on the unfiltered honesty of a child to get what they wanted in marriage. "With a childlike response you can, in a small moment, turn the night to day," Andelin explained. "You learn the right way to ask for things, and he responds by *wanting* to do things for you."[16] Once a wife learned what her husband truly wanted and gave it to him, she would then enjoy the benefits of what Andelin called "Celestial Love."

Celestial Love drew from the LDS theology of salvation and provided it a romantic dimension. Mormons believe that in the afterlife they will dwell not in heaven but rather in three degrees or kingdoms of glory with the Celestial Kingdom representing the highest realm. Mormons reach the Celestial Kingdom by living a righteous life and by entering into a temple marriage with a fellow Saint.[17] Since marriage is a requirement for exaltation—the highest degree of salvation—LDS theology understandably promotes the act of marriage with an unrelenting and sometimes dour fervor, and LDS teachings regarding marriage and family life at midcentury tended to emphasize religious obligation and eternal consequences rather than personal fulfillment and romantic happiness.

As much as Andelin's message responded to the general discontentment of the 1960s American housewife, it more directly reckoned with the particular crisis of the LDS woman, disillusioned by the married life that offered the essential path to exaltation. Celestial Love, then, promised LDS women a bit of heaven on earth. It did not escape the conventions of Mormonism's conservative theology of family life but rather fulfilled them. Instead of female sacrifice and self-denial as the path to godliness and the requisite component for a functioning family, as LDS leaders tended to preach, Andelin offered her readers a different lexicon of happiness, joy, and excitement. Even in affirming the moral responsibility of procreation and parenting, Andelin's encouragement that LDS women flirt, tease, and play with their husbands provided a rare reminder in Mormon circles that the marital relationship could have a pleasurable dimension. "Many women experience within a few weeks a more fulfilling sex life," she promised of her methods.[18] Still, Andelin's sexual advice, limited though it was, generally regarded sex as a tool women could use to gratify their men and make them more compliant and attentive to their own nonphysical needs. Celestial Love required that women utilize the dual nature of the Ideal Woman, as the "angelic arouses in man a feeling approaching worship and brings him peace and happiness" while her human appearance and actions, erotic and otherwise, "fascinate, captivate, amuse, enchant, and arouse a desire to protect and shelter."[19] A "fiery, saucy woman" was what men wanted, the workshops instructed. "You owe it to him to be this kind of woman."[20]

The only complaint Andelin's husband, Aubrey, had of her book was that it insufficiently addressed the marital sexual relationship, so he and Andelin authored *Fascinating Womanhood Principles Applied to Sex*, a fourteen-page pamphlet.[21] The pamphlet first established the divine gift of sex for marriage—and, conversely, nonmarital sex as a "defiance of God's clearly enunciated law." However, the pamphlet devoted most of its pages to the "many common sex problems" that arose from "an *imbalance of sexual desire* between husband and wife."[22] The pamphlet outlined different possible scenarios where one partner was "normal" while the other was "undersexed" or "oversexed," but even in imagining different possible sexual drives for husbands and wives, it still worked from the basic premise that it was "normal for men to be more highly sexed than women."[23] This basic biological fact, according to the Andelins, structured the sexual dynamics of married life. "Always remember," the pamphlet instructed, "the man is the pursuer, the woman the pursued, even after marriage. Always keep this straight."[24] Instead of pursuing sex, women were to present themselves in ways that aroused their husband's sexual interest. "Remember, it is femininity to which masculinity responds," the pamphlet advised. "When a woman loses her womanliness, to a great extent she loses her ability to arouse a man sexually." This referred not only to appearance and dress but also to her behavior: "For example, when a woman acquires the masculine traits of aggressiveness, boldness, drive, masculine efficiency and independence, she can 'turn a man off' sexually."[25] As *Fascinating Womanhood* had taught, the responsibility for achieving marital bliss depended on the wife "making your husband number one in your life." "To live this fully," the pamphlet extended the logic, "you must also make your husband's *needs* number one. Since sex is an important need, it is vital for the wife to keep this in a priority position."[26] But as *Fascinating Womanhood* always argued, these responsibilities were not a burden for women but rather their only pathway to true fulfillment and pleasure. "When a woman places her husband's sex needs in top priority," the pamphlet promised, "she will awaken a greater desire in herself. Once again, rewards come when she gives it her all."[27]

Helen and Aubrey developed their thoughts on sexuality in other publications addressed to young women and to men. In *The Secrets of Winning Men*, later renamed *The Fascinating Girl*, Helen sought to prepare women for happy marriages by making them into Fascinating Women before they became brides. Throughout were warnings that girls avoid premarital sex because it was both a sin against God and an impediment to marriage. "A man's desire for you as a sexual partner is no indication he desires you for a marriage partner.... It can, in fact, drive them away," she warned.[28] Aubrey's message to men, *Man of Steel and Velvet: A Guide to Masculine Development*, stressed that masculinity had to be cultivated for a successful marriage, including a healthy sexual relationship, but also as a guard against children becoming homosexuals. Aubrey theorized that homosexuality developed in "unisex" homes where children did not see their fathers and mothers demonstrating proper masculine and feminine roles, respectively.[29] By the 1970s, such ideas about homosexuality had little purchase in professional circles—the American Psychological Association would declassify homosexuality as a mental illness in 1973—but they resonated with religious conservatives struggling with the era's rapid social transformations of sexuality and gender. These ideas would inform religious conservatives' political responses to the "unisex" or "sexless" society they believed the Equal Rights Amendment would create.

As much as she believed in her message, Andelin could have hardly predicted her book's success, especially after the struggles she had encountered in finding a publisher. *Fascinating Womanhood* sold quickly through Mormon circles, bolstered by the workshops Andelin held in LDS wards. The LDS Church's Deseret Book Store chain could not keep *Fascinating Womanhood* in stock, ordering the book in batches of one thousand copies at a time. That first year, Andelin sold over forty thousand copies of her book.[30] Ten years later, nearly 1.2 million copies had flown off the shelf. By then four hundred thousand women across the country, including many non-Mormons, had also completed the FW workshop, paying twenty dollars for the ten-week experience.[31] As demand grew, Andelin trained women throughout the country to lead FW workshops, equipping them with her detailed lesson outlines for the program.[32] With this franchise model, FW expanded beyond its Mormon base, attracting Catholic and evangelical women who appreciated its conservative worldview. FW had no explicit references to LDS theology or the Book of Mormon. Andelin used only Bible verses to support her arguments, giving FW a broad Christian basis that aided its appeal. Shorn of any Mormon characteristics, FW fit smoothly into the conservative religious outlooks of evangelical and Catholic women alike. So many women wrote Andelin long, detailed letters of how FW had positively changed their lives and marriages that she had these "success stories" published as a book in 1973. "My prayer is that every woman could know and accept Fascinating Womanhood," one woman happily wrote to Andelin.[33]

JAQUIE DAVISON AND THE TURN TO POLITICS

One early adherent of Fascinating Womanhood, Jaquie Davison of Kingman, Arizona, became politicized by FW's message. Like Andelin, Davison belonged to the LDS Church, and also like her mentor, Davison presided over a large family with seven children. Born to a single mother in Kentucky, Jaquie had grown up impoverished. At the age of eight, she had joined the LDS Church with her mother. But at sixteen, Jaquie became pregnant after being raped by her boyfriend. After a failed first marriage, Jaquie struggled with four children and an alcohol problem. While waiting tables, she met Ronnie Davison, a chiropractor with two sons. After marrying in 1962, Davison gave birth to a boy, the seventh child in their combined family (they would ultimately have eight), and she and Ronnie settled in Kingman to raise their family. Ronnie soon converted to Mormonism, and the married couple immersed themselves in the church.[34]

As a young housewife in the LDS Church in the 1960s, Davison heard frequently about Fascinating Womanhood. Though her marriage had given her life personal stability and financial security, Davison still felt overwhelmed by motherhood and unfulfilled by her marriage. Just as her LDS sisters did, Davison grabbed onto Andelin's book and enrolled in a Fascinating Womanhood workshop at church, hoping to find happiness as a wife and mother. FW's teachings resonated with Davison. In short time, Davison was leading FW seminars and had become a close confidant of Andelin's.[35] In many ways, Davison was the perfect example of Andelin's Ideal Woman. As a mother of seven and a devout Mormon, Davison exhibited the requisite devotion to family and faith. But Davison was no shrinking violet, nor a typically demure Mormon housewife. She had a vivacious personality and cut a striking figure, topped by her platinum blonde bouffant hairdo. Davison loved describing herself to reporters as a "Jayne Mansfield type," an intentional swipe against the era's sexless feminists with their straight hair and pants that Andelin and Davison both so despised.[36] Press accounts fixated on Davison's appearance, describing her "elaborately curled, bleached hair, heavy, skillfully applied makeup, buxom figure, [and] flashing smile."[37] Another reported that she looked "as if she has just stepped out of a magazine centerfold" and asked if she ever felt like a sex object. "Oh no . . . no," Davison protested, "and even if I do, that's OK too."[38] All of this was calculated strategy based on her (and Andelin's) conviction that women's greatest power came from their physical attributes. "I do not have to be told the power of femininity," Davison wrote in her 1972 best-selling book, *I Am a Housewife!* "The way those [reporters] looked at me reminded me once more of that priceless possession."[39]

Davison's assertive sexuality unusually positioned her in the cultural terrain of the 1970s.[40] Her frank, open, and often playful discussion of sexuality seemed unsurprising in the era of sexual revolution. Yet Davison's message was deeply conservative, contending all sexual relations could take place only within monogamous heterosexual marriage. Even more than Andelin, Davison characterized marital intimacy as a thrilling pleasure and "God-given joy," a rebuke to the era's calls for experimentation and loosening mores outside of the traditional bonds of marriage.[41] Still, as a devout Mormon, Davison's ideas also diverged from the LDS Church's serious and utilitarian treatment of marital sex, a product of the church's turn from its polygamous past. Although some Mormons had practiced plural marriage in the nineteenth century, church leaders banned the practice in 1890 under pressure from the federal government. In remaking the Mormon image and positioning itself as a mainstream religious faith, the LDS Church in the twentieth century actively suppressed the history of polygamy in Mormonism's religious identity and cultural memory. This entailed glorifying the traditional heterosexual family unit in Mormon theology and culture, coupled with negative depictions of sexuality. LDS leaders, predictably, condemned all extramarital sex as sinful and dangerous, but even married sex suffered joyless treatment from LDS authorities who characterized it almost solely as a religious obligation to procreate.[42] (This treatment also contrasted in tone and message from that given by the mainline Protestant leaders described in Samira K. Mehta's chapter in this volume who argued "Christian duty" required married couples to use contraceptives to control their family size in an overpopulated planet.) As the sexual revolution escalated, the LDS Church doubled down on its teachings against, as one LDS leader described, "the wanton sex permissiveness of our day."[43] But unlike Davison and Andelin, the LDS Church did not accompany these jeremiads with encomiums about the joy of proper marital relations. As LDS president Spencer W. Kimball declared in 1974, "The Lord did not give sex to man for a plaything." Instead, he reminded them of the LDS scripture "For [virgins] are given unto [man] to multiply and replenish the earth, according to [God's] commandment."[44] As a mother of seven, Davison clearly understood the procreative nature of sex, but in her workshops and book, Davison esteemed a "good sexual relationship" as a critical and enjoyable component of marriage.[45] In the context of midcentury Mormonism, Davison's treatment of sexuality provided LDS women with a positive and playful alternative to the church's sometimes bleak message.

Still, Davison shared her church's sexual conservatism and worried about the nation's shifting social mores and political developments. Participating in Fascinating Womanhood unexpectedly had awakened her to politics as Andelin encouraged women to become active in local issues. Davison, however, had far bigger concerns. In 1970, when she discovered Congress was considering the Equal Rights Amendment, Davison set out to stop its ratification, convinced her two daughters would be drafted to serve in Vietnam should the ERA become law. Sitting at her kitchen table with a few friends, Davison created Happiness of Womanhood, a grassroots political organization to oppose the ERA. Davison explained she had chosen her group's name so its acronym would resemble that of the feminist National Organization for Women. "And so it turns out to be the H.O.W. versus the N.O.W.," Davison joked.[46] Yet Davison did not think this was an even match, characterizing feminists as representing only 3 percent of American women.[47] HOW activists repeated the line frequently with reporters, arguing 97 percent of women agreed with them—another "silent majority" now stirred to defend its values. "With their abortions and sterilizations they will soon become extinct," a HOW newsletter predicted of feminists. "In the meantime we must protect our children from their immoral teachings."[48]

With Andelin's blessing, Davison recruited FW members to join HOW, quickly building a strong Mormon base in Arizona, California, and Utah.[49] After Congress sent the ERA to state legislatures to vote on its ratification, HOW was one of the few groups mounting an organized campaign against it.[50] "I was in on it two years before Phyllis Schlafly and her 'Stop ERA,'" she later bragged when Schlafly started getting all the attention.[51] Davison traveled the country, testifying against the ERA in state legislatures. (She also spoke at antiabortion rallies in states considering liberalizing their abortion laws before *Roe v. Wade*.)[52] In Pennsylvania, Davison testified in a miniskirt and blew a toy whistle "to get my equal time in the presence of women's lib." She also presented a lock and key that she said represented the relationship between men and women, arguing that the ERA "would make us all locks with no keys," an allusion to the unisex society that Fascinating Womanhood had warned against.[53]

Davison's tactics often displayed her wit and knack for publicity. One stunt involved presenting California legislators with live mice after they had voted for the ERA. "This is our way of saying you're mice, not men," a HOW member explained.[54] "How could a good looking man like you be such a rat?" one HOW woman asked a senator.[55] When Davison learned the feminists of NOW had planned a Washington, D.C., rally for the ERA, she scheduled a countermarch in Los Angeles where HOW women would carry satin pillows representing "the life of ease women have thanks to their husbands."[56] Pleased with the results, Davison then launched a "Satin Pillow Tour," crisscrossing the country from 1971 to 1972 speaking out against the ERA, abortion, gay rights, and sex education to enthusiastic audiences.[57] The tour also included competitions for the prettiest satin pillow brought by a housewife and male judges' picking the most feminine woman in attendance, bringing together Davison's unique blend of sexual suggestiveness and conservative politics.[58]

Like many religious conservatives of her time, Davison believed sexually fulfilling heterosexual marriages served as a bulwark against the nation's moral decay and the key to social stability. At the same time, fears over nonmarital sexuality stood at the core of Davison and HOW's opposition to the ERA, as participants believed the amendment would unleash sexual permissiveness, promote abortion, and encourage gay rights, including same-sex marriage. No sooner had Fascinating Womanhood warned about the dangers of the "unisex" marriage to the healthy workings of the home than the nation was about to ratify an amendment HOW believed would eradicate gender distinctions, emboldening the "New Morality" of "promiscuity . . . homosexuality . . . and bestiality" that HOW foresaw.[59] In the logic of FW and HOW, proper sexuality, marital happiness, and even healthy childhood development required heightened gender differences from men and women.[60] In the HOW worldview, gender was sexualized and sexuality was gendered, but the ERA threatened to sever that relationship. Disentangling gender, sex, and sexuality promised dangerous results. Rapists would attack women in non-sex-segregated bathrooms. Abortions on demand would be legalized since men never faced the unequal responsibility of pregnancy. And homosexuals would gain all rights accorded to heterosexuals, including parenting, adoption, and marriage, since the law would now require two "persons" rather than a man and a woman to enter such arrangements.[61] In the ERA's language of equality, Davison heard only the possibility of sexual anarchy where women and particularly men were cut free from the reciprocity and mutual obligation of traditional heterosexual marriage to pursue the worst impulses of personal liberation, including unrestrained sexuality. "It is no wonder we have disposable relationships with each other," a HOW newsletter lamented.[62] A whole social order built upon heterosexual marital monogamy would collapse if the ERA became law, HOW warned its members.

Although its largest influence remained in Davison's home state of Arizona, HOW grew quickly, claiming ten thousand members in all fifty states by 1973.[63] While HOW had Mormon origins, its national expansion crossed religious lines, drawing in women from other conservative religious groups, many already active in conservative causes.[64] In Texas, Wanda Schultz, a longtime member of the John Birch Society, helmed HOW's state chapter made up mostly of evangelical women who worked closely with another anti-ERA group, Women Who Want to Be Women, a Fort Worth organization with deep ties to the conservative Church of Christ.[65] Three hundred largely Catholic women in Michigan's HOW chapter also worked with the local John Birch Society and Lifespan, a pro-life organization, to rescind Michigan's ratification of the ERA.[66] In Nebraska, the wife of an evangelical Lutheran minister directed the state chapter.[67] Claire Middleton, New York's state leader, led family planning workshops in her Catholic diocese and volunteered for her church's pro-life ministry. Her husband, John, served as chairman of the New York State Right to Life Committee.[68]

The religious diversification of HOW depended in part on Davison's promotion of a shared Christian identity with fellow women over her own

Mormon faith, a move that other religious right figures would adopt in the coming years as they built a cross-denominational political movement of religious conservatives. In the absence of explicit Mormon language or theology, HOW newsletters trafficked in generic Christian discourse and imagery. God, faith, the Bible, and prayer were routinely invoked; the scourges of sin and disobedience, particularly of a sexual kind, earned constant lamentations. This broad Christian ethos invited wide participation from conservative religious women without alienating any through overt sectarianism. Still, HOW chapters tended to reflect the local religious demographics and friendship networks of their members, such as the heavily Catholic Michigan group or the largely evangelical chapters in the South. And many Catholic women learned about HOW through Catholic circles. Patrick Frawley Jr., publisher of the reactionary Catholic publication *Twin Circle*, frequently promoted Happiness of Womanhood and Davison's book in his weekly newspaper.[69] Clarence Manion, the conservative Catholic radio host, had Davison on his show several times to speak out against the ERA and publicize her organization to his audience. One of those interviews, conducted by Father Daniel Lyons, a conservative Jesuit priest who also served as editor of *Twin Circle*, featured no mention of Davison's Mormonism. Instead, Lyons and Davison spoke generically of "the Creator" who had made women and men different in order to serve particular functions in the family, a difference now threatened by passage of the ERA.[70] In the end, the Catholic, evangelical, and Mormon women of HOW united around a traditional Christian identity recognizable more by its sexual and cultural conservatism than by any particular theology.

HOW chapters spearheaded the work against the ERA in their states. They also supported anti-ERA work elsewhere. For example, HOW members from other states sent money to the small chapter in Louisiana that helped prevent the ERA's ratification there.[71] At the state level, HOW chapters also addressed local political issues relating to sexuality and morality. The Michigan chapter helped defeat two sex education bills there.[72] In California, HOW held antipornography marches and opposed the distribution of birth control information to minors.[73] In battling the ERA, HOW warned that the amendment allowed the federal government to intrude into the private marital and sexual relationship between husband and wife. Similarly, HOW interpreted public school sex education and the providing of contraceptives and abortions to minors as "another usurpation of parent's [sic] rights" to shape and control their children's sexuality.[74] In its ten-point platform, HOW proposed to "restore morality... and return dignity and respect to sex in marriage. *We* will teach our sons and daughters to be morally clean."[75] The ERA had activated Davison at first, but it had also exposed her and other HOW women to a range of political issues in the 1970s concerning sexuality that they organized against. As a HOW pamphlet in 1980 explained, the group would oppose "any and all legislation concerning any issue which threatens our ... traditionally moral way of life."[76]

CONCLUSION

The personal had become political for conservative anti-ERA women. Helen Andelin and Jaquie Davison had transformed their messages of wifely submission and heightened femininity into a political cause, fighting the amendment they believed would threaten a wife's superior status with a downgraded equality and rendering women into sexless automatons for the socialist state rather than domestic goddesses of the hearth and home. Andelin's Fascinating Womanhood franchise had spun a virtual cottage industry of conservative women, including the evangelical Marabel Morgan, author of *The Total Woman*, and the Mormon Laura Snyder, author of *A Woman's Fulfillment*, who crafted their own version of the Andelin brand, writing books and leading workshops that combined religious orthodoxy with beauty lessons, cooking tips, and instructions for the marital bed.[77]

If these women's works avoided directly engaging the political issues of the day, they still advanced their own politics as they advocated traditional marriage arrangements, highly gendered notions of male and female roles and responsibilities, and a general sexual conservatism. That message, of course, had heightened meaning and deep resonance for conservative religious women in an era of women's liberation and sexual permissiveness. Religious conservatives had witnessed the advent of the birth control pill, the legalization of abortion, and the near-ratification of the Equal Rights Amendment. They had lamented the culture's loosening sexual mores, the rise in venereal disease and divorce, and the increasing visibility of homosexuality. They had worried about what they saw as legal challenges to sexual difference and the traditional marriage arrangement that they believed protected rather than oppressed them, and they had fretted about what their children were learning in sex education courses at school. At the same time, they shared the feelings of frustration and lack of fulfillment in their married lives that more liberal women had decried, but they refused to believe the solution could be found in challenging the patriarchy, seeking professional opportunity outside the home, or throwing off the customs and practices of traditional married life. Turning to Helen Andelin, Jaquie Davison, Marabel Morgan, and others, these women sought solace and strength in reforming marriage from within by a reevaluation of their own attitudes and behaviors. Embracing the gospel of wifely submission, these women believed they were not accepting a circumscribed life of self-effacement but instead finding the "fascinating" and "happy" life of their dreams.

Even if Andelin did not want to distract Fascinating Womanhood with a turn to politics, her devotees could not help but connect her message to the political issues of the day. LDS women had picked up Andelin's book and enrolled in her seminar to address the personal crises they felt in their homes and marriages; as Americans confronted domestic transformations, these women believed Andelin's message of male authority, female submission, and marital sexual fulfillment offered the only model of reform and the perfect antidote to the nation's ills. In the end, what they received from Andelin was not merely a personal instruction for how to run their homes and marriages but rather a call to arms to push back at the nation's changing social and sexual landscape. Jaquie Davison, herself an FW devotee, harnessed the impulse for personal and social reform coming out of Andelin's movement. With her own book, seminar, and grassroots organization, Davison translated Andelin's efforts into the political arena, mobilizing thousands of Mormon and other conservative religious women to oppose the Equal Rights Amendment, abortion, and sex education. By the end of the 1970s, the LDS Church would become one of the most powerful forces against the ERA, using its women to prevent the amendment's ratification through a nationally orchestrated movement. But thousands of these women had already become politically active thanks to Davison, and still thousands more had been primed to the politics of sexual conservatism through the writings and lectures of Andelin and Davison. Fascinating and happy, they stepped onto the nation's political stage to protect their marriages, their families, and, ultimately, the nation they believed the sexual revolution sought to destroy.

NOTES

My thanks to Gill Frank, Heather White, Bethany Moreton, Natalia Petrzela, Samira Mehta, Whit Strub, and Anthony Petro for their feedback and suggestions on various drafts of this essay.

1. Julie Debra Neuffer, *Helen Andelin and the Fascinating Womanhood Movement* (Salt Lake City: University of Utah Press, 2014).

2. Robert O. Self, *All in the Family: The Realignment of American Democracy since the 1960s* (New York: Hill and Wang, 2012), 255–57, 280–81; Jennifer Heller, "Marriage, Womanhood, and the Search for 'Something More': American Evangelical Women's Best-Selling

'Self-Help' Books, 1972–1979," *Journal of Religion and Popular Culture* 2 (Fall 2002): 17–20, 44; Daniel K. Williams, *God's Own Party: The Making of the Christian Right* (New York: Oxford University Press, 2010), 110. See also Rebecca L. Davis, *More Perfect Unions: The American Search for Marital Bliss* (Cambridge, Mass.: Harvard University Press, 2010), 207–8.

3. Rebecca L. Davis, "Eroticized Wives: Evangelical Marriage Guides and God's Plan for the Christian Family," in *The Embrace of Eros: Bodies, Desires, and Sexuality in Christianity*, ed. Margaret D. Kamitsuka (Minneapolis: Fortress Press, 2010), 165–79; Amy DeRogatis, "What Would Jesus Do? Sexuality and Salvation in Protestant Evangelical Sex Manuals, 1950s to the Present," *Church History* 74, no. 1 (March 2005): 97–137; Susan Hardin, "Family Reform Movements: Recent Feminism and Its Opposition," *Feminist Studies* 7, no. 1 (Spring 1981): 57–75; David Harrington Watt, *A Transforming Faith: Explorations of Twentieth-Century American Evangelicalism* (New Brunswick: Rutgers University Press, 1991), 131–36; Daniel K. Williams, "Sex and the Evangelicals: Gender Issues, the Sexual Revolution, and Abortion in the 1960s," in *American Evangelicals and the 1960s*, ed. Axel R. Schäfer (Madison: University of Wisconsin Press, 2013), 97–118.

4. Neil J. Young, "'The ERA Is a Moral Issue': The Mormon Church, LDS Women, and the Defeat of the Equal Rights Amendment," *American Quarterly* 59, no. 3 (September 2007): 623–44. See also Neil J. Young, *We Gather Together: The Religious Right and the Problem of Interfaith Politics* (New York: Oxford University Press, 2015).

5. Historians of conservative evangelical, Catholic, and Mormon women alike have shown how these women did not see a paradox between their traditional religious beliefs and practices and their political activism. For a sampling, see R. Marie Griffith, *God's Daughters: Evangelical Women and the Power of Submission* (Berkeley: University of California Press, 1997); Michael Lienesch, *Redeeming America: Piety and Politics in the New Christian Right* (Chapel Hill: University of North Carolina Press, 1993); Kristin Luker, *Abortion and the Politics of Motherhood* (Berkeley: University of California Press, 1984); Stacie Taranto, *Kitchen Table Politics: Conservative Women and Family Values in the Seventies* (Philadelphia: University of Pennsylvania Press, forthcoming); and Young, "'ERA Is a Moral Issue.'"

6. There has been a robust scholarship on conservative women from both sociologists and historians, particularly related to anti-ERA activism and other social concerns of the 1970s. See Rebecca Klatch, "Coalition and Conflict among Women of the New Right," *Signs: A Journal of Women in Culture and Society* 13, no. 4 (Summer 1988): 671–94; Theodore S. Arrington and Patricia A. Kyle, "Equal Rights Amendment Activists in North Carolina," *Signs: A Journal of Women in Culture and Society* 3, no. 3 (Spring 1978): 666–80; David W. Brady and Kent L. Tedin, "Ladies in Pink: Religion and Political Ideology in the Anti-ERA Movement," *Social Science Quarterly* 56, no. 4 (March 1976): 564–75; Rebecca Klatch, *Women of the New Right* (Philadelphia: Temple University Press, 1987); Susan E. Marshall, "Ladies against Women: Mobilization Dilemmas of Antifeminist Movements," *Social Problems* 32, no. 4 (April 1985): 348–62; Lisa McGirr, *Suburban Warriors: The Origins of the New American Right* (Princeton: Princeton University Press, 2001); and Catherine E. Rymph, *Republican Women: Feminism and Conservatism from Suffrage through the Rise of the New Right* (Chapel Hill: University of North Carolina Press, 2006).

7. Mary Frances Berry, *Why ERA Failed: Politics, Women's Rights, and the Amending Process of the Constitution* (Bloomington: Indiana University Press, 1986); Janet K. Boles, *The Politics of the Equal Rights Amendment: Conflict and the Decision Process* (New York: Longman, 1979); Donald G. Mathews and Jane Sherron de Hart, *Sex, Gender, and the Politics of ERA: A State and the Nation* (New York: Oxford University Press, 1990). For special emphasis on Phyllis Schlafly's role, see Hillary Frayne Slevin, "The New Right and the Defeat of the Equal Rights Amendment" (MA thesis, Hampshire College, 1992); and Patricia A. Tilson, "The Defeat of the Equal Rights Amendment: A Propaganda Analysis of Phyllis Schlafly's STOP ERA Campaign" (MA thesis, University of Houston, 1996).

8. Steven Mintz and Susan Kellogg, *Domestic Revolutions: A Social History of the American Family* (New York: Free Press, 1988), 207.

9. Betty Friedan, *The Feminine Mystique* (New York: W. W. Norton, 1963), 20.

10. Ibid., 15.

11. For Andelin's biographical details, see Neuffer, *Helen Andelin*.

12. Helen B. Andelin, *Fascinating Womanhood: Lesson Outlines* (n.p., 1965), 10, 17. Capitalization and italics in the original.

13. Helen Andelin, *Fascinating Womanhood*, rev. ed. (New York: Bantam Dell, 2007); Andelin, *Fascinating Womanhood: Lesson Outlines*.

14. H. Andelin, *Fascinating Womanhood: Lesson Outlines*, 60.

15. Aubrey P. Andelin, ed., *Fascinating Womanhood Success Stories* (Santa Barbara: Pacific Press, 1973), 106.

16. H. Andelin, *Fascinating Womanhood*, 395.

17. "Celestial Kingdom," "Exaltation," and "Salvation" in Bruce R. McConkie, *Mormon Doctrine* (Salt Lake City: Bookcraft, 1958), 109–10, 238–40, 602–3; Douglas J. Davies, *The Mormon Culture of Salvation: Force, Grace and Glory* (Aldershot, UK: Ashgate, 2000).

18. H. Andelin, *Fascinating Womanhood*, 62.

19. Ibid., 216.

20. H. Andelin, *Fascinating Womanhood: Lesson Outlines*, 73.

21. Neuffer, *Helen Andelin*, 64. Although both Helen and Aubrey were listed as the authors, Neuffer argues that Aubrey wrote the pamphlet alone.

22. Aubrey P. Andelin and Helen B. Andelin, *Fascinating Womanhood Principles Applied to Sex* (Santa Barbara: Andelin Foundation for Education in Family Living, 1974), 1, 5. Italics in the original.

23. Ibid., 5.

24. Ibid., 10.

25. Ibid.

26. Ibid., 8. Italics in the original.

27. Ibid.

28. Helen Andelin, *The Fascinating Girl*, rev. ed. (1970; Bloomington: AuthorHouse, 2003), ix.

29. Aubrey P. Andelin, *Man of Steel and Velvet: A Guide to Masculine Development* (Santa Barbara: Pacific Press Santa Barbara, 1972).

30. Neuffer, *Helen Andelin*, 45, 69.

31. Louise Farr, "Peddling the Pedestal," *New Times*, October 17, 1975, 49; Ellie Grossman, "Marriage Can Be Fascinating," *Sumter (S.C.) Daily Item*, September 16, 1975.

32. H. Andelin, *Fascinating Womanhood: Lesson Outlines*.

33. A. Andelin, *Fascinating Womanhood Success Stories*, 93.

34. Jaquie Davison, *I Am a Housewife! A Housewife Is the Most Important Person in the World* (New York: Guild Books, 1972), 4–20.

35. Ibid., 21–34.

36. Farr, "Peddling the Pedestal," 52.

37. "HOW Founder, However Apologetic, Is an Activist," *Daily Independent* (Long Beach, Calif.), June 12, 1974.

38. Doug Shuit, "Two Mothers Cast Ballots for Home, Femininity, Frills," *Toledo Blade*, August 26, 1970.

39. Davison, *I Am a Housewife!*, 42.

40. Nancy F. Cott, *Public Vows: A History of Marriage and the Nation* (Cambridge, Mass.: Harvard University Press, 2000), 200–214.

41. Davison, *I Am a Housewife!*, 54.

42. J. B. Haws, *The Mormon Image in the American Mind: Fifty Years of Public Perception* (New York: Oxford University Press, 2013), 74–98. See also Sarah Barringer Gordon, *The Mormon Question: Polygamy and Constitutional Conflict in Nineteenth-Century America* (Chapel Hill: University of North Carolina Press, 2002). For an example of LDS leaders' dour treatment of marital sex as a religious duty during the same time of Andelin's and Davison's influence, see Victor L. Brown, "The Meaning of Morality," General Conference, April 1971, https://www.lds.org/general-conference/1971/04/the-meaning-of-morality; Spencer W. Kimball, "God Will Not Be Mocked," General Conference, October 1974, https://www.lds.org/general-conference/1974/10/god-will-not-be-mocked; and Steve Gilliland, "The Psychological Case for Chastity," *Ensign*, July 1975, 54.

43. Spencer W. Kimball, "Voices of the Past, of the Present, of the Future," *Ensign*, June 1971, https://www.lds.org/ensign/1971/06/voices-of-the-past-of-the-present-of-the-future.

44. Spencer W. Kimball, "Guidelines to Carry Forth the Work of God in Cleanliness," General Conference, April 1974, https://www.lds.org/general-conference/1974/04/guidelines-to-carry-forth-the-work-of-god-in-cleanliness. The scripture comes from Doctrine and Covenants 132:63. Brackets in the original.

45. Davison, *I Am a Housewife!*, 54.

46. Ibid., 36.

47. Ibid., 71.

48. Happiness of Womanhood newsletter, June 1974, box 113, folder 15, Carl [Charles Curtis Jr.] McIntire Manuscript Collection, Princeton Theological Seminary (hereafter PTS).

49. Davison, *I Am a Housewife!*, 35–37; Doug Shuit, "Mother of 7 Fights Women's Lib Drive," *Los Angeles Times*, August 22, 1970; Neuffer, *Helen Andelin*, 107–8.

50. Davison, *I Am a Housewife!*, 67–72; Berry, *Why ERA Failed*, 65.

51. Farr, "Peddling the Pedestal," 52.

52. "300 Rally in Abortion Bill Protest," *Traverse City(Mich.) Record-Eagle*, May 17, 1971.

53. "Equal Rights Bill Need Disputed," *Pittsburgh Press*, June 23, 1972.

54. "Mouse Caper Sparks Stir," *Toledo Blade*, November 11, 1972.

55. Keith Kathian, "Meet Happiness of Womanhood, Inc. (HOW)," *Life Lines*, December 11, 1972, reproduced in HOW newsletter, n.d., PTS.

56. "Feminist Marches Scheduled," *Corpus Christi Times*, August 26, 1971.

57. Jack Webb, "Birth Control vs. Satin Pillows," *Sterling (Ill.) Daily Gazette*, October 26, 1973; Self, *All in the Family*, 255–56.

58. Marie E. J. Rosenwasser, "Growing Up from Another Perspective: The Countermovement," paper presented at the Annual Meeting of the Speech Communication Association, Chicago, December 1972, http://files.eric.ed.gov/fulltext/ED073503.pdf.

59. HOW newsletter, n.d., PTS.

60. For example, see "A Second Look at the Equal Rights Amendment," November 1977, folder: Happiness of Womanhood, Inc., Wilcox Collection, Spencer Research Library, University of Kansas.

61. William Weddon, "Happiness of Womanhood Her Concern," *Jackson (Mich.) Citizen Patriot*, March 21, 1974; and Patt Barbour to Michigan State Legislators, October 15, 1973, both in folder: Happiness of Womanhood, Inc., 1973–1983, box 1, Shirley Wohlfield Papers, 1972–1988, Bentley Historical Library, University of Michigan.

62. HOW newsletter, "Parents—Act Now!," June 1977, Wohlfield Papers.

63. Eileen Shanahan, "Opposition Rises to Amendment on Equal Rights," *New York Times*, January 15, 1973.

64. One way of ascertaining HOW's religious diversity is through the biographies of state leaders. I was able to determine the religious affiliation of thirteen of sixty-one state leaders and officers identified in HOW newsletters. These included three LDS, two Catholics, and eight Protestants, including Lutheran, Southern Baptist, Seventh-day Adventist, Pentecostal, and nondenominational fundamentalist. The three LDS leaders were in Arizona, Nevada, and Wyoming—states with significant Mormon populations. As HOW expanded into the Southeast and Midwest, the organization incorporated mostly Catholic and evangelical members.

65. Betty Barnes, May 12, 1975, Houston Oral History Project, http://digital.houstonlibrary.org/oral-history/betty-barnes_OH007.php; "Me Too, Please," *Houston Daily Cougar*, February 11, 1975; Kaye Northcott, "Fighting the ERA: The Ladies Mobilize," *Texas Observer*, November 15, 1974, 1–5; Nancy E. Baker, "Hermine Tobolowsky: A Feminist's Fight for Equal Rights," in *Texas Women: Their Histories, Their Lives*, ed. Elizabeth Hayes Turner, Stephanie Cole, and Rebecca Sharpless (Athens: University of Georgia Press, 2015), 447.

66. Letters to the editor, *Hillsdale (Mich.) Daily News*, July 5, 1977; *Michigan in Books*, vols. 12–13 (Lansing: Michigan State Library, 1971), 3.

67. "Against Equality," *Columbus Telegram*, February 24, 1973.

68. "Family Planning Classes Set in Ticonderoga," *Plattsburgh (N.Y.) Press-Republican*, May 15, 1982; "Bishop LaValley to Confer Pro Ecclesia et Pontifice Cross December 8," *North Country Catholic*, November 20, 2013, http://northcountrycatholic.org/Articles/2013/11_20ProEcclesia.html.

69. Mary A. Delsman, *Everything You Need to Know about *ERA (*the Equal Rights Amendment)* (Riverside, Calif.: Meranza Press, 1975), 74, 76.

70. "Another Silent Majority Becomes Vocal," Broadcast No. 916, April 30, 1972, box 84, folder 4, Clarence E. Manion Papers, Chicago History Museum. I am grateful to Nicole Hemmer for sharing this source with me.

71. HOW newsletter, June 1974, PTS.

72. Ibid.

73. "HOW Founder, However Apologetic, Is an Activist."

74. "Parents—Act Now!"

75. Davison, *I Am a Housewife!*, 90. Emphasis is mine.

76. HOW pamphlet, 1980, folder: Happiness of Womanhood, Inc., Wilcox Collection.

77. David White, "Fulfilling Marriage: Camarillo Housewife a Happy Author," *Oxnard Press Courier*, August 23, 1970.

THE MAKING OF GAY AND LESBIAN RABBIS IN RECONSTRUCTIONIST JUDAISM, 1979–1992

REBECCA T. ALPERT
AND JACOB J. STAUB

Since the mid-nineteenth century, most American Jewish leaders have been trained in seminaries and ordained as rabbis. A rabbi is a teacher, preacher, pastor, prayer leader, and interpreter of Jewish life and customs to both secular and other faith communities. Rabbis serve in a variety of institutional contexts but primarily in synagogues, schools, hospitals, and communal organizations. Rabbis were all men (with a few exceptions) until the 1970s. Today, excluding the Orthodox, half of American rabbis are women. The vast majority were (and still are) married and raising children in keeping with Jewish pronatalist values.[1]

Until the 1980s, it was also presumed that all rabbis were heterosexual. We have little way of knowing how many rabbis might have hidden their same-sex desires or behaviors during the decades—and centuries—before the emergence of modern gay and lesbian identities.[2] But just as the second-wave feminist movement enabled Jewish women to imagine that they too could be rabbis, so did the gay and lesbian movement of the same era also encourage Jews who were coming out as gay or lesbian to consider the rabbinate as a career option.[3] The entrance of women—heterosexual and lesbian—and gay men into the rabbinate posed a great challenge to the Jewish community in that era, making Jews question their assumptions and beliefs about religion and sexuality. While the story of women entering the rabbinate has been told many times over, the struggles of gay men and lesbians to achieve acceptance has yet to be explored in depth.[4]

This chapter tells how one Jewish denomination, the Reconstructionists, came to accept gay men and lesbians in their school for training rabbis, adopting the following policy: "An openly gay or lesbian orientation shall not in itself constitute adequate grounds for the rejection of an otherwise qualified applicant for admission to the College or for dismissal from the College of a student otherwise in good standing, or for denial of graduation of a student who otherwise meets all requirements for graduation."[5] This policy, adopted in 1984, made the Reconstructionist Rabbinical College (RRC) the first school for training rabbis to admit and ordain openly gay and lesbian students and only the second denomination in the United States to formally allow gay and lesbian religious leadership.[6] This move was particularly bold at a time when other religious organizations, even liberal ones, were actively barring gay men and lesbians from the clergy.

The story of RRC's shift in policy between 1979 and 1992 reveals the tangled and uneven nature of institutional and ideological change in sexual and religious mores. In practice, the changes in RRC as a religious institution look very similar to other kinds of organized policy change. They took place through committee meetings, communal debate, and democratic vote. Individuals' ideas about same-sex sexuality and their experiences with gay and lesbian identities shaped how they participated in this process. And some of those participants were gay and lesbian themselves. At first glance, much about this process does not seem "religious"—if by that term we mean formal teaching, ritual practice, or textual interpretation. But these institutional practices and decisions about policy were also deeply tied to, shaped by, and productive of religious meanings. The story of how RRC came to accept the ordination of gays and lesbians as rabbis highlights the complicated relationship between policy and practice.

The debate over including gays and lesbians began in 1979 when RRC rejected its first openly gay applicant. The policy change in 1984 permitted ordination, but hostility toward gays and lesbians as well as the efforts to transform the heteronormative culture of the school and the denomination at large continued until 1992, when the Reconstructionist movement officially affirmed the policy for its congregations. These struggles ultimately resulted in open acknowledgment and solidarity, in which the Reconstructionist movement has taken great pride. By the beginning of the twenty-first century, this landmark decision would be interpreted as a cornerstone of the Reconstructionist movement's platform on inclusive community.[7]

RECONSTRUCTIONIST JUDAISM

Given its history, it is not surprising that Reconstructionist Judaism moved relatively quickly to embrace religious rights for gay men and lesbians. Reconstructionism is a denomination of Judaism that began in the United

States in the 1920s, based on the teachings of Mordecai Kaplan, a Jewish philosopher and rabbi. Kaplan's followers call themselves Reconstructionists based on his idea that the customs and traditions of Judaism can be brought to life for every generation of Jews, who must "reconstruct" their Jewish heritage in ways that both incorporate the Jewish past and are in keeping with the best values of contemporary society. When it comes to making changes in Jewish tradition, the past, as Kaplan phrased it, "has a vote, but not a veto." Reconstructionists affirm that American Jews must straddle two worlds—the American and the Jewish. They maintain Jewish observances (celebrating holy days, keeping kosher) while simultaneously bringing the values of America (like democracy and women's rights) into Jewish organizational life. Kaplan famously called this effort "living in two civilizations."[8]

On this basis, Reconstructionist leaders were often supportive of progressive causes. In the 1930s and 1940s when the movement first got underway, Kaplan and his circle were politically outspoken in support of socialism, unions, and workers' rights. They published an influential magazine, the *Reconstructionist*, where they debated matters of interest to the general society as well as Jewish life. From its inception, Reconstructionism supported gender equality and is perhaps known best as the originator of the bat mitzvah in 1922. Until this time, the rite of passage at puberty had been restricted to boys. Reconstructionist Jews are innovative in their worship practices, tending toward an informal style of prayer while at the same time preserving the traditional Hebraic character of Jewish liturgy. This comfort with innovation would provide the backdrop for the willingness to tackle difficult social issues like gay and lesbian equality.[9]

Although Reconstructionism began as a philosophical approach, by the 1950s its followers organized into a structured denomination, culminating in the establishment of a school to train rabbis in 1968 in Philadelphia. As a product of its times and of the movement of which it was a part, the school defined itself as progressive. Women were admitted into the rabbinical program as soon as they applied, in its second year of operation.[10] Because democracy was an important value, students were included in decision-making processes. The progressive agenda, however, did not yet include openness to homosexuality, and there was no written policy about admitting homosexuals to the school.

JEWISH VIEWS OF HOMOSEXUALITY

The absence of such a policy was not surprising. Jewish texts and traditions, as historian Daniel Boyarin argues, did not conceptualize same-sex behavior in the terms and definitions of modern homosexuality.[11] And as Rebecca L.

Davis shows in this volume, the pronatalist concerns of twentieth-century Jews contributed to an increasing emphasis on marital heterosexuality. As a result, there was virtually no discussion of homosexuality in the Jewish community; if asked, most Jewish leaders probably were unaware that some Jews were homosexual. Moreover, the American Jewish press had little to no coverage of homosexuality until the 1970s. However, the emerging concern about homosexuality as a distinct area of deviance led Jewish leaders to formulate teachings and textual interpretations that specifically addressed this issue.

In 1968, Norman Lamm, a renowned rabbi and professor of philosophy at Yeshiva University (the Orthodox rabbinical school), was among the first to raise the topic in public, responding negatively to Christian clergy (and a few rabbis) who spoke in support of homosexual rights.[12] The most important addition to Jewish learning, *The Encyclopaedia Judaica*, was published in 1971–72 but did not include an article about homosexuality in its initial sixteen volumes. Indicative of the growing visibility of gay men and lesbians in American society, the subsequent first volume of the *Encyclopedia Judaica Yearbook* (1974) included what is now the classic explication of traditional sources forbidding homosexual relations, "Judaism and the Modern Attitude to Homosexuality," that Norman Lamm was invited to write. This thorough explication of the few references to homosexuality in ancient texts was the first of its kind. There were virtually no other resources available.

The mid-twentieth-century gay and lesbian identity movement also crystallized a challenge to this newly explicit antihomosexual tradition. Individual Jews were leaders in the homophile movement of the 1950s and in the beginnings of gay liberation in the 1960s, including in Philadelphia.[13] Jews in the gay liberation movement fought for social issues like decriminalization and destigmatization of their sexuality. Religious rights were not on their agenda, and the homophile movement in Philadelphia had little bearing on Jewish life in the 1950s and 1960s. The lack of connection stemmed from the fact that mainstream synagogues, with their intense focus on heterosexual marriage and child-rearing, were unwelcoming to gay and lesbian congregants.

THE EMERGENCE OF GAY JEWISH IDENTIFICATION

Not all gay and lesbian Jews were willing to relinquish their connections to Jewish religion. Gay-welcoming Christian churches like the Metropolitan Community Church provided a model for gay and lesbian Jews. In the early 1970s, several gay-welcoming synagogues and lesbian-feminist communities were founded. These groups did not affiliate with mainstream denominations.

The exception was the first gay synagogue, Beth Chaim Chadashim, founded in Los Angeles in 1972, which was supported from its inception by the Reform movement's regional leader, Rabbi Erwin Herman, the father of a gay son.[14]

As gay and lesbian Jews created visible Jewish institutional spaces, it was inevitable that rabbis too would begin to create spaces for sexual diversity within Jewish institutions. Doing so meant "coming out"—publicly declaring a gay or lesbian identity as a signature act of liberation. This decision symbolized, as historian John D'Emilio explains, "the shedding of the self-hatred that gay women and men internalized, and consequently it promised an immediate improvement in one's life."[15] However, when gays and lesbians came out, they also risked open stigma and the loss of family ties, jobs, and friends. Having created welcoming spaces where it was possible to come out, newly emboldened gay and lesbian Jews began to put more pressure on liberal Jewish institutions for validation and acceptance.

Rabbis, leaders, and teachers who publicly identified as gay would be an important next step in this process. Of course there were many mainstream rabbis who were "in the closet," and they rightly feared that coming out publicly would end their rabbinic careers. The first closeted rabbi came out in 1979. Alan Bennett, who had been ordained at Hebrew Union College (HUC) in 1974, decided to leave closeted mainstream life and take a job at Sha'ar Zahav, the gay synagogue in San Francisco. The demand by gay and lesbian Jews to be accepted into the liberal schools that trained rabbis was the beginning of a process of institutional change at the Reform movement's Hebrew Union College–Jewish Institute of Religion and the Reconstructionist Rabbinical College. Their applications triggered institutional discussions about the place of gays and lesbians within Judaism and as leaders in the community.

THE FIRST "OUT" GAY APPLICANT

In 1979 RRC received its first application from a gay man who chose to remain out because he was unwilling to live in fear of being outed and expelled. The applicant, Jordan Barbakoff, was well credentialed—a graduate of the Orthodox Crown Heights Yeshiva, the recipient of a BA in Judaic studies from the State University of New York at Albany, and a master's student in Jewish history at the Jewish Theological Seminary—and would have made an ideal candidate.[16] As part of the application process at HUC, Barbakoff had a preliminary screening interview, at which he was advised not to apply. Even though HUC later accepted several out gay men and lesbians in the early 1980s, institutional closeting persisted among the Reform denomination, and

HUC cautioned them that being public as students would jeopardize their career options and could result in their not being ordained.[17]

Rejected by HUC, Barbakoff turned to the Reconstructionist Rabbinical College. He was encouraged by Stanley Isser, his undergraduate academic adviser, who thought that the progressive heritage of the Reconstructionist movement would lead to his admission to RRC. The initial institutional response was not outright rejection; in keeping with the philosophy that the past "has a vote, but not a veto," RRC's administration began a process of study and reflection on the place of same-sex sexuality. RRC's academic dean, Ronald Brauner, an Orthodox scholar, decided to turn Barbakoff's application into an opportunity for an open discussion of the issue at RRC, although the applicant's identity was not revealed. While not resulting in an affirmative reply, the internal debate over this openly gay candidate began unanticipated transformations.

Even as an openly gay applicant pushed for reform, closeted lesbian and gay students within RRC began to challenge the admission process. This activism was profoundly difficult for gay and lesbian students at the school. Linda Holtzman, who was in her final year of the RRC program, had begun exploring her lesbianism one year earlier. She remembers being "so unsure of my own identity and so uncertain about the direction of my own career" that she could not take a leadership role in the conversations.[18] Classmates to whom she had revealed her situation, however, supported her and circulated a letter to the students in favor of admitting openly gay and lesbian students despite the negative message in the traditional texts. Approximately half of the student body (nineteen students) signed the letter. Students who did not sign based their reluctance on both practical considerations and concerns about Jewish law.

RRC faculty met to decide on Barbakoff's candidacy on March 9, 1979. They unanimously passed the motion "The RRC will not consider the candidacy of an avowed homosexual."[19] Their refusal came from a range of theological and cultural sources. For some faculty members, homosexuality was "inimical to the survival of the Jewish people," in keeping with the common assumption in this era that gay people could not have children. After the Holocaust, any threat to producing the next generation of Jews, from intermarriage to abortion, was often perceived in this light. Other faculty members were supportive of civic equality for gay and lesbian people, and RRC president and founder, Ira Eisenstein, was unequivocal in his support of homosexual civil rights.[20] But they, too, voted against admission. For them the issue of visibility within the Jewish community was at the heart of the matter. The fear of being condemned by traditional Jews outweighed their desire to welcome gay and lesbian Jewish leadership.

RRC was now on record as opposing the ordination of openly gay men and women, but this formal statement had unintended effects. The initial result, of course, was the candidate's rejection: Barbakoff received a simple letter, accompanied by a sympathetic phone call and verbal apology from Brauner.[21] However, the debate also emboldened openly gay men and lesbians to put more pressure on liberal Jewish institutions for acceptance. Several developments of the early 1980s also put new weight on this pressure for change. These years witnessed the founding of gay and lesbian synagogues in most large cities, a flourishing of progressive conversations about the place of homosexuality in Judaism, and efforts among gay and lesbian Jews to reconcile these identities within mainstream Judaism.[22] The topic of homosexuality, itself once closeted, was out in the open, and the demand for acceptance was growing.

A NEW POLICY

It took only five years for the faculty of RRC to reverse the policy. In March 1984, the faculty voted to admit openly gay and lesbian students. Change in the RRC leadership was primarily responsible for reconsidering the policy. A new president, Ira Silverman, came to RRC in 1982. His vision of Reconstructionism emphasized gender equality, ritual experimentation, and engaging a broader range of voices. Sweeping personnel changes brought in new liberal faculty and thus an opportunity to reconsider gay and lesbian admission and ordination.

At a fall 1983 faculty meeting, two of these new faculty members—left-wing Conservative rabbi Hershel Matt and Reconstructionist rabbi Linda Holtzman—volunteered to draft a position paper for the faculty's consideration on admitting gay and lesbian students. Holtzman, a 1979 graduate of RRC, was already well known to the Philadelphia Jewish community as a public advocate for lesbian and gay inclusion. She also made history as the first woman rabbi to serve a mainstream Conservative movement congregation. (That movement was not yet ordaining women as rabbis.) Although not out to her congregation, she had begun living an openly lesbian life and worked with the lesbian and gay congregation in Philadelphia, Beth Ahavah. In contrast, Matt was an elder statesman. He was widely respected throughout the Jewish world as a traditionalist but also known to be willing to take liberal stands on controversial issues.

Matt had already published an essay that offered support for gays and lesbians within traditional Jewish language. Published in 1978 in *Judaism*, "Sin, Crime, Sickness, or Alternative Life Style? A Jewish Approach to Homosexuality" advocated for a change in halacha (Jewish law) based on the idea that homosexuality was not a choice but innate. If gay men and lesbians are "born that way," he argued, they should be treated compassionately. He applied the halachic category of *ones* (compulsion), reasoning that if you cannot act otherwise, you are not culpable for your actions. Matt argued that homosexuals could even become rabbis (a startling idea in 1978). But he held out one proviso—that the homosexual rabbi "honestly hold the conviction—and would conscientiously seek to convey it to others—that, in spite of his or her own homosexuality, the Jewish ideal for man and woman is heterosexuality."[23]

Despite the inferior status for gay men and lesbians that this position assumed, Matt's argument also created an unprecedented place within Judaism for gays and lesbians. Presenting homosexuality as an innate and unchangeable identity rather than a sinful choice—and making this argument from halachic premises—made a powerful case for accepting gays and lesbians within Jewish traditions.

Many of these ideas would appear in Matt and Holtzman's position paper, which also responded to the vocal challenge from Rabbi Ivan Caine, one of the two faculty members remaining from 1979. Caine circulated a substantial and dense position paper arguing against a change in policy, "On the Admittance of Overt Homosexuals to the RRC."[24] He expressed concern that the faculty was not considering the weight of halacha, and thus not in his opinion honoring the position of Reconstructionist founder Mordecai Kaplan, that the past "should have a vote." Kaplan tied this defense of Jewish tradition to fears about the social dangers of the "homosexual life style" as a source of promiscuity, hedonism, and seduction. He argued that overt homosexuals would not accept Matt's position granting them lesser status and was skeptical that homosexual role models would not be inclined to persuade undecided young people to become homosexual. Caine also argued that this would begin a "slippery slope" for the admission of comparable groups: prostitutes, bigamists, transvestites, brother-sister incestuous couples, drug users, the intermarried, non-Jews. He cautioned the faculty about consequences. Shouldn't the other arms of the movement, the rabbis and lay leaders, be included in this decision that would affect them? Wouldn't the activist and militant overt homosexuals turn RRC into the "gay seminary"? Shouldn't the faculty be concerned about what would happen when congregations refused to hire an openly gay rabbi? Or would congregations be required to do so? In language that mirrored broader antigay discourses, Caine presented homosexuality as a threat to Jewish traditions in general and a threat to the survival of RRC in particular.

Matt and Holtzman's position paper, "Proposed RRC Policy Statement on Gays/Lesbians," responded to many of Caine's criticisms. They argued against traditional positions that associated homosexuality with idolatrous worship as a misinterpretation of the Hebrew Bible. They supported Jewish pronatalism but argued that procreation was not the only avenue to preserve the Jewish people; gay men and lesbians could contribute as teachers, following the rabbinic idea that "whoever teaches another person's child Torah is as one who has borne or begotten a child."[25] The statement emphasized that gay and lesbian families would create nurturing relationships. It asserted, as Matt suggested in his earlier work, that "the basic question is not whether people should *be* homosexual but whether they can live openly and with integrity what they *truly* are." This perhaps was the most persuasive point of all. Furthermore, a gay or lesbian rabbi could be an asset, helping congregants acknowledge and come to terms with their true sexual orientation and "reduce prejudices and stereotypical thinking" of heterosexual congregants. They acknowledged that a change in the policy might be detrimental to the college's reputation and fund-raising ability but also suggested that some people would "be moved and impressed by the moral courage and forthrightness of such a policy," and they advocated the change as the "most truly moral, Jewish, Reconstructionist thing to do."[26]

The faculty vote on the Matt-Holtzman paper was held in June 1984 after the students had left for summer vacation. Silverman and the incoming academic dean, Arthur Green, spoke in strong support. Caine reiterated his opposition at length, but only one other faculty member voted with him (10–2 by secret ballot). The majority vote was based on a belief that admitting openly gay and lesbian students was the moral and therefore the correct Jewish position, even if it contradicted Jewish legal precedent. Despite their conviction, faculty members were aware that this position was not shared by most of the Reconstructionist community who would need to be convinced that this change would not destroy the Reconstructionist movement by placing it outside the mainstream and subjecting it to the criticism of traditional Jews. But President Silverman was willing to handle the fallout and wanted the policy in place for the following year.[27] To allay fears about adverse publicity, the report recommended that the decision not be publicized with a press release. The faculty would inform only the Board of Governors, students (although not until the following fall), and the rabbinic leadership of the movement, as well as "individual prospective students who inquire"[28] prior to the fall announcement. The policy would not appear in the RRC catalog (and did not until 1993). Thus, RRC passed an internal policy that permitted gay and lesbian admission and ordination but as an institution was itself not publicly "out" about this new policy.

INSTITUTIONAL AMBIVALENCE

The 1984 policy offered an important symbolic step toward ending the injustice of homophobia at RRC. But it was only a first step in a much longer process of creating institutional change within RRC and within the Reconstructionist movement as a whole.

In many ways the gay-inclusive policy served as an unintentional litmus test that revealed the Reconstructionist movement's pervasive heterosexual biases. The initial backlash from movement leaders was powerful, and acclimation would be slow. People who agreed with Caine's moral position (mostly, but not only, Orthodox and Conservative Jews) were outraged. The rabbinic and lay bodies of Reconstructionism were angry that they had not been consulted. Employment issues were a concern, both for students and congregations. While the passage of the admissions policy was significant, it was the beginning of a long process rather than its culmination.

The formal policy of inclusion also compelled many gays and lesbians—and supportive allies—to look more critically at the institutional culture of the seminary and the Reconstructionist movement as a whole. On the face of it, the policy made one thing clear: once gay men and lesbians matriculated as rabbinical students, it was no longer acceptable for faculty or students to question the legitimacy of the ordination of gay or lesbian rabbis. However, even the working of the policy suggested that this legitimacy came at a cost, and those who wanted equal respect were not pleased with Matt's argument that heterosexuality was the preferred way of life. In addition to stated matters of policy, there was also the larger question of practice. The symbolic statement of inclusion did nothing to address the homophobia of faculty and students or the heteronormative culture of the school. The faculty had assumed that a lesbian or gay student would apply, be admitted, and be treated like everyone else. They had given no thought to the possibility that closeted students and applicants might feel more vulnerable because of the policy. Could the students who were out be trusted to respect the closets these students had so carefully built? The faculty also did not consider how to address students who had never met an out gay person or who disapproved of the "homosexual lifestyle." The formal gesture of inclusion did nothing to change the everyday practices that made gays and lesbians feel like trespassers in straight space.

Students who arrived on campus from more radical corners of the counterculture quickly noticed this gap between policy and practice. Jane Litman and Julie Greenberg, incoming students who were public about their respective bisexual and lesbian identities, found themselves in an environment that was less welcoming than they had anticipated. Both Litman and Greenberg had come to RRC from the lesbian separatist group Dyke Shabbos,[29] where they were exploring new lesbian-feminist approaches to Jewish life. They wanted a similar environment at RRC. However, RRC's atmosphere had not changed much from the one Greenberg described when she came for her interview the year before. Finding only "one closeted student and one closeted faculty member," Greenberg decided to keep quiet about her sexuality as a student.[30]

The vast majority of queer students made similar choices about obscuring their sexual identity despite the formal inclusivity of the seminary.[31] Yet all were out in their personal lives and came out to at least some faculty and students during their student years. Among them was Sharon Kleinbaum, who would later become the leading student advocate for the policy and the first full-time rabbi of the gay synagogue of New York, Congregation Beth Simchat Torah, where she has served for over twenty-five years. At the time of her matriculation in 1985, however, she was astonished at how deeply closeted many of the RRC students and faculty were and was "overwhelmed by heterosexual assumptions" she found. Coming from a place where she, too, had been quite open and moving to Philadelphia with her partner, she nonetheless decided, at least temporarily, to "go back into the closet" at RRC.[32]

These decisions about coming out publicly also posed unique challenges for faculty and administration at the seminary. The institution's reticence to make its inclusion policy public placed unique demands for silence on those who represented it as authorities. Faced with the high cost of making their sexual identity public, these leaders found less public strategies for advocating change. Linda Holtzman, coauthor of the 1984 policy, was going through her own coming-out process. When renegotiating her synagogue contract in 1985, she told her Conservative congregation that she would need "two weeks of co-parenting leave to 'help my housemate when she gave birth' written into my next contract."[33] The congregation refused to provide a contract with that provision, and Holtzman left the congregation and increased her time working at RRC. The role she took there would be crucial to the next steps in the process of helping the public acclimate to the new policy. Along with Matt she became the trusted confidant of many of the students who were encouraged to explore their sexuality in this changing environment.

Jacob Staub, another faculty member, used his role as the editor of the *Reconstructionist* magazine to support the policy even as he felt it necessary to be circumspect about his own gay identity. As editor of a special issue on Judaism and homosexuality in October 1985, Staub urged the Reconstructionist movement to further support the inclusion of gay men and lesbians in Jewish life:

> Many of us probably wish that a Jew's sexual preference could remain private and that the subject could be closed right there. The facts are otherwise, however.... Gays and lesbians now seek to live their lives out of the closet. They are forming congregations where they can celebrate their *semakhot* [life cycle events] openly and can confront honestly the hostility of Jewish tradition. They want to consecrate their relationships in public Jewish ceremonies, and they want to raise their families with Jewish communal support.... There should be no question that the needs of gay and lesbian Jews deserve our full attention.[34]

The issue included reviews of the current literature and of halachic (legal) positions, an essay by Janet Marder about her positive experience as the rabbi of a gay synagogue, and two personal essays by mothers advocating for their gay children. And yet this groundbreaking public discussion of lesbian and gay inclusion not only did not mention the editor's personal investment in the topic but also did not mention the change in RRC's admission policy.

Neither did *Exploring Judaism: A Reconstructionist Approach*—the introduction to Reconstructionism coauthored by Rebecca Alpert and Jacob Staub and also published in 1985. Tellingly, the only mention of homosexuality was a suggestion that in keeping with the Reconstructionist value of "living in two civilizations" (the Jewish and the American), Jews should adopt the American value of "decent treatment of homosexuals."[35] Neither the authors nor the movement was ready to be more public, yet. In the fall of 1986, Alpert, then dean of students, began the process of leaving her marriage and coming out. Arthur Green, who became president after Silverman's departure in 1986, worried about the adverse publicity the policy was receiving in the traditional community. Seeing the sexual identity of the seminary's leaders as a reflection of its institutional identity, Green informed Alpert that if she chose to be public about her sexual orientation, she would have to leave her position.

Green's concerns reflected genuine conflicts. RRC as an institution risked being marginalized within broader Jewish communities by publicly staking out a stance of sexual inclusion. In December 1986, RRC student Jane Litman gave an interview about her views on Jewish feminism to the *Boston Jewish Advocate*, where she was quoted as saying that Judaism is homophobic and patriarchal and explaining that her interest in goddess worship was meant to overcome the absence of sexuality outside "heterosexual monogamy" in traditional Judaism.[36] The article provoked intense reactions. Conflating feminism and lesbianism, Rabbi Samuel H. Dresner, a faculty member at the Conservative movement's rabbinical training institution, the Jewish Theological Seminary, concluded that the ordination of lesbian and gay rabbis was a return to paganism. Quoting Litman's interview, he argued that Judaism, to separate from pagan sexuality, gives primacy to family as the "moral, eventually monogamous" container for the "sexual impulse."[37] Real Judaism, according to Dresner, was defined by its promotion of heterosexual marriage and family.

Dresner also suggested that RRC, by this measure, was not truly Jewish. Dresner not only faulted Litman but also accused RRC of supporting "an anti-family, sexually free goddess-cult." He viewed Litman as dangerous not because of her views but because a rabbinical student holding such views *remained* a rabbinical student. In response, RRC countered that it was open to students' experimentation, which prompted Dresner to describe a slope even slipperier than the one Rabbi Caine had outlined: "Does it entail a new type of rabbi who will expect a couple to live together before marrying them? Does it include the worship of a goddess or becoming a witch? ... Does it mean rabbis who see the family of husband-wife-and-child as 'very limiting' and 'homophobic'? Does it include homosexual or lesbian rabbis? ... Where will it end?"[38]

Dresner, like Caine, was expressing views that were not uncommon in the Jewish community in the mid-1980s, even in liberal circles.[39] Homosexuality, seen as a wholesale challenge to family and child-rearing, also seemed to pose an insidious threat to the integrity of Judaism itself.

CHANGING RRC CULTURE

The absence of a strong institutional response to these inflamed worries sent a different message to gay and lesbian Jews: it reinforced the implicit feeling that they were outsiders to a religious tradition normatively defined as heterosexual. Inside RRC, however, things were beginning to change. In

In 1993 *Bridges: A Journal for Jewish Feminists and Our Friends* hosted a Havdalah service and benefit concert at the National March on Washington for Lesbian, Gay and Bi Rights and Liberation, called "An Evening of Jewish Lesbian Entertainment," at the New York Presbyterian Church in Washington, D.C. The Havdalah service was written and conducted by Rabbi Linda Holtzman and lesbian students at the Reconstructionist Rabbinical College, including Elizabeth Bolton, pictured here. Photo by Linda Eber.

spring 1988, Sharon Kleinbaum had been working as a student rabbi at Bet Haverim, the gay outreach synagogue in Atlanta. Emboldened by that experience, Kleinbaum wanted to make a contribution to changing the culture at RRC.[40] She and Staub convened the "What Now?" Group to talk about what needed to change. It consisted of Staub, Holtzman, and Alpert representing the faculty and Kleinbaum and two other students.[41]

The group began discussions with the acknowledgment that the policy change, now nearly four years old, did not in itself achieve genuine inclusion. Gay and lesbian students at RRC needed support. Their privacy was not being protected. Some were being outed without their consent. Even supportive classmates often did not understand the complexities of living a double life and made damaging assumptions about what they could say to whom. The first class that had entered under the new policy was nearing their final year. What was RRC going to do about job placement? Would the school honor congregational requests for only straight candidates? The conversation also raised broader questions about the nature of the policy itself. The policy stated a right to be included. However, that statement did not amount to a moral position with broad implications about the equality of gay men and lesbians or the holiness of their sexuality.[42]

In the fall of 1988, members of the "What Now?" Group invited Felice Yeskel of Cold Spring Educational Consultants to help them think about culture change. They began by producing a packet of materials for the rabbinical students to use. The packet explained how to respond to provocative questions, such as these: Isn't Judaism against homosexuality? Shouldn't I worry about my kids being molested? Aren't Jews obligated to "be fruitful and multiply"? Is RRC really a hotbed of gay activity? These were questions that in 1988 were still difficult for RRC faculty and students to answer.[43] Presenting clear, factual, and nondefensive responses to these questions helped to redress gay and lesbian students' sense of being besieged.

In 1989–90, the "What Now?" Group planned a daylong seminar for the RRC community. Christie Balka and Andy Rose had just published an edited anthology, *Twice Blessed: On Being Lesbian or Gay and Jewish* that included articles by several Reconstructionist rabbis and other local Philadelphians who were invited to speak. The highlight of the day was a conversation with leaders of the Reconstructionist movement, "Where Do We Go from Here?," where difficult questions were raised about the movement's plans for inclusion.[44]

These actions helped to achieve the "What Now?" Group's goal of culture change. Beginning with the class of 1989, graduating seniors agreed among themselves not to discuss their personal lives with prospective employers at their initial interviews so that lesbian and gay students would not be rejected before the search committees even considered them. Additionally, the 1990 graduating class passed a resolution to be forwarded to the Reconstructionist Rabbinical Association, demanding that the association's representatives on the Joint Federation of Reconstructionist Congregations and Havurot–RRA Placement Commission "insist that guidelines require all listing congregations to refrain from discrimination."[45] These policies and practices took important steps beyond symbolic inclusion. They presented sexual inclusivity as a shared value that was also supported in pragmatic ways by Reconstructionist Jews of all sexual orientations.

These changes at RRC also slowly influenced the broader Reconstructionist movement. Employment in the mainstream Jewish community for out gay and lesbian rabbis was still a work in progress. Until 1996, no RRC graduates came out when they interviewed for their first rabbinic positions. Leila Berner graduated from RRC in 1988 and took a congregational job at a Reconstructionist synagogue in the Philadelphia suburbs but did not come out to members. Her partner functioned as the rebbitzin (rabbi's wife); their relationship was an open secret. Berner's article under the pseudonym La Escondida ("the hidden one") in *Twice Blessed* described the difficulties of living a double life.[46] Julie Greenberg found a solution by starting her own organization, the Jewish Renewal Life Center, in 1990.[47]

Ultimately, things would need to change within the movement at large. The Reconstructionist Commission on Homosexuality, comprising representatives from all arms of the movement, was convened in 1990 and met five times for three days, discussing every nuance of every issue. The commission's report was published in 1992. The document, passed unanimously, is an example of the signature Reconstructionist approach to values-based decision-making. In contrast to the family values ascribed to Judaism by thinkers like Samuel Dresner, the document lists the key Jewish values (human dignity, equality, variety of family forms, good sex, children, and many others) as the reasons for full religious and civil equality for gay men and lesbians. In keeping with the Reconstructionist value of giving the past "a vote, but not a veto," the document balances current social science and traditional texts and enumerates guidelines for full inclusion and education, including endorsing same-sex wedding ceremonies. Going beyond the earlier views of Hershel Matt, the document concludes, "We recognize the bias in Jewish and American culture that deems homosexuality as less desirable than heterosexuality. As we affirm that heterosexuality and homosexuality are both normal expressions of human diversity, we affirm that both are ways of being which offer fulfillment."[48] With this statement of full inclusion, the Reconstructionist movement was now ready to accept its gay and lesbian rabbis as equals.

CONCLUSION

The events that took place at the Reconstructionist Rabbinical College illustrate the complexity of creating welcoming religious spaces in the 1980s, a slow process that involved challenging social practices and institutional culture as well as formal teachings and policies. The Reconstructionist movement spent over a decade on the process that made it possible for gay men and lesbians to win full religious equality. These policies eventually met with broad acceptance in the non-Orthodox Jewish world. The Reform movement officially approved of gay and lesbian ordination in 1990, and the Conservative movement did so in 2006. Gay men and lesbians who are willing to accept the values and mores of Judaism as it is practiced in liberal religious communities are now fully welcome and included. Bisexuality (and other nonnormative sexual behaviors) has never been accepted. In the last decade, transgender men and women have been admitted to rabbinical programs in the Reform and Reconstructionist movements. In 2016 they are welcomed, but not fully and not everywhere. Not yet.

From a distance, the inclusion of LGBTQ people and clergy within religious denominations appears to occur suddenly: after millennia of exclusion, policies are reversed with a majority vote. A close look at the process undergone in the Reconstructionist movement suggests otherwise. The shift that occurred from 1979 to 1992 was gradual. Initially, queer clergy were unimaginable. It required a great deal of courage for queer and straight individuals, as well the Reconstructionist Rabbinical College as a whole, to stand up for the policy change against fierce hostility. Liberals with heteronormative assumptions had to be willing to accept the possibility that lesbian and gay Jews were full members of the Jewish people and were not threatening. As lesbian and gay rabbis and rabbinical students began to come out, prejudices evaporated. Over a decade, the conversation progressed to the point in 1992 that members of a representative, movement-wide Commission on Homosexuality could unanimously conclude that the traditional Jewish values they most treasured led them to affirm that lesbians and gays should be fully and unequivocally embraced. Ultimately, Reconstructionist Jews came to embrace queer inclusion as something that was itself an important part of their collective Jewish identity.

NOTES

1. See Rebecca L. Davis's chapter in this volume, which illuminates the importance of pronatalist thinking in Jewish life at the time.

2. We attended rabbinical school together in the 1970s, were both closeted in that era, and certainly knew of other rabbinical students who were dealing with issues related to

their sexuality at the time. But we will never know about past generations of rabbis who were compelled to hide their sexual desires. For a suggestive exploration of this question, see Shaun Jacob Halper, "Coming Out of the Hasidic Closet: Jiří Mordechai Langer (1894–1943) and the Fashioning of Homosexual-Jewish Identity," *Jewish Quarterly Review* 101, no. 2 (Spring 2011): 189–231. Langer, the subject of this article, was a homosexual Jewish writer in Prague who wrote about homoerotic relations between men in the history of Hasidic Judaism, *Die Erotik der Kabbala* (1923).

3. John D'Emilio's afterword in this volume suggests a different pattern: that those who came out as gay in that era simply left their religious commitments behind. But as books like Heather White's *Reforming Sodom: Protestants and the Rise of Gay Rights* (Chapel Hill: University of North Carolina Press, 2015) suggest, many gay men and lesbians in that era sought ways to make sense of both religious and sexual identities.

4. See Pamela Nadell, *Women Who Would Be Rabbis: A History of Women's Ordination, 1889–1985* (Boston: Beacon Press, 1998).

5. "Proposed RRC Policy Statement on Gays/Lesbians, drafted by a subcommittee consisting of Hershel Matt and Linda Holtzman, for consideration by the faculty at its meeting on 5/29/84," Jacob Staub personal files.

6. The Unitarian-Universalists led the way in 1980.

7. Rebecca Alpert and Jacob Staub, *Exploring Judaism: A Reconstructionist Approach*, expanded and updated ed. (Wyncote, Pa.: Reconstructionist Press, 2000), 135–37. This work is a basic introduction to Reconstructionist Judaism.

8. See Mordecai Kaplan, *Judaism as a Civilization: Toward a Reconstruction of American-Jewish Life* (New York: Schocken Books, 1967).

9. See Alpert and Staub, *Exploring Judaism*, chap. 9.

10. Rachel Kranson's chapter in this volume discusses the trajectory of the ordination of women in the Reform and Conservative denominations. Sandy Sasso, the first Reconstructionist woman rabbi, was ordained two years after Sally Priesand in the Reform movement and eleven years before the ordination of Amy Eilberg in the Conservative movement.

11. Daniel Boyarin, *Unheroic Conduct: The Rise of Heterosexuality and the Invention of the Jewish Man* (Berkeley: University of California Press, 1997).

12. See Norman Lamm, "The New Morality under Religious Auspices," *Tradition: A Journal of Orthodox Thought* 10, no. 2 (Winter 1968): 17–30.

13. Jews in Philadelphia were actively engaged in the struggle for gay rights, and Frank Kameny, Mel Heifitz, Carole Friedman, Laurie Baron, Mark Segal, Malcolm Lazin, and Clark Polak were important national and local leaders in the 1950s–1970s. While publicly identified as gay and lesbian, they had little or no connection with institutional Judaism. Beth Ahavah, the gay synagogue in Philadelphia, was founded in 1975. Rebecca Alpert and Linda Holtzman made connections between RRC and Beth Ahavah beginning in 1977, but there was no formal affiliation with the Reconstructionist movement.

14. See http://www.bcc-la.org/about/history/ (accessed August 3, 2016).

15. John D'Emilio, *Sexual Politics, Sexual Communities: The Making of a Homosexual Minority in the United States, 1940–1970* (Chicago: University of Chicago Press, 1998), 235.

16. Jacob Staub, personal communication with Barbakoff, July 8, 2014.

17. Ibid.; with Eric Weiss, February 1, 2010; and with Yoel Kahn, February 15, 2010. Weiss refused to remain closeted as a condition of admission.

18. "Struggle, Change, and Celebration: My Life as a Lesbian Rabbi," in *Lesbian Rabbis: The First Generation*, ed. Rebecca T. Alpert, Sue Levi Elwell, and Shirley Idelson (New Brunswick: Rutgers University Press, 2001), 41.

19. Minutes of RRC Faculty Meeting, March 9, 1979, Jacob Staub personal files.

20. RRC's founding president, Ira Eisenstein, retired in 1981. Writing in the 1983 *Judaism* symposium, Eisenstein was unequivocal in his support of civic equality for homosexuals, but he was silent on the question of reconstructing Jewish practice. "Discrimination Is Wrong," *Judaism* 32, no. 4 (Fall 1983): 415–16.

21. Personal communication with Barbakoff, July 8, 2014.

22. There were an increasing number of gay synagogues that became part of a network, the World Congress of Gay and Lesbian Jewish Organizations. See Aliza Maggid, "Joining Together: Building a Worldwide Movement," in *Twice Blessed: On Being Lesbian or Gay and Jewish*, ed. Christie Balka and Andy Rose (Boston: Beacon Press, 1989), 157–70. Another rabbi (Lionel Blue, a graduate of the Leo Baeck Institute in London) came out in 1981. See Lionel Blue, "Godly and Gay," in *Jewish Explorations of Sexuality*, ed. Jonathan Magonet (London: Berghahn Press, 1995), 117–34. A book of essays by Jewish lesbians was published in 1982: *Nice Jewish Girls: A Lesbian Anthology*, ed. Evelyn Torton Beck (Trumansburg, N.Y.: Crossing Press, 1982)]. A symposium on Judaism and homosexuality in the influential journal *Judaism* (32, no. 4 [Fall 1983]) included ten articles on the subject. Also that year the gay synagogue in Los Angeles hired Janet Marder, a graduate of HUC, as its first full-time (and not gay-identified) rabbi. Through her supportive writings, Marder would play a major role in the developing acceptance of gay and lesbian Jews. See "Getting to Know the Gay and Lesbian Shul," *Reconstructionist* 51, no. 2 (October–November 1985): 20–25; Janet Marder, "Getting to Know the Gay and Lesbian Shul: A Rabbi Moves from Tolerance to Acceptance," in *Twice Blessed: On Being Lesbian or Gay and Jewish*, ed. Christie Balka and Andy Rose (Boston: Beacon Press, 1989), 209–17; and "Our Visible Rabbis," *Reform Judaism* 1/2 (Winter 1990): 5–11.

23. Hershel Matt, "Sin, Crime, Sickness, or Alternative Life Style? A Jewish Approach to Homosexuality," *Judaism* 27, no. 1 (Winter 1978): 21.

24. Caine's position paper is appended to the faculty meeting agenda of May 29, 1984, Jacob Staub personal files.

25. Babylonian Talmud 19b.

26. "Proposed RRC Policy Statement." See above (note 5) for the proposal.

27. Minutes of the Faculty Meeting of June 12, 1984, n.p., Jacob Staub personal files.

28. Ibid. An open lesbian had submitted an application for admission, and while Silverman did not mention this fact to the entire faculty, he conveyed to other administrators that there was urgency to the question. Jane Litman identifies herself as this applicant. Jane Litman, "Kol Sason v'kol simcha, Kol Kalah v'Kol Kalah: Same Gender Weddings and Spiritual Renewal," in *Queer Jews*, ed. David Shneer and Caryn Aviv (New York: New York University, 2002), 114.

29. Part of the growing movement of gay synagogues and Jewish lesbian-feminist separatist groups, Dyke Shabbos was a weekly gathering of Jewish lesbians and bisexual

women in the San Francisco Bay area that provided a safe space for them to experiment and blend Jewish and gay identities.

30. Julie Greenberg, "My Piece of Truth," in *Lesbian Rabbis: The First Generation*, ed. Rebecca T. Alpert, Ellen Sue Levi Elwell, and Shirley Idelson (New Brunswick: Rutgers University Press, 2001), 182.

31. With one exception, queer students who were admitted in the years 1984–90 of whom the authors are aware were not out at their admissions interview.

32. Sharon Kleinbaum, "Gay and Lesbian Synagogue as Spiritual Community," in *Lesbian Rabbis: The First Generation*, ed. Rebecca T. Alpert, Ellen Sue Levi Elwell, and Shirley Idelson (New Brunswick: Rutgers University Press, 2001), 141–51.

33. Linda Holtzman, "Jewish Lesbian Parenting," in *Twice Blessed: On Being Lesbian or Gay and Jewish*, ed. Christie Balka and Andy Rose (Boston: Beacon Press, 1989), 133.

34. *Reconstructionist* 51, no. 2 (October–November 1985): 2.

35. Rebecca Alpert and Jacob Staub, *Exploring Judaism: A Reconstructionist Approach* (Wyncote, Pa.: Reconstructionist Press, 1985), 43.

36. Judith Antonelli, "Rabbinical Student Reconstructs Judaism from a Feminist Perspective," *Boston Jewish Advocate*, December 12, 1986, 1, 16.

37. See Samuel H. Dresner, "The Return to Paganism," *Midstream* 34 (June/July 1988): 36. Dresner further elaborated on these ideas in "Homosexuality and the Order of Creation," *Judaism* 40, no. 3 (Summer 1991): 309–21.

38. Dresner, "Return to Paganism," 37.

39. These concerns are echoed in the reluctance of the Women's League of Conservative Judaism to support abortion rights in this same time period. See Rachel Kranson's essay in this volume.

40. Kleinbaum, "Gay and Lesbian Synagogue as Spiritual Community," 145.

41. Sharon Kleinbaum personal files.

42. Report of the Spring 1988 "What Now" Group, June 21, 1988, Sharon Kleinbaum personal files.

43. Minutes, "What Now?" Group Meeting, October 10, 1988, Sharon Kleinbaum personal files.

44. Program, "The What Now Committee Presents a Three Part Seminar Day, Gays, Lesbians and the Jewish Community," February 21–22, 1990, Sharon Kleinbaum personal files.

45. "A Resolution for the Fuller Acceptance of Gay and Lesbian Jews in Our Community," Sharon Kleinbaum personal files.

46. La Escondida [Leila Berner], "Journey Toward Wholeness: Reflections of a Lesbian Rabbi," in *Twice Blessed: On Being Lesbian or Gay and Jewish*, ed. Christie Balka and Andy Rose (Boston: Beacon Press, 1989), 218–28.

47. "My Piece of Truth," 182.

48. Bob Gluck, ed., *Homosexuality and Judaism: The Reconstructionist Position*, (Wyncote, Pa.: Federation of Reconstructionist Congregations and Havurot and the Reconstructionist Rabbinical Association, 1992–93), 37.

FOUNDING NEW SODOM

Radical Gay Communalist Spirituality, 1973–1976

DANIEL RIVERS

"I'm so tired of the city, of the gay treadmill, recyclable people and city trips."[1] This complaint, from a gay man writing from Berkeley, California, appeared in *RFD*, a magazine devoted to celebrating rural gay life.[2] The focus of this criticism was the increasingly visible "gay urbanism" of the 1970s. In the early 1970s, distinct gay male neighborhoods developed, such as San Francisco's Castro District, Greenwich Village in New York, and West Hollywood in Los Angeles, offering new opportunities for men to live in communities that celebrated same-sex intimacy and sexuality. Some of these neighborhoods had been home to queer communities for decades by this point, but in the era of liberation these gay enclaves emerged as unprecedentedly open gay male neighborhoods. As a new, televised politics of visibility brought awareness of gay and lesbian communities and political activism to the living rooms of mainstream America, these neighborhoods became quickly legible to millions of people as gay male spaces. Consequently, men who saw the possibility of living openly gay lives migrated to these neighborhoods from across the country.

A frequent criticism in *RFD* addressed changes brought by this new migration. The newcomers, often middle- or upper-class professional white men, differed from the liberation-era residents of these neighborhoods. In San Francisco's Castro District, for example, Harvey Milk had arrived in the neighborhood ready to be a local business owner and with a reformist perspective on civil rights that would lead him to enter municipal politics. These new arrivals, though, were different from the revolutionary gay liberationists who had espoused an anticapitalist, antiwar politics in the first few years after the Stonewall Riots of June 1969. At the same time, these neighborhoods saw a rapid growth in commercialism, as business enterprises emerged to take advantage of a market created by the new immigrants. As these neighborhoods and the electoral-based civil rights movement that grew out of them changed the political and social culture of gay male districts, these shifts often alienated members of these communities who had been sympathetic to the revolutionary ethos of gay liberation.

In defiance of this shift to urban gay neighborhoods, another group of gay men migrated in the opposite direction. They created rural gay communes devoted to the practice of radical gay liberation brotherhood as an alternative to the mid-1970s gay bar scenes of the cities. As they did so, they often grounded their vision of gay country space in an ethos of free sexual expression amid nature conveyed in spiritual terms, which they saw as capable of revolutionary action and as the true successor to early gay liberation. They criticized the urban gay world for its commercialized sexuality while developing notions of sexual freedom and transcendence rooted in experiences of rural life.[3] This liberatory gay spirituality wedded the erotic with an ecofeminism that questioned both straight and gay male assumptions of power. At times, it involved a loose politics of gay male separatism developed in dialogue with neighboring lesbian communes and was connected for many of these rural gay men to an appreciation for a male energy that they felt flowered in rural spaces. In gay male rural communes of the early 1970s, all of these perspectives contributed to a gay New Age worldview that embodied many of the revolutionary ideals of gay liberation at the same time as it embraced a rural, sexually vibrant, and often pagan cosmology.

This essay looks at the worldview of gay male communalists across the United States in the mid-1970s as seen in the rural gay magazine *RFD* in the critical years from 1973 to 1976 as well as in other extant archival sources related to gay communalism. As a clearinghouse for gay men involved in radical, back-to-the-land ventures, *RFD* provides a complex view of the creation of a largely white, gay male counterculture spirituality that fused the sexual politics of early gay liberationists with ecofeminist, animist, New Age understandings of sexuality, the natural world, and spirit. Gay men who were or who wanted to live in communal spaces nationwide sent letters and stories in to *RFD*, which was published in a variety of gay male communal spaces during these years, including Wolf Creek, Oregon; Grinnell, Iowa; and a communal farm in rural central New England.[4] At least thirteen gay communes existed in the mid-1970s, in Massachusetts, Oregon, Washington, North Carolina, New York, Tennessee, and Virginia. The broadly dispersed readership of *RFD* also shows the appeal of these communal and spiritual visions to those dwelling in other locales: to rural gay men not living on communes as well as to gay men in urban settings intrigued by gay communal country spaces.[5]

The gay spirituality developed and debated in the pages of *RFD* and on gay communes nationwide circulated well beyond the participants in these rural gay communes. It came from and expressed elements of early gay liberation—the notion of a revolution in both gender and sexual expression; commitment to a loving brotherhood, connected erotically and energetically in gay communal spaces; and a celebration of personal authenticity expressed through gay identity. At the same time, gay spiritualities and communal life also led directly to the founding of the Radical Faerie movement, the national network of Faerie space and ritual celebration founded in 1979 by Harry Hay, John Burnside, Don Kilhefner, and Mitch Walker.[6]

The Radical Faeries were both the specific brainchild of these four men as well as the consequence of previous rural gay organizing throughout the 1970s more generally that includes *RFD* and its original publishers. Harry Hay, John Burnside, Carl Wittman, and Allan Troxler had spent time on Wittman's Wolf Creek land in 1975 and had talked about gay consciousness.[7] By the mid-1980s, *RFD* was being published at Running Water, gay male–occupied rural land in North Carolina. This land, along with Short Mountain, Tennessee, was a center of queer rural life in the South.[8] Short Mountain itself, east of Nashville, had developed over time as countercultural queer land by the late 1970s. At the same time as the initial discussions were underway that led to the first Faerie gathering in Arizona in 1979, a gathering of radical rural gay men was held at Running Water. The owner of the land had returned from a conference on rural gay men and organized a retreat around ways of thinking that were remarkably similar to those that were discussed in Arizona.[9] Throughout the country, in a variety of spaces, rural gay male radicalism was emerging.

Gay radical communalists of the 1970s like Carl Wittman, Allan Troxler, and Stewart Scofield bridged the post-Stonewall radical, urban liberation moment to a utopian, sex-radical, gay male mysticism while also appealing to rural gay men alienated by the urban centers. Their gay communalism was a rejection of the male-oriented gay identity visible in the urban areas and centered on the creation of a gay liberational identity grounded in an erotic nature-magic and a sense of gay brotherhood that was at times separatist—the natural world served both as inspiration and path toward authenticity and escape from the commodification of the cities. A historical analysis of this rural liberationist spirituality expands our understanding of early gay liberation and revolutionary sexualities of this period and deepens our appreciation of the American

New Age movement in the late twentieth century. While most scholarship on the New Age has focused on the late nineteenth century and the fin-de-siècle, relatively newer work now extends this analysis into the late twentieth century as well.[10] The world of early 1970s gay male political, rural spirituality is linked to these histories, grounded in nature religions and appropriations of Asian and Native American religious traditions while at the same time expressing a revolutionary erotics of gay liberation and personal transformation.[11]

A LOVING BROTHERHOOD

A central facet of the spirituality that gay rural communalists crafted in the early 1970s was a sense of a loving brotherhood of men. This brotherhood was understood as revolutionary in its commitment to sexual freedom, to interpersonal communication, and to a celebration of a feminist masculinity that offered an alternative to normative aggressive, heteronormative male identity. This notion of a loving network of men contrasted with both the reformist, commercial gay male neighborhoods forming in the cities and the homophobic, sexist, countercultural vision of the rural heterosexual communes. It also offered the promise of an alternative source of spiritual information—a gay male mysticism in which an open-hearted, communally focused sexuality, informed and supported by deep study of and sensitivity to the natural world, offered access to an energetic, psychic, or metaphysical wisdom.

The idea of a gay brotherhood engaged in communal living was uniquely exciting to gay men who had been raised in rural spaces. Olaf, who had grown up in rural Wisconsin, wrote of feeling the possibility of a gay brotherhood outside of the cities after he drove to Iowa to help with the production of *RFD*. His time in rural Iowa had shown Olaf that "we could choose the rural life and need not feel alone. We can find ways to communicate, to gather our tribes in many ways, to expand the circle of our friends."[12] Peter, a rural gay man who had just recently come out two years earlier, wrote, "Folks who are seeking some sort of alternative by moving back to the earth will be the creators of things good for posterity." For Peter, gay people had a unique potential because they had "broken through some of the strongest and all-pervading of norms."[13]

Others excited about the possibilities of gay communal living and the sense of gathering that it held came from urban counterculture communities. Caradoc, a "poet/shaman" from Berkeley, California, "hatched out of the egg of a Haight-Ashbury street freak," wrote that he and another man in conjunction with two women wanted to buy land near Eugene, Oregon, to "create a communal family of gay people living and working and growing together in harmony with each other and the Earth our mother in the flow of Tao."[14] A sense of a spiritual family bound by their connection to nature imbued many of these radical gay communal projects.

Men like Caradoc connected with gay men in rural America who had never been attracted to the urban metropoles, offering them a vision of gay community that would not demand they sacrifice their rural roots. The urban men who founded these communal experiments were predominantly white with experience in the New Left, and they brought with them an antiracist, anticapitalist, feminist, sexual liberationist politics that caused them to be critical of both the gay neighborhoods they left behind and the heterosexual, countercultural communities that often treated them with homophobic disdain. As these men attempted to create rural spaces defined by the ethics of early gay liberation, they also developed new ways of understanding themselves, communities, and environments, articulated in part through a lexicon of spirituality.

Gay men on the land had a sense that they were part of a distinct communalist brotherhood, a tribe of individuals living in contradiction to constrictive norms, connected beyond physical proximity and form, and interconnected with the world of spirit that existed alongside it. Jeff, taking part in the production of the fourth issue of *RFD* in McLeansville, North Carolina, wrote that he and the others putting the magazine together were "buoyed by a thousand spirits in the woods, on the mountains, by the sea, in the desert, and yes in the cities waiting for *RFD* #4. I hope we don't disappoint them."[15] For the men working on this rural gay magazine, there was a sense of responsibility to an invisible but palpable and real community of spirit.

This sense of a communal brotherhood tied countercultural gay communes of the early 1970s to earlier gay communal, spiritual projects. In 1965, the United Order of the Family of Christ, a gay Christian commune, was founded in Oregon. In a 1975 letter, a member of the United Order described the "small farm" that the group ran, detailed their goals of raising Vietnamese orphans and learning sign language to work with deaf children, and stated that the members of the order "live together and share all things in common for the common good of our brothers." The order defined itself as Christian and eschewed drinking, smoking, and drug use—elements of a monastic life that later gay liberationist communalists might have found restrictive. The group represented an earlier form of gay spiritual, communalist brotherhood that predated those emerging from early gay liberation and also predated the development of LGBT movements within mainstream religious traditions discussed in the chapters by Lynne Gerber and by Rebecca T. Alpert and Jacob J. Staub in this volume.[16]

For many gay men in the 1970s, this sense of a spiritual and sexual brotherhood offered the possibility of fulfilling the promise of early gay liberation in its celebration of an affective connection between men. Doug Beckwith, from Lincoln, Nebraska, wrote, "By pooling our spiritual resources we could generate new approaches to fulfilling human potential that are truly creative alternatives to the ever-present and increasingly straight lifestyle." For Beckwith, writing to *RFD*, one of the most important elements of the magazine was the portrayal of "gay men enjoying each other's presence—erotic perhaps but more important, warm, tender, and caring. We see so little of this and it's such a beautiful sight." Beckwith believed that rural gay communal living encompassed "new lifestyles that embody the very meaning of gay liberation/awareness."[17] Steve DiVerde, who hitchhiked from his home in Santa Rosa, California, to the Northwest Faggots Gathering outside of Port Angeles, Washington, experienced "so much real positive energy that it was easy to stay high." During the gathering, he kept returning to the "need to live in the country with some people I could share and work with on some sort of collective basis."[18] The loving and committed network of rural gay communalists would embody the liberational possibilities of men loving men that these men felt had been lost in the commercialization of gay urban life.

Across the country, gay communes were conceived in this vision of a radically, emotionally, and spiritually interconnected gay community. Hop Brook Commune, founded on land near New Salem, Massachusetts, was a gay commune that saw itself as anti-consumerist and anti-competition. Its nine members lived in a large farmhouse on thirty-one acres and saw the commune as an anarchistic alternative to "gay subcultures," which they critiqued as objectifying. The commune had few rules but did ban meat, weapons, and murder from the house. The members of the Hop Brook Commune were clearly inspired by Walt Whitman's vision of an erotic brotherhood grounded in the natural world; they renamed their road "Walt Whitman Way" and grew calamus plants to sell in honor of Whitman's exhortation for young men to engage in a phallic brotherhood.[19]

In South Salem, New York, a group of "anti-racist, anti-sexist activists working for a nonviolent, revolutionary social change" envisioned a "Gay New Age Community." The goals of the group included "survival, liberation, spiritual growth and healing" through "organic living and organic farming, vigorous exercise and massage, music and dance, yoga and meditation and consciousness raising."[20] George Bamberger, a man about to be released from prison in Tulsa, Oklahoma, wrote that he and a few others were working on a "'Church-Farm-Commune for Gays' idea" that would focus on "seeking higher planes of consciousness," the "knitting together of souls," and "helping friendships form on a more lifetime basis," goals that were seen by many gay communalists as intertwined.[21] In Redmond, Oregon, a group announced the formation of a "Gay Religious Community" modeled after the "14th and 15th century religious communities of Europe."[22] By the mid-1970s, radical gay communes with alternative spiritual understandings of community were emerging across the country, even as a gay civil rights movement was becoming more mainstream and reformist.

SEXUAL REVOLUTIONARIES

A crucial part of this new socio-spiritual vision of gay male community was the expression of a sexual freedom distinct from the commercialized sex of the bathhouses and bars in urban gay male neighborhoods. Gay rural communalists saw sexuality as a fundamental part of their immanent connection to the land and to each other and always as part of a rich and complex relationship between men that included emotional and psychic communication, in addition to the physical. This bond was seen as one of the energetic ties between the members of the network of radical gay men on the land, as well as with their urban brethren who were still in the cities.

For some gay men on the land, sexuality presented a direct and intimate way of relating to nature. Jay Schraeter, writing from an apartment in San Francisco's countercultural Haight Street neighborhood, described the summer of 1974, when he and Arthur Evans lived for three months on New Sodom, their land in eastern Washington. The summer was very difficult for Schraeter, as he and Evans engaged in backbreaking labor to dig latrines, clear the land, and construct rudimentary log buildings. On his next to last day on the land, however, Schraeter wandered into a sunlit meadow on the property and had a personal epiphany. There, amid the "clusters of bushy Douglas maples, and tall succulent grasses," he had a sexual relationship with the land itself. Deciding this would be the spot for their new home, he took off his clothes and was brought to orgasm by the energy between his own body and the natural world he and Evans were in communication with.[23] For Schraeter, sexual expression was a way to commune as a radical gay man with the natural world of eastern Washington.

Gay men living in collective rural spaces often saw sexuality in urban gay enclaves and sexuality on the communes as being distinctly different, though both brought valuable experiences. In a discussion about sexuality printed in *RFD*, twelve men living in gay rural communities on the West Coast talked about their sexual experiences in relationship to communal life. Several of the men spoke about living in San Francisco for short periods of time, enjoying the anonymous sexuality of the gay scenes there. One man explained how he "wanted to explore San Francisco so I rented a room for two weeks, spending a lot of time walking and sensitive to the sexual energy. I responded to it, almost daily." Another man in the group described going "to the baths for only the second time in my life. I met a man I was into. We went upstairs and had sex. Whoosh, it was so liberating, to share that with each other, to expect and demand no more."[24]

However, at the same time, the men in the group tended to discuss the sexual relationships they had with friends and lovers in gay rural communal space as different—as more emotive, complex, and rich. One man described the night he arrived in Iowa to work on the magazine *RFD*: "I had come to be with other faggots. I felt the loneliness and despair which I had grown to know all winter long. . . . I no longer listened. Instead followed my strong feeling for another male. . . . A sweet and powerful feeling overwhelmed me. . . . My right hand was folded inside another hand. I did not sleep alone." Other men in the discussion spoke of intense relationships with lovers on their communes, negotiating group sexuality, jealousy, and feelings of deep friendship.[25] Jerry, who lived on a predominantly gay communal farm in New England called Butterworth Farm, interviewed in 1975, said, "I think that my sexuality has gone through a lot of changes living out in the country. When I lived in cities, I always had a lot of sexual partners. . . . It was such a casual thing. . . . You're out here and you very seldom get to relate to people on that level. . . . Whenever you do find someone you can relate to . . . almost always you have to be their friend."[26] There was a commitment among gay communalists to sexuality as a complex form of communication between friends and lovers in the intense and intimate atmosphere of the rural spaces in which these men lived.

Men involved in gay rural networks saw radical sexuality as a part of the new world they were helping into being. Peter, writing in 1974, said, "We may well be able to start to shape the new society with a new and healthier perspective on sexuality."[27] This perspective sometimes transcended clear homo/heterosexual identities. The Hop Brook Commune declared that "most of us are homo-erotic and/or homo-hetero erotic, even pan-erotic."[28] Jim, living in a home in Mendocino County, was planning on building a cabin but longed for someone to share his life with "as a friend; for lover is too possessive."[29]

For some men, sexuality was a powerful part of the natural seasons, and erotic love between men was a celebration of those cycles. "Knowin' when and how to dig some dude an' get it on good without regrets is sort of special knowledge," Dan Fee wrote on Valentine's Day 1975, evoking the history of tacit and coded gay cruising before going on to compare it with the maintenance of fruit trees: "Like knowin' how to set the trees right an' protect 'em from frost an' see 'em through drought an' more or less live with the fruit grove."[30] Sexual desire and communication could become a kind of intuitive wisdom—cultivated through deep and careful study, much like attentive horticultural practices.

Rural gay male communalists also brought erotic expression into well-established New Age metaphysical practices, infusing them with a queer sensibility. In Carl Wittman's revisioning of the tarot in which he used the classic Crowley deck but tried to rewrite its insistent heterosexism, Wittman focused on the dialogue of sexual engagement as a way to understand the cards. The four suits of tarot become organized around the sexual pleasing of self and other and the coming into consciousness of gay identity as a way of marking points of spiritual reference.[31] For gay men on the land, reimagining New Age spirituality and engaging with the natural world of rural spaces meant infusing both with the sexual expression of early gay liberation movements.

THE NATURAL WORLD

An animistic sense of the natural world around them was a critical part of the way that rural gay communalists viewed the world. In this, gay communalist New Age spirituality was connected to the set of Native American and Anglo North American cultural traditions that Catherine Albanese has collectively identified as nature religion. As Albanese argues about a larger tradition among late twentieth-century New Age practitioners, gay communalists saw the natural world as imbued with symbol and meaning.[32] An ecofeminist commitment to seeing the earth and all of its inhabitants as one interconnected living, breathing entity led them to experience the natural world as teeming with spirit. This natural vibrancy was often part of a comparison between the activity of the urban life and the more subtle interactions of the country; this distinction was part of the way that rural gay men navigated the social isolation that could be a part of rural life.

Like other manifestations of ecological consciousness in this period, this understanding of gay men as stewards of the earth involved the appropriation of Native American symbols and traditions. Gay communalists on the land sometimes saw their responsibilities to the natural world as mediated through Native American symbols and rituals. Three "men of the land" who smoked hallucinogenic mushrooms together reported becoming aware of "a Native American brother with a red blanket over his shoulder" who told them that if they kept the laws of "non-harm and balance" and helped all creatures, then they would be blessed.[33] Native American–inspired imagery was frequently used in the pages of *RFD*, including a psychedelic teepee on the cover of the summer 1976 issue. One man wrote from West Lynn, Massachusetts, that he wanted to "hear from a 'New-Age' spiritual brother into yoga, meditation, and outdoor living" who would be "interested in living a simply . . . organic existence based on a 'Traditional' South-West Native American way of life."[34] The psilocybin-induced vision, the use of Native-inspired imagery, and the letter all fuse an appropriated countercultural, stereotypical, non–tribally specific notion of Native authenticity with a gay settler-colonialist, communalist vision to communicate the responsibility that gay men felt as shepherds of the environment and its ties to spiritual experience.[35]

A strong element of ecofeminism ran throughout radical, rural gay male communal culture. "There is a great deal we have to say and give each other[,] . . . we who love mother earth and brother man," Sandy Lowe wrote from rural California. "The gay city ghetto may make us appear marginal[,] but if survival[,] . . . restoring a respect for the harmonies of nature[,] and learning to love one another are still important, then we rural faggots are on the front line."[36] In this man's words, the connections made between rural gay men were part of a new way of being in harmony with nature. Mountain Bear, from Mendocino, California, wrote of looking for other gay men with whom to live and "learn to live together with nature."[37]

At times, this ecological spirituality was part of a larger separatist, political consciousness. The members of Mulberry House, a gay male urban commune in Fayetteville, Arkansas, defined themselves as feminists and hoped to organize a "fairy farm—free from the oppressions of straight society" on land in the Ozarks. The goal was to create a "free space" committed to saving the earth, which they saw as "raped by speculators, poisoned by chemicals, and carved up by nuclear-family breeders." The Mulberry House members believed that their politics required "separating ourselves from straight male energy" and noted that as white, working, and middle-class men they were "aware of the power that comes with money and want to be supportive of other poor and nonwhite faggots." The collective saw the natural world of the Ozarks as a way to purify spiritually and stand apart from a homophobic, patriarchal, racist, and capitalist society.[38]

The natural world could also sometimes serve as a way of thinking about the solitude of rural life and the energy that flowed between men who loved each other. Edward, from New York, wrote, "Love flows out of me like a spring its water; the water is taken freely by all, and the spring makes no choice.... No one need fear a solitary country life, if one can love."[39] The ebb and flow of the natural world spoke to rural gay men of the transitory and permanent aspects of love and affirmed lives lived outside of the normative heterosexual patterns of domesticity. For gay men who moved back and forth between communal gay life and the urban enclaves, the natural world and its spirit presence was a powerful marker of the difference between the two. Felix (Lee) Mintz, who lived part-time in Lavender Hill, a gay commune in upstate New York, and the rest of the year in San Francisco and New York, wrote of "the magick of the moon on my soul" and reflected that "I forget to look up in San Francisco. It could be one among the many street lights."[40]

Rural gay communalists felt the spirits of the natural world as their companions and protectors. After returning from a trip to Europe, George discovered that his cabin had burned to the ground, his lover had abandoned him, and the four goats they had raised together were dead. When he came to the spot where his cabin had stood, grief overtook him, and he "went to the holy places deeper in the forest and wailed and chanted and screamed and called on all my friends to help me."[41] In his despair, George turned to the woods and the spirits there for solace. In his journal, detailing rituals with other gay men in rural space and celebrating his coming into acceptance of his love for men, Don Tevel-Treelove wrote, "Nine of us sitting, equals. Feeding each other, comforting each other, rejoicing in the magic of faggotry. Faggot Magic/Faggot Spirit/Faggot Power. In direct contact with the Energy of the Earth."[42] For Tevel-Treelove, the spirits of nature and the power of gay male community and sexuality fused into a magic that was at the same time resonant of his own coming-out struggle and the actualization of his true desire.

A CRITIQUE OF THE CITIES

To many gay men who made the journey from urban gay worlds to rural life, urban gay neighborhoods seemed like safe, homogeneous, false, and spiritually empty enclaves. Gary Menger, a man who grew up in Vermont and upstate New York and then traveled across the country to finally end up in rural Boonville, California, remembered San Francisco as a "safe, artificial little world," a "Nirvana" of "gay bars, gay baths, gay restaurants, gay churches."

Menger, who had been expelled from a religious order in Vermont as a teen for having sex with another novitiate and then struggled with his own attraction to other men while cruising in Lincoln, Nebraska, had come out to himself as a gay man after going to the Stud, a well-known gay bar in San Francisco. But then he went on to find a world more in keeping with his sense of self in rural Northern California.[43] Upon returning to Wolf Creek, Oregon, from a trip to New York with his lover, Carl Wittman reflected on how "gay men in the city are deprived of much of what we have here ... as a homosexual the space and time to pursue a relatively open and honest loving relationship without the constantly destructive and distracting city phenomena."[44]

Part of this critique of the urban gay world was a sense that it had fostered the emergence of a commodified gay male sexuality at odds with the original gay liberation vision of a sexual freedom based on deep affective bonds between gay men challenging patriarchal, militaristic, homophobic mainstream America. Anonymous sexuality in bathhouses and other cruising spaces often seemed to these men to represent a desensitized sexual gratification to the detriment of a notion of radical sexual, social, and spiritual brotherhood. Stewart, living in a communal household in rural Iowa, reflected on his coming out in San Francisco and initial reluctance to leave the city for the Midwest where he had grown up: "I didn't want to leave the safety of numbers of Castro Street.... I had yet to get my yah-yahs out in Babylon."[45] Tom Lauria, who had left Buffalo, New York, for the desert in Arroyo Seco, New Mexico, wrote that he had "got out of east coast bars, and with it, the whole mentality of cruising, clothes, all of it so much wasted effort."[46] Jay Jackson described sitting in Portland, where he was visiting from his rural home in Monmouth, Oregon, and reflecting on how "dependent gays are on the city bar games (sexual and social) to meet other gays."[47] Many gay men living in countercultural, rural spaces found the sexual spaces of urban gay neighborhoods to be alienating and removed from their vision of gay male possibilities.

Gay communalists who were learning about Eastern spiritual traditions sometimes incorporated their understanding of these perspectives into their critiques of the commodification of gay male sexuality. David, a member of the Hop Brook Commune in New Salem, Massachusetts, who had recently read *The Nameless Experience* by Rohit Mehta, wrote in 1975 that "some of us have become incapable (through conditioning) of knowing the difference between thrill and joy." For David, thrill, embodied by cruising, contrasted with joy, which came from the absence of self.[48] He links a critique of cruising and mid-1970s bar culture with a notion of the falseness of the self and its desires that he had come to through reading Mehta.[49]

This vision of gay male urban spaces was not an absolute one, however; many gay men who spent considerable time in rural gay communal situations also found themselves still needing the social and sexual networks of the urban gay scenes. This created a dichotomy in their lives between these two worlds. Lee Mintz spent the first half of the 1970s moving back and forth from gay urban households in San Francisco and New York and Lavender Hill, gay communal land in upstate New York, outside of Ithaca. While the rural gay communal space and the experience of building a house with other gay men was intensely uplifting and gave him "high, warm ties of togetherness," Mintz cyclically felt the need to return to the gay urban world for the stimuli of "gay politics and dances and meeting new people and struggling with each other."[50] In describing his ambivalence about a trip to New York from the commune in Wolf Creek, Oregon, Carl Wittman described his delight at seeing a new queer theater in the city and expressed "various contradictory stances about cruising and anonymous sex."[51] Jay Schraeter and Arthur Evans would spend months alternating between New Sodom, their gay communal space in rural Washington State, and the gay urban neighborhoods of either Seattle or San Francisco.[52]

For many gay men who found a spiritual and political haven in rural communalism, the urban gay world was nonetheless a critical and important place. This dual-geography life choice was specific and significant to the spiritual commitments of gay liberationists; these gay men made their homes in both places. Regularly moving between the two facilitated continued connections between the nature and land-oriented socio-spiritual brotherhood of rural communal spaces and the urban gay male communities that had been shaped by but were steadily moving away from the values of gay liberation.

STRAIGHT COUNTERCULTURE HOMOPHOBIA

The socio-spiritual vision of ecofeminist brotherhood in imminent relation with nature and spirit was forged not only in contrast or reference to changing gay urban communities; in the early 1970s, when gay men seeking an alternative to the emerging gay neighborhoods in the metropoles moved to rural areas, they encountered homophobia from heterosexual, back-to-the-land communal movements. When gay communalists from rural Iowa sent in an announcement to *Mother Earth News*, the counterculture periodical well known as a clearinghouse for hippie communal information, asking for inclusion in the Position and Situations section that ran notices from individuals interested in forming alternative rural living collectives, they were told that the magazine did not print gay announcements.[53] The gay men in Iowa were not alone. *Mother Earth News* had turned down or failed to run announcements from gay men in Oklahoma, Nebraska, and Florida. The ad from Joel in Florida had read "Gay brothers and Sisters who are interested in beginning preparations toward the organization of a rural based gay people's commune, please drop Southern Gay Liberator a line." *Mother Earth News* refused to run the ad, reiterated its policy of not running gay ads, and wrote, "Joel, I hope you don't dislike us now.... We're really on your side, you know."[54] Other gay men living in rural spaces noted the racist and sexist vision of countercultural rural living. Jim, from Mendocino, wrote that he had long "been disenchanted by their folksie and old timey put on and of course their obvious racist and sexist stand."[55]

The animosity these aspiring gay communalists experienced was part of a larger expression of homophobia by heterosexual communalists who often maintained a vision of a rural counterculture based on traditional gender roles and heterosexual nuclear families. While Allan Troxler found the older rural communities in Plainfield, Vermont, where he tried to create a communal living situation as a gay man, to be friendly and forthcoming with information about planting practices and other important tips, he felt a deep hostility from the countercultural men who were establishing their own communal spaces in the area: "For the male freak, self-respect and respect from the community meant coming on rugged, self-sufficient, knowledgeable, and potent." In Troxler's experience, this left little room for male identities that lay outside of a macho, countercultural vision of rural entrepreneurial success. After he relocated to Wolf Creek, Oregon, Troxler encountered the same rough manifestation of heterosexual, countercultural masculinity: "In the bar at Wolf Creek Inn it's not clear where the knife-toting loggers stop and the knife-toting hippies begin."[56] Often, gay rural communalists found themselves outnumbered by these heterosexual counterculturalists. Mark and Andy, two gay men living on the land in the Ozark Mountains outside of Fayetteville, Arkansas, complained that most of the young communalists who surrounded them were "new pioneers" who were "young, family-oriented people, into a Steve Gaskin's 'The Farm' trip."[57] Gay men interested in forming radical, rural communes were alienated by the preponderance of heterosexual communes based on traditional, gender-essentialist notions of the nuclear family. The alternative vision of a loving, feminist brotherhood living in sexual and spiritual communion with nature and the invisible world of spirits was forged in part in opposition to these heterosexual rural communes.

RURAL GAY COMMUNALISM AND THE COUNTERCULTURAL HERITAGE OF GAY LIBERATION

In the summer of 1976, Tom Kennedy from San Francisco wrote to *RFD*. Kennedy chastised the magazine for "promoting counter-culture consciousness." In his view, the rural gay communalists who used the magazine for a forum seemed like "white men who have dropped out of school and then society and then into a quiet life in the country." For Kennedy, the pursuit of gay communal living was a privileged one that ignored the fact that there remained "those of us here in the city who are trapped ... in a vicious circle of attempting to survive in a racist, classist, and sexist society." Kennedy believed that gay male communalism represented an irresponsible and indulgent turning away by white gay countercultural men in the face of the struggle on the part of "some of us who are poor, transsexual, [and] non-white-working-class" to survive in urban spaces.[58]

Kennedy was not wrong. The move toward the rural by largely white gay men was in part a move away from urban politics. They criticized the racist, heterosexist, countercultural vision of *Mother Earth News* but themselves appropriated Native American aesthetics and concepts to express their ideas of communalist spirituality while founding homogeneous, white gay male rural enclaves. But their movement was more than that, as well. These gay male liberationists were also engaged in a complex spiritual/political renegotiation of the politics, centered on neighborhoods and municipal, civil rights–based politics that grew out of the activist successes of the early 1970s as well as the heterosexual counterculture. Their spiritual visions actively fused New Age spiritualities, an ecofeminist understanding of the natural world, and a radical ethic of erotic freedom while mediating a reciprocal play between the increasingly consolidated gay male urban world and a rural spiritual and social network that insisted on the revolutionary power of emotive and erotic connections between men.[59]

Radical gay communalist spiritualities of the 1970s appropriated from multiple sources—medieval Christian communities, ecofeminism, Native American ritual, Asian religions, and nature religions—in the project of achieving an authentic and sacred "gay" identity. This spiritual revolution grew directly out of both the rural gay experience and radical gay liberationist politics and represented an alternative to what the communalists and their sympathizers saw as a commodified, assimilated gay urban world. The spirituality they developed centered on an erotic and personal gay authenticity as the foundation for a sacred brotherhood.

NOTES

1. "Letter from Caradoc," *RFD*, Spring 1975, 37.
2. The three-letter name of the magazine, a play on Rural Farm Delivery, was said to stand for an ever-changing array of titles, including *Rustic Fairy Dreams* (Issue 1), *Reckless Fruit Delight* (Issue 2), and *Really Feeling Divine* (Issue 3).
3. In his book *Another Country: Queer Anti-urbanism* (New York: New York University Press, 2010), Scott Herring describes *RFD* as having an "aesthetic of anti-urbanism" expressive of what he calls a "critical rurality." For Herring, critical rurality grew out of both gay liberation political commitments and rural lesbian feminist critics of urbanity (63). As Judith Weisenfeld's essay on the followers of Father Divine in this volume shows, the insularity of communal spirituality can often allow for sexual and social expressions other than what is allowed in mainstream society. In part, the separatism of a spiritual communal impulse allowed gay radicals to continue to develop an oppositional sexual/social politics.
4. The circulation of *RFD* during these early years is difficult to determine exactly, as is the case with many counterculture periodicals from the era. However, material in the magazine itself and correspondence between those publishing it allow some speculation. Letters between Carl Wittman, Allan Troxler, and Stewart Scofield from 1974 to 1976 indicate that five hundred copies of the first issue were printed, and steady demand pushed this number up to eight hundred copies of the second issue. For this correspondence, see "RFD" folder, Collection 2011.072, Stewart Scofield Special Collection, ONE National Gay and Lesbian Archives, Los Angeles. Copies were distributed to bookstores and coffee shops in both rural and urban settings, to subscribers, and to prison inmates, free of charge. A map titled "RFD Country" illustrating the distribution of *RFD*'s readers indicates that they lived in all U.S. states with the exceptions of Nevada, Nebraska, West Virginia, Arkansas, Louisiana, and Mississippi, although correspondence later printed in the magazine from gay communalists in Arkansas indicates that *RFD* did in fact make it there. "RFD Country," *RFD*, Winter 1974–75, 3.
5. Almost all of these thirteen communes were predominantly gay male, with some being exclusively so and at least one, Butterworth Farm in Massachusetts, being a mixed space that celebrated gay male rural life while also including lesbians and heterosexual men and women. Materials on Butterworth Farm can be found in the Butterworth Farm Special Collection at the New York Public Library, and for Gay Liberation Arizona Desert's communal experiment, see "Communalists," *Life*, December 1, 1971, 66. All other locations cited come from material in *RFD*. Examples of urban communes that wanted to establish gay male rural communal spaces would be Mulberry House in Fayetteville, Arkansas, and a communal household of "3–5 gay men" in San Francisco with aspirations of buying land in rural California. On Mulberry House, see material in "Communes" subject file, ONE National Gay and Lesbian Archives, and for the San Francisco commune, see "Letter from Steve Ginsberg," *RFD*, Spring 1975, 46.
6. On the founding of the Faeries and the organizing of the first gathering in Arizona in 1979 by Hay, Kilhefner, Walker, and Burnside, see Mark Thompson, ed., *The Fire in Moonlight: Stories from the Radical Faeries, 1975–2010* (Maple Shade, N.J.: White Crane

Press, 2011). For other material on the Faeries, see Scott Lauria Morgensen, *Spaces between Us: Queer Settler Colonialism and Indigenous Decolonization* (Minneapolis: University of Minnesota Press, 2011), 127–60; and Mark Thompson, "This Gay Tribe: A Brief History of Fairies," in *Gay Spirit: Myth and Meaning* (New York: St. Martin's Press, 1987), 260–78.

7. On Harry Hay and John Burnside's 1975 visit with Carl Wittman and Allan Troxler, see *RFD*, Autumn 1975, 40.

8. Ron Lambe, "RFD: Gay Men Living the Good Life in the Country," *In Touch for Men* #105, undated, copy of article in "RFD" subject files, ONE National Gay and Lesbian Archives.

9. Gabby Haze, "Short Mountain Sanctuary: Where We Came from & Where We're Going," *White Crane*, Winter 2008/9, 25, 27.

10. In his book *The New Age Movement: The Celebration of the Self and the Sacralization of Modernity*, anthropologist Paul Heelas argues that the diverse manifestations of New Age spirituality are united in their focus on self-authority amid received wisdom. Working in American religious history, Catherine Albanese links New Age spiritual movements to various and competing traditions of nature religion in American and Native American history, while sociologist Courtney Bender has compellingly argued in her study of modern-day Cambridge, Massachusetts, that the New Age is part of an American focus on the self-mediated spiritual experience. Bender importantly asks that we see New Age spiritual traditions, as well as the very questions of what spirituality and religion are, as part of a mutable discourse; in her book, *The New Metaphysicals: Spirituality and the American Religious Imagination* (Chicago: University of Chicago Press, 2010), she shows how the New Age values the unmediated spiritual experience while still seeking disciplinary verification and ties with the American academy.

11. Heelas, *New Age Movement*. For an organizational history of counterculture communes in the 1960s, see Timothy Miller, *The 60s Communes: Hippie and Beyond* (Syracuse: Syracuse University Press, 1999).

12. Olaf, "Forest Folk: Assorted Tales—If You Are Very Quiet You Can Hear the Sounds of Fairies in the Woods," *RFD*, Winter 1974–75, 21.

13. "Letter from Peter," *RFD*, Autumn 1974, 6.

14. "Letter from Caradoc," *RFD*, Spring 1975, 37.

15. Jeff, "Layout on the Lake," *RFD*, Summer 1975, 23.

16. On the United Order of the Family of Christ, see letter dated July 2, 1975, in "Communes" subject file, ONE National Gay and Lesbian Archives, and an advertisement for the group that read "Gay Christian Commune—live together in love and in brotherhood" in the *Berkeley Barb*, July 5–11, 1974, A9.

17. "Letter from Doug Beckwith," *RFD*, Autumn 1975,5.

18. "Letter from Steve DiVerde," *RFD*, Autumn 1975, 20.

19. On Hop Brook Commune, see the collection of its publication, *Gay Community Pamphlets*, in the Beinecke Rare Book and Manuscript Library, Yale University. One of these pamphlets was also printed in *RFD*, Autumn 1974, 4.

20. "Letter from New Age Community Clearing House," *RFD*, Summer 1975, 17.

21. On George Bamberger's proposal for a Christian gay commune, see "Contact Page," *RFD*, Autumn 1974, 26; and "Letter from George Bamberger," *RFD*, Winter 1974–75, 4.

22. "Letter from George A. Beadle," *RFD*, Autumn 1975, 3.

23. Jay Schraeter, "Some of My Best Friends Are Cedar Trees," *RFD*, Spring 1975, 15.

24. For the notes from this group discussion, see "Sexual Tension," *RFD*, Autumn 1975, 6–11.

25. Ibid.

26. "As the Butter Churns," *RFD*, Spring 1976, 17.

27. "Letter from Peter," *RFD*, Autumn 1974, 6.

28. "Hop Brook Commune," *RFD*, Autumn 1974, 11.

29. "Letter from Jim," *RFD*, Spring 1975, 28.

30. "Sometimes I Sits and Thinks, but Mostly I Sits," *RFD*, Winter 1975, 42. Donald Boisvert, in his work on gay male spaces in Montreal, has suggested that sexuality and the erotic is uniquely central to a gay male spirituality: "Gay religion remains rooted in desire. It represents a form of spiritual practice that draws its inspiration and sustenance from the erotic and emotional needs that men have for other men." I would agree and add that in these gay male communal counterculture spaces, sexuality became a spiritual relationship that tied men to each other, to the natural world, and to an immaterial world of spirit. Donald Boisvert, "The Spirit Within: Gay Male Culture as a Spiritual Venue," in *Gay Religion*, ed. Scott Thumma and Edward R. Gray (New York: Altamira Press, 2005), 366.

31. Carl Wittman, "In Search of a Gay Tarot," *RFD*, Winter 1974–75, 32–37.

32. Catherine Albanese, *Nature Religion in America* (Chicago: University of Chicago Press, 1990).

33. "Letter from Haia," *RFD*, Winter 1975, 3.

34. "Letter from Arthur," *RFD*, Spring 1976, 2.

35. On the appropriation of the Native American as symbol by the 1960s counterculture and environmentalist movement more generally, see Phil Deloria, *Playing Indian* (New Haven: Yale University Press, 1998), 154–80; and Sherry L. Smith, *Hippies, Indians, and the Fight for Red Power* (Oxford: Oxford University Press, 2012), 43–77. On the appropriation of Native symbol by the modern New Age, see Shari Huhndorf, *Going Native: Indians in the American Cultural Imagination* (Ithaca: Cornell University Press, 2001), 162–98. For an important discussion of the appropriation of Native symbol by white queer activists, see Morgensen, *Spaces between Us*.

36. "Letter from Sandy Lowe," *RFD*, Summer 1976, 18.

37. "Letter from Mountain Bear," *RFD*, Winter 1975, 2.

38. See typewritten letter signed by the members of Mulberry House in "Communes" subject file, ONE National Gay and Lesbian Archives.

39. "Letter from Edward," *RFD*, Summer 1976, 2. R. Marie Griffith has suggested that one compelling element of queer religion and the intersections of sexuality and spirituality more broadly is the interplay of belief and the body. Here, in Edward's description, his emotion, his sexuality, and possibly his body itself become linked to the natural world. Griffith, "Conclusion: Gay Religion as a Cultural Production," in *Gay Religion*, ed. Scott Thumma and Edward R. Gray (New York: Altamira Press, 2005), 374.

40. Felix (Lee) Mintz, "The Magick of the Moon," *RFD*, Spring 1975, 40.

41. George, "Yellow Flickers," *RFD*, Autumn 1975, 16.

42. Don Tevel-Treelove, "Spring, Spirit, and Faggotry," *RFD*, Spring 1975, 44.

43. Gary Menger, "Full Circle," *RFD*, Autumn 1974, 8, 10, 12.

44. Carl Wittman, "Coming Home," *RFD*, Autumn 1974, 20. Wittman had already famously reflected on the constraints of a "gay ghetto" and the importance of an erotic freedom and objectification grounded in a notion of radical brotherhood in the groundbreaking essay "Refugees from Amerika: A Gay Manifesto" that was published in the *San Francisco Free Press* in 1970 and was reprinted by Gay Liberation Front New York as *Gay Flames* pamphlet #9. In the essay, Wittman presages his later involvement in a rural gay male communalist movement in a call for independent gay community structures that has nationalist undertones: "Rural retreats, political action offices, food cooperatives, a free school, unalienating bars and after hours places—they must be developed if we are to have even the shadow of a free territory." Carl Wittman, "Refugees from Amerika: A Gay Manifesto," in *The Homosexual Dialectic*, ed. Joseph A. McCaffrey (Englewood Cliffs: Prentice Hall, 1972), 169.

45. Stewart, "Road to Malcom," *RFD*, Winter 1974–75, 41.

46. "Letter from Tom Lauria," *RFD*, Winter 1974–75, 46.

47. "Letter from Jay Jackson," *RFD*, Spring 1975, 2.

48. As Kathi Kern's essay on Winnifred Wygal in this volume shows, LGBT individuals marked as outsiders by orthodox religious practitioners found Eastern spiritual traditions compelling throughout the twentieth century.

49. See "Gay Relationship," *Gay Community Pamphlets* 1, no. 1 (1975), Beinecke Rare Book and Manuscript Library, Yale University.

50. Lee Mintz, "City/Country," *RFD*, Spring 1975, 8–9.

51. Carl Wittman, "Coming Home," *RFD*, Autumn 1974, 20.

52. See "A Letter from New Sodom," *RFD*, Autumn 1974, 22; and "Two Tales of New Sodom," *RFD*, Spring 1975, 14–17.

53. Allan Troxler, "A Rejection," *RFD*, Autumn 1974, 14–18.

54. "More From MEN," *RFD*, Winter 1974–75, 11.

55. "Letter from Jim," *RFD*, Spring 1975, 28.

56. Troxler, "Rejection," 15, 17.

57. "Letter from Mark and Andy," *RFD*, Spring 1975, 3. The letter here is referring to The Farm, a commune in Tennessee founded in 1971 by a group of people led by Stephen Gaskin. The Farm was one of the most famous of the counterculture communes of the era and here serves as a prototypical example of a patriarchal, heterosexist vision.

58. "Letter from Tom Kennedy," *RFD*, Summer 1976, 3.

59. These contradictions and complexities would be passed on to the Radical Faerie movement, founded in 1979 out of some of these radical gay communal spaces. For histories of the Radical Faeries, see Morgensen, *Spaces between Us*, 127–60; and Thompson, "This Gay Tribe."

WE WHO MUST DIE DEMAND A MIRACLE

Christmas 1989 at the Metropolitan Community Church of San Francisco

LYNNE GERBER

The first Christmas service at the Metropolitan Community Church (MCC) of San Francisco (MCCSF) in 1989 was a candlelight service on Christmas Eve 1989. The *Bay Area Reporter* (*BAR*), San Francisco's largest gay and lesbian newspaper, warned readers to arrive early to get good seats.[1] The "pink and purple church on Eureka Street," three blocks from the center of San Francisco's famed gay neighborhood, the Castro, had a reputation for great music, great singing, and a progressive gay preacher. As on most Sundays in the 1980s and 1990s, the people who attended this Christmas Eve were mostly men, mostly white, and many were ill—newly, gravely, or somewhere in between—with AIDS.[2] They came by themselves or in the nontraditional kinship groups they formed as gay and lesbian people in a largely gay neighborhood. But there were also some traditional family members at this service, parents, siblings, and others who accepted their loved ones' sexuality or were trying to. And there were likely more visitors, gay people from the neighborhood or the city, estranged from their families or from Christianity but looking to be somewhere that felt homelike on Christmas.

The service started with an extended piano medley of Christmas carols, and then the singing began. It was so crowded that the choir director asked everyone to share hymnals; there were not enough to go around. The carol sing went through many of the season's classics—"Joy to the World," "Angels We Have Heard on High"—before the service formally began with the call to worship, read responsively by the congregation and the pastor, Jim Mitulski. "Comfort, comfort my people says your God," read Mitulski. "And the glory of God shall be revealed, and all flesh shall see it together," they responded. After a rousing version of "O Come, All Ye Faithful," Mitulski welcomed the congregation and made some announcements, including two about church members currently hospitalized and asking for visitors. One, Mitulski told the audience, wished to express his praises to God for the healing he had been experiencing with his family, who were coming to San Francisco to visit him for the first time. There was more singing before a reading of the story of Jesus's birth from the gospel of Luke. And there was more singing still before Mitulski stood to begin his sermon.

In the 1980s and 1990s, gay religious leaders and communities faced a challenge that stretched their physical, emotional, spiritual, and theological resources past their limits. The emergence of AIDS forced them to address the familiar challenges of integrating sexuality and faith in a new—life or death—context. It would prove a critical testing ground for whether and how the radical experiment of explicitly gay religiosity could sustain people and communities "in trouble."[3] This chapter tells the story of how one gay-identified congregation and its pastor drew on a combination of liberation theology, LGBT literature, and what David Halperin calls a "queer sensibility" to forge gay religious life in a time of both immense possibility and immense suffering and loss. It does so by looking at one moment in the church's life—the sermon given by the congregation's minister on Christmas Eve of 1989—and using it as a lens to examine how liberation theology and LGBT literature were brought to bear on this particular moment in the AIDS crisis in order to make gay Christianity a usable tradition in a time of crisis and change.

WE GAY CHRISTIANS

The Metropolitan Community Church of San Francisco was part of a larger experiment in gay Christianity, the Universal Fellowship of Metropolitan Community Churches (UFMCC). UFMCC was founded as a denominational home to congregations inspired by the Reverend Troy Perry to forge an independent Christian space that affirmed homosexuality and recognized gay relationships.[4] Perry founded the first UFMCC congregation in his home in Huntington Beach, California, in October 1968. A preacher in the Pentecostal Church of God in Prophecy, Perry had been removed from his Florida congregation a few years earlier when his homosexuality was disclosed to denominational authorities. After openly exploring gay life apart from church life, he believed he heard God call him to start a church for gays and lesbians, people deemed sinful by the vast majority of Christian groups at the time. In addition to providing a home for churchless gay Christians, Perry and other denominational leaders sought to demonstrate the compatibility between Christianity and homosexuality to the Christian world through UFMCC.

The founding of UFMCC marked an early point in a period from the mid-1960s to the mid-1970s when many gay Christian experiments began. There were a number of historic precedents to these efforts by homosexually oriented people to claim Christianity as their own, including the Old Catholic/Independent Orthodox movement that started reaching out to gay people as early as 1946 and shaped San Francisco's gay religious ecology through the leadership of Bishop Mikhail Itkin. By the 1960s, these experiments were more often undertaken in tandem with an increasingly self-aware political and social movement for gay rights, one that put gay self-identification, in the form of "coming out," at its center. One of the earliest of these efforts, the Council on Religion and the Homosexual (CRH), convened in San Francisco in 1964 and saw homophile activists stand with liberal clergy to challenge church teachings on homosexuality.[5] A few months after Perry's first MCC service, the events at Stonewall moved gay activists away from the homophile model of political engagement, which was hesitant about public sexual identification, to the gay liberationist model, which practically demanded it.[6] Many of the gay religious experiments that followed tried to reconcile gay identity and religious identity within a specific denominational context, such as the Reconstructionist debate over the admission of gay and lesbian students to the Reconstructionist Rabbinical College, discussed by Rebecca T. Alpert and Jacob J. Staub in this volume. Other gay religious experiments, such as the rural gay spiritual projects that Daniel Rivers explores in his chapter, sought to discover and/or create a gay form of spiritual expression outside of Christianity.[7]

UFMCC was distinguished by its gathering of gay believers from across the spectrum of American Christianity, independent of preexisting denominational contexts and outside of preexisting denominational limitations.[8] This distinction was the source of its greatest challenges and innovations.[9] Through UFMCC, gay Christians from churches and denominations as theologically and culturally distant as Catholics and Baptists, Lutherans and Pentecostals, Mormons and Methodists tried to make church together, resulting in a pragmatic or lived ecumenism. On the congregational level, this forced cooperation and compromise across deep personal differences. On the denominational level, it generated an affinity with ecumenical Christianity, one that competed and at times conflicted with the cultural and theological affinity with evangelicalism bestowed by Perry and inspired by his work. This pragmatic ecumenism was perhaps exemplified in the denomination's practice, from its very first worship service, of having an open Communion table where people of any faith, at any stage of ritualized Christian participation, or of no faith or Christian identity, were equally welcome to participate.[10] Institutionally, it led to numerous efforts at membership in the National Council of Churches, the nation's ecumenical body, efforts that consistently failed because of UFMCC's position on homosexuality.[11] In a sermon delivered at MCCSF, Perry described his simultaneous delight and horror when he discovered that his invitation of Communion MCC-style during a service with the leadership of the National Council of Churches was the first time the leaders of that organization had ever taken Communion together.[12] Finally, this lived ecumenism resulted in diversity not only within UFMCC congregations but between them as well. These congregations, particularly in this period before the welcoming and affirming movement helped secure gay recognition in mainline liberal churches, ran the theological gamut from conservative evangelical (except for homosexuality) to liberal, progressive, and liberationist.

MCCSF was at the far left of this spectrum. The church was founded in 1970 at Jackson's Bar in the city's North Beach District. It faced the complexities of lived ecumenism early on when church leaders debated whether or not the congregation's second pastor, Jim Sandmire, needed to be baptized before beginning his pastorate: Sandmire was a Mormon.[13] The congregation met in numerous churches throughout the city, including one that was burned down in an arson attack directed at MCCSF. In 1979 it purchased a small church building on Eureka Street from a Pentecostal congregation, painted it pink and purple, and made its home in the Castro District. The congregation changed leaders almost as often as it changed church buildings. By the time of its move to the Castro, the church was on its fifth minister in under a decade; for a year in the mid-1980s, it was run entirely by lay leaders.

Jim Mitulski was hired as the church's pastor in 1986. He was twenty-seven years old and had been raised Catholic in the Detroit area. He had a background in political organizing and received on-the-ground pastoral training at MCC New York, then in Greenwich Village, which introduced him to AIDS ministry and AIDS activism. He arrived in San Francisco with his then-partner, Bob Crocker, who became the congregation's longtime music director. During his first years at the church, Mitulski was a student at the Pacific School of Religion, from which he received a master of divinity degree in 1990. Mitulski pastored in one of the few cities with more than one UFMCC congregation. In the late 1970s Jim Sandmire, MCCSF's Mormon former pastor, returned to the city after a hiatus in Los Angeles working for the denomination and founded a second UFMCC congregation, Golden Gate MCC.

One of the questions UFMCC continually grappled with was whether it was primarily gay or primarily Christian. Early UFMCC publications reflected a diversity of opinion on this question, but for Troy Perry personally and for the denomination formally, the answer was clear: Christian came first. "We are not the 'Gay Church,'" Perry wrote in 1970. "We are the 'Church of the Living God.' Metropolitan Community Church is much more than some 'gay' organization: we are born again believers!"[14] In formal statements, UFMCC took pains to present itself as a Christian denomination with a special outreach to the homosexual community.[15] Jim Sandmire expressed similar sentiments in MCCSF magazine *Cross Currents*. He wrote, "MCC is not a gay church. We are very supportive of gay organizations as a means of directing effectively our efforts at community self-help and liberation.... But MCC is a Christian Church, directed first to our brothers and sisters long ignored or oppressed by that Church."[16]

But under Mitulski's leadership, MCCSF took a different position. "The thing that I think that we did that was dynamic," he said in an interview for the church's thirty-fifth anniversary, "was that we took our gay experience first and then looked at how Christianity fit that rather than trying to cram our gayness into a Christian lens."[17] The decades between this statement and those by Perry and Sandmire notwithstanding, they reflect both a generational change represented by Mitulski and his cohort and a change in the culture of the Castro neighborhood and in the church as a result of its relocation there. This gay-first position was in sharp contrast to many other gay Christian experiments of the period, including others within UFMCC, which made greater efforts to demonstrate their compatibility with Christianity as their referent tradition or denomination understood it. But it had a great deal of affinity with the liberation theology approach that was popular in many liberal Christian communities and that Mitulski used in building the congregation and preaching to it.

The Christmas 1989 sermon was in many ways emblematic of the liberation approach that Mitulski took to homiletics during his tenure at MCCSF. Liberation theology, which had its origins in Latin American Catholicism, aimed to encourage the economically poor and socially marginalized to engage both with the church and with larger political issues in order to effect social justice. It did this through the related pedagogical strategies of showing marginalized communities their affinity with the gospel story and giving them voice to speak back to scripture in order to develop revolutionary interpretations of it. In the United States, left-leaning theologians adapted this approach with communities at the edges of social power and legitimacy who may or may not have been materially poor. Mitulski and MCCSF were at the forefront of this effort, building a gay church and an AIDS church on these principles.

The Christmas 1989 sermon exemplified two critical dimensions of a gay liberation theology approach to preaching in an epidemic. First, it made connections between the biblical story and the congregation's story by reading scriptural narratives using contemporary figures, phrases, and issues; by adding the voices of gay people as scriptural commentary; and by continually evoking a sense of place and time through references to San Francisco, the Castro, and the pink and purple church. Making these connections was a strategy aimed at helping people alienated from the tradition to see and understand it as their own. Doing so then gave marginalized people the discursive space from which to begin making demands on society and on the tradition itself: demands for social recognition and for social justice, for angels and for miracles.

WE WHO MUST DIE

Mitulski brought his Christmas Eve sermon to a close with a quote from W. H. Auden's Christmas oratorio *For the Time Being*. Auden, a major figure in English literature, was part of a cohort of English homosexual writers of the period, including Christopher Isherwood and E. M. Forster, with interests in writing and religion. Homosexuality was rarely an explicit theme in Auden's work, but gay liberation thinkers included him in their developing canon of writers they were reclaiming as predecessors and trailblazers whose work culminated in that movement. "In the portion about Christmas, this is what W. H. Auden says," Mitulski told the audience "'We who must die demand a miracle. How can the eternal do a temporal act, how could the infinite become a finite fact? Nothing can save us that is possible. We who must die demand a miracle.'"[18]

Auden's poem, written after his mother's death and the dissolution of a relationship with a man he considered his spouse, includes all humans when evoking "we who must die." Death is a fate all people share, one that is consigned to us by the fact of our birth. Although written by a devout Christian who was also a gay man, the poem expresses a universalizing impulse in Christianity; it is a gay Christian experiment that does not explicitly evoke "gay." But in Christmas 1989 in the Castro, this poem could be read, and was likely heard, as a very particular reflection of the experience of this community of gay men, many of whom were consigned to death not just because of their universal experience of birth but because of a devastating disease that was under-researched, undertreated, and often ignored because of the particular groups of people it affected.

The use of Auden is reflective of the way Mitulski frequently used gay literature in his sermons. His approach to liberation theology was deeply informed by *The Gospel in Solentiname*, itself an experiment in liberation theology albeit in a very different social context. Compiled and edited by Catholic priest and theologian Ernesto Cardenal, the book is a set of commentaries on gospel passages by a community of Nicaraguan peasants or campesinos. The commentaries were developed during masses in which, rather than giving a traditional sermon, Cardenal read the gospel reading one verse at a time and invited people to make observations, ask questions, and interpret meaning. Cardenal wrote, "The campesinos' discussions were often more profound than those of many theologians, but they reflected the simplicity of the gospel readings themselves. That is not surprising. The *gospel*, or good news (good news to the poor), was written for them, by people like them."[19]

Mitulski wanted to do something like the Solentiname practice at MCCSF, but the size and complexity of the congregation did not permit that approach during sermons at worship services. Rather than literally asking the community to comment during the sermon, he used voices from gay writers, gay poets, gay theologians, and MCCSF congregants alongside scripture as a way of asserting to a sometimes skeptical congregation that, despite the church's marginalization of gay people, the scripture was in fact written for them, as it was for all marginalized people. Auden was just one of many gay writers who appeared in Mitulski's sermons over the years. Adrienne Rich, James Baldwin, Jeanette Winterson, Audre Lorde, Alice Walker, Paul Monette, Sarah Schulman, Dorothy Allison, and many others were evoked with some regularity, and a number of these writers visited the congregation, preaching or giving readings there.

Auden's poem spoke directly and hauntingly to the community's context. By Christmas 1989 the community had been living with AIDS for more than eight years. San Francisco did not have the highest number of AIDS cases in the country, but it did have the highest density of cases, and that density was highest in the Castro.[20] The disease changed everything, from individual lives to alternative kinship structures to neighborhood and city politics. After an initial period of denial and suspicion, the gay community in San Francisco began to take AIDS very seriously, albeit with much disagreement over strategy and tactics. Grassroots AIDS organizations such as the Shanti

Project and the Kaposi's Sarcoma Foundation (later the San Francisco AIDS Foundation) were formed early in the epidemic to care for people with AIDS and to agitate for research, education, and safe sex. Together these organizations created the San Francisco model of AIDS care focused on meeting the pragmatic needs of people with AIDS, keeping them socially connected, and minimizing hospitalization. The first public forum about the disease took place at MCCSF, as did many in the years that followed.[21]

In the mid-1980s, the controversy over bathhouse closures took center stage in San Francisco, with some gay activists siding with public health officials arguing for closure while others insisted that the baths were an important site of public education about AIDS and that sexual freedoms were too valuable and too hard-won to abandon.[22] The pastors of the two UFMCC congregations in the city at the time took the latter position, publishing a letter in the *BAR* expressing concern that closing the baths would be "ill-advised and unproductive."[23] That controversy died down in 1985, just as more direct political action regarding AIDS began, with the start of the AIDS/ARC Vigil and the founding of Mobilization for Action, an organization that took public protest as its mission.

By the time of the Christmas 1989 sermon, there was a great deal of discouragement in the AIDS community along with a modicum of hope. It was a moment of significant and growing AIDS fatigue. Many local AIDS groups were deep in or just coming out of a period of crisis, with a scandal at the Shanti Project and leadership changes at the San Francisco AIDS Foundation as two examples. They were also facing increased competition for funding from more established and better organized public health organizations that had recently turned attention to AIDS after years of looking away. As a result, the San Francisco model was giving way. The *BAR* published editorials throughout 1989 on the sorry state of AIDS organizations in the city. In December it reported on the "New San Francisco model," an effort by fifty grassroots AIDS organizations to regroup and move to the next stage of AIDS service provision.[24] "That initial feeling of 'crisis' is over," wrote HIV columnist Michael Botkin, "and caring for the sick and dying now seems less like a sacred vocation and more like dirty, hard work."[25]

It was also a time of increased tension between gay organizations and AIDS organizations. The week before Christmas saw an article in the *BAR* about efforts on the part of some gay organizations to "re-gay" AIDS.[26] In order to attract money and political attention, a number of AIDS organizations sought to present AIDS as a disease that could affect anyone, not just homosexuals. They highlighted stories of people with AIDS who were not gay—mothers, children, hemophiliacs—and were successful in gaining funds and passing critical legislation as a result. But some gay organizations felt this was a strategic error, one potentially harmful to the gay rights movement.[27] A few months after Christmas, Eric Rofes, director of the Shanti Project and occasional preacher and retreat leader at MCCSF, published an article in *Out/Look* titled "Gay Groups vs. AIDS Groups: Averting Civil War in the 90s."[28] It reflected the tension many activists felt as AIDS organizing and gay organizing, once deeply fused, began moving apart. In analyzing this moment in the organizational life of gay San Francisco, sociologist Elizabeth Armstrong argued that, contrary to conventional wisdom, the AIDS crisis did not strengthen gay organizations in San Francisco. Rather, AIDS organizations established a competing field that drained gay organizations of financial resources, volunteer time, and organizational expertise.[29] In December 1989, gay and AIDS organizations were feeling that competition and asking themselves whether it was possible to be both or if at some point they would have to choose.

MCCSF was asking itself similar questions. The congregation began as a gay community group, and that remained its primary identification, especially at the denominational level. But by the late 1980s the church began to understand and articulate just how deeply AIDS was affecting its community—that it was, in fact, becoming an AIDS church. Because it was one of the first gay organizations to own property in the city, the church was the site of the earliest public meetings and information sessions in the Castro regarding AIDS. Many AIDS organizations had offices in the church at some point, and groups rented the space to hold trainings, safe-sex education sessions, and other AIDS-related events. But before Mitulski's pastorate, the church had not engaged AIDS much directly as a congregation.

Upon his arrival it became clear that if the congregation wanted to respond authentically to the needs of the community, it would have to take on AIDS as a central issue and concern. At Mitulski's first Easter service, Communion was consecrated by Bill Knox, a congregant with visible Kaposi's sarcoma lesions, the bodily sign of AIDS. This intentional integration of AIDS into the liturgy represented the congregation's dual commitments to AIDS and Christian witness. By his second year, Mitulski, with the help of Steven Clover, another congregant with AIDS, developed a relationship with Double Rock Baptist Church, an African American congregation that was also being affected by AIDS. Despite that congregation's objection to homosexuality, the two churches sponsored joint worship services and gospel concerts for many years. In 1988 Mitulski and associate pastor Kittredge Cherry coauthored an article in the mainline Christian magazine the *Christian Century* describing how MCCSF had become not a church serving people with AIDS but "a

Church with AIDS" itself.[30] And earlier in 1989 MCCSF hosted a delegation from the National Council of Churches' Faith and Order Commission, which was conducting a study of AIDS.[31] Ron Russell-Coons, a UFMCC clergy person with AIDS, delivered the sermon. Russell-Coons had retired from his Seattle pastorate when diagnosed and affiliated with MCCSF to conduct ongoing educational campaigns about AIDS in the National Council of Churches and UFMCC, work he did until his death in 1990. Years later Mitulski reminded congregation members that they did not have a Communion service that evening, not because the delegates were afraid of sharing the sacrament with gay people or people with AIDS, but because the organization could not come to theological agreement on how to partake in Communion together.[32] In 1989 MCCSF was a gay church, with a strong commitment to gay issues and organization, but it was also an AIDS church, and the two priorities were often held in generative tension.

WE SUBJECTS/CITIZENS

Mitulski's use of the Auden poem came at the end of a sermon focused on the story of Jesus's birth according to Luke. Throughout, Mitulski made explicit links between the time of the gospel story and the present, using current names in scriptural stories, employing current categories, and telling the story in a way that resonated with the specificity of MCCSF and its struggles. "The story begins," Mitulski explained, "'In those days a decree went out from Caesar Augustus that all the world would be enrolled.' And contextualizing, placing that in history, it could just as much say, not just Caesar and Quirinius and the governor of Syria but also in those days when George Bush was president, and George Deukmejian was governor and Art Agnos was mayor of San Francisco. God picks specific times in history to involve, to be involved and to make a difference. And I believe just as God chose that specific time God is choosing now and every time."[33]

The biblical passage denotes not just a time and a place but an oppressive political regime. MCCSF was a congregation deeply aware of the political regime within which it was living. The year 1989 was a moment in which gay people in San Francisco were caught in a number of political crosswinds, with both forward movement and near-simultaneous reversal on several critical issues. Gays, lesbians, and people with AIDS seemed to be constantly on the brink of greater social acceptance and political legitimacy, only to be pushed back into subjection rather than into citizenship.

The gay community and the AIDS community in the San Francisco Bay Area faced two particularly difficult political setbacks on the Election Day preceding Christmas: the defeat of domestic partnership legislation in the city of San Francisco and the repeal of an ordinance outlawing AIDS discrimination in the Bay Area city of Concord. Discussion of domestic partnership legislation, designed to give gay couples and other nontraditional families some of the financial and social benefits of legal marriage, began in San Francisco in 1982 under the leadership of supervisor Harry Britt, a colleague of Harvey Milk's and a former Methodist minister. The first version of a domestic partnership bill passed that year by the city's board of supervisors was vetoed by then-mayor Dianne Feinstein after an intense campaign against the legislation waged by the Catholic Church. Britt took leadership again in 1989, revising domestic partnership legislation and helping get it passed by the board of supervisors and signed into law by Mayor Art Agnos. But just as the legislation went into effect in July, it was suspended in response to a petition to put it to a popular vote as a ballot referendum, an effort again spearheaded by conservative religious groups including the Catholic Church. "Prop S" initially seemed to be an easy win, but as the election approached, prospects began to dim. In an October *BAR* article on the measure, which doubled as a plea for support, Eric Rofes attributed those dim prospects to a dispirited campaign, burnout on the part of the legislation's natural supporters, and political distraction on the part of the mayor. The measure was defeated on Election Day by fewer than twelve hundred votes.

The second major setback the community faced on Election Day 1989 was the repeal of Concord's anti-AIDS discrimination legislature. A city in the East Bay with a large population of conservative evangelicals, Concord was the site of many skirmishes between gay and AIDS activists and an increasingly emboldened Christian right. Concord supervisors resisted the latter in April by unanimously passing a law outlawing discrimination against people with AIDS and earning the gratitude of the *BAR* "for their courageous resistance to bullying."[34] In a parallel process to Prop S, conservatives in the region, with support from national conservative organizations such as the Traditional Values Coalition, put a repeal measure on the ballot. That measure was approved by voters, leaving gay people and people with AIDS with the visceral sense that whatever rights remained for them were precarious at best.

This sense of political precariousness hit alarmingly close to home in another event that affected the community in the weeks before Christmas 1989. On October 6, the city's AIDS Coalition to Unleash Power (ACT-UP) chapter organized a protest at city hall, a march to Castro Street, and a rally there to agitate for increased AIDS funding. As the march approached the Castro district, the crowd took note of an unusually high number of police officers monitoring the event. When the march arrived, it was met by hundreds of officers in riot gear mobilized to break up the rally and clear the streets. The marchers protested, staging spontaneous sit-ins and die-ins, and were beaten off the streets in a riot the scale of which had not been seen in the Castro since the 1979 murder acquittal of city supervisor Dan White in the assassinations of Supervisor Harvey Milk and Mayor George Moscone. Gay leaders demanded a full investigation into what became known as "the Castro sweep," including Mayor Agnos's role in ordering it. Residents of the Castro, many of whom were confined indoors by police for the duration of the events, were deeply shaken by the events, seeing a brutal reminder that gay people could not feel at home even in their own neighborhood. This sense of dislocation was intensified further by the Loma Prieta earthquake, which took place eleven days later, disorienting the entire city and adding fuel to the fire of religious conservatives who claimed that God was surely speaking clearly to the sins of San Francisco. In evoking the connections between the time of Herod and the time of Art Agnos, Mitulski underscored his own belief that God was, in fact, talking in San Francisco and the Castro in 1989. But Mitulski's God was saying very different things.

WE UNCONVENTIONAL FAMILIES

One of the things Mitulski believed God was saying through the story of Mary and Joseph was that God picks unusual people to be God's messengers in the world, people whom churches would not always recognize as partners in God's earthly endeavors. Gay Christians, he claimed, were more like those unlikely people than one might think:

> The thing in this first part that I think is also our story [is] where it says, "Joseph went to be enrolled with Mary, his betrothed who was with child." Now it's amazing that this is in our Christian scriptures. And in fact as we study the scriptures we know that people in subsequent generations have tried to take this verse out, or change it, 'cause if you heard what it said, it said "enrolled with Mary his betrothed who was with child." Not Mary his wife. Mary his betrothed. Mary was an unmarried woman. An unwed mother. That is the scandal of Christianity, that our origin is in an unconventional family. ... Mary and Joseph were domestic partners and in that time there was no place for them.[35]

He went on to explain that when the scripture says there was no place for them at the inn, it meant that there was literally no space, that the inn was full. But it also meant that there was no place for people such as Mary and Joseph among the respectable people of their society. Mary was, in Mitulski's words, "an offense to their sensibilities," and because of that they made no space for this unwed mother carrying the incarnation of God or her domestic partner.

The emotional, cultural, and legal questions of family were palpable in MCCSF, and the fate of domestic partnership legislation was only one of them. Many gay people came to the Castro from towns and cities around the country in order to live openly gay lives and realize gay dreams. This often entailed breaking with their families of origin, who frequently did not know of their loved ones' sexual orientation or disapproved of it to the point of estrangement. Churches like MCCSF were migrant churches of a sort, made up of internal migrants pushed or pulled away from their communities of origin and disconnected from traditional kinship networks.[36] They were also sites that formed alternative kinship networks through rituals that validated gay relationships by bestowing on them the rites of the church. UFMCC performed gay "holy union" ceremonies from its earliest days, and MCCSF clergy performed countless gay marriages alongside the countless AIDS funerals that marked this period. Gay marriages and funerals were closely connected, argued anthropologist Ellen Lewin, and in many cases pending death sharpened the desire for formal relationship recognition.[37] Mitulski spoke of how he often performed these so-called deathbed weddings days, and sometimes hours, before one partner's death.[38] MCCSF funerals were often the only sites where bereaved partners were recognized as spouses; congregational anecdotes tell of people who had funeral services in mainline churches where partners went unrecognized and memorial services at MCCSF where they were treated as rightful mourners. The emotional salience of family was especially strong at the holidays. By seeing Mary and Joseph as a domestic partnership and reading their betrothal as evidence of a scandal of unconventional familial structures at the heart of the Christian faith, Mitulski was saying yet again to his congregation that this story was theirs in a deep and integral way: not just in the extension of its precepts to the gay community but at the very center of how the Christian faith came to be and what it represents.

WE ANGELS

Mitulski made further connections between the congregation and the story by telling members that their experience could be seen not just in Mary and Joseph's unconventional family but in the angels that delivered the message that a savior had just been born in Bethlehem:

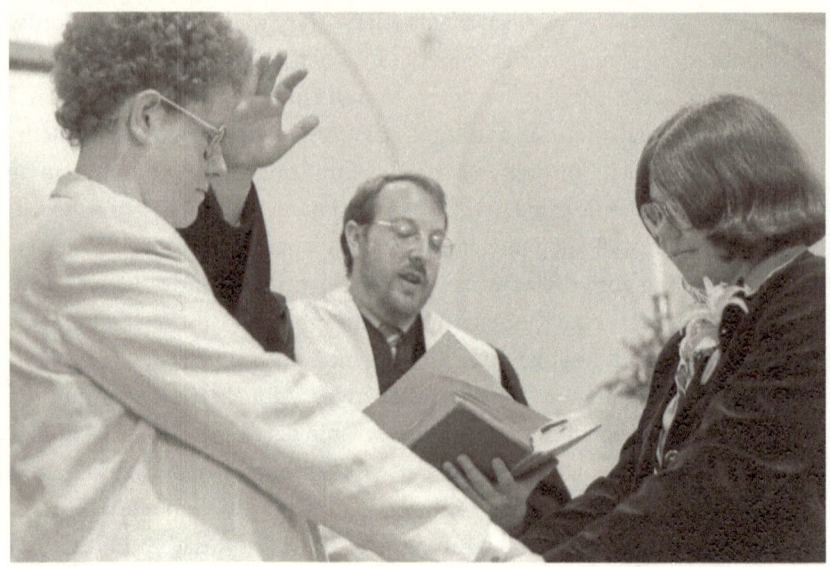

Kittredge Cherry, *right*, and Audrey Lockwood were united in a "holy union" wedding ceremony conducted by Jim Mitulski at Metropolitan Community Church of San Francisco on April 11, 1987. Photo by Lisa Wigoda.

>Another point of contact with the story, that I believe is so important and uniquely ours: the angels appearing and giving these words to the shepherds, "Be not afraid." The word for angels means "messenger." ... Messengers from God saying "be not afraid." And I believe we are messengers in the very same way for one another when we can assure one another, so that we can take away one another's fear. This church is a messenger to a much larger community than you can see tonight. People come in here all week long and say, they start off by saying, "I have feelings," you know. "I have feelings for someone, for someone of the same sex." And it's a coming out. That's how coming out starts for many people. And when we as a church are able to say to every person who has ever loved another person, "That's okay, that's good, don't be afraid," then we are being angels, messengers of God, to an entire, to an entire world, to all people.[39]

MCCSF congregants, he suggested, were like angels whenever they soothed the fears of others, something they did often at the height of the AIDS crisis. But in 1989 they likely needed reassurance about their own ministries.

The year 1989, as we have seen, marked a moment of extreme dejection, challenge, and change among AIDS organizations in San Francisco. It was a similar moment for MCCSF in relation to its own AIDS ministry. In 1989 the church endured a public scandal with its clergy, one that received national attention and shook the congregation to its core. In January, Lynn Griffis was installed as MCCSF's AIDS ministry chaplain, the church's first paid position focused exclusively on ministry to people with AIDS. In July she claimed to have been the victim of a homophobic attack in which she had been beaten and her home vandalized. The perpetrators made it clear that she had been subject to attack specifically because of her work with gay men with AIDS. The story made all of the city's newspapers. There was a unified call to find the attackers and bring them to justice, and the story was used to raise the issue of public safety for gays and lesbians. The next week she reported that she was attacked again, this time claiming abduction in a car by two skinheads who cut her and warned her against continuing working with people with AIDS. The Sunday after the second attack the congregation was addressed by, among others, San Francisco supervisor Harry Britt, denominational leader Troy Perry, and San Francisco police chief Frank Jordan, who assured the community that he was doing everything he could to apprehend those who had committed these acts. Griffis served Communion at that service and addressed the congregation, saying, "If anything were to happen to me, I want you to spread the message loud and clear, far and wide, that I was proud. That if anything happens to me that I died happy."[40]

A few days later, inconsistencies in Griffis's account were noted by police, and investigators raised questions. At the next Sunday's worship service, the chair of MCCSF's board of directors, Linton Stables, read a statement revealing that Griffis's injuries had been self-inflicted, that she had retracted and revised her police statement, and that in the wake of those actions she had resigned from MCCSF and left San Francisco. No one knew where she was. The scandal was deeply humiliating for the congregation, especially for Mitulski, and the period after Griffis's departure was one of intense personal and institutional reflection on how those events came to pass and how to understand the value of MCCSF's AIDS ministry in light of them. Whether and how MCCSF could continue to serve as angels to each other and the community was a live question at the moment of this Christmas Eve sermon. The members of the congregation needed assurance that they need not be afraid going forward.

Angels were salient to this congregation in another way, one that Mitulski also addressed in this sermon.

> Another way that we experience angels that are so real. We have these Christmas carols that we sing all year long, I really think of them as Christmas carols. The two songs. "Surely the presence of our God is in this place. I can hear the brush of angel's wings, I see glory on each face" and the other one: "We are standing on holy ground, and I know that there are angels all around." A member of our church, Art Plaskett, who died just a few months ago, said that when he was sick and all of his friends from here and from Sonoma County came around him he said, "Where did all the angels come from?" Where did all the angels come from? People who have gone before us, would assure us that we have nothing to be afraid of.[41]

This evocation of angels speaks to the visceral sense many people in the congregation had that their dead were present with them in worship, during their illnesses, and at their deaths. Their presence was evoked by the songs Mitulski referenced, songs that came to signify the congregation's dead. Over time this group became known as the Great Cloud of Witnesses and was called upon in a range of congregational contexts, from worship services to business meetings. Using the voices of the beloved dead in sermons was another strategy Mitulski employed to evoke the dead and keep them in conversation with the living. Reviving the voices of congregants like Art Plaskett brought other marginalized voices to the Christian conversation, voices that reminded congregants that the Christian story was their own. It also kept memories of specific individuals alive, something that became increasingly valuable as the numbers of dead increased and the specificity of those lost began to blur into that Great Cloud. Former pastor Jim Sandmire was just one of many close community members the congregation lost in 1989.

The question of how to remember the AIDS dead was also faced by the gay community at large at every stage in the crisis. The most visible effort at memory was the Names Quilt, which was organized by San Francisco activist Cleve Jones and displayed at the 1987 March on Washington for Gay and Lesbian Rights. MCCSF heeded Jones's call to commemorate the dead by quilting memorial panels for those they had lost, displaying them in the congregation, and praying over them publicly at the worship service preceding the march. After the march, the congregation continued to contribute to the quilt, including a 1988 panel for the church's founding pastor, Howard Wells. By 1989 the question of where to permanently house the quilt was pressing. In November an announcement was made that construction would begin on a building that would house all of the neighborhood's AIDS programs along with the quilt.⁴² This project, which was never completed, was part of the strategy for reviving the San Francisco model of localized care for people with AIDS. It was also a rival to MCCSF, whose building had housed many gay and AIDS organizations, making it a community center of sorts for the neighborhood. Remembering the dead raised live political issues in the community about the legitimate carriers of memory, the institutional infrastructure necessary for collective memory, and the public rituals that would keep people from forgetting.

WE SHEPHERDS

The last point of identification Mitulski made between the congregation and the gospel story was with the recipients of God's angelic message.

> And finally the shepherds, I think we can connect with.... The shepherds are people who are poor, materially poor, who are not allowed in the religious assemblies because they were dirty and because they smelled bad. They were not allowed to be in church if you will because of their poverty.... That's who God chooses to make a revelation to. Not the powerful but those shepherds who were the least esteemed in that civilization. And I believe that God is still making revelations to people who are on the margins.... Sometimes, people in our community who make protests about injustices, people who say that the cost of AZT is a sin and an offense to God, the ways they choose to make their protests known seem to be shocking and inappropriate to us. Even though they're pointing out a truth that in itself is an injustice. That AZT is so expensive. That health care is not available to all. When we see these protests in our community, and we hear the things that are said about people who choose radical means to draw attention to an injustice, it's the same way people used to talk about shepherds, who did desperate things out of their poverty. But those are the ones whom God chose to make revelations to.⁴³

In this case, Mitulski connected characters in the gospel story to a very specific group of people in the congregation and the gay community. In doing so, he came close to putting the rest of that community in the position of those who do not recognize the one whom God uses to convey God's messages.

One bit of hope regarding AIDS in the late 1980s was AZT, the protease-inhibiting drug. The drug was approved by the FDA for use in treating AIDS in 1987, and in 1989 there were reports that it was successful in delaying the onset of AIDS.[44] The problem was price: it was prohibitively expensive and out of reach for many people. Another bit of hope regarding AIDS in this moment, at least in the eyes of some, was the emergence of ACT-UP and its use of public protest to demand increased research, treatment, and access to both. ACT-UP began in 1987 with a sit-in on Wall Street protesting AIDS drug prices that made its presence viscerally felt, if not universally loved. Other protest targets included the Food and Drug Administration building, *Cosmopolitan* magazine's headquarters, and the New York Stock Exchange.

On December 10, 1989, two weeks before Mitulski's sermon, ACT-UP, in partnership with Women's Health Action and Mobilization, staged an event that would be its most controversial: Stop the Church. The action took place during the midmorning mass at St. Patrick's Cathedral in New York City. It aimed to protest positions taken by the Catholic Church on AIDS, homosexuality, abortion, and condom use and the actions of Cardinal O'Connor as the representative of those positions. After announcing to the world and to the church that St. Patrick's would be the target of ACT-UP's protest, activists attended the mass and interrupted it by blowing whistles, calling out the ways in which they saw the church as complicit in the spread of AIDS, and staging a "die-in." Protesters were carried outside by police, where they were greeted by additional protesters staging a parallel event outside the building.

The action was received differently in different communities. Those outside of the gay world largely saw it as disrespectful and offensive. The AIDS activist world deemed it a success, in part because, in the words of theologian Mark Jordan, "it refuse[d] to observe the curious immunity granted religious speech."[45] But the gay world, especially the gay Christian world, was ambivalent. The *BAR* published letters pro and con. At MCCSF, there were vocal defenders of the protest and vocal critics. In the Christmas Eve sermon, Mitulski walked a delicate line. In identifying the shepherds, those outcasts often unwelcome in religious communities, with "people in our community who make protests about injustices," he made the point that God may well be using those unnamed but clearly referenced ACT-UP activists to deliver God's message of justice. He also made the subtle inference that those who do not recognize them as such may be in the same position as those respectable people who did not recognize the divine events that were unfolding in Bethlehem. This could have been directed not only at the straight world but also at ACT-UP critics within the gay community and even within the congregation.

Yet neither ACT-UP nor the Stop the Church action was explicitly named. Jordan pointed out the affinities between Stop the Church protesters and church reformers. "The suffering refused to let religion remain the possession of those institutions that manage God for the sake of established powers," he wrote. "That is the essence of church reform."[46] Mitulski and MCCSF embodied that refusal in many ways, week after week, throughout the crisis. But this invocation of shepherds reflected the ways in which management was still necessary in the face of the at-times conflicting powers of reforming activists and reforming congregants.

WE DEMAND/WE ARE

In his conclusion to the Christmas sermon, Mitulski brought together all of these various connections between the gospel story and MCCSF's gay Christian experiment on Eureka Street.

> I read a W. H. Auden poem this time of year that I always like to read called "A Christmas Oratorio." "For the Time Being" it's called. In the portion about Christmas, this is what W. H. Auden says, "We who must die demand a miracle. How can the eternal do a temporal act, how could the infinite become a finite fact? Nothing can save us that is possible. We who must die demand a miracle." All of the world needs redemption. That's what we say, that's what we mean by saying "All who must die demand a miracle." We demand a miracle and we deserve a miracle. This is Christmas in the Castro like Christmas in Palestine 2000 years ago. This is the highest concentration of lesbian and gay people in the world. And in this place, the pink and purple church, the humble place where Christ is born anew just as God chose shepherds, we hear our angel choirs sing to us, peace to you. Good will to you. The promises of God will be fulfilled in you, if you will say yes. We hear the promises of God fulfilled in the miracles that we see about us. We who must die demand a miracle. And we are that miracle. We are that miracle. This church, this community, each person in this place, this night, for tonight, and every night if we chose to. We are that miracle that can redeem the world. Amen.[47]

In this conclusion the connections are made and made again: the Castro and Palestine, the pink and purple church and the inn where Christ was born, the shepherds whom God chooses and our angelic choir. This story is ours, he insisted, and our story is one of God's miracles. This was also the moment where the value of these connections became clear. The purpose of rendering the gospel story in such a way that it spoke directly to a community of gays and lesbians with AIDS in San Francisco was not just to give that community access to that tradition or to assure them that they had a place there. Rather, building connections to the tradition provided an opportunity for a certain audacity in relation to the tradition: the audacity to demand and the audacity to make claims.

Christmas of 1989 was an auspicious moment to be demanding miracles. It was after the early stages of AIDS, past the moment of early denial, and past the first burst of creative responses. There was some hope on the horizon and some evident success but a great deal of defeat as well. The community and the congregation both needed to reimagine themselves to encounter the next stage. But it was before the hopes for AZT were dashed, before the dissolution of ACT-UP in the early 1990s ended the most visible public expression of rage about AIDS, before deaths from AIDS in San Francisco reached their peak in 1992 and MCCSF reached its own peak of funerals. The defeat of Prop S and the Concord anti-AIDS discrimination bill were defeats indeed, but they were also seen as a backlash to a tide of political possibility that may have been, from the perspective of that time, still rising. It takes a certain combination of suffering and possibility to make demands. And a kind of faith.

MCCSF's experiment with gay Christian faith was different from Auden's. Auden did not speak directly to the tradition's prohibitions on homosexuality and did not make demands on it as a gay man. But he found a space within it, as a man who loved men, to express desires, longings, and hopes that demonstrated a continuity rather than division between such men and Christianity. Using the terms in David Halperin's sense, Auden brought to the Christian tradition, if not a gay identity, then a queer subjectivity.[48] MCCSF's gay Christian experiment was much more explicit about its gay identity, invested in putting it into conversation with the Christian tradition and challenging the tradition when necessary. But a similar air of mourning pervaded both experiments, and there was a similar queerness in the quality of their faith. Mitulski and the MCCSF experiment combined a commitment to theological reason and criticism with an affirmation of some of the mysteries of the faith: mysteries such as angels, resurrection, and miracles, hopes for which were heightened in a community facing an epidemic.[49] Writer Edward Mendelson describes Auden's Christianity as similarly idiosyncratic: "He... thought that all religious statements about God must be false in a literal sense but might be true in metaphoric ones."[50] Mitulski's use of Auden's demand for a miracle and his assertion that MCCSF was such a miracle can be read as a similar balance between the literal and the metaphorical.

In 1989 the congregation and the community were exhausted, grief-ridden, and somewhat adrift. People were still dying, cures distant, and literal miracles scarce: "nothing can save us that is possible." But there was something of the miraculous in how the little church on Eureka Street pulled together gay culture and the Christian tradition, forged something possible from the two, and used it to face AIDS. Searching for truths in metaphor may be a queer sensibility of sorts. Living them, or trying to, was at the heart of MCCSF's strategy for Christmas, and gay Christian life, in the midst this epidemic.

NOTES

Many people and institutions helped support work on this chapter. My thanks to Kent Brintnall, Sarah Quinn, and Susan Stinson, steadfast readers of many versions of this essay. Thanks also to Gil Frank, Bethany Moreton, and Heather White for encouraging this work, reading it so thoughtfully, and including it here. Three great research centers at the University of California, Berkeley, have supported this project over many years: the Beatrice Bain Research Group, the Institute for the Study of Societal Issues, and the Religion, Politics, and Globalization Program. The Congregational Studies Team also provided much-appreciated support, personal, intellectual, and financial. Finally, I was privileged to share earlier versions of this work at the Global Perspectives on Religion and AIDS seminar at the American Academy of Religion and at Fordham University at the kind invitation of Orit Avishai. An earlier version of this essay, titled "How to Have Christmas in an Epidemic," received honorable mention for the 2015 Religious History Award sponsored by the LGBT Religious Archives Network.

1. Allen White, "Don We Now Our Gayest Apparel," *Bay Area Reporter* (hereafter *BAR*), December 21, 1989, 1.

2. In this period the term ARC, or AIDS-related complex, was also in wide use indicating people in early stages of HIV infection. For the purposes of this chapter I will use the term AIDS exclusively.

3. Sarah Schulman, *People in Trouble* (New York: Plume, 1991).

4. Troy Perry recounted the founding of the church in two autobiographical works: *The Lord Is My Shepherd and He Knows I'm Gay*, with Charles L. Lucas (Austin: Liberty Press, 1972) and *Don't Be Afraid Anymore: The Story of Reverend Troy Perry and the Metropolitan Community Churches*, with Thomas L. P. Swicegood (New York: St. Martins Press, 1992). Much of the academic work on the denomination has been written by sociologists. One of the earliest such analyses of UFMCC took the San Francisco congregation as its major case study: Ronald M. Enroth and Gerald E. Jamison, *The Gay Church* (Grand Rapids: Wm. B. Eerdmans, 1974). More recent sociological work on UFMCC includes R. Stephen Warner, "The Metropolitan Community Churches and the Gay Agenda: The Power of Pentecostalism and Essentialism," in *Sex, Lies and Sanctity: Religion and Deviance in*

Contemporary North America, ed. Mary Jo Neitz and Marion S. Goldman (Greenwich: JAI Press, 1995), 81–108; Melissa M. Wilcox, "Of Markets and Missions: The Early History of the Universal Fellowship of Metropolitan Community Churches," *Religion in American Culture* 11, no. 1 (Winter 2001): 83–108; and Melissa M. Wilcox, *Coming Out in Christianity: Religion, Identity, and Community* (Bloomington: Indiana University Press, 2003). Recent historical work on the denomination includes Mark Jordan, *Recruiting Young Love: How Christians Talk about Homosexuality* (Chicago: University of Chicago Press, 2011), 116–20; and Heather White, *Reforming Sodom: Protestants and the Rise of Gay Rights* (Chapel Hill: University of North Carolina Press, 2015).

5. Jordan, *Recruiting Young Love*, 102.

6. John D'Emilio, *Sexual Politics, Sexual Communities: The Making of a Homosexual Minority in the United States, 1940–1970*, 2nd ed. (Chicago: University of Chicago Press, 1998); Elizabeth A. Armstrong, *Forging Gay Identities: Organizing Sexuality in San Francisco, 1950–1994* (Chicago: University of Chicago Press, 2002).

7. Dignity, the Catholic gay affinity group, started at roughly the same time as UFMCC. Most Protestant gay affinity groups were founded in the early 1970s, including Integrity (Episcopalian, 1974), More Light (Presbyterian, 1974), and Affirmation (United Methodist, 1972). For more on the history of mainline churches and struggles for gay recognition, see White, *Reforming Sodom*. The first gathering of the gay pagan group the Radical Faeries was in 1979.

8. UFMCC also brought together believers from other faith traditions. The first gay Jewish congregation, Beth Chayim Chadashim in Los Angeles, emerged from the UFMCC congregation there and shared space with them. Moshe Shokeid, *A Gay Synagogue in New York* (New York: Columbia University Press, 1995), 16.

9. On the theological diversity in UFMCC, see Warner, "Metropolitan Community Churches and the Gay Agenda"; and Wilcox, "Of Markets and Missions."

10. Jordan retells the story of this first Communion in *Recruiting Young Love*, 119.

11. For a brief discussion of this effort, see Warner, "Metropolitan Community Churches and the Gay Agenda," 93.

12. Troy Perry, sermon delivered at MCCSF, October 21, 1990, morning service, transcript in possession of the author.

13. Author interview with Lynn Jordan, March 16, 2012. Sandmire was not rebaptized before taking the MCCSF pulpit.

14. Troy Perry, "Dr. King and the Homosexual Community," *In Unity* 1, no. 2 (May 1970): 3. For a different opinion from that period, see Howard Wells, "A Justification for Gay Separatism," *In Unity* 3, no. 2 (Spring 1973): 8. Wells was the founding pastor of MCCSF. For more on this question, see Wilcox, "Of Markets and Missions," 100–101.

15. There are echoes of this decentering of homosexuality in UFMCC's self-presentation in its current efforts to identify itself globally as a human rights church. See http://mccchurch.org/overview/history-of-mcc/human-rights-protocol/.

16. James Sandmire, "Pastor's Corner," *Cross Currents* 1, no. 1 (Fall 1972): 4.

17. Interview with Jim Mitulski by Cheryl Rosenthal, True to Life Films, 2005, DVD (raw footage made for a documentary) in possession of the author.

18. Jim Mitulski, sermon delivered at MCCSF, December 24, 1989, evening service, 10, transcript in possession of the author. Mitulski's reading is not verbatim from the original

text, which appears in the Advent section of the poem, not the Christmas section. For the original text, see W. H. Auden, *For the Time Being: A Christmas Oratorio* (Princeton: Princeton University Press, 2013), 8.

19. Ernesto Cardenal, *The Gospel in Solentiname* (Maryknoll, N.Y.: Orbis Books, 2010), xi.

20. Willi McFarland, ed., *Atlas of HIV/AIDS in San Francisco, 1981–2000*, HIV Statistics and Epidemiological Section, San Francisco Department of Public Health, 2002. New York had the highest number of cases, but the overall population was larger and the gay community was not as tightly concentrated in gay neighborhoods.

21. "KS Forum at MCC," *BAR*, July 29, 1982, 4.

22. Randy Shilts took the former view, which is evident in the criticism of gay leaders in his classic account of the early AIDS years, *And the Band Played On: Politics, People and the AIDS Epidemic* (New York: St. Martin's Press, 1987). The *BAR* formally took the latter view, as is evident in its editorials, including Paul Lorch, "Killing the Movement," *BAR*, April 5, 1984, 6–7.

23. "MCC Responds to Closings," *BAR*, April 5, 1984, 12.

24. See, for example, the following from the *BAR*: Eric Rofes, "Time to Rebuild at Shanti Project," May 4, 1989, 6; Eric Rofes and Tim Wolfred, "A Prescription for Healing: Saving San Francisco's AIDS Service Model," June 22, 1989, 8; editorial, "The 'San Francisco Model' under Stress," July 27, 1989, 6; and Pat Christen, "The Crumbling San Francisco Model," September 14, 1989, 6.

25. Michael Botkin, "The New San Francisco Model," ibid., December 7, 1989, 5.

26. Rex Wockner, "Activists 'Re-gay' AIDS to Boost Lib Movement," ibid., December 14, 1989, 19.

27. Ibid. John-Manuel Andriotte discusses the de-gaying controversy in *Victory Deferred: How AIDS Changed Gay Life in America* (Chicago: University of Chicago Press, 1999), 228–35.

28. Eric Rofes, "Gay Groups vs. AIDS Groups: Averting Civil War in the 90s," *Out/Look*, Spring 1990, 8–17.

29. Armstrong, *Forging Gay Identities*, 171.

30. Kittredge Cherry and James Mitulski, "We Are the Church Alive, the Church with AIDS," *Christian Century* 5 (January 1988): 85–88.

31. The Faith and Order Commission published a volume informed by that experience. Letty M. Russell, ed., *The Church with AIDS: Renewal in the Midst of Crisis* (Philadelphia: Westminster John Knox), 1990. Unlike with other sexual issues of the period, such as birth control, as Samira K. Mehta shows in this volume, the National Council of Churches had a contradictory relationship to homosexuality and UFMCC, rejecting the denomination's application for membership while at the same time seeking its guidance in addressing AIDS.

32. Jim Mitulski, sermon delivered at MCCSF, January 5, 1992, evening service, 2–3, transcript in possession of the author. Mitulski delivered his sermons in a style that combined preselected texts with extemporaneous speech. He did not read from a composed text and there are no formal transcripts. The transcripts used here were produced by me and a team of research assistants using sermon recordings as their source. They were transcribed verbatim, resulting in sentence fragments and other

grammatical anomalies that make sense in the spoken versions but may read as incorrect in this textual format.

33. Mitulski sermon, December 24, 1989, 5.

34. Editorial, "Courage in Concord," *BAR*, May 4, 1989, 6.

35. Mitulski sermon, December 24, 1989, 6.

36. Cymene Howe, "Sexual Borderlands: Lesbian and Gay Migration, Human Rights, and the Metropolitan Community Church," in *At the Corner of Bliss and Nirvana: Politics, Identity and Faith in New Migrant Communities*, ed. Lois Ann Lorentzen (Durham: Duke University Press, 2009), 39–68.

37. Ellen Lewin, *Recognizing Ourselves: Ceremonies of Lesbian and Gay Commitment* (New York: Columbia University Press, 1999).

38. Quoted in Lewin, *Recognizing Ourselves*, 202–3.

39. Mitulski sermon, December 24, 1989, 8.

40. MCCSF, July 30, 1989, morning worship service, transcript in possession of the author.

41. Mitulski sermon, December 24, 1989, 8.

42. Allen White, "Community, Quilt, PWAs Find Home," *BAR*, November 30, 1989, 1.

43. Mitulski sermon, December 24, 1989, 8–9.

44. David Smyth, "AZT Study Raises Hopes," *BAR*, August 24, 1989, 1.

45. Jordan, *Recruiting Young Love*, 188.

46. Ibid., 190.

47. Mitulski sermon, December 24, 1989, 10.

48. David Halperin, *How to Be Gay* (Cambridge, Mass.: Harvard University Press, 2012), 12.

49. On this juxtaposition of liberal reason and belief in angels at MCCSF in this period, see Mitulski quoted in Lewin, *Recognizing Ourselves*, 203.

50. Edward Mendelson, "The Secret Auden," *New York Review of Books*, March 20, 2014.

AFTERWORD
JOHN D'EMILIO

During a spring semester sabbatical in 2007, I spent a good chunk of time at the Gerber Hart Library in Chicago. As someone who had not done local community history before, I wanted to immerse myself in the materials of a city whose LGBT history had not yet received a great deal of attention. Working my way through the organizational newsletters and community-based newspapers produced in the 1970s, the first decade after the birth of a gay liberation movement, I was struck by how much content was related to religion.

Interestingly to me, as a historian of social movements, the material was not primarily what might be called opinion pieces. It went far beyond LGBT individuals expressing their views or recounting their experiences with organized religion. Rather, there was much activity to report. Groups had formed, meetings happened regularly, activities took place, and significant public events occurred. A Dignity chapter for LGBT Catholics formed in 1972, and Sunday Mass attendance frequently surpassed two hundred people. The Metropolitan Community Church established a congregation in 1970; its minister was the first person in Chicago paid to work for an LGBT organization. When Troy Perry, the founder of MCC, stopped in the city in 1974 as part of a book tour for his memoir, his presence provoked a media blitz. Integrity, an organization for LGBT Episcopalians, held its first national conference in Chicago in 1975. The city was also the site for a major gathering of Dignity chapters from across the Midwest.

As my file of notes on religion and LGBT life and politics grew, I found myself thinking back to my own experience as an out-of-the-closet gay man and activist living in New York in the 1970s. For instance, I remembered a talk that John McNeill, a Jesuit priest, gave on the topic of the Bible and homosexuality at a 1973 Gay Academic Union conference. I had also met and socialized on several occasions with William Johnson, who was challenging the United Church of Christ's ban on the ordination of gay men and who eventually became the first openly gay minister to be ordained in the UCC. I recalled as well an independent LGBT-centered religious congregation in New York, the Church of the Beloved Disciple, which made its space available for many LGBT public meetings. But for the most part, in my experience of the 1970s, religion barely figured at all. It was very much on the margins of community life and activism.

Three decades later, in the wake of what my research was uncovering about Chicago, I recognized my experience as a form not so much of selective memory—my recollections were reasonably accurate—but of selective experience. For myself, the process of self-acceptance and coming out was intimately involved with my struggles over religion. I was raised a devout Catholic. I was accepted into seminary in my senior year of high school but after much painful self-scrutiny decided against it because of my hidden conflicts over my sexuality. Embracing an identity as a gay man was thoroughly enmeshed for me with a simultaneous rejection of my religious upbringing and affiliation. Once I became active in the gay movement, religion became transformed into a key "oppressor." But, unlike some forms of oppression that required organized activism, such as that imposed by the state, its laws, and its police apparatus, the oppression of religious institutions could be ended, in my personal experience, simply by saying good-bye. Those views, I now realized as I sat at a desk in the Gerber Hart Library, went on to shape an unaware, but nonetheless real, process of selective networking and affiliations. The result? Religion really did not figure in my experience of the 1970s and its activism.

Now, many years later and using the Chicago material as a concrete example, I found myself speculating on the place of religion in the broader LGBT experience of the 1970s. Some key characteristics of that critical decade, for instance, were the growth of visibility, the proliferation of organizations, and the solidification of urban spaces identified as "gay." Clearly, in Chicago's case, one had to acknowledge that religious organizations had a major place in the mix since religious issues and leaders captured so much media attention and brought visibility. But perhaps one needed to go further than simply adding religion. Might an analysis of religion's presence and role also lead to a revised understanding of how things happened? For instance, a key change in Chicago over the course of the 1970s was the emergence of "Boystown," a queer neighborhood on the city's north side. Lakeview, as it is more formally called, had not been especially identified as gay before that. Why this neighborhood and not another? As it happens, the two largest LGBT religious organizations in the 1970s—Dignity and MCC—both had their meeting places in the neighborhood. Every week on Sundays, and sometimes on other evenings as well, very large numbers of gay men and lesbians were congregating together. Afterward, did they just scatter to the winds? Or, did the social networks that they were creating as they gathered for worship spread out onto the sidewalks afterward, as they walked the streets, went to a restaurant for a meal, or hung around for a drink? Did their visible concentrated presence in the area attract others? Did it make Lakeview seem more like the right place for queer-owned and queer-serving businesses to open?

Before long, my venture into local history and the unexpected discoveries I was making led me back to the narrative trajectory of *Intimate Matters: A History of Sexuality in America*, which I had coauthored with Estelle B. Freedman. Written in the 1980s, it drew heavily on the then-existing literature in a still very young subfield of history, which we supplemented by some selective ventures into primary sources. We constructed an interpretive framework that used sexual meanings, sexual regulation, and sexual politics to organize our broad survey of sexuality in U.S. history. In the centuries of settlement and colonization, religion figured strongly and centrally. It both shaped sexual meanings and played the leading role in the regulation of sexual behavior; it created such a strong consensus that there was no sexual politics to speak of. As we moved through the nineteenth century, religion became one among several players. It sometimes competed with and sometimes cooperated with the state and medical science as regulators of sexual behavior and shapers of meaning. And the growing domain of sexual politics had players who were deeply grounded in religious frameworks, players who welcomed church support, and players who opposed the sway of organized religion. By the twentieth century, religion seemed to shift to a back seat in the story, until the rise of the evangelical-based Christian right in the 1970s reinjected it powerfully into a contentious new era of sexual politics.

Was this another case of selective experience informing historical interpretation? So much of the early history of sexuality—the work produced in the 1970s and early 1980s—was created by a younger generation of historians deeply influenced by radical movements of the 1960s and how they spilled over into academic life. Did those influenced by radical secular versions of feminism, gay liberation, and the sexual revolution then interpret the recent history of sexuality through the lens of that experience? In writing about "olden" times, of course, it was impossible not to see the influence of religious outlooks and institutions. But, in moving into a twentieth-century world more familiar to personal experience, did the constraints of experience shape interpretive frameworks and narrative trajectories? Whatever the explanation might be, the impact of the Chicago-based research that I was doing and the speculations toward which it was leading pushed me to call, on panel after panel at conference after conference as well as in the informal conversations that historians have with each other, for more consideration of the role of religion in the history of twentieth-century sexuality.

Having laid out this background, do I need to say how pleased and excited I am to see an anthology like this? Spread across the twentieth century and covering an impressive array of topics, these essays address subjects and offer interpretations that can only widen and deepen our understanding of U.S. history. They take on stereotypes; they challenge common notions of center and margin; they force reflection on what has propelled change.

Rather than work my way through each essay in this volume and comment on them one by one, I will instead focus my comments on a few themes and insights that especially caught my attention. In their introduction, the editors themselves make a number of key points that I encourage every reader of history to take to heart. Religion, they remind, "has been a site for invention, contestation, and change during the twentieth century," not a singular entity or a timeless force. They urge us to reject the narrative of secularization. They make the unarguable yet easy-to-forget point that neither religion nor sexuality is a singular or unchanging entity and, therefore, the relationship between the two is not a fixed one and changes over time. Put all these perspectives together, and one is certain to emerge with "a far more complex account of the American past." The reward for taking all of this seriously will be the surprises that research into twentieth-century religion and sexuality will generate because, as they conclude, there will be no telling in advance what insights will emerge, how interconnected or separate these two areas may be, and what new story lines will surface.

Let me point to a few examples of the insights and surprises that essays in this collection provoked for me. As I suggested earlier, one of the key claims of many gay liberationists in the 1970s was that homophobia and oppression rested on a foundation constructed by religion. Two thousand years of Christianity had made the condemnation rock solid. In *Christianity, Social Tolerance, and Homosexuality*, published in 1980, John Boswell had challenged and revised this common assumption. According to Boswell, the hostility to homosexual behavior did not solidify within Christianity until the thirteenth century. But that still left a legacy of seven hundred years of undisputed sinfulness. By contrast, Kathi Kern's research into the life of a particular woman, Winnifred Wygal, uncovers a very different story. Kern demonstrates convincingly that, for Wygal, "religious faith created a venue for same-sex expression." Religion became a resource for affirming her passionate love for women; it became a pathway to acceptance of same-sex desire. Her essay serves as a reminder of the power of human agency, of the ability of individuals to carve out their own path in life, even in the face of strong contrary social forces. Other essays also ask us not to take for granted standard assumptions about the relationship between Christianity and same-sex love. Reading Judith Weisenfeld's study of Father Divine's Peace Mission, I was struck by how the combination of an emphasis on celibacy and the practice of sex-segregation could have the unintended consequence of sparking passionate love between women.

Many of the essays in the volume cover the topic of marriage and sexual expression during the era associated with the baby boom, the feminine mystique, and the heyday of what *Intimate Matters* describes as "sexual liberalism." For a number of reasons, I found these particularly interesting. Taken cumulatively, they constitute good examples of how the study of religion and sexuality can provide a much more nuanced picture of the past even as it can confirm a larger interpretive vision. Neil J. Young's essay on Mormon women inserts them prominently into the history of the sexual politics of the religious right, an important modification of the story as it has been told. But, in the process, he also reveals how these same women embraced an active, pleasure-oriented sexuality within marriage. Sex was not simply a duty one had to put up with as a route to childbearing or as a form of submission to patriarchal power. Rather, these women were sexual actors. The implicit support of an ethic of sexual satisfaction within marriage also appears in Samira K. Mehta's discussion of mainline Protestants and their endorsement of oral contraceptives. Although their encouragement of contraceptive use was framed in a language of responsible parenthood, it assumed that sexual expression rather than restraint represented the normative. Even a discussion of Charles Keating and his antipornography campaigns demonstrates, in Whitney Strub's telling, that an "antisex" ethic no longer had credibility in Cold War America. Sexual liberalism had quite a long reach.

Interestingly, what struck me especially strongly when I had finished the essays was something that is not a major focus of them. I came away from my reading of the anthology with a cumulative sense that, yes, a sexual revolution is indisputable. In scanning newspapers and popular magazines from the 1960s and early 1970s, one will encounter the phrase "sexual revolution" everywhere and recurringly. Starting in the form of warnings and predictions after oral contraceptives received FDA approval at the start of the decade and continuing as an urban singles culture and then a rebellious youth movement spread further with each succeeding year, the phrase is an integral component of the culture, social life, and politics of this era. Historians have stepped back from the simplistic renditions offered by the media and tried to identify more precisely what changed, what propelled change, and who was drawn into the orbit of this so-called revolution. Indeed, is "sexual revolution" even an appropriate term? Does it illuminate, or does it confuse?

I will not even pretend to address such indisputably important questions. But several of these essays demonstrate both the power of a sexually liberal consensus at the start of the 1960s and how unmistakably that consensus had dissolved by the mid-1970s. Faced with this evidence I find myself saying yes, the changes provoked in this decade and a half were profound and unsettling, whether we consider such a "revolution" or not. And the lines of conflict that emerged then are still operative today. We can see religious activists and constituencies on both sides of many key issues, and we can see conflict not simply between various communities of faith but within many as well. Will we ever fully understand this last half century of change and conflict without a deep exploration of the intersections between religion and sexuality? And, can anyone dare to pretend that such explorations are *only* about religion, sexuality, and their relation to one another? The impact upon American politics, culture, and community life has been profound.

Like any good anthology, this one engenders a call for more, not because of any insufficiency in the essays but because they offer so many insights and stimulate so many questions that can be answered only through even more research and writing. I hope *Devotions and Desires* inspires some of you reading this to plunge into the field.

RECOMMENDED READING

Alpert, Rebecca T. *Like Bread on the Seder Plate: Jewish Lesbians and the Transformation of Tradition.* New York: Columbia University Press, 1998.

Balka, Christie, and Andy Rose, eds. *Twice Blessed: On Being Lesbian or Gay and Jewish.* Boston: Beacon Press, 1991.

Beck, Evelyn Torton. *Nice Jewish Girls: A Lesbian Anthology.* Boston: Beacon Press, 1989.

Best, Wallace. *Passionately Human, No Less Divine: Religion and Culture in Black Chicago, 1915–1952.* Princeton: Princeton University Press, 2005.

Black, Gregory D. *The Catholic Crusade against the Movies, 1940–1975.* New York: Cambridge University Press, 1997.

Botham, Fay. *Almighty God Created the Races: Christianity, Interracial Marriage, and American Law.* Chapel Hill: University of North Carolina Press, 2009.

Boyarin, Daniel. *Unheroic Conduct: The Rise of Heterosexuality and the Invention of the Jewish Man.* Berkeley: University of California Press, 1997.

Briggs, Laura. "From Refugees to Madonnas of the Cold War" and "Gay and Lesbian Adoption in the United States." In *Somebody's Children: The Politics of Transracial and Transnational Adoption,* 129–59, 241–68. Durham: Duke University Press, 2012.

Brown, Angela. *Mentsh: On Being Jewish and Queer.* New York: Alyson Books, 2004.

Buss, Doris, and Didi Herman. *Globalizing Family Values: The Christian Right in Global Politics.* Minneapolis: University of Minnesota Press, 2003.

Butler, Anthea D. "Prohibitions." In *Women of the Church of God in Christ: Making a Sanctified World,* 75–95. Chapel Hill: University of North Carolina Press, 2007.

Byrne, Julie. "Hearing a New Call." In *The Other Catholics: Remaking America's Largest Religion,* 255–86. New York: Columbia University Press, 2016.

Cady, Linell Elizabeth, and Tracy Fessenden. *Religion, the Secular, and the Politics of Sexual Difference.* New York: Columbia University Press, 2013.

Chauncey, George. "Christian Brotherhood or Sexual Perversion? Homosexual Identities and the Construction of Sexual Boundaries in the World War One Era." *Journal of Social History* 19, no. 2 (December 1985): 189–211.

Curtis, Edward E., IV. "Islamizing the Black Body: Ritual and Power in Elijah Muhammad's Nation of Islam." *Religion and American Culture: A Journal of Interpretation* 12, no. 2 (July 2002): 167–96.

Dailey, Jane. "Sex, Segregation, and the Sacred after *Brown.*" *Journal of American History* 91, no. 1 (June 2004): 119–44.

Davis, Rebecca L. *More Perfect Unions: The American Search for Marital Bliss.* Cambridge, Mass.: Harvard University Press, 2010.

———. "'My Homosexuality Is Getting Worse Every Day': Norman Vincent Peale, Psychiatry, and the Liberal Protestant Response to Same-Sex Desires in Mid-Twentieth Century America." In *American Christianities: A History of Dominance and Diversity*, 347–65. Chapel Hill: University of North Carolina Press, 2011.

Davis, Tom. *Sacred Work: Planned Parenthood and Its Clergy Alliances*. New Brunswick: Rutgers University Press, 2005.

DeRogatis, Amy. *Saving Sex: Sexuality and Salvation in American Evangelicalism*. New York: Oxford University Press, 2014.

Deutsch, Nathaniel. *Inventing America's "Worst" Family: Eugenics, Islam, and the Fall and Rise of the Tribe of Ishmael*. Berkeley: University of California Press, 2009.

Dubow, Sara. "Defining Fetal Personhood, 1973–1976." Chap. 3 in *Ourselves Unborn: A History of the Fetus in Modern America*. Oxford: Oxford University Press, 2010.

Dzmura, Noach, ed. *Balancing on the Mechitza: Transgender in Jewish Community*. Berkeley: North Atlantic Books, 2010.

Erzen, Tanya. "Testimonial Politics: The Christian Right's Faith-Based Approach to Marriage and Imprisonment." *American Quarterly* 59 (September 2007): 991–1015.

Espinosa, Gastón. "Mexican Madonna: Selena and the Politics of Cultural Redemption." In *Mexican American Religions: Spirituality, Activism, and Culture*, 359–80. Durham: Duke University Press, 2009.

Frank, Gillian. "'The Civil Rights of Parents': Race and Conservative Politics in Anita Bryant's Campaign against Gay Rights in 1970s Florida." *Journal of the History of Sexuality* 22, no. 1 (January 2013): 126–60.

———. "The Color of the Unborn: Anti-abortion and Anti-busing Politics in Michigan, 1967–1973." *Gender and History* 26, no. 2 (August 2014): 351–78.

Ginsburg, Faye D. *Contested Lives: The Abortion Debate in an American Community*. Berkeley: University of California Press, 1998.

Goodwin, Megan. "Thinking Sex and American Religions." *Religion Compass* 5, no. 12 (2011): 772–87.

Gordan, Rachel. "Alfred Kinsey and the Remaking of Jewish Sexuality after the Holocaust." *Jewish Social Studies* 20, no. 3 (Spring/Summer 2014): 72–99.

Gordon, Sarah Barringer. *The Spirit of the Law: Religious Voices and the Constitution in Modern America*. Cambridge, Mass.: Harvard University Press, 2010.

Greenberg, Steven. *Wrestling with God and Men: Homosexuality in the Jewish Tradition*. Madison: University of Wisconsin Press, 2005.

Griffith, Marie. "The Religious Encounters of Alfred C. Kinsey." *Journal of American History* 95, no. 2 (September 2008): 349–77.

———. "Sexing Religion." In *The Cambridge Companion to Religious Studies*, edited by Robert A. Orsi, 338–59. Cambridge: Cambridge University Press, 2011.

Gualtieri, Sarah. "Marriage and Respectability in the Era of Immigration Restriction." In *Between Arab and White: Race and Ethnicity in the Early Syrian American Diaspora*, 135–54. Berkeley: University of California Press, 2009.

Gustav-Wrathall, John. *Take the Young Stranger by the Hand: Same-Sex Relations and the YMCA*. Chicago: University of Chicago Press, 2000.

Gutierrez, Laura. "Sexing Guadalupe in Transnational Double Crossings." In *Performing Mexicanidad: Vendidas y Cabareteras on the Transnational Stage*, 31–63. Austin: University of Texas Press, 2010.

Henold, Mary. *Catholic and Feminist: The Surprising History of the American Catholic Feminist Movement*. Chapel Hill: University of North Carolina Press, 2008.

Herman, Didi. "Devil Discourse: The Shifting Constructions of Homosexuality in *Christianity Today*." In *The Antigay Agenda*, 25–59. Chicago: University of Chicago Press, 1997.

Hoffman, Scott. "'Last Night, I Prayed to Matthew': Matthew Shepard, Homosexuality, and Popular Martyrdom in Contemporary America." *Religion and American Culture: A Journal of Analysis* 21, no. 1 (Winter 2011): 121–64.

Hoffman, Warren. *The Passing Game: Queering Jewish American Culture*. Syracuse: Syracuse University Press, 2009.

Howard, John. "The Library, the Park, and the Pervert: Public Space and Homosexual Encounter in Post–World War II Atlanta." *Radical History Review* 62 (March 1995): 166–87.

———. "Politics and Beliefs." In *Men Like That: A Southern Queer History*, 230–56. Chicago: University of Chicago Press, 2001.

Irvine, Janice. *Talk about Sex: The Battles over Sex Education in the United States*. Berkeley: University of California Press, 2002.

Jakobsen, Janet R., and Ann Pellegrini. *Love the Sin: Sexual Regulation and the Limits of Religious Tolerance*. New York: New York University Press, 2003.

Johnson, E. Patrick. "Gayness and the Black Church." In *Sweet Tea: Black Gay Men of the South*, 182–255. Chapel Hill: University of North Carolina Press, 2008.

Johnson, Val Marie. "Protection, Virtue, and the 'Power to Detain': The Moral Citizenship of Jewish Women in New York City, 1890–1920." *Journal of Urban History* 31, no. 5 (July 2005): 655–84.

Jordan, Mark D. *Recruiting Young Love: How Christians Talk about Homosexuality*. Chicago: University of Chicago Press, 2011.

———. *The Silence of Sodom: Homosexuality in Modern Catholicism*. Chicago: University of Chicago Press, 2000.

Klassen, Pamela. "Evil Spirits and the Queer Psyche in an Age of Anxiety." In *Spirits of Protestantism: Medicine, Healing, and Liberal Christianity*, 137–68. Berkeley: University of California Press, 2011.

León, Luis D. "Cesar Chavez, Christian Love, and the Myth of the (Anti-)Macho: Toward an Ethic of the Religiously Erotic." In *Out of the Shadows, into the Light: Christianity and Homosexuality*, 88–103. St. Louis: Chalice Press, 2009.

Leon, Sharon Mara. *An Image of God: The Catholic Struggle with Eugenics*. Chicago: University of Chicago Press, 2013.

Lofton, Kathryn. "Queering Fundamentalism: John Balcom Shaw and the Sexuality of a Protestant Orthodoxy." *Journal of the History of Sexuality* 17, no. 3 (2008): 439–68.

Lyons, Andrew, and Harriet Lyons. "The Reconstruction of 'Primitive Sexuality' at the Fin de Siècle." In *Irregular Connections: A History of Anthropology and Sexuality*, 100–130. Lincoln: University of Nebraska Press, 2004.

McCartin, James P. "The Church and Gay Liberation: The Case of John McNeill." *U.S. Catholic Historian* 34 (Winter 2016): 125–41.

McGarry, Molly. "'The Quick, the Dead, and the Yet Unborn': Untimely Sexualities and Secular Hauntings." In *Secularisms*, 247–79. Durham: Duke University Press, 2008.

McGinity, Keren R. *Still Jewish: A History of Women and Intermarriage in America*. New York: New York University Press, 2009.

McGreevy, John T. *Catholicism and American Freedom: A History*. New York: W. W. Norton, 2004.

Michaelson, Jay. *God vs. Gay? The Religious Case for Equality*. Boston: Beacon Press, 2011.

Moreton, Bethany. "Why Is There So Much Sex in Christian Conservatism and Why Do So Few Historians Care Anything about It?" *Journal of Southern History* 75 (August 2009): 717–38.

Oh, Arissa. "A New Kind of Missionary Work: Christians, Christian Americans, and the Adoption of Korean GI Babies, 1955–1961." *Women's Studies Quarterly* 33, nos. 3–4 (2005): 161–88.

Orsi, Robert A. "Events of Abundant Evil." In *History and Presence*, 215–48. Cambridge, Mass.: Belknap Press, 2016.

Pascoe, Peggy. "Gender Systems in Conflict: The Marriages of Mission-Educated Chinese American Women, 1874–1939." *Journal of Social History* 22, no. 4 (1989): 631–52.

Petro, Anthony. *After the Wrath of God: AIDS, Sexuality, and American Religion*. New York: Oxford University Press, 2015.

Retzloff, Tim. "'Seer or Queer?' Postwar Fascination with Detroit's Prophet Jones." *GLQ: A Journal of Lesbian and Gay Studies* 8, no. 3 (2002): 271–96.

Rosen, Christine. *Preaching Eugenics: Religious Leaders and the American Eugenics Movement*. New York: Oxford University Press, 2004.

Russell, Thaddeus. "The Color of Discipline: Civil Rights and Black Sexuality." *American Quarterly* 60, no. 1 (2008): 101–28.

Satter, Beryl. *Each Mind a Kingdom: American Women, Sexual Purity, and the New Thought Movement, 1875–1920*. Berkeley: University of California Press, 1999.

Schimel, Lawrence, ed. *Found Tribe: Jewish Coming Out Stories*. Santa Fe: Sherman Asher, 2002.

Schmidt, Leigh. *Heaven's Bride: The Unprintable Life of Ida C. Craddock, American Mystic, Scholar, Sexologist, Martyr, and Madwoman*. New York: Basic Books, 2010.

Shneer, David, and Caryn Aviv, eds. *Queer Jews*. New York: Routledge, 2002.

Smith, Andrea. "'Without Apology': Native American and Evangelical Feminisms." In *Native Americans and the Christian Right: The Gendered Politics of Unlikely Alliances*, 115–99. Durham: Duke University Press, 2008.

Spickard, Paul R. *Mixed Blood: Intermarriage and Ethnic Identity in Twentieth-Century America*. Madison: University of Wisconsin Press, 1989.

Stein, Marc. "The Objectionable Walt Whitman Bridge." In *City of Sisterly and Brotherly Loves: Lesbian and Gay Philadelphia, 1945–1972*, 138–54. Chicago: University of Chicago Press, 2000.

Stone, Amy L., and Jane Ward. "From 'Black People Are Not a Homosexual Act' to 'Gay Is the New Black': Mapping White Uses of Blackness in Modern Gay Rights Campaigns in the United States." *Social Identities* 17, no. 5 (September 2001): 605–24.

Strub, Whitney. "The Homophile Is a Sexual Being: Wallace de Ortega Maxey's Pulp Theology and Gay Activism." *Journal of the History of Sexuality* 25, no. 2 (May 2016): 323–53.

Tentler, Leslie Woodcock. *Catholics and Contraception: An American History*. Ithaca: Cornell University Press, 2004.

Urban, Hugh. *Magia Sexualis: Sex, Magic, and Liberation in Modern Western Esotericism*. Berkeley: University of California Press, 2006.

Vidal-Ortiz, Salvador. "Religion/Spirituality, U.S. Latina/o Communities, and Sexuality Scholarship: A Thread of Current Works." In *Latina/o Sexualities: Probing Powers, Passions, Practices, and Policies*, edited by Marysol Ascensio, 173–87. Rutgers: Rutgers University Press, 2009.

Waller, James. "'A Man in a Cassock Is Wearing a Skirt': Margaretta Bowers and the Psychoanalytic Treatment of Gay Clergy." *GLQ: A Journal of Lesbian and Gay Studies* 4, no. 1 (1998): 1–16.

Wenger, Beth S. "Mitzvah and Medicine: Gender, Assimilation, and the Scientific Defense of 'Family Purity.'" *Jewish Social Studies* 5, no. 1/2 (Autumn 1998–Winter 1999): 177–202.

Wenger, Tisa. "Dance Is (Not) Religion: The Struggle for Authority in Indian Affairs." Chapter 4 in *We Have a Religion: The 1920s Pueblo Indian Dance Controversy and American Religious Freedom*. Chapel Hill: University of North Carolina Press, 2009.

White, Heather R. "Proclaiming Liberation: The Historical Roots of LGBT Religious Organizing, 1946–1976." *Nova Religio* 11 (May 2008): 102–19.

———. *Reforming Sodom: Protestants and the Rise of Gay Rights*. Chapel Hill: University of North Carolina Press, 2015.

Williams, Daniel K. *Defenders of the Unborn: The Pro-life Movement before Roe v. Wade*. New York: Oxford University Press, 2016.

———. "The GOP's Abortion Strategy: Why Pro-choice Republicans Became Pro-life in the 1970s." *Journal of Policy History* 23 (2011): 513–39.

———. "Sex and the Evangelicals: Gender Issues, the Sexual Revolution, and Abortion in the 1960s." In *American Evangelicals and the 1960s: Revisiting the "Backlash."* Madison: University of Wisconsin Press, 2014.

Young, Neil J. "'The ERA Is a Moral Issue': The Mormon Church, LDS Women and the Defeat of the Equal Rights Amendment." *American Quarterly* 59, no. 3 (2007): 623–44.

———. "Mormons and Same-Sex Marriage: From ERA to Prop 8." In *Out of Obscurity: Mormonism since 1945*, 144–69. New York: Oxford University Press, 2016.

———. *We Gather Together: The Religious Right and the Problem of Interfaith Politics*. New York: Oxford University Press, 2015.

———. "'Worse Than Cancer and Worse Than Snakes': Jimmy Carter's Southern Baptist Problem and the 1980 Election." *Journal of Policy History* 26, no. 4 (2014): 479–508.

CONTRIBUTORS

REBECCA T. ALPERT, a professor of religion and senior associate dean of the College of Liberal Arts at Temple University, was among the first women in America ordained as a rabbi, at the Reconstructionist Rabbinical College in 1976. She is the author of five books, including *Like Bread on the Seder Plate: Jewish Lesbians and the Transformation of Tradition*; *Whose Torah? A Concise Guide to Progressive Judaism*; and *Out of Left Field: Jews and Black Baseball*.

REBECCA L. DAVIS is an associate professor of history at the University of Delaware, where she has a joint appointment in the women and gender studies department. She is the author of *More Perfect Unions: The American Search for Marital Bliss* and is coediting a collection of essays on the history of heterosexuality.

JOHN D'EMILIO is an emeritus professor of history and gender and women's studies at the University of Illinois at Chicago. His books include *Sexual Politics, Sexual Communities: The Making of a Homosexual Minority in the United States, 1940–1970*; *Intimate Matters: A History of Sexuality in America* (with Estelle B. Freedman); *Lost Prophet: The Life and Times of Bayard Rustin*, a finalist for the National Book Award; and three volumes of his collected essays.

GILLIAN FRANK is a managing editor of *NOTCHES: (re)marks on the History of Sexuality* and a visiting fellow at the Center for the Study of Religion at Princeton University. His work has appeared in a number of venues, including *Journal of the History of Sexuality*, *Gender and History*, and *Journal of Religion and Popular Culture*. He is currently working on two book manuscripts: *Save Our Children: Conservative Sexual Politics in the United States, 1965–1990* and *Making Choice Sacred: Liberal Religion and Reproductive Politics in the United States before* Roe v. Wade.

LYNNE GERBER is a visiting scholar at Harvard Divinity School's Women's Studies in Religion Program and the author of *Seeking the Straight and Narrow: Weight Loss and Sexual Reorientation in Evangelical America*. Her current research, tentatively titled *A Church Alive: AIDS and the Metropolitan Community Church of San Francisco*, focuses on the first two decades of the

AIDS epidemic and the Metropolitan Community Church of San Francisco, a gay/lesbian congregation that engaged AIDS as a religious issue.

ANDREA R. JAIN is an associate professor of religious studies at the Indiana University School of Liberal Arts and the author of *Selling Yoga: From Counterculture to Pop Culture*. She is a regular contributor to *Religion Dispatches* and cochair of the Yoga in Theory and Practice Group of the American Academy of Religion.

KATHI KERN is the director of the Center for the Enhancement of Learning and Teaching and an associate professor of history at the University of Kentucky. She is the author of many articles as well as the book *Mrs. Stanton's Bible*.

RACHEL KRANSON is an assistant professor of religious studies at the University of Pittsburgh. She is the author of *Ambivalent Embrace: Jewish Upward Mobility in Postwar America* and, with Hasia Diner and Shira Kohn, a coeditor of *A Jewish Feminine Mystique: Jewish Women in Postwar America*. Her current project traces American Jewish engagement in national debates over abortion.

JAMES P. MCCARTIN is an associate professor of the history of Christianity at Fordham University. He is the author of *Prayers of the Faithful: The Shifting Spiritual Life of American Catholics* and is currently at work on a history of U.S. Catholics and sex from the 1830s to the 1980s.

SAMIRA K. MEHTA is an assistant professor of religious studies at Albright College. She is the author of *Beyond Chrismukkah: The Christian-Jewish Interfaith Family in the United States*.

BETHANY MORETON is a professor of history at Dartmouth College and a series editor for Columbia University Press's Studies in the History of U.S. Capitalism. She is the author of *To Serve God and Walmart: The Making of Christian Free Enterprise* and is at work on *Jesus Saves: Christians in the Age of Debt* as well as on *Our Lady of the Market: Catholicism and the Conservative Search for a Moral Economy*.

DANIEL RIVERS is an associate professor in the Department of History at the Ohio State University and an enrolled citizen of the Choctaw Nation of Oklahoma. His first book, *Radical Relations: Lesbian Mothers, Gay Fathers, and Their Children in the United States since World War II*, was published in 2013. He is currently at work on a second book project on the history of LGBT/Two-Spirit Native Americans from 1940 to the present.

JACOB J. STAUB is a professor of Jewish philosophy and spirituality at the Reconstructionist Rabbinical College and the codirector of *Bekhol Levavkha: A Training Program for Jewish Spiritual Directors*. He is the author of *The*

Creation of the World According to Gersonides and a coauthor, with Rebecca T. Alpert, of *Exploring Judaism: A Reconstructionist Approach*.

WHITNEY STRUB is the director of the Women's and Gender Studies Program at Rutgers University-Newark and an associate professor in the history department. He is the author of *Perversion for Profit: The Politics of Pornography and the Rise of the New Right* and *Obscenity Rules:* Roth v. United States *and the Long Struggle over Sexual Expression* and is a coeditor of *Porno Chic and the Sex Wars: American Sexual Representation in the 1970s.*

AIKO TAKEUCHI-DEMIRCI is a lecturer in the Program in Feminist, Gender, and Sexuality Studies at Stanford University. She is the author of *Conceiving National Bodies: The Transpacific Politics of Birth Control in the United States and Japan, 1920–1960*.

JUDITH WEISENFELD is the Agate Brown and George L. Collord Professor of Religion at Princeton University, where she is also associated faculty in the Department of African American Studies and the Program in Gender and Sexuality Studies. She is the author of *New World a-Coming: Black Religion and Racial Identity during the Great Migration*; *Hollywood Be Thy Name: African American Religion in American Film, 1929–1949*; and *African American Women and Christian Activism: New York's Black YWCA, 1905–1945*.

HEATHER R. WHITE is a visiting assistant professor at the University of Puget Sound with a joint appointment in the Department of Religious Studies and the Gender and Queer Studies Program. Her first book, *Reforming Sodom: Protestants and the Rise of Gay Rights*, was published in 2015.

NEIL J. YOUNG is an affiliated scholar with George Mason University's Schar School of Policy and Government. He is the author of *We Gather Together: The Religious Right and the Problem of Interfaith Politics*.

INDEX

Page numbers in italics refer to illustrations.

Abortion, 3, 145, 147; Catholic views of, 9, 83, 123, 135, 138, 180, 270; Jewish views of, 63, 64, 170–86, 219, 233n39; as antipornographers' target, 136; Protestant views of, 138, 162; religious right's opposition to, 171–72; Mormon opposition to, 193, 194, 195
Ackerman, Edward, 117, 120, 123, 124
ACLU (American Civil Liberties Union), 124, 139–40, 142
ACT-UP (AIDS Coalition to Unleash Power), 263, 270–71
Adultery, 56, 76
Affirmation (Methodist gay affinity group), 274n7
African Americans, 57
African religion, 13
Agnos, Art, 262, 263, 264
AIDS, 11, 253–73
AIDS/ARC Vigil, 260
AIDS Coalition to Unleash Power (ACT-UP), 263, 270–71
Albanese, Catherine, 242, 250n10
Alexander, John, 155
Allison, Dorothy, 259
Alpert, Rebecca T., 65, 66, 225, 228
America (magazine), 139
American Baptist Church, 153
American Civil Liberties Union (ACLU), 124, 139–40, 142
American Institute of Family Relations, 61
American Medical Association, 121
American Psychiatric Association, 59
American Psychological Association, 200
American Sex Revolution (Sorokin), 144

Americans for Moral Decency, 139
American Theosophical Society, 43
Andelin, Aubrey, 199–200
Andelin, Helen, 193–208
And the Band Played On (Shilts), 275n22
Anglican Communion, 156
Another Country (Herring), 249n3
Antimiscegenation laws, 57
Animism, 235, 242
Anthropology, 6
Armstrong, Elizabeth, 261
Asian religion, 13
Asians, 57
Atomic weapons, 121–22
Auden, W. H., 258, 271, 272–73
Augustana Evangelical Lutheran Churches in America, 156
Awful Disclosures of the Hotel Dieu Nunnery (Monk), 74
AZT (protease-inhibiting drug), 269–70

Bailey, Beth, 154
Baldwin, James, 259
Balka, Christie, 228
Balter, Bernice, 184, 185
Baltimore Cathechism, 77
Bamberger, George, 239–40
Barbakoff, Jordan, 218–20
Baron, Laurie, 231n13
Bay Area Reporter (*BAR*), 253, 260, 263, 270
Beatles, 46
Beckwith, Doug, 239
Belstrom, LaVere, 108–9
Bender, Courtney, 250n10
Benedict XV (pope), 80

293

Bennett, Alan, 218
Bernard, Pierre, 38–40, 43, 44
Berner, Leila, 229
Besant, Annie, 43
Beth Ahavah, 220
Beth Chaim Chadashim, 218, 274n10
Beth Simchat Torah, 224
Bikram Yoga, 47
Bill of Rights, 50n5
Bills, Arthur, 140
Birth control, 3, 8, 57; Catholic views of, 9, 83, 84, 113–25, 138, 139, 158, 160–61, 164; Craddock's views of, 36, 37; condoms for, 37, 78, 136, 270; Jewish views of, 60, 63, 64, 115, 116, 139, 176–78; Protestant views of, 63, 115–16, 138, 139, 152–67, 281; in postwar Japan, 113–25; as antipornographers' target, 136. *See also* Family size
Bisexuality, 230
Black, Gregory, 137
Blavatsky, Helene, 42
Boisvert, Donald, 251n30
Bolton, Elizabeth, 227
Borderland (magazine), 36
Boswell, John, 280
Botkin, Michael, 260
Boyarin, Daniel, 216
Boys Beware (film), 145
Brahmo Samaj, 40
Brauner, Ronald, 219, 220
Brav, Stanley R., 54, 60–62, 63, 66
Breen, Joseph, 137
Brennan, William, 142
Britt, Harry, 263, 267
Bryant, Anita, 64–65
Buddhists, 20, 66
Burkhart, Roy A., 61
Burnside, John, 236
Bush, George H. W., 262
Butler, Jon, 4
Butterworth Farm, 249n5

Caine, Ivan, 221–22, 223, 226
Canaday, Margot, 4
Canadian Council of Churches, 162
Cana Movement, 84
Cardenal, Ernesto, 259
Carter, Jimmy, 180–81
Casanova, José, 114
Casti Connubii (1931), 83, 84, 116
Catholics, 2, 7–8, 71–85; birth control viewed by, 9, 83, 84, 113–25, 138, 139, 158, 160–61, 164; abortion viewed by, 9, 83, 123, 135, 138, 180, 270; in postwar Japan, 113–25; pornography opposed by, 133–47
CDL (Citizens for Decent Literature), 8, 133–47
"Celestial Love," 193, 198–99
Celibacy, 23–24; among yoga practitioners, 35, 42, 44, 45, 46, 47; among Catholic clergy, 73, 74–75, 76, 79; criticisms of, 74–75, 91; in Father Divine's movement, 90, 93–94, 95, 100–101, 109, 281
Censorship, 134, 136–37, 138, 141–44. *See also* Pornography
Central Conference of American Rabbis (CCAR), 60, 65
Chauncey, George, 28
Chaurasi Kutia (ashram), 46
Cherry, Kittredge, 261, 266
Children's Aid Society, 135
China, 115, 124
Choudhury, Bikram, 47
Christian Century (*CC*; magazine), 140, 153, 154, 159–61, 165, 261–62
Christian Crusade, 146
Christian Family Movement, 84
Christianity and Crisis (magazine), 154, 159–60, 161
Christian Mingle, 3
Christian right, 9, 135, 146–47, 171–72, 179–80, 182, 186, 194, 281
Christians and the Crisis in Sex Morality (Genné and Genné), 163
Christian Science, 34
Churchmen's Commission for Decent Publications, 142, 143
Church of Christ, 205
Church of Jesus Christ of Latter-day Saints, 2, 10, 44, 56, 180–81, 193–208, 281

Church of the Beloved Disciple, 278
Church of Yoga, 36
Circumcision, 64
Citak, Audrey, 192n35
Citizens for Decent Literature (CDL), 8, 133–47
Clarkstown Country Club, 39, 44
Clover, Steven, 261
Cohen, Gerson D., 180, 183–84, 186
Cold War, 9, 114, 123; homophobia during, 59, 144, 145; antipornography movement during, 138, 141, 143, 144
Colonialism, 40, 113, 114, 115, 122, 183
Commission of the Churches on International Affairs, 157
Committee on Marriage, Family, and the Home, 60
Communism, 113, 119, 121–22, 124–25, 144–45
Companionate marriage, 12, 17, 34, 42
Complex marriage, 56
Comstock, Anthony, 35, 36, 37, 133, 135–36, 141, 144
Comstock Act (1873), 50n6, 121, 135, 144
Concerned Women for America, 181
Condoms, 37, 78, 136, 270
Congregational Christian General Council, 156
Conservative Jews, 2, 9, 64, 170–86, 223, 230
Contraception. *See* Birth control
Cooper, John Montgomery, 80
Council of Trent (1545–63), 75
Council on Religion and the Homosexual (CRH), 255
Counseling, 54, 59
Counter-Reformation, 137
Cox, H. G., 33n57
Craddock, Ida C., 12, 35–38, 40, 44
Crocker, Bob, 256
Crusaders for Decency in Literature, 142

Davis, Rebecca L., 145, 171, 196, 216–17
Davison, Jaquie, 193, 194, 195, 201–8
Davison, Ronnie, 201
Daya Mata, 35, 43–44

D'Emilio, John, 3–4, 218, 231n3
Democratic Party, 65
Dennison, Martha, 28
Deukmejian, George, 262
DeVries, Blanche, 44–45
Dewey, John, 77
Diagnostic and Statistical Manual, Mental Disorders, 59
Diary of a Smut-Hound (Roth), 136
Dierenfeld, Bruce, 148n20
Dignity (Catholic gay affinity group), 274n7, 277, 278
DiVerde, Steve, 239
Divine Illius Magistri (1930), 82
Divorce, 75–76, 83
Domestic partnership, 263–65
Double Rock Baptist Church, 261
Douglas, Susan J., 47
Dower, John, 127n11
Drake, Gordon, 146
Dresner, Samuel H., 226, 229
Dyke Shabbos, 224

Ebony (magazine), 90
Ecofeminism, 235, 242, 243, 246, 248
Eilberg, Amy, 231n10
Eisenhower, Dwight, 173
Eisenstein, Ira, 219
Encyclopedia Judaica, 217
Endogamy, 62
Enlightenment, 6
Entertainment industry, 78, 118, 136–38
Episcopal Church, 153
Equal Rights Amendment (ERA), 178, 193, 194, 195, 200, 203–8
Esoteric Science and Philosophy of the Tantras, Shiva Sanhita, The, 36
Ethnicity: of Jews, 55, 57–58, 62, 63, 66, 137–38; of Catholics, 74, 75, 137–38
Eugenics, 57, 58, 60, 114, 115–17, 119, 124, 159, 166. *See also* Population growth; Sterilization
Evangelicals, 13, 36, 138, 194, 255, 256; same-sex marriage opposed by, 1–2; conservative Catholics allied with,

Index 295

9, 181, 201, 206; orthodox Jews allied with, 64; sex education opposed by, 146; in Christian right, 147, 171, 279; abortion opposed by, 180–81; Mormons allied with, 181, 201, 206; Equal Rights Amendment opposed by, 205–6
Evans, Arthur, 240, 246
Everson v. Board of Education (1947), 148n20
Exploring Judaism (Alpert and Staub), 225
Ezrat Nashim, 179–80

Fagley, Richard, 154, 157–59, 160, 161, 162
Faith and Order Commission, 262
Faithful Mary (Father Divine follower), 102
Falwell, Jerry, 147, 181, 183
Family size, 55, 64, 214, 217, 219, 222. *See also* Birth control
Farm (Tennessee commune), 252n57
Fascinating Girl, The (*The Secrets of Winning Men*; Andelin), 200
Fascinating Womanhood (Andelin), 194, 197, 200–201, 208
Fascinating Womanhood (FW), 193, 194, 202, 203, 204–5, 207–8
Fascinating Womanhood Principle Applied to Sex (Andelin and Andelin), 199–200
Father Divine, 10, 23, 90–109, 281
Father Divine (Harris), 90
FDA (Food and Drug Administration), 154, 155, 160, 269–70, 281
Federation of Jewish Men's Clubs, 175
Fee, Dan, 242
Feinstein, Dianne, 263
Feminine Mystique, The (Friedan), 196
Feminism, 4, 47, 57, 64, 214, 279; in Conservative Judaism, 174–75, 177, 178–79; Mormon opposition to, 195, 203; Eco-, 235, 242, 243, 246, 248
Fertig, Ruth, 21, 23, 24, 25, 26
First Amendment, 142, 170
Fischer, John, 137
Folan, Lilias, 47–48
Food and Drug Administration (FDA), 154, 155, 160, 269–70, 281

Forster, E. M., 258
Fortas, Abe, 146
For the Time Being: A Christmas Oratorio (Auden), 258, 271
Fosdick, Harry Emerson, 24, 27, 155–56
Foster, Gaines, 135
Foucault, Michel, 7, 18
Frank, Gillian, 30n6
Frawley, Patrick, Jr., 206
Freedman, Estelle B., 3–4, 279
Free love, 12, 56
Free Synagogue, 60
Freud, Sigmund, 136, 143
Friedan, Betty, 196
Friedman, Andrea, 133
Friedman, Carole, 231n13

Gamble, Clarence, 124
Gandhi, Mahatma, 20, 21, 22, 23
Gaskin, Stephen, 252n57
Gauer, Raymond, 133
Gay Christian Network, 2
Gay Liberation Arizona Desert, 249n5
Gays and lesbians: Jewish views of, 1, 11, 55, 61–62, 64–65; growing acceptance of, 11, 136, 253–73; among Reconstructionist rabbis, 11, 214–30, 255; urban vs. rural, 11–12, 134, 234–48; Cold War harassment of, 59, 144, 145; attempts to convert, 61; rights for, 64, 65, 145, 194, 195, 204, 263, 270; Catholic, 84–85; Christian right's opposition to, 147; Mormon opposition to, 193, 195, 200, 205, 207
Gender norms. 35, 46, 48, 181
Geneticists' Manifesto, 131n72
Genné, Elizabeth, 154, 163
Genné, William, 154, 162, 163
GI bill, 118
Globalization, 114
Golden Gate MCC, 256
Goldstein, Sidney E., 60
Goodridge v. Massachusetts (2003), 66
Gordis, Robert, 181–84, 185
Gospel Coalition, 2
Gospel in Solentiname, The (Cardenal), 259

Graham, Billy, 61
Great Depression, 60, 83, 115, 136
Green, Arthur, 222, 225–26
Green, Madeline, 96
Greenberg, Julie, 224, 229
Greenstidel, Christine, 42
Griffis, Lynn, 267
Griffith, R. Marie, 251n39
Gruenberg, Benjamin, 78
Guttmacher, Alan, 152

Halperin, David, 254, 272
Hamati, Sylvais, 38
Happiness of Womanhood (HOW), 193, 194, 195, 203–7
Harkness, Rebekah, 45
Harris, Sara, 90, 102
Hatha yoga, 36, 38, 39, 40, 41, 42
Havurot–RRA Placement Commission, 229
Hay, Harry, 145, 236
Hebrew Union College (HUC), 218
Heelas, Paul, 250n10
Hefner, Hugh, 139, 143
Heifitz, Mel, 231n13
Herberg, Will, 173
Herman, Erwin, 218
Herring, Scott, 249n3
Herzog, Jonathan, 138
Heterosexuality, 3–4; as new category, 5, 57; sexual liberalism and, 7; marriage linked to, 9–10, 12, 17, 37, 38, 42, 54–55, 57, 59, 90, 93, 193–96, 202–5, 217, 226; as Mormon ideal, 10; women's emancipation linked to, 28; as Protestant ideal, 34, 55; as Jewish ideal, 55, 59, 64, 65, 214, 217, 221–23, 224, 226, 229; as Catholic ideal, 55, 82, 83; procreation linked to, 144, 217; in counterculture, 237, 238, 246–48
Hindu American Foundation, 2, 48
Hindus, 20, 22, 23, 41, 48
History of Sexuality, The (Foucault), 18
Hollywood Production Code, 137, 138
Holocaust, 63, 64, 66, 114, 123, 172, 219
Holtzman, Linda, 219–22, 224–25, 228

Homosociality, 18, 101
Hoover, J. Edgar, 140–41
Hop Brook Commune, 239, 241, 245
Horan, Ellamay, 76, 80
HOW (Happiness of Womanhood), 193, 194, 195, 203–7
Huff, Louise, 27–28
Humanae Vitae (1968), 84
Husslein, Joseph, 81
Hyman, Paula, 179–80

I Am a Housewife (Davison), 202
Immigration, 12, 57, 58, 115, 118, 121
Independent Orthodox churches, 255
Index Librorum Prohibitorum, 137
India, 12, 21–23, 24, 124
Integration, racial, 97, 99, 103, 109
Integrity (Episcopalian gay affinity group), 274n7, 277
Interfaith marriage, 55, 58, 62, 66, 219
International Journal of the Tantrik Order, 38
International Missionary Council, 157
Interracial marriage, 3, 57
InterVarsity Christian Fellowship, 155
Intimate Matters (D'Emilio and Freedman), 3–4, 279, 281
Isherwood, Christopher, 258
Isser, Stanley, 219
Is the Schoolhouse the Proper Place to Teach Raw Sex?, 146
Itkin, Mikhail, 255
Iyengar, B. K. S., 45

Jackson, Jay, 245
Jacobs, Robert, 68n22
Janakananda, Rajarsi, 52n41
Japan, 9, 113–25
Jesus Christ, 25
Jewett, Paul King, 160
Jewish Renewal Life Center, 229
Jewish Theological Seminary, 180, 181, 183, 226
John, the Apostle, Saint, 25
John Birch Society, 146, 205
Johnson, Lyndon, 146

Johnson, William, 277
Joint Federation of Reconstructionist Congregations, 229
Jones, Cleve, 268
Jordan, Frank, 267
Jordan, Mark, 270, 271
Joseph (biblical figure), 264–65
Journal of Religious Education, 80
Judeo-Christian heritage, 8, 119, 134, 141, 144, 147, 173
Judge, William, 43
Jung, Leo, 62–63
Justice, Mary (of California), 96–97
Justice, Mary (of South Carolina), 96

Kainos Movement, 2
Kameny, Frank, 231n13
Kaplan, Mordechai Aaron, 58, 216, 221
Kaposi's Sarcoma Foundation (San Francisco AIDS Foundation), 260
Kaschmitter, William, 117, 121
Keating, Charles, 133–35, 138–47, 281
Kefauver, Estes, 141
Kellogg, Susan, 196
Kennedy, John F., 134
Kennedy, Tom, 248
Kern, Kathi, 93–94, 280
Khrushchev, Nikita, 144
Kilhefner, Don, 236
Kimball, Spencer W., 203
King, Martin Luther, Jr., 22, 61
Kinsey, Alfred C., 138, 143
Kleinbaum, Sharon, 224, 228
Knox, Bill, 261
Kosher Sex (Boteach), 3
Kranson, Rachel, 64
Krishnamacharya, Tirumalai, 45
Kriya Yoga, 44
Krohn, Ida, 175

La Guardia, Fiorello, 137
La Haye, Beverly, 181, 194
Lambeth Conference, 155
Lamm, Norman, 217
Langer, Jiří Mordechai, 230–31n2

Latter-day Saints, 2, 10, 44, 56, 180–81, 193–208, 281
Lauria, Tom, 245
Lavender Hill, 244, 246
Lazin, Malcolm, 231n13
Legion of Decency, 133, 136, 137, 138, 142
Lerner, David, 65
Lewin, Ellen, 265
Liberal Christianity, 28; countercultural challenges to, 34; marriage and family idealized by, 61, 156; contraception embraced by, 63, 155, 157; therapeutic language compatible with, 140, 145; ecumenism of, 153; publications of, 159, 161; gay recognition by, 256; liberation theology and, 257
Liberation theology, 254, 257–59
Lifespan, 205
Light on Yoga (Iyengar), 45
Lilias, Yoga and You! (television program), 47
Litman, Jane, 224, 226
Living Arts Center, 44
Lockwood, Audrey, 266
Lorde, Audre, 259
Love, Happy S. (Father Divine follower), 92, 95, 97, 99, 100–102, 106–9
Love, Peaceful (Father Divine follower), 101
Love and Sex: A Modern Jewish Perspective (Gordis), 182
Loving v. Virginia (1967), 2
Lyons, Daniel, 206

MacArthur Douglas, 118, 120, 122, 123–24
Maharishi Mahesh Yogi, 46
Mainline Christianity, 9, 183, 203, 265; sexual liberalism advanced by, 8; conservative Catholicism vs., 19, 138; in antipornography movement, 146; "responsible parenthood" espoused by, 152–56, 159–62, 165–67, 203, 281; gay recognition by, 256
Manion, Clarence, 206
Mann, Moshay, 142
Man of Steel and Velvet (Andelin), 200
Marchetti, Gina, 127n11

March on Washington for Gay and
   Lesbian Rights, 268
Marder, Jacob, 225
Marder, Janet, 232n22
Marital counseling, 59, 61
Mark, Saint, 25
Marks, Jeanette, 18–19
Mary (biblical figure), 264–65
Masturbation, 56, 61
Matt, Hershel, 220–22, 224–25, 229
Mattachine Society, 144–45
May, Elaine Tyler, 154
Mayo, Katharine, 21
MCC. *See* Metropolitan Community
   Church
McCartin, James P., 91, 137, 153
McDowell, Anne, 30n6
McGreevy, John, 119, 141
McLuhan, Marshall, 143
McNeill, John, 277
Meador, Keith, 140
Mehta, Rohit, 245
Mehta, Samira K., 63, 116, 203, 281
Mendelson, Edward, 272
Menger, Gary, 244–45
Metropolitan Community Church
   (MCC), 217; of San Francisco
   (MCCSF), 11, 253–73; Golden Gate
   MCC, 256; of Chicago, 277, 278
Meyer, Fulgence, 80–81
Michel, Matthew, 71–73
Middleton, Claire, 205
Middleton, John, 205
Mikvah (ritual bath), 56, 58
Milk, Harvey, 234, 263, 264
Mind cure, 41
Mintz, Felix (Lee), 244, 246
Mintz, Steven, 196
Miscegenation laws, 57
Mitulski, Jim, 253–73
Mobilization for Action, 260
Modern Use of the Bible (Fosdick), 27
Mohler, Albert, 48
Monette, Paul, 259
Monk, Maria, 73

Monogamy: sexual liberalism compatible
   with, 7; alternatives to, 29, 56; as Jewish
   ideal, 64, 65, 226; as Mormon ideal, 193,
   195, 202, 205
Moody Bible Institute, 2
Moore, Dorothy L. (Dot), 91, 95, 102–8, 109
Morality in Media, 146
Moral Majority, 146, 181, 183
More Light (Presbyterian gay affinity
   group), 274n7
Morgan, Marabel, 194, 207
Morgan, Sue, 32n43
Mormons, 2, 10, 44, 56, 180–81, 193–208, 281
Moscone, George, 264
Mother Earth News, 246–47, 248
Mother India (Mayo), 21
MOTOREDE (Movement to Restore
   Decency), 146
Muktananda, Swami, 35
Mulberry House, 243, 249n5
Muller, H. J., 131n72
Muslims, 13
Muslims for Progressive Values, 2

Nameless Experience, The (Mehta), 245
Names Quilt, 268–69
Narayanan, Vasudha, 51n27
National Association for the Repeal of
   Abortion Laws, 177
National Association of Evangelicals, 2
National Catholic Educational
   Association, 80
National Catholic Welfare Conference
   (NCWC), 117–18, 121
National Coalition of Black Pastors and
   Religious Leaders, 2
National Council of Churches (NCC), 153,
   154, 157, 161–62, 163, 165, 256, 262
National Day of Prayer, 138
National Federation for Decency, 146
National Hispanic Christian Leadership
   Conference, 2
National Organization for Decent
   Literature (NODL), 133, 136–37, 138, 139,
   141, 143

Index

299

National Organization for Women (NOW), 177, 204
National Review, 1
National Student Council Staff, 20
Native Americans, 13, 57, 237, 242–43, 248
Nature religion, 242, 248
Nazis, 114, 124
NCC (National Council of Churches), 153, 154, 157, 161–62, 163, 165, 256, 262
New Age movement, 11, 235, 236–37, 239, 242
New Age Movement, The (Heelas), 250n10
New Day (Peace Mission magazine), 108
New Deal, 60
New Left, 238
New Right, 8
New Sodom, 246
New Thought, 34, 36, 94–95, 100
New York Society for the Suppression of Vice, 35, 135–36
New York Times, 137
Nidah (family purity laws), 56, 58, 60, 62
Niebuhr, Reinhold, 19
Nixon, Richard, 144, 146, 180
NODL (National Organization for Decent Literature), 133, 136–37, 138, 139, 141, 143
Noguchi, Yone, 93
Northwest Faggots Gathering, 239
NOW (National Organization for Women), 177, 204
Noyes, John Humphrey, 37
Noyes, Theodore R., 50–51n12
Nuclear weapons, 121–22

Obergefell v. Hodges (2015), 1–3
O'Brien, John A., 158, 161
Obscenity, 121, 136, 141–42. *See also* Pornography
O'Connor, John, 270
O'Connor, Patrick, 117–18, 121–22, 123
Olcott, Henry Steel, 42
Old Catholics, 255
Oneida Community, 37, 56
Ordination: of gay and lesbian rabbis, 11, 55, 65, 214–30; of female rabbis, 177–80, 214, 216; of gay and lesbian ministers, 277

Orthodox Church, 161
Orthodox Jews, 55, 58, 59, 62–63; gay rights opposed by, 64, 223; women's participation resisted by, 174

Pagans, 11
Paramananda, Swami, 49n2
Parliament of the World's Religions, 40
Patanjali, 41
Patheos Progressive Christian, 2
Paul, the Apostle, Saint, 2
Paul VI (pope), 84
Peace churches, 161
Peace Mission Movement, 10–11, 23, 90–109, 281
Peale, Norman Vincent, 61, 140, 145
Penininah (first Mother Divine), 91
Perry, Frances, 17, 24, 25–27, 29
Perry, Troy, 254, 255, 256, 257, 267, 277
Perversion for Profit (film), 145
Petchesky, Rosalind Pollack, 187–88n3
Pius X (pope), 80
Pius XI (pope), 82, 83, 116
Planned Parenthood, 124, 152, 155, 164
Plaskett, Art, 268
Playboy, 139, 143
Pledge of Allegiance, 138
Pluralism, 5
Polak, Clark, 231n13
Polygamy, 56, 202–3
Popenoe, Paul, 61
Population Explosion and Christian Responsibility, The (Fagley), 154, 157–58
Population growth, 8, 63, 64, 155, 157–60, 161–62, 164, 166; in Japan, 113–25. *See also* Eugenics
Pornography, 8, 133–47, 193, 195, 206, 281. *See also* Censorship
Postural yoga, 46–47
Power of Positive Thinking, The (Peale), 140
Premarital counseling, 54, 61, 62
Premarital sex, 63
Presbyterian Church (USA), 153, 155
Presley, Elvis, 51n43
Price, Helen, 24, 26, 27, 29

Priesand, Sally, 179
Printed Poison (film), 145
Prisons, 94
Prohibition, 135
Pronatalism, 55, 64, 214, 217, 219, 222. *See also* Birth control; Population growth
Prop S, 263, 272
Prostitution, 38, 78, 79
Protestant, Catholic, Jew (Herberg), 173
Psychiatry, 5–6, 57, 140
Psychology, 5–6, 40
Putnam, George, 145

Rabbinical Assembly, 175, 177, 179, 181, 182
Racism, 119, 121
Radical Faeries, 236, 252n59
Raja yoga, 42–43
Raja Yoga (Vivekananda), 41
Ramakrishna (mystic), 40
Rappaport, Selma, 179
Reagan, Ronald, 173, 181, 195
Reconstructionist (magazine), 216, 225
Reconstructionist Commission on Homosexuality, 229, 230
Reconstructionist Jews, 11, 65, 174, 214–30
Reconstructionist Rabbinical Association, 229
Reconstructionist Rabbinical College (RRC), 65, 66, 215, 218, 219–26, 228–30, 255
Reed, Ralph, 147
Reforming Sodom (White), 231n3
Reform Jews, 2, 54–55, 58, 59–62, 63, 174; gay rights backed by, 65, 218, 230
Religious Coalition for the Freedom to Marry, 65–66
Religious liberalism, 20, 215, 255, 256, 257; Protestant, 28, 34, 61, 63, 140, 145, 153, 155, 156, 157, 159, 161; Jewish, 62, 65, 218, 220, 230
Religious pluralism, 5
"Religious right," 9, 135, 146–47, 171–72, 179–80, 182, 186, 194, 281
"Repressive hypothesis," 7
RFD (magazine), 234, 235–39, 241, 243, 248

Rich, Adrienne, 259
Ritchings, Edna Rose (second Mother Divine), 91, 92, 101
Rivers, Daniel, 100
Rock, John, 154, 155–56, 164, 166
Roe v. Wade (1973), 145, 177, 180, 186, 204
Rofes, Eric, 261, 263
Roosevelt, Eleanor, 124
Rose, Andy, 228
Roth, Samuel, 136
Roth v. U.S. (1957), 134, 141–42
RRC (Reconstructionist Rabbinical College), 65, 66, 215, 218, 219–26, 228–30, 255
Russell-Coons, Ron, 262

Same-sex marriage, 1–2, 55, 204; Jewish views of, 65; lay Catholic views of, 84–85
Sams, Crawford, 116, 122, 123, 124
Sandmire, Jim, 256, 257, 268
San Francisco AIDS Foundation (Kaposi's Sarcoma Foundation), 260
Sanger, Bill, 60
Sanger, Margaret, 78, 119–20, 123–24, 136
Sasso, Sandy, 231n10
SCAP (Supreme Commander of the Allied Powers), 113–24
Schlafly, Phyllis, 195, 204
Schmidt, Leigh, 36
School prayer, 193
Schraeter, Jay, 240, 246
Schulman, Sarah, 259
Schultz, Wanda, 205
Scofield, Stewart, 236
Second Vatican Council, 161
Secret of Fascinating Womanhood, The, 196
Secrets of Winning Men, The (*The Fascinating Girl*; Andelin), 200
Secularism: modern growth of, 3; sexual values linked to, 7, 8, 14, 72, 279; marriage and, 54, 62, 75; Jewish values and, 55, 58, 66; in education, 77; antipornography movement and, 135, 141, 143, 145; Protestant values conflated with, 153; in feminist movement, 173, 186, 279

Index

301

Seduction of the Innocent (Wertham), 141
Seelig, Evelyn, 176
Segal, Mark, 231n13
Segregation, 119
Sehat, David, 35
Self-Realization Fellowship, 44
Sex and the Family in the Jewish Tradition (Gordis), 182
Sex education, 7–8, 20, 72–73, 78–85, 137, 146, 193, 204, 206, 208
Sexual binary, 4, 8
Sexual liberalism, 3–8, 121, 134–35, 139, 143–45, 153, 281–82
Sexually transmitted diseases (STDs), 78, 79, 207
Sha'ar Zahav, 218
Shanti Project, 259–60, 261
Sheen, Fulton, 119, 138
Shilts, Randy, 275n22
Shiva Samhita, 36
Silverman, Ira, 220, 222, 225
Since Eve (Brav), 61
Singleton, Mark, 40
Snyder, Laura, 207
Social Gospel, 31–32n25
Society for Psychical Research, 36
Sorokin, Pitrim, 144
Southern Baptist Convention, 2
Southern Baptist Theological Seminary, 2, 48
Soviet Union, 144
Spiritualism, 40–41, 56
Stables, Linton, 267
State formation, 4, 135
Staub, Jacob J., 65, 66, 225, 228
Sterilization, 78, 116, 119, 123
Stoddard, Lothrop, 126–27n10
Stonewall Riots, 234, 255
STOP ERA, 195, 204
Stopes, Marie, 124
Stop the Church, 270–71
"Straight state," 58–59
Strub, Whitney, 85, 119, 281
Sueyoshi, Amy, 93
Sumner, John Saxton, 136

Supreme Commander of the Allied Powers (SCAP), 113–24
Sussman, Helen P., 175, 176

Tagore, Rabindranath, 20, 21, 22
Takeuchi-Demirci, Aiko, 76, 139, 159
Talmud, 58, 59, 64
Tantra yoga, 36–41, 44–45, 48
Tantrik Order in America, 39
Television, 138
Tevel-Treelove, Don, 244
Theosophical Society, 42–43
Theosophy, 34, 36, 41
Thompson, Warren, 117, 120, 124
Thornberry, David, 140
Tillich, Paul, 19
Torah, 58, 59, 185, 190n20
Total Woman, The (Morgan), 207
Traditional Values Coalition, 263
Transcendentalism, 34
Transcendental Meditation, 46
Transgender people, 230
Transnationalism, 114
Troxler, Allan, 236, 247
Twin Circle (newspaper), 206

UFMMC (Universal Fellowship of Metropolitan Community Churches), 254–57, 260, 262, 265
Union of Orthodox Jewish Congregations of America, 1
Union of Reform Judaism, 2
Union Theological Seminary, 19
Unitarian Universalist Association, 2, 36
United Church of Christ, 2, 153, 277
United Methodist Church, 152
United Nations, 121, 124, 157
United Order of the Family of Christ, 238
United States Conference of Catholic Bishops, 2
United States Federal Council of Churches, 156
U.S. News & World Report, 155
United States v. One Package of Japanese Pessaries (1936), 121

Universal Fellowship of Metropolitan
　Community Churches (UFMMC),
　254–57, 260, 262, 265

Vanderbilt family, 39
Van Waters, Miriam, 18
Vedanta, 40
Vedanta Society, 34, 41–42
Venereal disease, 78, 79, 207
Vivekananda, Swami, 12, 35, 40–42,
　43, 45, 48

Walker, Alice, 259
Walker, Jimmy, 137
Walker, Mitch, 236
Wedding Night, The (Craddock), 37, 39
Weisenfeld, Judith, 23, 281
Wells, Howard, 268
Wertham, Fredric, 141
"What Now?" Group, 228–29
White, Dan, 264
White, Heather, 231n3
Whiteness, 21, 57, 138
"White slavery," 38, 78
Whitman, Walt, 239
Wiegel, George, 1
Wilhelm II, Kaiser, 127n11
Williams, Ariam, 22

Winterson, Jeanette, 259
Wise, Stephen, 60
Wittman, Carl, 236, 242, 245, 246
Woman's Fulfillment, A (Snyder), 207
Women's Health Action and
　Mobilization, 270
Women's League for Conservative Judaism
　(Women's Religious Union of the
　United Synagogue), 9, 170–86, 233n39
Women Who Want to Be Women, 205
Wonderful Joy (Father Divine follower),
　91, 95, 97, 99, 100–106, 108–9
Woolley, Mary, 19
World Council of Churches, 157, 160
World's Columbian Exposition (1893), 36
World War I, 78
Wygal, Winnifred, 12, 17–30, 93–94,
　280–81

Yeskel, Felice, 228
Yoga, 12, 34–49
Yogananda, Paramahansa, 43, 44, 45
Yoga Sutras, 41, 42–43
Young, Neil J., 44, 281
Young Men's Christian Association
　(YMCA), 39, 135
Young Women's Christian Association
　(YWCA), 12, 17, 19, 21

www.ingramcontent.com/pod-product-compliance
Lightning Source LLC
Chambersburg PA
CBHW021651230426
43668CB00008B/584